Morality, Identity and Narrative in the Fiction of Richard Ford

GW00567615

COSTERUS NEW SERIES 176

Series Editors:
C.C. Barfoot, Theo D'haen
and Erik Kooper

Morality, Identity and Narrative in the Fiction of Richard Ford

Brian Duffy

 Amsterdam-New York, NY 2008

Cover photo: Le Jardin du Luxembourg, Paris. By Brigitte Le Juez

Cover design: Aart Jan Bergshoeff

The paper on which this book is printed meets the requirements of
"ISO 9706:1994, Information and documentation - Paper for
documents - Requirements for permanence".

ISBN: 978-90-420-2409-0
©Editions Rodopi B.V., Amsterdam - New York, NY 2008
Printed in the Netherlands

ACKNOWLEDGEMENTS

Most of this book was written during a year's sabbatical leave in 2006. I am grateful to Dublin City University for granting me this research time, but particularly to the School of Applied Language and Intercultural Studies in DCU. I would also like to acknowledge the travel grant I received from the Research Travel Programme of DCU's Faculty of Humanities and Social Sciences, which allowed me to travel to the United States to interview Richard Ford.

I am very grateful to my editor, Cedric Barfoot, for his meticulous editing and advice; his experience and guidance were invaluable to me throughout the editing of the manuscript. And I would also like to thank Esther Roth of Rodopi for her patience and assistance during the latter stages of bringing the book to publication. I greatly appreciated, too, the technical assistance of Shelly Barron in DCU.

There are, of course, personal debts that I am glad to be able to acknowledge. The reader's gratitude I felt towards Richard Ford took a more personal form when I had the opportunity to meet him and, later, to interview him. In all my contacts with him he has been courteous, attentive and exceptionally obliging in his responses. And my gratitude for this easy personal contact extends fully to Kristina Ford. Both of them welcomed me warmly into their home, where the interview with Richard Ford was conducted, a generosity that has extended well beyond the professional business of this book

I am grateful to Douglas Smith for his encouragement, and to my colleague Marnie Holborow for her support over a number of years.

This book is dedicated to Brigitte Le Juez, the person to whom I owe most.

CONTENTS

INTRODUCTION

Since the publication of *The Sportswriter* in 1986 Richard Ford has been recognized as one of America's leading writers of fiction. He has been awarded the Pulitzer Prize, the PEN/Faulkner Award and the PEN/Malamud Award for short fiction. His work has been celebrated by critics and fellow writers alike, and he has won the loyalty of a large and international readership. Yet, for such an important writer, there is relatively little scholarly work available on his novels and stories. At the time of writing, only three books devoted exclusively to his work have been published (a monograph, a book of essays and a collection of interviews), along with a limited number of articles in academic publications. The relative scarcity of scholarly work leaves Richard Ford's fiction seriously under-researched, not only in terms of general commentary but also with respect to important recurring themes in his writing. A new book on Ford's fiction, then, might hope to have a small contribution to make.

Richard Ford is most immediately identified with the trilogy of novels devoted to his character, Frank Bascombe. One of the objectives of this book is to provide a wide-ranging and integrated commentary on the trilogy, recently completed with the publication of *The Lay of the Land* (October 2006). Why "wide-ranging"? The Frank Bascombe novels are long novels, each successive book longer than its predecessor, with the final one not far short of five-hundred pages. The novels present us with a man and a nation, and take their leisurely time to explore both at three different moments, two in the 1980s and, finally, in the year 2000. Character and country are examined from a variety of perspectives. Frank features in his various roles as ex-husband, father (of two living children and one dead child), divorcee, lover, husband, abandoned husband, friend, sportswriter, real estate agent, suburbanite, citizen and, in the role that gives his narrative voice its great distinctiveness, inveterate philosopher of his own life.

Frank's life is, in exemplary fashion, the examined life. But Frank, as first-person narrator, also turns his inquiring mind to his country, and delivers himself of a rich stream of opinions on contemporary America, be it the experience of living in the suburbs, the influence of the economy on American culture and society, the understanding and practice of the values of the American republic, the condition of community life in America, the role of developers and the real estate profession in the transformation of the American urban landscape, or the influence and relevance of American history on contemporary life. Frank takes his status and responsibility as citizen seriously, and examines his country with the tough love of a critical patriot. At this under-developed stage of Richard Ford studies, then, there is a need to cast one's analytical net fairly wide in order to do justice both to the thematic scope of the trilogy and to the intellectual curiosity of Ford's reflective narrator, whose mind is ceaselessly turned to either self or country (often, it should be emphasized, to great comic effect).

As for "integrated", while it is indeed true that Richard Ford wished to maintain a certain creative independence when he began the second and third novels of the trilogy, this did not in any important way undermine the ultimate identity of the project as a trilogy, as three novels indissolubly connected in a number of vital ways. This is not to say that a reader may not profitably read only one of the novels, but it is to insist that there is continuity and a consistency of theme in the three books. There also develops, for the reader of the entire trilogy, an increasing familiarity with characters, settings and situations that has a powerful cumulative effect as the novels progress. In support of the integrated analytical approach to the novels, one might cite the trilogy's evolving interest in, *inter alia*, Frank's conceptualization of time, his relationship with members of his family, his ambivalence about intimacy, the condition of interpersonal relations in America and the atomization of American society. To these recurring thematic concerns one might add the emerging sense in the reader, particularly by the third novel, of being a privileged witness to a life evolving through time and the inevitable losses and accommodations of adulthood.

The case for an integrated reading receives its most potent support in the relationship between Frank and his dead son, Ralph. The opening scene of *The Sportswriter*, and therefore of the trilogy, finds Frank at Ralph's grave, there to pay his respects on what would have been his son's thirteenth birthday. Move forward to *The Lay of the Land*, and Ralph is still very present in Frank's mind. His relationship with his dead son, in fact, becomes one of the important themes of the last novel, occasioning a profound emotional upheaval, and one that has a decisive effect on Frank's trilogy-long conceptualizations of time and experience. Only an integrated reading of all three novels can do justice to this unexpected return of Ralph, which is also powerfully the case, one might add, where Frank's relationship with his ex-wife and son are concerned.

Beyond the objective to offer a general integrated reading of the Frank Bascombe novels, the title of this book also identifies three specific themes in Richard Ford's fiction that it wishes to investigate – those of morality, identity and narrative. The focus on these themes, along with the demand to place a manageable limit on the scope of this study, immediately influenced the texts to be analysed. It would be difficult to justify a monograph on Richard Ford's fiction that excluded the Bascombe trilogy; that reality accepted, other texts quite readily either attached themselves to, or detached themselves from, the undertaking, particularly with regard to the theme of morality, an important concern in Ford's fiction. In an interview published in 2000 Ford was asked about "the idea of moral vision in fiction". His reply, that such a vision must be "foremost",[1] is but one of several statements that could be adduced to underline the importance for Ford of a moral dimension in his fiction, a perspective that immediately calls forth the stories of *Women with Men* and *A Multitude of Sins*. Ford has characterized the novellas and stories of these two collections as "much more morally stringent" than his previous work. In the two Paris novellas of *Women with Men* and in the novella and nine stories of *A Multitude of Sins* Ford explores the moral dimension of relations between men and women, and in particular the responsibilities and consequences attendant upon the failure of people to remain faithful to each other, or to love each other in the way they have undertaken to do. Yet Ford's investigation of this aspect of human relations in these collections is merely a more explicit articulation of what had been preoccupying him in his fiction for years: the three Frank Bascombe novels are also deeply concerned with a moral vision, notably through Frank's relationships with members of his family and various women. And the trilogy's vision of contemporary America also has an ineradicable moral dimension to it in its focus on the values, practices and failings of American society.

---

[1] *Conversations with Richard Ford*, ed. Huey Guagliardo, Literary Conversations Series, Jackson, MS: UP of Mississippi, 2001, 192.

The thematic complementarity of the trilogy and the aforementioned collections of stories is reinforced by other important shared characteristics: the protagonists in all of these narratives are urban, well-educated, middle-class professionals. It is as if Ford placed his middle-class characters – in contrast to, say, those of the Montana stories in *Rock Springs* – beyond material need in order to better isolate the moral dimension of their behaviour. Furthermore, these characters are, as befits their professional circumstances, well able to articulate their emotions. It is worth pointing out in this regard that Richard Ford himself has noticed obvious demarcations in his writing output. In one interview he gave, he sets apart his first two novels, then goes on to identify the different "ways" of writing that he has practiced since then, discerning three such "thrusts" in his work, namely the "Montana stories", the "New Jersey" (Frank Bascombe) novels, and the "less personable stories" of *Women with Men* and *A Multitude of Sins*.[2] There is a concordance of theme and characters' concerns in the five books consisting of the Frank Bascombe trilogy, *Women with Men* and *A Multitude of Sins* to which neither Ford's first two novels nor the Montana stories of *Rock Springs* and *Wildlife* lend themselves.[3]

The themes of identity and narrative are not those commonly associated with Ford's fiction, nor do they feature particularly in Ford's own comments on his work. Yet it is remarkable the extent to which the issue of identity becomes either an explicit concern for Ford's characters, or an indispensable analytical concept for understanding their dilemmas. In *The Sportswriter* Frank cultivates difference and non-permanence in his life and personality to the point that, by the end of the novel, his identity remains strangely elusive, a condition that serves well his instinct to evade responsibility. In all three novels Frank's temporal manipulations, his highly conceptualized pigeonholing of his experience in time, seek above all to diminish, and even efface, the impact of the past in favour of the present. But precisely because we are beings who construct ourselves in time, who leave the trail of our emerging selves in the past, any attempt to cut our present off from our past will produce distorting effects on our identity. This is indeed what has happened to Frank by

---

[2] *Ibid.*, 202.
[3] One of the stories of *Women with Men*, "Jealous", is a Montana story, and is thus not considered in this study.

late middle age, the time of his life recounted in *The Lay of the Land*, making identity another of the important themes of the final novel.

In the story "Charity", Nancy Marshall is forced out of her comforting identity as a happily married woman and is obliged to question the old certainties upon which that identity was constructed. In the transitional phase between the unravelling of her old identity and the construction of a new identity as a solitary woman, she must confront the destabilizing experience of her being as "an *ebbing*" and as "something going out of her",[4] and must forge a new sense of self from the threatening new unnamability that has enveloped her. As she finds herself wondering at one point: "What was that thing she was? Surely it was a thing anyone should be able to say."[5] At a national level, important articulations of American identity are brought to light in the practice of such strong American values as freedom and independence (*Independence Day*), in the contrasting commitments to community and consumerism (all three novels of the trilogy), in the country's political choices (*The Lay of the Land*), in the attitudes to and assimilation of immigrants in contemporary America (*The Lay of the Land*), in the country's mythology and tradition of violence (*Independence Day*, but particularly *The Lay of the Land*), in the general demeanour of citizens as they celebrate important national holidays (*Independence Day* and *The Lay of the Land*), and in the attitude of Americans to intercultural contact when abroad ("Occidentals").

The theme of identity, however, is not only of relevance in its own right as a recurring theme. It would have been necessary to consider it in any case by virtue of its important relationship to morality. Charles Taylor, one of the philosophers upon whose work this study draws to elucidate the exchange between morality and identity, proposes that the answer to the question, "Who am I?", is arrived at by way of "an understanding of what is of crucial importance to us. To know who I am is a species of knowing where I stand."[6] Taylor wishes to emphasize "the essential link between identity and a kind of orientation". He continues: "To know who you are is to be oriented in

[4] Richard Ford, *A Multitude of Sins*, New York: Knopf, 2002, 195.
[5] *Ibid.*, 187.
[6] Charles Taylor, *Sources of the Self: The Making of the Modern Identity*, Cambridge, MA: Harvard UP, 1989, 27.

moral space."[7] Taylor's thesis resonates with remarkable regularity and force in Richard Ford's fiction, and becomes an exceptionally productive source of insight in the "morally stringent" stories of *Women with Men* and *A Multitude of Sins*. Martin Austin, the protagonist of "The Womanizer", wonders at the end of the story whether, by straying from the "good" represented by his wife and marriage, he has not moved away from the "fixed" identity through which he had understood himself, and has not "altered the important linkages that guaranteed his happiness and become detached, unreachable".[8] It is made absolutely clear in the text that it is his moral failings that have altered his sense of, and the reality of, who he is. The female protagonist of "Abyss" is thrown into a crisis of identity on account of the unhappy course of her affair: Frances Bilandic identifies her sense of feeling "strange" as one of not feeling "really like who she was",[9] as the betrayal of her husband, her life and values pulls her away from the sense she has of her own identity.

The theme of narrative imposes itself on the discussion by virtue of its role both in the articulation of morality and in the dynamics of identity. Charles Taylor insists that the understanding of our moral condition "can never be exhausted for us by what we *are*, because we are always also changing and *becoming*". He goes on:

> [The] sense of the good has to be woven into my understanding of my life as an unfolding story. But this is to state another basic condition of making sense of ourselves, that we grasp our lives in a *narrative*.[10]

For Taylor, life is a movement, both in the obvious sense of a temporal unfolding, but also in the moral sense of a continual self-orientation towards the good, an orientation that accords our lives a moral direction. And we comprehend that movement, understand that orientation and chart that direction by way of narrative.

The mechanics of narrative in this temporal and moral understanding and articulation of self are explored later in this study through the work of French philosopher, Paul Ricoeur, through his theory of narrative identity. For the moment, suffice it to say that the

---

[7] *Ibid.*, 28.
[8] Richard Ford, *Women with Men*, New York: Knopf, 1997, 92.
[9] Ford, *A Multitude of Sins*, 256.
[10] Taylor, *Sources of the Self*, 47 (italics in the original).

relationship between moral identity and narrative is one that Frank Bascombe consistently resists in the trilogy: he seeks to demarcate his temporal experience in order to minimize his past and achieve a fullness of being, identity and sensation in the present. Indeed, it is through systematically evading his past that he attempts to evade moral responsibility for his actions and behaviour. It comes as no surprise to the reader, then, but as something of a shock to Frank, to discover by *The Lay of the Land* that, some years earlier, he had begun to feel disturbingly inessential, and that he yearned for a recognizable self, for a sense of permanence and substantiality of identity. As Frank puts it himself: "Here, for a man with no calculable character, was a hunger for *necessity*, for something solid, the thing 'character' stands in for."[11]

The interdependence of morality, identity and narrative becomes all the more visible and unavoidable in a trilogy of novels covering the events of twenty years or more of Frank's adult life. And narrative is a recurring theme elsewhere in Ford's work, and on one occasion is central to the resolution of a specific dilemma confronting a character: the adult narrator of "Calling" recounts a series of events from his adolescence of thirty years previously that he manifestly has not fully come to terms with. In turning to narrative he seeks both an understanding of his relationship with his father and a means of connecting – through a bearable narrative account of that troubled relationship – his subsequent life to formative events in his youth.

A word of explanation ought to be offered about the modality of the readings offered in this study. Richard Ford's fictional texts are heavily character-based, a function of his realist fiction, his desire to explore the moral dimension of human relations and his desire, too, to render in his work what he terms "lived life".[12] As Charles Taylor reminds us, life is lived as an experience of *becoming* in time; characters move through time in their temporal trajectories, leaving the past, inhabiting the present and tending towards the future. The dominant narrative temporal structure in Ford's fiction is the simple chronology of events. There are, of course, analepses in his stories, but, in terms of structure, Ford is generally happy for the narration of events to proceed chronologically: in the Frank Bascombe trilogy, for

---

[11] Richard Ford, *The Lay of the Land*, New York, Knopf, 2006, 54.
[12] *Conversations with Richard Ford*, 28.

instance, the narratives all take us from the beginning of a holiday period to its end, a structure that emphasizes both the teleological and moral nature of Ford's fiction – the author wishes to transport his readers to the insights of the conclusion, to the lessons of the experiences just recounted (which is why he likes to, as he puts it, "load up the end" of his stories[13]).

Ford's fictional texts resemble so many journeys, charting the twists and turns, the losses and gains, the blindness and insight, and, above all, the changes that characterize human becoming in time. Moreover, because the time-frames in which events and experiences in Ford's stories occur are relatively short, and because his characters are reflective and anxious to justify their actions (two features that reach their extreme degree in the trilogy, in which several hundred pages are devoted to a few days), the various stages of characters' evolutions are thoroughly scrutinized. On account of this narrative practice, it is important to accompany Ford's characters on their journeys in order to identify and understand the stages they pass through in their movement towards whatever fate Ford reserves for them. This accompaniment is all the more necessary as Ford places so much emphasis in his fiction on the causal relation between acts and their moral consequences. It has, therefore, been one of the goals of this study to follow and capture the transformations, small and large, that ensue from the application of this simple but powerfully rendered logic in the fiction of Richard Ford.

---

[13] Robert Birnbaum, Interview with Richard Ford, "Richard Ford", *identity theory: the narrative thread*, http://www.identitytheory.com/people/birnbaum37.html (31/05/2005).

CHAPTER 1

THE SPORTSWRITER

I: FLEEING THE PAST

With *The Sportswriter* Richard Ford set himself the task of writing a novel "about a decent man" and about "a certain stratum of life that I knew, which was life in the suburbs".[1] The novel's tone also emerged out of Ford's desire "to write something that was optimistic".[2] These are untypical ambitions for the contemporary writer of fiction, a form whose themes, moral vision and narrative dynamic normally develop out of the exploitation of conflict, failure and a focus on the exceptional, even the extreme. Yet Ford remained true to his ambition: he wrote a novel about a tolerant, fair-minded man, Frank Bascombe, living a generally contented life in the New Jersey suburbs, and who, while enduring the unavoidable aggravations and tragedies of a life, retained an unshakable faith in the potential of life to bring mystery and pleasure.

That Ford's novel did indeed seem committed to exploring such a character and such a life caused the irony-detecting antennae of critical readers to quiver: surely this benign and apparently sympathetic view of the unexceptional life of a white male in the boring suburbs of central New Jersey was not to be taken at face value? In the postmodern, ironic age in which the novel was published

---

[1] *Conversations with Richard Ford*, 29.
[2] *Ibid.*, 172. Ford recalls that, in his first two novels, *A Piece of My Heart* and *The Ultimate Good Luck*, he "had begun, out of youthful ignorance and ardor, to associate darkness—emotional, spiritual, moral darkness—with high drama". He came to realize that he "could no longer sustain identifying darkness with drama. I just sort of ground to a halt." It was this creative impasse that propelled him to seek drama elsewhere, and he found it in the less self-consciously dramatic travails of Frank Bascombe.

the question was – and remains today – a relevant one. Critics, indeed, have not been able to agree about the dominant register of the novel. Jeffrey J. Folks finds many targets of satire in *The Sportswriter*, among which political liberals and conservatives, Frank's "grandiose philosophizing"[3] and expressions of sentiment in general, and sees Ford, through Frank's celebration of suburban life, as carrying out an interrogation of the "superficiality and oppressiveness of the suburbs".[4] Folks, however, does not read the novel exclusively in an ironic mode, noting, for example, how Frank – whom Folks sees as the target of much of the novel's satire – is depicted as a character "with serious ethical concerns".[5] Other critics see no irony in the novel at all. Edward Dupuy finds Ford's portrait of Frank free of "bitterness and irony",[6] while Fred Hobson distances himself from the "several reviewers" who detected an ironic intent in Ford's representation of mass culture, and goes so far as to assert that it is precisely Ford's refusal to indulge in facile irony in dealing with "popular culture" that distinguishes him from "numerous other contemporary writers".[7]

The discerning reader of a fictional text quickly becomes conscious of and attuned to its overall tone, and is alert to ironic possibilities and intentions, from subtle inconsistencies and contextual underminings to more direct satire and caricature. One does not have this sense of a structural irony in *The Sportswriter*, of a clear authorial invitation to the reader to collude at the expense of Frank Bascombe's life and environment: one understands Frank to be the generally contented and hopeful man he appears to be, living the life he likes in a community he appreciates, and doing a job he finds pleasurable. And while authorial intention is a much-discredited notion nowadays, one would do well to take seriously Ford's own comments on what he thought he was doing when writing about suburban life in *The Sportswriter*:

---

[3] Jeffrey J. Folks, "The Risks of Membership: Richard Ford's *The Sportswriter*", *Mississippi Quarterly*, LII/1 (1998-99), 77.
[4] *Ibid.*, 85.
[5] *Ibid.*, 84.
[6] Edward Dupuy, "The Confessions of an Ex-Suicide: Relenting and Recovering in Richard Ford's *The Sportswriter*", in *Perspectives on Richard Ford*, ed. Huey Guagliardo, Jackson, MS: UP of Mississippi, 2000, 71.
[7] Fred Hobson, "*The Sportswriter*: Post-Faulkner, Post-Southern?", in *Perspectives on Richard Ford*, 87.

There are lots of things to dislike about the suburbs, and the New Jersey suburbs in particular, but people don't dislike them. And that's just the truth. The suburbs have been written about ironically so often that I thought it might be a more interesting surgery on the suburbs to talk about them in unironic terms.[8]

While Ford's "surgery" metaphor may seem to suggest a deconstructive desire to expose the contradictions and conceits of suburban existence, the context makes it clear that he saw an unironic treatment of the suburbs as the means to better understand their appeal. In neither his protagonist nor his setting, then, does Ford seek to collaborate with the reader from an ironic position of superiority, or to try to flatter the reader's discernment at the expense of the world he portrays. Equally, however, he does not collaborate with his protagonist to promote the values that the latter proclaims, such as, for example, Frank's celebration of suburban existence. Ford, almost unfailingly, simply gives full expression to his creation and allows his character to narrate his life and proclaim the pleasures of suburban existence without directing the reader to the fault-lines in that ideology, while nonetheless exposing the values and meanings of that world to the harsh examination of experience. In this sense Ford is more disinterested scientist than ruthless ironist.

The personal nature of Frank's narrative is announced in the opening lines of the novel: "My name is Frank Bascombe. I am a sportswriter."[9] Both the novel's title and its opening lines refer to a profession, but also to an individual. Ford chose essentially the device of character through which to explore the social and moral world he deals with in *The Sportswriter*; whatever we learn of this world, we do so through the perspective of the main character, Frank Bascombe, a novelistic device of focus and partiality that is reinforced by employing Frank as a first-person narrator. The views presented to us

---

[8] *Conversations with Richard Ford*, 54.

[9] Richard Ford, *The Sportswriter*, New York: Knopf, 1996, 3. *The Sportswriter* was originally published in paperback by Vintage in March 1986. The Knopf edition was the first American hardcover edition of the novel. Further references to *The Sportswriter* will be indicated parenthetically in the text.

of, for example, the suburbs, middle-class culture, the relationships between men and women, and, at a more personal and overtly moral level, the vision presented to us of a worthwhile life, are those imparted to us from the exclusive perspective of the novel's narrator. This narrator, moreover, engages with his world and understands his place in it on the basis of a highly self-conscious and rigorously conceptualized set of convictions and dispositions, and the events and experiences he narrates are filtered through a very particular sensibility and a very personal perspective. It is for these reasons that the discussion in the two chapters devoted to the novel focuses on the first-person narrator and protagonist whose vision constructs the world we discover in *The Sportswriter*, and on this character's notions of the kind of man he is and on how he engages with the world. It is through this examination of the character of Frank – and of Frank's character – that we will come to an awareness of an evasive and disingenuous side to his personality that runs counter to the sense of identity he narrates for himself and the place in the moral world he would aspire to occupy.

There is another feature of the narrative that should be highlighted from the outset. It will emerge that Frank's account has been written some months after the events described in it, yet the narrative does not draw attention to its status as a worked-over, retrospective account. Not only is there no metanarrative commentary, but the novel, critically, is narrated in the present tense, feeding the illusion and narrative conceit that events are being recounted more or less as they occur, and are thus relatively, and almost naturally, free of but the merest of interventions by the narrator. It is only at the end of the account that the conditions surrounding the writing of the narrative become an important issue, to the point, indeed, that they have a decisive influence on our understanding of Frank's view of the events he has just narrated and even of the sense he has of his own identity.

From a number of perspectives, and certainly in the early chapters, the reader willingly assents to the proposition that Ford has written a novel about an essentially decent man. Frank is tolerant, amiable, rarely unfair in his judgements and willing to acknowledge his shortcomings when be becomes aware of them. It is these very qualities that accord the narrative its open-minded and affable tone. That Frank possesses all of these qualities, that he is free of bitterness and cynicism and is staunchly optimistic, is all the more admirable given the calamities that have befallen him: his son, "my sweet boy Ralph Bascombe" (204), died at the age of nine from Reye's syndrome (four years before the Easter weekend events narrated in the novel) and his marriage ended in divorce in the aftermath of this tragedy and Frank's loss of bearings. Frank is now coping with this double burden, attempting with his ex-wife to maintain the semblance of a normal childhood for their two other children. He can even find it in himself to conclude that it is sometimes through loss that we "become adults" (9) and that "things sometimes happen for the best" (29). And, in an admirably transcendent view, he can find comfort in life's ephemerality: grief and loss, like joy and passion, will pass, and time will move us on, perhaps to something better. As Frank puts it: "In all cases things are here and they're over, and that has to be enough" (16).

It is significant that Frank espouses this philosophy at this particular moment – at the beginning of his narrative and as he meets up with his ex-wife (referred to throughout as X) at their son's grave to commemorate what would have been Ralph's thirteenth birthday. In other words, Frank is keen from the outset to proclaim his philosophy of optimism, and can still do so despite the painful and sobering act of memory that he and his wife are about to perform. It is this context of the continued experience of loss that renders Frank's rejection of melancholy, his unself-pitying optimism and his instinct to survive so forceful: "We can make too much of our misfortunes" (207), he declares. As he approaches his thirty-ninth birthday Frank can survey the twelve years since he became a sportswriter unbowed by the tragedies of his past and able to look undeterred towards the future:

> In most ways it's been great. And although the older I get the more things scare me, and the more apparent it is to me that bad things can and do happen to you, very little really worries me or keeps me up at night. I still believe in the possibilities of passion and romance. And I would not change much, if anything at all. I might not choose to get divorced. And my son, Ralph Bascombe, would not die. But that's about it for these matters. (4)

In light of the above – Frank's winning personal qualities and his refusal to dwell on the tragedy and loss that have scarred his life – the reader might wonder about the urgencies and issues from which the novel draws its *raison d'être*. The answers to these speculations may be found initially in Richard Ford's conception of the purpose of fiction and of the burden of justification he insists that fiction must bear. Asked by an interviewer for his opinion "about the idea of moral vision in fiction", Ford replied:

> It's everything to me that the stories be about the most important things the writer knows about. And that a writer contracts with his reader, to use all of his power ... to go on and invent something new and of moment from those important issues .... I read a lot of novels this year. And when I decide one's not very good, it's because this sense of moral vision is not foremost in the story.[10]

Fiction, of course, simply by representing human existence, cannot but possess a moral dimension.[11] But Ford demands a "moral vision" and insists that this vision be "foremost" in fiction. And although perhaps less explicitly than in some of his later work, such a moral vision is indeed on display in *The Sportswriter*, and is realized through the character of Frank, whose voice, thoughts and actions dominate the text. That the novel, however, presents more than just a moral "vision" has been the subject of a certain amount of critical commentary: Frank's character and his relationships with others have given rise to the discussion of moral issues. Huey Guagliardo concludes that Frank "resists genuine intimacy",[12] while William G. Chernecky writes that Frank "alienates him[self] from the world around him",[13] which he attributes to his objectification and abstraction of people. Playing on Frank's name, Fred Hobson finds him "anything but frank, anything but candid and reliable", to the point, indeed, that he is not convinced that Frank is the "happy man"

---

[10] *Conversations with Richard Ford*, 192. This interview was first published in 2000.

[11] As Paul Ricoeur puts it: "Literature is a vast laboratory in which we experiment with estimations, evaluations, and judgments of approval and condemnation" (Paul Ricoeur, *Oneself as Another*, trans. Kathleen Blamey, Chicago: U of Chicago P, 1992, 115).

[12] Huey Guagliardo, "The Marginal People in the Novels of Richard Ford", in *Perspectives on Richard Ford*, 16.

[13] William W. Chernecky, "'Nostalgia Isn't What It Used To Be': Isolation and Alienation in the Frank Bascombe Novels", in *Perspectives on Richard Ford*, 159.

he claims to be.[14] Moreover, Hobson considers Frank to be philosophical in "a facile sort of way",[15] and he is not alone in questioning the sincerity of Frank's account. For Folks, Frank's "grandiose philosophizing seems trivial and inconsequential"[16] and his manner "irresolute and flippant".[17] Elinor Ann Walker opens a lengthy discussion on the novel with the observations that Frank's "efforts at truth-telling result mostly in further obfuscation" and that, due to his deployment of certain novelistic devices while at the same time condemning them, "the possibility of untruth" is built into his narrative.[18]

One is immediately struck in this critical commentary by the extent to which it contradicts the initial impression one gains of Frank (as well as Richard Ford's own description of his character). A close reading of the novel, then, would appear to transform Frank from a decent and admirable man into one who is glib, detached and possibly untrustworthy. And while the critical commentary also allows Frank many of the creditable qualities already accorded him, the charge remains that all is not as it seems where the central character of the novel is concerned. Two questions immediately suggest themselves: first, to what extent, and in what exact manner, is Frank less admirable than initially indicated, and that has him appear to be other than he believes himself to be, or other than he claims to be? And, second, what, if any, are the moral implications of this less admirable behaviour, or, to frame the question in light of Ford's concerns with morality in his work, how does the portrayal of Frank's behaviour contribute to the moral vision presented in the novel?

These considerations ultimately resolve themselves into questions about the personal and moral identity of Frank and about the foundation and construction of these self-conceptions. Richard Ford has observed, responding to an interview question about the importance to him of "the development of character", that "we

---

[14] Hobson, "*The Sportswriter*: Post-Faulkner, Post-Southern?", 93.
[15] *Ibid.*, 94.
[16] Folks, "The Risks of Membership", 77.
[17] *Ibid.*, 84.
[18] Elinor Ann Walker, *Richard Ford*, Twayne United States Authors Series, New York: Twayne, 2000, 63.

wouldn't have moral dilemmas and conflicts without [characters]".[19] Ford remains true to his conviction about the function and potential of fictional character in the manner in which he presents his protagonist in the novel as a moral agent. He accords Frank a philosophical disposition and a capacity to conceptualize his life into a series of guiding principles that are as much moral as practical, and it is precisely this vision that is seen to inform the conduct of Frank's life. Ford also lays open for our scrutiny the construction and justification of Frank's moral views and identity, almost explicitly inviting his readers to attend to the moral dimension of the novel.[20] Finally, Ford devotes detailed attention to Frank's daily actions, in a manner consistent with his view that we do not "sin in thought, only in our deeds";[21] his novel develops in part, therefore, from the obligation to provide adequate exposition of Frank's behaviour.

It is to these moral considerations that we now turn, by exploring, first, Frank's character and the provenance and nature of the principles that inform his engagement with the world; second, the application of these principles to his life; and, third, the consequences they have for him and for others. This will oblige us to look back before considering the present: while the events of the novel take place over the Easter weekend, long portions of the narrative are devoted to Frank's past, and particularly to the four years between the death of his young son and the Easter weekend he is about to narrate. It becomes clear that the weekend events take place in the mournful shadow cast by what has occurred in Frank's life in the years preceding this Easter weekend. The Frank Bascombe we meet on Good Friday morning, then, is a man heading into the holiday weekend sustained by a very precise view of his values and goals in life, yet is also a man marked

---

[19] Bonnie Lyons, Interview with Richard Ford, "Richard Ford: The Art of Fiction CXLVII", *Paris Review*, 140 (Fall 1996), 46.

[20] In an interview Ford agreed with the interviewers' observation about how characters' decisions in *The Sportswriter* and *Independence Day* "reflect a philosophy of life, a world view" (Imre Salusinszky and Stephen Mills, "An Interview with Richard Ford", *Heat Magazine*, 15 [2000], 171). The philosophical and moral framework that Ford provides for Frank in *The Sportswriter* is indeed one of the defining features of the novel, making it all the more difficult to avoid a moral reading of Frank's behaviour.

[21] "Richard Ford: The Art of Fiction CXLVII", 68.

by painful recent experiences from whose effects he has not yet liberated himself.

The defining event in Frank's life has been the death of his nine-year-old son. This was the turning point in a life that, until then, had been enjoyable and fulfilling, and that Frank remembers "fondly". It was a "generic" life in which Frank and X worked, loved and played while having three children, and where Frank was "happy as a swallow" (9) living the "normal applauseless life of us all" (10). When Ralph died, Frank drifted into a state of detachment, both from himself and his life, and became distant from X, leading, two years later, to divorce. In a manifestation of his reluctance to confront troublesome facts and reality, and to acknowledge that actions and events can produce direct consequences, Frank is unwilling to attribute his period of detachment, which he calls dreaminess, to his son's death, despite an irrefutable chronology and causation: "my son Ralph got Reye's syndrome some years later and died, and I launched off into the dreaminess his death may or may not have even caused" (41). At the very end of his narrative Frank will recognize obliquely that his period of dreaminess was one expression of his grieving for his son, which, when combined with other reactions and dispositions of character, imprisoned him in a narrow, delusionary view of his life and his relations with others. It is precisely this brittle frame of mind into which Frank retreated that must first be examined, by exploring the various manifestations of Frank's engagement with the world in the aftermath of Ralph's death.

The most striking feature of the opening passages of Frank's narrative is the juxtaposition of tragedy and optimism. Frank has suffered an almost unbearable loss, yet seems able to surmount this and to proclaim that, all things considered, life is good. One does not for a moment doubt Frank's sincerity, yet his resilience in the face of his child's death and his own divorce seems hardly credible, and almost unnatural. One is led to wonder how, if life before tragedy struck was so happy, Frank can now be so serene and optimistic. The clue to this jarring optimism is to be found in the final comments of his opening remarks: "for your life to be worth anything you must sooner or later face the possibility of terrible, searing regret. Though you must also manage to avoid it or your life will be ruined" (4). The regret that Frank has in mind is the pain and loss associated with the twin calamities in his life, and it is these that he decided he must avoid, perhaps at all costs. But avoidance of regret in Frank became evasion, an unwillingness or inability to confront the reality of loss; instead, Frank's reaction to pain and loss was to wall himself up in an impermeable, self-protective carapace, a response that was itself but a symptom of his wider, deeply rooted tendency to shun the unpalatable facts of reality, and of which his dreaminess was but one expression.

The opening scene in the novel, when Frank and X meet at Ralph's grave, allows a telling contrast to be drawn between Frank and X's respective responses to tragedy. X is sad and unhopeful, and cries in her unhappiness. She seems defenceless against the emotions triggered by the anniversary of her son's death and is invaded by a pessimism linked to getting old, to an unanswered existential anxiety about "what we should all be doing" (16), and to a grief-ridden feeling that has her wonder if "anyone can be happy anymore". In her experience of grief she refuses to take comfort in the optimistic sentiments of the poem Frank begins to read at Ralph's grave, cutting him off by telling him that she "just [doesn't] believe it" (19). X is confronting terrible loss because it is an unavoidable reality for her; her reaction seems true, appropriate and convincing. Frank, on the other hand, seems to have anaesthetized himself to his grief, and counters X's pessimism with glib, calendar-quotation pieties and chirpy assertions of his optimistic frame of mind. His attitude seems forced and facile. To X's question about whether he laughs enough these days, Frank's "You bet I do" (13) response sells his optimism a little too hard. X, indeed, is struck by Frank's sunny pronouncements, telling him, euphemistically, that he is "very adaptable", and, at his fatuous response to this, feels obliged to be more explicit: "Do you feel like you're at the point of understanding everything that's happened—to us and our life?" (21). The implication of her question is clear, and the accusation justified, but they fail to penetrate Frank's defensive shield.

The scene ends with X walking away sadly at another of his happy-grin assertions of his belief in optimism. Frank has already claimed that he feels he is now emerging from his detached phase, but this opening scene discloses that he is still deeply immersed in the emotional consequences of tragedy. So, too, is X, but she knows that she is, knows why this is so and is facing up to loss. Frank believes that he is now beyond grief, an illusion engendered by his avoidance of a slow, direct and lengthy confrontation with loss.

Frank's avoidance of regret is, as I have suggested, only one aspect of a complex and systematic defensive strategy that infiltrates every part of his emotional and intellectual being, affecting his perspective on his life, both personal and professional, and his very identity. The most instinctive and immediate aspect of this defensive response has been his condition of dreaminess. As Frank conceives it, it is a state of detachment or disconnectedness from himself, producing in him the urge "to 'see around the sides' of whatever I was feeling" (64), a state in which everything became contingent and arbitrary. This psychological and philosophical disengagement allows feelings and actions to be viewed from any number of different perspectives, but mostly ironically, leading Frank to behave erratically and liable to utter, as he acknowledges himself, "the most sinister lie or the most clownish idiocy known to man" (218). His dreaminess did not begin as a willed or calculated refusal of reality, but seems rather to have been a response to deep psychological shock, yet it has now become an important part of his avoidance mode of behaviour. It estranges Frank from the present reality of his life in a number of ways: it substitutes a rootedness in and possession of his own life with a pleasurable basking in the vague possibilities of a different life; it replaces the responsibility of knowledge with the giddiness of anticipation; and, as "a response to too much useless and complicated factuality" (42), it encourages Frank to take refuge in fantasy: "For a time … I … thought I was onto something big—changing my life, moorings loosed, women, travel, marching to a different drummer" (42). When Frank most needed to be fully attentive to his emotions and most aware of the influence of cause and effect in his life, he was, at the worst stages of his dreaminess, "light years away from everything" (16), afloat in a spectral existence, at once present and absent in his own life.

Frank is highly self-conscious and self-reflective; he is the great philosopher of his own existence, and his account is littered with maxims and principles about the conduct of his life. If dreaminess was an instinctive or uncalculated response to his grief, it was nonetheless consistent with an intricate set of concepts and theories he had consciously developed, and through which he has come to understand his life and sense of self. Although Frank passes these off as no more than the accumulated wisdom of the thoughtful man of experience, his notions of literalism, factualism and mystery represent the conceptual foundations of his philosophical world-view and constitute a vital part of his self-protective strategy of avoidance. Frank's notions of literalism and factualism are interdependent, and represent opposing philosophies of apprehending and dealing with one's experience. The literalist, which is what Frank considers himself to be, takes life as it comes, is at home with his emotions, is serene in the present moment and does not bedevil his life with useless complication. The factualist is the opposite of this, letting himself get bogged down in immutable facts and in the wider context of causes and consequences, thus restricting possibilities and limiting the simple pleasures of the moment. Frank explains the difference between the two as follows:

> A literalist is a man who will enjoy an afternoon watching people while stranded in an airport in Chicago, while a factualist can't stop wondering why his plane was late out of Salt Lake, and gauging whether they'll still serve dinner or just a snack. (132-3)

Frank, as a literalist, advocates the simple pleasure of appealing emotions, to be fully appreciated in the moment of their occurrence; the unfortunate factualist, on the other hand, will situate events within the wider temporality of past and future, thus exposing himself to the responsibilities and consequences attendant upon cause and effect. Frank has codified these attitudes into the conflicting modes of serenity and fretfulness, and would have us endorse his obvious preference. His concept of factualism, however, is no more than his derisive codeword for reality and the unpalatable facts of life – factualism denotes the reality that Frank is committed to avoiding. The obdurate reality of brute facts is Frank's constant target in the novel. In his eyes they reduce the world to the impoverished condition of the knowable and the sayable; they are restrictive, immutable, anti-anticipation and anti-possibility. As Frank puts it: "I hate for things to get finally pinned down, for possibilities to be narrowed by the shabby impingement of facts" (83).

When one of his acquaintances, Walter Luckett, confesses a homosexual encounter to Frank, it is not any moral aspect of the incident that bothers Frank, but simply that Walter has brought him a form of news about the world, "a set of facts-of-life", that he would "have been happy never to know about" (98). And Walter, like the airport factualist, compounds his mistake in Frank's eyes by trying to insert the brute facts of his isolated homosexual encounter into a wider story of causes and consequences. To Frank's response that "most things are better if you just let them be lonely facts", Walter pleads that he "needed a context" (94), by which he means the wider story of his life into which his homosexual experience could be made to fit, and out of which might emerge a bearable explanation of his behaviour, or at least some important knowledge about the kind of man he is. But Frank is closed to Walter's distress, a characteristic response when the responsibility of knowledge and unpalatable facts threaten to penetrate his serene world-view: "when the facts are made clear, I can't bear it, and run away as fast as I can" (83), declares Frank.

The governing concept in Frank's life, his commanding value, is mystery, "the *only* thing I find to have value at this stage in my life". He defines it as "the attractive condition a thing (an object, an action, a person) possesses which you know a little about but don't know about completely". This condition of partial knowledge and the "promise of unknown things" (101) free the mind to anticipate without constraint, presenting the imagination – and feeding one's desires – with unlimited possibilities. Its most dubious manifestation in Frank are his visits to a palmist, Mrs Miller, whose ritual pronouncements Frank claims to see through but whom he continues to visit for the sense of mystery these same pronouncements procure. Mystery represents the fullest and ultimate expression of a philosophy already articulated in his concepts of dreaminess, literalism and anti-factuality. Although dreaminess became a destructive condition for Frank, and too destabilizing in its insubstantiality, its attraction lay in the anticipation of possibilities and in the freedom to think beyond one's mundane existence. This vestige of dreaminess has evolved into his notion of mystery and its valorization of pleasurable anticipation. And factuality, in its turn, is the enemy of mystery, in that awkward facts limit the choices that give birth to mystery and anticipation:

> Choices are what we all need. And when I walk out into the bricky warp of these American cities, that is exactly what I feel. Choices aplenty. Things I don't know anything about but might like are here,

possibly waiting for me .... And what could be better? More
mysterious? More worth anticipating? Nothing. Not a thing. (7-8)

In his casual indifference to considering the possible consequences
of such an attitude, it has not dawned on Frank that the precondition of
mystery, namely the refusal of knowledge, may have had a vital
bearing on his divorce. Knowledge, like facts, exacts responsibility;
we are changed, made different, drawn into a web of responsibilities,
causes and consequences by the acquisition of knowledge. But
responsibility, and things becoming "pinned down" through
knowledge, are what Frank most dreads. This extends to the
knowledge of people, and even to X. As a general rule Frank
considers that it is not "a good idea to want to know what people are
thinking", one awkward consequence of which could be that "you will
run the risk of being told the *very* truth of what someone is thinking,
which can turn out to be something you don't want to hear" (76).
Frank likes to believe that his marriage failed because of the dreamy
detachment he lapsed into, a condition he did not control but rather
suffered from. This is partly true, but is also convenient, as it allows
him to elude responsibility and to ignore the implications of the fact
that, as he tells the incredulous Walter, he never confided in X when
they were married.

The catalyst for their divorce illustrated how emotionally
unreachable Frank had become for X. She discovered letters that
Frank had been receiving from a woman he had met on one of his
sportswriting trips. Peggy Connover and Frank had done nothing but
talk long into the night on that occasion, but Peggy had continued
their conversation in her "chatty, normal over-the-fence-sounding"
letters (148). X concluded that these letters, and those she correctly
assumed Frank was sending back, represented the kind of exchange
that she had long been deprived of in her relationship with Frank; her
reward for remaining faithful to him had been, as Frank himself puts
it, his "lying charitably to avoid full disclosure" (131). The discovery
of the letters provoked the crisis that led to divorce. Yet two years
later Frank has not progressed in his reflections on the state of his
marriage or the causes of the divorce. He professes to love and admire
X and, in what is close to disingenuousness, wonders "How could I
have ever loved her and let her go" (11). He thinks reconciliation with
X is possible and would gladly remarry her. Such is his systematic

avoidance of harsh facts and the reasons attending his marriage and divorce that he felt that, "if she could've simply trusted just that I loved her", their marriage could have been saved, as Frank considers that he would have "come around before too long" (131).

Frank's dreaminess was the immediate condition that estranged him from X, from himself and his own life. This short-term circumstance, however, was bolstered by the conscious and codified philosophy of Frank to privilege anticipation over reality, mystery over facts, and unknowing over knowledge. Frank's philosophy of avoidance of reality and his airy disengagement from complexity played a major part in his decision to abandon literature in favour of sportswriting. He offers various explanations for his decision not to pursue a promising literary career following the publication of a well-received book of short stories, among which his feeling of being "washed up" (40), his "failure of imagination" (46) and the more immediate reason of being offered a job on a sports magazine. But a decisive factor was Frank's increasing wariness of the "complicated and enigmatic" (42) nature of "complex literature" (43). When offered a sportswriting job, therefore, the essential attraction for Frank lay in exchanging the potentially troubling complexity of literature for the simplicity and superficiality of sportswriting. Being a sportswriter, for Frank, is "more like being a businessman, or an old-fashioned traveling salesman with a line of novelty household items, than being a genuine writer" (42).

Frank's subject is now athletes, whom he considers to be superficial, one-dimensional and focused on themselves to the point of selfishness, and to whom doubt and complexity are utterly alien. Athletes' capacity to avoid complexity, indeed, is a quality that Frank admires "more than almost any other I can think of" (63), and one he subscribes to in his own life. The ultimate appeal of the world of sport to Frank is that it allows him to live out his essential values, and he eventually reaches the quite logical, and profound, conclusion about his affinity with his profession: "I am content ... to think of sportswriting not as a real profession but more as an agreeable frame of mind, a *way* of going about things rather than things you exactly do or know" (312). Sportswriting, then, has come to articulate an important aspect of Frank's value system: through it, he can depict the world in the simplistic and – as we will see – fabricated terms that his literalist, avoidance philosophy demands and through which he understands his own life.

Frank's embracing of the superficiality of sportswriting is of a piece with his commanding ideology of mystery. Their affinity lies in what they oppose – explanation, complexity, disclosure, knowledge. Frank rails constantly against these: they remove mystery (and therefore anticipation) from the world, and they are the antithesis of the literalist mode in which he wishes to live. "Explaining is where we all get into trouble", proclaims Frank, before continuing: "Some things can't be explained. They just are. And after a while they disappear" (223). This lamentable urge to explain was the source of Frank's irritation with his former colleagues at the college he taught while deep in his dreaminess phase: Frank castigates them all as "anti-mystery types" because they were "expert in the arts of explaining, explicating and dissecting" (222). And he worries, too, about X not taking his children to church, as they risk becoming "perfect little factualists and information accumulators with no particular reverence or speculative interest for what's not known" (204).

The final component of Frank's strategy of self-protection against the intrusion of inconvenient reality and unwanted facts and explanation – all of which threaten his responsibility-free status of present-moment serenity and anticipation of the future – is his dismissal of any reliable explanatory or predictive mechanisms in respect of human behaviour, or in the progression of human lives. This doctrine takes the radical form of Frank's refusal to concede any principle of causality in human affairs. We have seen that he is reluctant to posit his son's death as the cause of his dreaminess, declaring himself "unwilling to say" that "anything is ever the sole cause of anything else" (10). But what is offered initially as perhaps no more than normal circumspection in attributing precise causes to specific effects evolves into a comprehensive refusal to allow the past any causal function or explanatory role in human behaviour:

> All we really want is to get to the point where the past can explain nothing about us and we can get on with life. Whose history can ever reveal very much? In my view Americans put too much emphasis on their pasts as a way of defining themselves, which can be death-dealing ....
>
> My own history I think of as a postcard with changing scenes on one side but no particular or memorable messages on the back. You

can get detached from your beginnings ... just by life itself, fate, the tug of the ever-present .... at some point we are whole and by ourselves upon the earth, and there is nothing that can change that for better or worse. (24)

Frank seems to recognize that the past has indeed the power to exercise a decisive influence on the understanding of our lives; his goal, therefore, is to break free of that potential power and potential burden. This is particularly so where the family story is concerned. Frank's father died when he was fourteen, and he did not see a lot of his mother after that, and he is happy to consign his parents to that distant, and now forgotten, past. For Frank, family narratives succeed only in nourishing perceived slights, producing "a list of problems and hatreds to brood about—a bill of particular grievances and nostalgias that pretend to explain or trouble everything" (29). Frank acknowledges that "We all have histories of one kind or another", by which he means that we all have a potential narrative of how we got to "where we are" (41), but insists that "nobody's history could've brought another Tom, Dick or Harry to the same place. And to me that fact limits the final usefulness of these stories" (42). For Frank, the very individuality of such stories disallows the predictive or explanatory competence of personal narratives. He returns indirectly to the narrative theme elsewhere in the novel, intent on undermining both the past and narrative as sources of knowledge. He lists the important events that can occur in a life, any one of which "would be enough to send you into a spin", concluding that "it is hard to say what *causes* what, since in one important sense *everything* causes everything else" (132). And he points to the "minor but pernicious lie of literature" that reduces the confused emotional aftermath of important events to an exclusive, knowable emotion, or to the "falsehood" of an epiphany (119). In both cases Frank's intention is to undermine the past as a source of knowledge and explanation, and to deny that narrative knowledge or explanation are either possible or desirable.

If Frank insists that the past can neither explain nor define him in any useful way, it is largely because he has a vested interest in promoting the temporality that serves his own philosophy of mystery and anticipation. In particular Frank's narrative is obsessed with the present, a tendency already visible in his literalist philosophy. At

several points in his account – narrated, let us recall, in the present
tense – Frank's only desire is for time to stop so as to allow the
pleasure of the moment to endure. As he is about to take the plane to
Detroit with his girlfriend, Vicki Arcenault, a sudden sensation of
well-being has him yearn: "And if I could make the moment last, ... I
would, and never leave this airport" (73). He pops into the Haddam
First Presbyterian church on Easter Sunday morning for his spiritual
fix and comes away with what he was seeking, some "*pro tempore*"
salvation (238). These are small instances of the manner in which
Frank has systematically delimited his temporality to the present and
the future, and into a child-like demand that the world provide him
with either immediate pleasure or the anticipation of pleasure. "New
today. New tomorrow" is how he formulates this expectation of what
he calls "Eternal renewal" (148). One of the attractions of
sportswriting, he realizes, is "how often I am with people I don't
know", granting him "a clean slate almost every day of my life" (152).
This is the clinical, frictionless temporality of Frank's existence,
where the past is actively effaced ("what *I* am a proponent of is
forgetting", 144), the present moment venerated, and the future of
commitments and consequences dissolved into the anticipation of
mystery, into the "bright, softened future awaiting us" (140).

On the threshold of the Easter weekend at which his narrative
begins, Frank Bascombe is a man who has developed a perspective on
his life and a relation to reality that demand an ultimate flexibility and
freedom. He seeks an existence which offers unlimited choices
promising future delights; which soothes the present with the pleasure
of anticipation, and beckons it enticingly towards the future; which
liberates the present and the future from the pull of the past; and
which lightens reality of constraining facts and causal explanations.
This is the depthless world – temporally, emotionally, morally – that
Frank has constructed for himself and in which he conducts his life.
These expectations and dispositions inform the principles that have
fixed the moral coordinates for his action in the world, and that will,
therefore, direct his behaviour and relationships with others over the
Easter weekend.

CHAPTER 2

THE SPORTSWRITER

II: IMPERMANENCE AND THE PRESENT

Having considered Frank's character and the provenance and nature of the principles that inform his engagement with the world, we may now turn to the second and third objectives we set ourselves in the previous chapter – the application of these principles to his life and the consequences they have for him and for others. If there is a danger in this approach, it would be to slip into a facile moralizing mode. It would simply not be good enough, however, merely to pronounce judgement on Frank on the basis of some unspoken but conventional moral code, as if it were transparently obvious where Frank's moral shortcomings lay. One needs, rather, to understand how Frank's personal philosophy leads to a particular kind of behaviour, and then to specific moral consequences. Tracing this trajectory, in turn, demands a philosophical and moral perspective that not only elucidates Frank's attitudes and behaviour but that is also conceptually equipped to move beyond mere moral evaluation and on to the wider issue of the interaction between moral behaviour and personal identity. Such a conceptualization is provided by the theory of moral action and moral identity formulated by Alasdair MacIntyre in his book, *After Virtue: A Study in Moral Theory*, and by the analysis of modern identity carried out by Charles Taylor in his *Sources of the Self: The Making of the Modern Identity*. In their different ways both works illuminate the moral dimension of Frank's character, highlight the inescapably temporal features of moral action and articulate a concept of personal identity that is indissociable from moral identity.

Alasdair MacIntyre's moral theory differs from those of many of his contemporaries in his insistence that human behaviour must be considered within the context of a human life, within, that is, the unity of a life as a whole, and that human behaviour cannot be dissected into individual actions. For MacIntyre, it makes no sense "to think atomistically about human action",[1] as actions that are disconnected from each other in this manner are simply not intelligible. Without the context of the agent's intentions, motives and beliefs, and the settings of actions,[2] all of which have their own histories, a basic action cannot become an intelligible action. And the intelligibility conferred by these histories of intentions, beliefs and settings, MacIntyre insists, is a narrative one: "Narrative history of a certain kind turns out to be the basic and essential genre for the characterization of human actions."[3] It is also this narrativized intelligibility that renders agents accountable for the actions they author: because, precisely, actions derive from a human agent's motives and intentions, they are carried out and apprehended by others within an intelligible moral context, within which an account of these actions can then be demanded. And it is narrative, too, that gives the whole of a human life its unity, and that constructs the personal identity of an individual. These come together in the notion of selfhood, the "concept of a self whose unity resides in the unity of a narrative which links birth to life to death as narrative beginning to middle to end".[4]

Charles Taylor arrives at the same conclusion from a different perspective: he wishes to emphasize the sense we have of our lives as a movement, which in turn leads to our concern with the direction of our lives, and specifically with how we are "'placed' or 'situated' in relation to the good".[5] These notions of movement and direction immediately situate us in time, and this constant obligation to

---

[1] Alasdair MacIntyre, *After Virtue: A Study in Moral Theory*, 2nd edn, London: Duckworth, 1985, 204.

[2] By "setting", MacIntyre means the context within which an action takes place. He gives the example of a man working outside, the explanation of whose actions could fall within the different intelligible contexts of "Digging", "Gardening", "Taking exercise", or "Pleasing his wife". In other words, several contexts, or settings, could render his actions intelligible, as these actions would be situated within a wider history of a connected set of intentions and consequences. In the above example, the setting could be the "annual cycle of domestic activity" (*ibid.*, 206), or that of the social setting of a marriage. Clearly, an action can belong to several settings at once.

[3] *Ibid.*, 208.

[4] *Ibid.*, 205.

[5] Taylor, *Sources of the Self*, 42.

orientate ourselves morally in time has us understand life "as an unfolding story" and has us "grasp our lives in a *narrative*". And it is also because of this dynamic dimension of our lives that the questions of who we are and how we are situated in relation to the good "can never be exhausted for us by what we *are*, because we are always also changing and *becoming*".[6] The sense we have of who we are, then, cannot be achieved uniquely in the present, but necessarily involves the whole of our life, embracing the past, the "history of my maturations and regressions, overcomings and defeats", and the future, as it is "On the basis of what I am [that] I project my future".[7] In this regard Taylor cites the example of those who seek to redeem their dubious moral past through their actions in the future.

MacIntyre, for his part, also focuses on our past and our future, but links it specifically to the social nature of our identity. In stating that "What I am … is in key part what I inherit, a specific past that is present to some degree in my present", he sees us as "bearers of a tradition":[8] "I am someone's son or daughter, someone else's cousin or uncle; I am a citizen of this or that city, a member of this or that guild or profession."[9] And the historical and social aspects of identity coincide also in our projections into the future:

> We live out our lives, both individually and in our relationships with each other, in the light of certain conceptions of a possible shared future …. There is no present which is not informed by some image of some future and an image of the future which always presents itself in the form of a *telos* – or of a variety of ends or goals.[10]

For Taylor, too, a social identity is the *sine qua non* of the very notion of identity: there cannot be a person without there being language, and an embeddedness within language presupposes a language community: "We first learn our languages of moral and spiritual discernment by being brought into an ongoing conversation

---

[6] *Ibid.*, 47.
[7] *Ibid.*, 50 and 51.
[8] MacIntyre, *After Virtue*, 221.
[9] *Ibid.*, 220.
[10] *Ibid.*, 215.

by those who bring us up." We define ourselves as selves within the context of our interlocutors, within the linguistic and moral space inhabited by these selves. Taylor's understanding of a social identity, then, is quite simple: "One is a self only among other selves. A self can never be described without reference to those who surround it."[11]

In their discussions of personal, but particularly moral, identity, MacIntyre and Taylor concur on two important points. First, identity can be understood only within the context of the whole life of a person, or, to formulate this with an eye to the discussion on Frank Bascombe, identity cannot be articulated in the present alone. If located uniquely in the present, both individual actions and moral orientation lack the necessary temporal context: individual actions will be unintelligible, and moral orientation impossible. Second, being a self, having an identity, implies a social context: we are who we are in relation to others, that is, as a function of our interaction with a community of other selves. If there is an implicit moral imperative embedded in MacIntyre's and Taylor's concepts of moral identity, it is that of responsibility, and this in two senses. First, there is the responsibility to one's own past and future, in which one must pay attention to the obligations of the personal and social self that have emerged out of the past, and be responsible for the goals one forms for the future. Second, there is the responsibility that lies in our accountability to others, the obligation that comes with our existence within a society, with our constant interaction with other selves.

As it happens, this is also the moral context within which Richard Ford likes to situate his characters. Speaking in an interview about why he preferred to write about adults rather than children in his fiction, he observed: "the real events take place in the lives of people who are responsible, who bear the consequences of action as fully as it can be borne."[12] As we will see, Ford will remain true to this moral imperative where Frank is concerned: it is precisely in the area of responsibility that Frank's philosophy leaves him exposed, a consequence of his refusal of a causal, narrative understanding of his life, of his avoidance of unwelcome reality, and of his philosophy of the primacy of the present over the past.

---

[11] Taylor, *Sources of the Self*, 35.
[12] *Conversations with Richard Ford*, 116.

Frank's most important and intimate relationship in the novel is with his girlfriend, Vicki Arcenault, and a good part of the text is taken up with the time they spend together. Vicki is altogether different from X, sentimental and kitschy one moment, suspicious and aggressive the next. Frank claims to be much taken with her, although this seems due more to Vicki's physical attractions and to Frank's need to have a woman in his life than to any deep complicity between them. He describes her as a "sweet, saucy little black-hair" (6), and as a "little bundle" (7). One wonders how Frank could be involved with Vicki after having happily spent most of his adult life with X, whose fidelity, steadfastness and sober intelligence are qualities that Frank claimed to love. However, it is precisely the complete contrast offered by Vicki that explains Frank's infatuation with her. We have said that Frank's defining characteristics are his evasion of constraining reality and his striving towards mystery. This impels him to search for modes of escape, leading him, in what has become an instinctive reaction, to seek refuge in both physical flight and fantasy. He tells us that the "first thing" he did after Ralph's burial was to "take off driving west" (117) on a Harley-Davidson motorcycle he had just bought, before he eventually turned back; and he finally did leave home, and his wife and children, after Ralph's death to teach for three months in a private college in western Massachusetts. He took flight from his life, too, in the fantasy worlds he created through his contact with the lives of the eighteen women he slept with in the two years after Ralph's death, "longing with all my worth to be a part" of their lives (129), and in the process creating "an illusion of life" (132) that was different from the one from which he was fleeing. Grief was at the origin of the flight into the illusory world of the lives portrayed in shopping catalogues in which Frank immersed himself after Ralph died.

That escapist tendency continues: when he arrives with Vicki in Detroit (where he has an assignment), he immediately lapses into sentimental fantasy mode, imagining in detail the life he could lead there, seeing himself as "a perfect native" (115) of, in turn, Detroit, Michigan and the Midwest. In all of these moments, as in his straining towards the future, Frank is running away from his life, and yearning for another spiritual and emotional place to inhabit. Vicki embodies this other place and other life, and Frank willingly escapes into her embrace. Yet the perpetually edgy nature of their conversations suggests a mismatch of sensibilities and expectations, and although Vicki's "matter-of-factness with her raptures" can make Frank "cry out in the night for longing" (6), his relationship with her is founded more on fantasy than affinity.

Frank's relationship with Vicki takes on a moral dimension due to the attenuated sense of responsibility he brings to their relationship. Frank subscribes to the view that "you don't need to be held responsible for what you think" (77). This self-absolution from responsibility in thought does not in itself seem so shocking: thoughts arrive in one's mind uninvited, and are not always noble. The problem with Frank is that self-absolution from responsibility in thought leads to self-absolution from responsibility in speech and deed, and does so in those moments when neither past nor future is allowed to inform his actions, and when the opinions of the other person are neither known nor sought. There are fewer more hallowed words pronounced between human beings than "I love you", yet Frank found himself saying this routinely to the many women he slept with after his divorce. But his relationship with Vicki is supposed to be different; on his own account Frank is now coming out of his emotionally unstable period and has thoughts of marrying Vicki, noting with optimism, as he anticipates the trip with her to Detroit, that "I am already pretty certain I'm in love with her" (6). In the light of his previous tendency to declare his love to whichever woman he happened to be with, Frank very pointedly obliges himself to consider both the depth of his feelings for Vicki and the language that would express these feelings: "how can I say I 'love' Vicki Arcenault? How can I trust my instincts all over again?" (132). With the full weight of this self-conscious and very deliberate reflection behind him, Frank concludes, drawing on his creed of the valorization of the present moment: "Who cares if I don't love her forever? Or she me? Nothing persists. I love her now, and I'm not deluding myself or her" (133).

Neither Frank's experience in the past nor the possible future consequences of his words allows him to see beyond the narrow temporal parameters of present gratification. But in his refusal to take responsibility for the profound implications of his words, in rejecting any principle of cause and effect, he is indeed deluding both Vicki and himself, as the depiction of the two extended periods of time they spend together over the Easter weekend demonstrates (the Good Friday overnight trip to Detroit and the Easter Sunday visit to Vicki's family). Both end in disappointment, and the latter in recrimination and bitterness. It dawns on Frank fairly quickly in Detroit that he is "lost in strangerville with a girl I don't know well enough and can't figure how to revive an interest in" (168). If Frank does not know Vicki well enough, it is simply because his values of superficiality, anti-complexity and anti-explanation have allowed him to live an illusion, and, moreover, to draw someone else into the consequences of that illusion. But if he does not want to know others, nor reveal himself, and if he cuts himself off from the past and ignores the possible implications of his actions in the future, there is little left to offer Vicki but the superficial consolations of immediate gratification This is indeed what Frank falls back on when the inevitable moment of truth arrives, when his systematic evasion of moral responsibility finally corners him. When Vicki announces to Frank in their Detroit hotel that their relationship isn't "working out" (172) and that friendship might be all there can be between them, Frank's only recourse, in an all-singing, all-dancing performance of emotion, is to distract Vicki from seeing what has been – and continues to be – absent from his "love" for her:

> My only hope now is to deny everything—friendship, disillusionment, embarrassment, the future, the past—and make my stand for the present. If I can hold her close in this cold-hot afternoon, kiss her and hug away her worries with ardor, so that when the sun is down and the wind stops and a spring evening draws us, maybe I will love her after all, and she me, and all this will just have been the result of too little sleep in a strange town. (172)

Frank's philosophy has deprived him of everything he could have brought to bear to convince Vicki of his worth: he can neither draw on the lessons of the past – his divorce from X and his many post-divorce relationships with women – nor look responsibly to the future to counter Vicki's insight into their relationship. From the perspective of MacIntyre and Taylor, he has deprived himself of the vital narrative context and temporality of moral action and orientation, and has chosen instead what MacIntyre calls the "individualist mode".[13] In so

---

[13] MacIntyre, *After Virtue*, 221.

doing, he has elected "to think atomistically" about his behaviour, thus isolating his actions from causes and consequences. In Taylor's terms, he is concerned uniquely with "is", and has no thought for "becoming".

MacIntyre's theory of action is particularly appropriate to Frank's behaviour. MacIntyre proposes, let us recall, that, if we fail to understand the narrative dimension of action, we give up on the concept of an intelligible action. And it is indeed remarkable how Frank's relationships with the two women with whom he is involved in the novel, Vicki and X, are transformed abruptly and detrimentally following what appears to the two women to be unintelligible, and therefore morally unacceptable, behaviour by Frank. When Frank visits Vicki's family for dinner on Easter Sunday, she makes it clear to him that their relationship has no future. Despite this being obvious since Detroit, and despite the evidence that Vicki is right, Frank, stranded in the present moment and present emotion, can only persist in wanting the relationship to continue. The news of Walter's suicide obliges Frank to leave the Easter Sunday dinner early, yet, as he is saying goodbye to Vicki, he makes the shocking suggestion to her that they "just go get a motel room right now". His proposition is utterly consistent with his non-narrative, non-contextualized, present-moment mode of immediate gratification; for Vicki, however, in the immediate context of her having ended their relationship and of the news of Walter's suicide, Frank's suggestion is a morally unintelligible, and therefore morally reprehensible, action. It is highly significant, too, that Vicki's response to Frank's proposition is indeed at a moral level, as she tells him that she would "be ashamed" to go along with what he suggests (293).

Frank causes X, too, to turn definitively away from him towards the end of the novel. We have seen X to be affectionate to Frank and concerned about his welfare, and it is precisely in that spirit of generosity that she agrees to accompany Frank to visit Walter's apartment on the evening of the latter's suicide, although very reluctant to do so. When she suggests "in a friendly way", after Frank has had a look around the apartment, that they should leave, Frank's knee-jerk response to present-moment impulses, and in his rejection of responsibility for his own thoughts, has him make an even more shocking proposal: "'You know,' I say, 'I suddenly had this feeling we should make love. Let's close the door there and get in bed'"

(335). For X, functioning within the normal narrative context of settings, causes and consequences, this is an incomprehensible suggestion, and is, in particular, morally incomprehensible. She reacts accordingly and, horrified, leaves Frank in Walter's apartment. As for Frank, it is simply another instance of how his entire philosophy deprives him of the moral co-ordinates that would allow him to evaluate the moral implications of his actions. He has atomized his behaviour into disconnected, individual actions, emptied of cause or consequence, creating the illusion that present actions do not reverberate beyond the present moment. It is little wonder that a number of critics use the term "solipsistic" to describe Frank, this character who reduces the world to the narrow dimensions of his self-centred perspective, and who seems, at the moment of action, unable to imagine any perspective other than his own.

The moral consequences of Frank's philosophy is but one expression of the wider issue of Frank's engagement with the reality of his life; the greater issue from this perspective would be one of truth, and more precisely Frank's quest for truth. If Frank's rigidly conceptualized understanding of reality is exposed through the moral consequences of his personal relationship with Vicki, its deficiencies are equally revealed in his professional life. The distortion of the truth in this case is caused by Frank's forced optimism. It is one thing to have an optimistic demeanour; it is quite another to force reality to fit this optimistic world-view. The most revealing elaboration of the inadequacies of Frank's forced optimism occurs during his encounter with Herb Wallagher, the ex-football player on whom Frank has been assigned to write a story. Herb has been confined to a wheelchair following a waterskiing accident, but – so goes Frank's cosy narrative as he anticipates his interview with Herb – "has become an inspiration to his former teammates by demonstrating courage and determination" (5). Frank disapproves of the probing, in-depth interviews practised by some of his fellow sportswriters, preferring to "pull a good heartstring" (65) with his optimistic reports of disadvantage and adversity overcome. But Herb, in his interview with Frank, immediately begins to evoke his pre-accident life, disconcertingly so for Frank, whose instinct is to ignore the past: "I am sorry to hear Herb referring to his life in the past tense. It is not an optimistic sign" (154). Thereafter, Frank's dogmatic optimism runs up everywhere against the brute factuality of Herb's past and circumstances, and of Herb's own telling of his story, one told from a wheelchair about a life destroyed and adversity not overcome.

Herb is undoubtedly disturbed and unstable, but he sees through Frank's glib superficiality, and turns on him for his insulting, trite optimism: "This is goddamn real life here, Frank. Get serious!" (157), he shouts, banging on his wheelchair. But Frank just digs himself deeper into his hole, patronizing Herb with his platitudinous questions, until Herb spells out to Frank that he is not "going to get any inspiration" out of him, and dismissing Frank as "an asshole" (159). Frank is well able to recognize in Herb "the sadness of elusive life glimpsed and unfairly lost" (164), but is unwilling to face the harsh reality of Herb's life, and has no other thought than to make a quick getaway. He will ultimately fail to write Herb's story. He had intended to find in Herb the survivor that he aspires to be himself: both men had overcome personal tragedy, faced down regret, and, as Frank wanted to see it, just got on with their lives. But shaping the world to suit his preconceptions is a greater priority for Frank than facing the truth, particularly when that truth would oblige him to confront the implacable influence of the past. Frank's professional life, in other words, is an extension of his personal life. He had noted at the beginning of his narrative that "there is much truth to [sportswriting] as well as plenty of lies" (4). In his approach to Herb, the lie is all his own.

With regard to the truth, as in everything, Frank has a theory, or at least a few facile maxims, to justify his attitude. "Too much truth can be worse than death" (139), he reflects during a difficult conversation with Vicki. She has just told him that he "lie[s] about things", something Frank accepts that he does, as it is "better than confiding" (137). Frank's relationship to the truth is probably, indeed, the greatest moral issue in the novel. He has so insulated himself in his protective layers of self-justificatory dogma that he has either lost sight of the importance of the truth, or has convinced himself of the infallibility and truth of his approach to life. In his professional capacity as a sportswriter this matters little as Frank essentially imposes his optimistic world-view on everything he writes about, and passes this on as the truth of the world without risk of contradiction. But the consequences in his personal life are more serious, and, again, significantly, it is women who see through Frank and call him to account.

The issue is one of sincerity, one that Frank is aware of, yet is either unable or unwilling to address. He allows that he has different voices for different occasions, and wonders, for instance, as he meets up with X in the graveyard, which of his voices will speak, "a convincing, truth-telling voice" or "a pseudo-sincere, phony, ex-husband one that will stir up trouble" (11). This is a rather disingenuous formulation for Frank to use to absolve himself of responsibility, as if the voice he spoke in were something over which he had no control. As with his behaviour, the problem arises because Frank is less concerned with the truth of what he says than with the immediate effects it will procure; Frank's voice, therefore, is often the voice of calculation and expedience rather than that of sincerity. Vicki chastises him for speaking in one of his insincere voices over dinner in her family's house, a voice that, Frank has learned, "Women hate" (283); it indeed aggravates Vicki, and X used to "turn hawk-eyed with suspicion" (283) when she heard it. Both women have learned that, as Vicki puts it bluntly to Frank, he is "liable to say anything" (295), and this plays a large part in both of them having cut themselves off from Frank by the end of the Easter weekend.

We have noted how MacIntyre and Taylor stress the importance of the relationship with others in the construction of a moral identity, the manner in which, as MacIntyre puts it, the self finds "its moral identity in and through its membership in communities such as those of the family, the neighborhood, the city and the tribe".[14] It is here that we may gauge the personal consequences for Frank (as distinct from moral consequences) of his rigid attachment to a set of private dogmas that pass for moral principles. His insistence on superficiality in his relations with others and his hostility to exchanging confidences or explaining himself have already contributed to his isolation. To these may be added further unbending maxims about human relationships. Frank pronounces that "Friendship is a lie of life" (195) and that "Some people were not made to have best friends, and I might be one". As with the voice he does not control, this is another example of

---

[14] *Ibid.*, 221.

Frank's determinism, or, rather, of a self-serving choice dressed up as an immutable law of human nature. But it is Frank who chooses to isolate himself. "Acquaintanceship usually suffices for me" (215), he proclaims, a self-conception that is ideal for one who wishes to keep a distance from others. In this regard, one of the very striking features in the novel is the nature of Frank's face-to-face interaction with others. Due to his fundamental solipsism, one aspect of which is a lack of interest in others, Frank seems to endure rather than participate in conversations: he constantly reacts to what others say, an essentially defensive mode of interaction.

This is particularly noticeable with women, with whom Frank, of course, has good reason to be defensive, yet it is also the case with men, for example in his long exchanges with Walter Luckett and Wade Arcenault (Vicki's father), with both of whom Frank is content merely to bat back the comments addressed to him. He comes across as evasive and disengaged in these conversations, as if he had little to say to either of these men, and seeks only to keep them at bay with his eager-to-agree, non-committal responses. Frank is, moreover, perfectly aware of his isolation from others. He keeps a boarder to "ward off awful loneliness" (30), and, to X's remark that he has "awfully odd relationships", Frank responds: "I don't have any relationships at all" (328). The Easter weekend will only serve to confirm this remoteness of Frank from others. He has been rejected by – or has driven away – two women, Vicki and X, who had been prepared to offer him all the affection they could, and he has had wary contact with a series of other alienated men, with Herb, Walter, Wade (who spends his time deep in his basement restoring an old car that he drives one foot forward and one foot back), and with Vicki's brother, Cade. Frank himself is one in a line of lost and lonely men in the novel who are no longer ministered to by women, and who cope poorly as a result: Walter has killed himself, unable to deal with being abandoned by his wife and the destabilizing feelings triggered by the homosexual encounter that ensued; we learn that Wade kidnapped a baby after his wife died; and the men in the Divorced Men's Club to which Frank belongs are "lost" (80) and are "full of dread and timidness" (79) whenever they get together.

On his Easter Sunday evening drive home to identify Walter's body after his disastrous visit to Vicki (which had culminated in her punching him in the mouth), Frank's isolation receives vivid expression. In a typical response to unpalatable reality, Frank does not seek to face up to his behaviour with Vicki, but rather takes flight from it, and, typically again, it is to a woman that he turns for solace and escape. He stops to phone Selma Jassim, the woman with whom he had an affair during his three-month teaching stay at the Massachusetts college three years earlier. Their conversation stutters along the way it does between people who no longer have anything to connect them, and therefore to say to each other, although, in his usual impulsive way, Frank tries (but fails) to have Selma agree to see him again. Frank makes the call from a phone booth on an empty Acme parking lot. During the conversation a young show-off driver hits a shopping cart that smashes into Frank's phone booth, shaking him up and cutting him on the knee.

The weekend that promised so much is captured now in a telling image: Frank, shaken and cut, still sore from Vicki's punch in the mouth, stands alone in the desolation of an empty parking lot on the outer edge of an anonymous town "sunk in the secular aimlessness" (305) of an Easter Sunday, the debris of the phone booth and the shopping cart strewn around him. As an expression of Frank's aloneness and isolation, the confrontational nature of his human contact over the weekend, and the failure of his relations with others, it is a powerful and appropriate tableau. Out of this desolation "emerges a Samaritan" (307), a girl who works at the aptly named Ground Zero Burg burger restaurant across the road, who brings Frank a restorative root beer, chats to him in a disinterested way until he has recovered, and with whom Frank has the most rewarding adult contact of the entire weekend. She is a stranger who simply helps him, from whom he wants nothing, and with whom his conversation becomes an honest, non-defensive exchange. It is entirely fitting, and surely not a coincidence, that the final two words of their conversation are the utterance of Frank's first name – the girl asks for his name, which he tells her and she repeats – a play on "Frank" that seems to pronounce their satisfied verdict on their unexpected and rewarding contact.

Whenever his life is in turmoil, or whenever things do not work out as he wishes, Frank, as we have seen, either flees or seeks a refuge. The great reliable refuge in his life, now that he is no longer married, and in the absence of another woman to provide a sanctuary, is his life in

Haddam. The town's first identity for Frank was indeed that of a refuge, when he and X originally settled there following Frank's sudden feeling that he had to get away from New York. In the fourteen years he has lived there Frank has come to identify closely with the town, and, particularly since his divorce, it has come to represent a haven for him. In part, it was the town's very suburban blandness and absence of assertive character that appealed to Frank in his instability after the shock of death and divorce. Haddam is lost in the depths of central New Jersey, located "midway between New York and Philadelphia" (48), a suburb of both, and is a town that barely rises to the status of a centre in its own right. But it functions as a refuge from what Frank himself refers to as the "real world", which is "a worse and devious and complicated place to lead a life in" (51). Frank is comfortable in the "out-of-the-mainstream feeling" (48) that exists in Haddam and is reassured by its distance from the "genuine woven intricacy" of big cities and its absence of "challenge or double-ranked complexity" (103). In keeping with his aversion to complexity, Frank feels at home in its "façades-only" landscape (31).

Frank also claims to find in the suburban simplicity of Haddam a repository of civic, social and moral values that engender in him a sense of tribal belonging and identification. Haddam represents solid middle-class values that foster and protect the living out of a particular notion of the American dream: having one's piece of real estate in a community where property prices are stable, crime low, services good, and where the social-class and racial hierarchy is understood and respected by all. One aims to live in peace with one's neighbours, behaving discreetly but nonetheless looking out for each others' interests – if you lose your wallet, Frank proudly asserts, it will quickly be returned to you, contents untouched, by "someone's teenage son", and without any mention of a reward. The manifestation of such a consensual social order assumes, for Frank, the power of a moral force, as, for example, when family and friends gather together in the evening in their houses, "windows lit with bronzy cheer" and with the sound of laughter and "spirited chatter floating out". On the occasions he apprehended his neighbourhood in this manner, Frank was "stirred to think all of us were living steadfast and accountable lives" (51).

Yet, even in the full flow of what Folks refers to as Frank's "unctuous ode" to the suburbs,[15] the evidence of a potentially different identity and character seeps through, an effect of the "surgery on the suburbs" that Richard Ford is carrying out. The town's very spatial organization exposes its lack of character and reveals it as a soulless place to live. The town square reminds Frank of "life pictured in catalogs", and he notes that Haddam is not a town that "seems very busy". It has "no real main street" and its residents have a superficial attachment to where they live: "most people who live here work elsewhere", Frank observes, and many are not "residents year-round" (49), escaping when they can to their summer or winter homes. Surface appearance everywhere seeks to hide the illusion upon which the town exists, from the "suburban chlorine bouquet" (14) of swimming pools to the "pseudo-colonial Square" (31), and on to the artifice of the "theme-organized housing development" (53) outside the town. Haddam's deceptive veneer is an appropriate expression of the nature of human contact there. People are friendly but "in a distant way" (5), and Frank has been quietly frozen out of his and X's circle of friends and neighbours since his divorce. The inhabitants of this "town of mailers and home shoppers" (49) wall themselves up in their homes, happy to have the Post Office and "the UPS truck" (196) replace personal contact and exchange with their community. And while Frank might airily suppose that the "servant classes, who are mostly Negroes, seem fulfilled" (50) in their segregated lives in Haddam, X, for one, takes a less sanguine view of race relations in the town, finding the sight of black maids being dropped off at a street corner, "waiting for their white ladies to come and pick them up" for their day's work, the "saddest thing you ever saw" (21).[16]

This is the refuge to which Frank returns on Easter Sunday evening. But he is immediately struck by the "unfriendliness of the town" and the indecipherability of its centre-less dispersion, as if the town had been deliberately constructed to remain impenetrable to unwelcome outsiders. Frank sees again that "it can be a sad town, a

---

[15] Folks, "The Risks of Membership", 85.

[16] Ford will deal with the race question much more comprehensively in *Independence Day*, as indeed he will with life in the suburbs and the condition of community life in America.

silent, nothing-happening, keep-to-yourself Sunday town" (314), closed to those who have not already staked out their holiday-weekend sanctuary there. Ford is being true here to his belief that people create the meaning of places rather than places speaking their predetermined meanings to us. Ford puts it thus: "I think one's sense of locatedness represents the claim you make on place, rather than the claim it supposedly makes on you."[17] And if we impose meanings on a place, these meanings can change as our moods and circumstances change. Alone, and worn down by the weekend's events, Frank is suddenly defenceless against the grief at the loss of his son and Walter that now wells up in him, making Haddam feel "unexpectedly a foreign place", invaded by a "crusty death's smell" (314). This ghost-town feel of Haddam on Easter Sunday evening is reinforced by Frank's failure to find any of those he seeks out for comfort – his palmist's house is closed up, his boarder is not around, and X is not at home. The only sign of life is the three messages left on his answering machine, two of them from people, Vicki and Walter, whose voices now can speak to him only of loss and death. The anonymous town of Adelphia at least produced a Samaritan to rescue Frank. Haddam, his own town, this ostensible source of moral and spiritual comfort, remains cold and indifferent, true to its soulless superficiality.

By the end of Easter Sunday in Haddam Frank has reached his nadir. His dogmatic attachment to his beliefs and values has been a calamitous guide to moral behaviour: he has behaved harmfully with the people closest to him, constantly misread people and situations, drifted easily into lies and insincerity, and habituated himself to a permanent mode of evasion and escapism. Not for the first time in the novel, state of mind and spatial location mirror each other. Frank sees himself as "a man with no place to go" (338), and finds himself in a town that is no place to be, for, in Frank's eyes now, lifeless Haddam offers no potential for consolation. He should be able to go home, but even home seems closed to him, a symbolic loss of centre and attachment that reflects the loss of moral centre and identity to which he has brought himself. And his homelessness and moral death is mirrored in the only thing he can do, drive aimlessly around empty Haddam, an "invisible man", a ghostly figure "beyond all hopes"

---

[17] *Conversations with Richard Ford*, 142.

(339), disconsolately at one with the death he senses everywhere in the town.

This empty moment is a decisive one for a lonely man. It is a moment where things could go either way for Frank, but Richard Ford remains true to the unshakeable optimism he has granted his character and true to the symbolism of Easter weekend, and he allows Frank a chance at salvation. But Ford also remains true to the evader in Frank. His demoralizing experiences with others over the previous days, the catalysts of this empty moment, should be the occasion for Frank to face up to his failings, yet he experiences these only as an unwanted burden to be cast off. So it is that he addresses the effects rather than the causes of his situation: the problem, as Frank sees it, is the empty moment itself, not what has brought it into being. The optimist in Frank prevails: he construes his spiritual and moral unmooring, and his absolute isolation in the empty streets of the Haddam night, as a condition of absolute freedom – he is free of responsibility now and free to do whatever he wishes. If his invisibility, from the perspective of his moral behaviour and of those he has harmed, symbolizes Frank's isolation and exile, it represents for him, mystery-obsessed and responsibility-free as he is, a condition in which one is "loosed from body and duty, left to drift on the night breeze, to do as we will, to cast about for what we would like to be when we next occur" (339). In the immediate aftermath of X's rejection of him in Walter's apartment and her withdrawal of the invitation to him to spend the evening with her in her home, Frank is yet again straining towards the future, as oblivious to the past as if it had never happened.

Frank's aimless driving through Haddam brings him to the train depot, seeking comfort there as he often did after his divorce when he would go to witness the affectionate evening rituals of homecoming and welcome. Appropriately, Frank's physical expression of his absolute freedom, his return to visibility, is triggered by his instinct for flight in the face of unwanted reality. Thinking that one of the passengers alighting from the Philadelphia train is Walter's sister, arriving to deal with the funeral arrangements, Frank flees the human entanglement that such an encounter with her would involve and jumps into the New York-bound train, a city at night that he has always avoided in the past. Frank has always appreciated Haddam for the many ways in which it was not New York. He had fled to Haddam from New York years earlier, just as he used to flee the city in the evening after work, afraid of its "demoralizing firestorm of speeding cabs, banging lights and owl-voiced urban-ness".

Now, however, New York's very excess of urban energy is the welcome antidote to Haddam's suburban blandness, a city of excitement and extremes, where he can return to being, perhaps through the "exhilaration of a woman" (352). Frank noted earlier that women had always "lightened" his burdens (61), and as he finds himself in his New York office, failing to write his story on Herb, he thinks of people he could call, all six of whom are women. Of these, four are former lovers, though Frank is "almost certain none of [these six women] would particularly want to" talk to him. But Frank's faith in the future brings another one to his shoulder, with "a face to save a drowning man" (357). Catherine Flaherty may be another woman prepared to offer him a form of salvation and perhaps even an opportunity for redemption. The latter, however, would demand atonement, born of the awareness of past failings, but Frank is now fully back in the present, and it is immediate salvation that he seeks.

At the end of his Easter weekend, despite the human and moral damage he has left in his wake, Frank seems to have learned nothing: his initial conversation with Catherine is marked by the ingratiating tone of one of his insincere voices and his customary self-serving platitudes. As he processes everything in his mind at the point where he might ask Catherine to go for a bite to eat with him, he falls back instinctively on his pieties and impregnable self-image:

> And what's my attitude? At some point nothing else really matters *but* your attitude—your hopes, your risks, your sacrifices, your potential islands of regret and reward—as you enter what is no more than rote experience upon the earth.
> Mine, I'm happy to say, is the best possible. (364-65)

He offers to buy Catherine a sandwich, and she accepts. The pleasure of the present moment prevails again, and the events of the weekend are instantly effaced as everything in Frank inclines towards the anticipation and mystery that another attractive woman holds out: "there is no nicer time on earth than now—everything in the offing, nothing gone wrong, all potential" (365). His faith in mystery and his effacement of the past seem to have triumphed in the end.

Frank, we have said, is evasive; he is also, partly as a consequence of this, elusive. It is possible to say many things about Frank's character, but what do all of these amount to in the end? Do the individual parts constitute a whole, which would be the self, the personal and moral identity, of Frank Bascombe? Our only witness to Frank has been Frank himself. He has said many things about himself, has given a detailed account of his values, thoughts, motives, ambitions and actions, yet, at the end of his narrative of the Easter weekend, he remains strangely ungraspable. One has as much a sense of dispersal as of wholeness, of discreteness as of unity, where Frank's identity is concerned. The French philosopher, Paul Ricoeur, in his work on identity and narrative, focuses on two understandings of the term "identity", namely the choice between identity as sameness and identity as selfhood, or between identity as permanence, and identity as a dialectic between permanence and change within a life. It is the latter concept, the understanding of identity as a dynamic exchange between permanence and non-permanence in time, which, Ricoeur insists, is appropriate to identity understood as selfhood. The construction of identity as selfhood is facilitated through the discourse of narrative, through the dynamic structure of the story, specifically in the identity of the operation of emplotment (*la mise en intrigue*),[18] which Ricoeur sees as the mediator in the exchange between the competing forces of permanence and non-permanence. Out of this dynamic exchange, this balancing act between sameness and difference, emerges our personal identity, the self constantly reconfigured by way of the stories we tell about ourselves.[19]

Identity as an exchange between permanence and non-permanence is played out in the character of Frank. Elinor Ann Walker observes that Frank "constructs himself in such a way as to exaggerate his differences".[20] Another way of saying this is that Frank seems constituted more by difference than by sameness, or by non-permanence more than permanence. All Frank's efforts, in fact, are directed at thwarting a permanence of identity. And, significantly, this

---

[18] Literally *la mise en intrigue* means "the putting into plot".
[19] See in particular Ricoeur's *Oneself as Another* for a full discussion of the correlation between *la mise en intrigue* and identity.
[20] Walker, *Richard Ford*, 68.

is a highly self-conscious gesture on his behalf. We have already
noted this tendency in Frank, in, for example, his desire for "Eternal
renewal" on a daily basis, as well as in the provisional nature of his
"love" for Vicki. This resistance to permanence is a consistent trait in
Frank. One of the things he hated about the semester he spent teaching
in the Massachusetts college was the danger, when lecturing to
students, of "reducing *yourself,* your emotions, your own value
system—your life" (217) to a permanent, knowable core. Elsewhere in
the college it was the lecturers' rage to explain and dissect, "and by
these means promoting permanence" (222), that ultimately drove him
away, as was their reduction of literature to "permanent explanations;
monuments to themselves" (223). What made his time there bearable
was his affair with fellow literalist Selma Jassim, in which they gave
themselves up to the pleasures of the present moment and "reveled" in
the "frothiest kind of impermanence" (224). Above all, however, it is
through the downplaying of his past, and of the past as part of an
ongoing life- and self-narrative, that Frank seeks to frustrate a sense of
permanence and fixity of identity. The evidence mounts that what
Frank is trying to evade in the minimizing of his past is the
permanence of a recognizable identity. With a strong sense of identity,
a core of sameness through which one may be identified and re-
identified, comes the responsibility to be accountable for, and true to,
that identity. Remarkably, Frank himself makes this explicit link
between morality and identity, noting at one point: "I feel a conviction
that I have no ethics at all and little consistency" (120). This brings us
back to MacIntyre's and Taylor's idea of a moral identity and to the
obligations of responsibility. And it also brings us full circle, back to
Richard Ford's use of character in his novel and his concern that
fiction should contain a moral vision. Ford has noted that he thinks of
characters as "changeable, provisional, unpredictable, decidedly
unwhole", and that he avails of this mutability to create characters that
are "morally provoking",[21] a conception that accords strikingly with
Ricoeur's notion of fiction as a "vast laboratory" where moral
experiments are carried out.[22] Frank's character has indeed evolved in
the novel in such a way as to promote perpetual difference and

[21] "Richard Ford: The Art of Fiction CXLVII", 46-47.
[22] See note 11.

avoidance of constancy, creating a personal identity that is morally provoking but that demands a moral appraisal. The suspicion grows that Frank's disconnecting himself from his past, his rejection of permanence, his idealization of the present moment and his taking refuge in self-serving theories are so many strategies directed at avoiding a permanence of identity, and whose ultimate objective is the achievement of a supreme form of freedom, the freedom from moral responsibility.

The End

Just before Frank flees to New York on Easter Sunday evening, the person who knows him best, his ex-wife, delivers a devastating verdict on his character, after what she considers to be his repugnant suggestion to make love in Walter's apartment:

> I remember why I divorced you now .... You've really *become* awful. You weren't always awful. But now you are. I don't like you very much at all. (335)

Although Frank, locked into his blindly optimistic mode, seems to be able to take setbacks in his stride (a few short hours after being severely rejected by two women who were important to him he is immediately alert to the charms of Catherine Flaherty), we learn that the events of the Easter weekend have nonetheless left their mark on him. The novel has an epilogue. Five months have passed, and Frank is now in Florida, and seems to have spent most of the time there since Easter. It is now that the narrative act itself is foregrounded:

> I realize I have told all this because unbeknownst to me, on that Thursday those months ago, I awoke with a feeling, a stirring, that any number of things were going to change and be settled and come to an end soon, and I might have something to tell that would be important and even interesting. (369)[23]

---

[23] At the beginning of his account Frank situates this anticipation of change on Good Friday, rather than on Thursday, morning. Announcing that "Good Friday today is a special day for me", he continues: "When I woke in the dark this morning, my heart pounding like a tom-tom, it seemed to me as though a change were on its way, as if

Although he does not say so explicitly, the "feeling" that indicated
to him that "things were going to change" seems to have been that he
was emerging from the period of mourning for his dead son. This was
confirmed to him some months later when, on reading a newspaper
report in Florida about the death of a boy, he notes: "I realized that my
own mourning for [my son] is finally over" (374). This sense of a
moment of transition in his life seems to have been what prompted
Frank to write his account, but it is the writing of the narrative itself
that is credited with effecting the important change in him that he now
proclaims: "Things occur to me differently now, just as they might to
a character at the end of a good short story. I have different words for
what I see and anticipate, even different sorts of thoughts and
reactions; more mature ones, ones that seem to really count" (369-70).
Frank has discovered the function and transformative power of
explicit self-narration, the operation of which is described by Paul
Ricoeur:

> The structure of narrativity demonstrates that it is by trying to put
> order on our past, by retelling and recounting what has been, that we
> acquire an identity. These two orientations – towards the future and
> towards the past – are not, however, incompatible. As Heidegger
> himself points out, the notion of "repeating" (*Wiederholung*) the past
> is inseparable from the existential projection of ourselves towards our
> possibilities. To "repeat" our story, to retell our history, is to re-collect
> our horizon of possibilities in a resolute and responsible manner. In
> this respect, one can see how the retrospective character of narration is
> closely linked to the prospective horizon of the future. To say that
> narration is a recital which orders the past is not to imply that it is a
> conservative closure to what is new. On the contrary, narration
> preserves the meaning that is behind us so that we can have meaning
> before us.[24]

Frank has "put order" on his past by "recounting what has been",
and has "[preserved] the meaning" of what has happened, thus
allowing him to face into the future with the wisdom and lessons these

---

this dreaminess tinged with expectation, which I have felt for some time now, were
lifting off of me into the cool tenebrous dawn" (5).
[24] Richard Kearney, *Dialogues with Contemporary Continental Thinkers: The
Phenomenological Heritage*, Manchester: Manchester UP, 1984, 21-22.

meanings have brought to light. It is notable, too, that Ricoeur speaks of the obligation to be "responsible" in this narrative construction of meaning. In this regard, too, Frank is changing: "Walter's death, I suppose you could say, has had the effect on me that death means to have; of reminding me of my responsibility to a somewhat larger world" (366). Walter's death, now inserted into the narrative of Frank's life, gains the meanings that narrativized actions can gain: they are connected with other events, circumstances, motives, intentions and actions, in other words with all the diverse dimensions of experience that narrative brings together in coherent, meaning-creating connections, forging the intelligibility promoted by MacIntyre. One reason that Walter's death has shaken Frank may well be that he recalls the occasion that Walter tried to narrate his homosexual encounter to him as part of a wider story. "We've all got our stories, don't we?" (96), Walter pleaded to Frank at the time, but he got no help from Frank that evening in constructing a bearable explanatory narrative of his homosexual act. In Frank's acknowledgment now of responsibility to a wider world may lie the beginnings of a sense of a social identity and an end to his personal isolation.

But before Frank can recount his story, before he can take responsibility for the construction and preservation of meaning in narrative that Ricoeur demands, he has to take responsibility for the past, has, indeed, to acknowledge the past. This, ultimately, is the most significant change in Frank. During his stay in Florida he found that he had relatives there, cousins of his father, and is happy to have linked up with these Bascombes, particularly as they are able to tell Frank about his father, whom he hardly remembered. In embracing the notion of family ("I'm proud to be the novelty member of their family" [371]), Frank is moving towards the temporality of MacIntyre's and Taylor's concept of identity, and is becoming what MacIntyre calls the inheritor and bearer of a tradition. And more than simply acknowledging his past, Frank is even beginning to see the benefits of having one. Whenever he takes his leave of the Florida Bascombes, he records that:

> I am usually (if only momentarily) glad to have a past, even an imputed and remote one. There is something to that. It is not a burden, though I've always thought of it as one. I cannot say that we all need a

past in full literary fashion, or that one is much useful in the end. But a
small one doesn't hurt, especially if you're already in a life of your
own choosing. (371)

All the signs suggest that Frank has come a long way from the
events of the Easter weekend. There is evidence that he is now facing
up to his behaviour with Walter, Vicki and X. The grief and mourning
at his son's death, which triggered his loss of bearings, are in the
process of being overcome. And it would appear that the protective
framework of rigid attitudes through which he seems to have tried to
stabilize himself following adversity, and through which he came to
exclusively understand his life, is loosening its grip on him. There are
signs that Frank is less obsessed with himself and more aware that
consideration is due to others, too. The seeds are being sown,
therefore, for Frank's genuine resurrection, not a symbolic Easter
weekend one, but one possible now through the retrospective narrative
of that weekend's events. The act of narrative has had a redemptive
effect. Now Frank speaks the language of change and renewal – the
final image is of a shedding of the restrictive accretions of a life, the
"residue or skin of all the things you've done and been and said and
erred at" (374), as if a new being was being born out of the narrative
of the experiences of the old. A new identity is being constructed and
neglected responsibilities are being accepted. In the end, *The
Sportswriter* has narrated a highly moral tale.

CHAPTER 3

INDEPENDENCE DAY

I: FROM UNITY TO FRAGMENTATION

Independence Day, the sequel to *The Sportswriter*, takes up the story of Frank Bascombe five years after the events of the first novel. It is now 1988. We soon learn that, as intimated in the epilogue to *The Sportswriter*, the events of Easter weekend 1983, and particularly the narrative reconfiguration of those events, had a somewhat cathartic effect on Frank. The psychological term is warranted as Frank now speaks of his having "suffered what must've been a kind of survivable 'psychic detachment'".[1] The temporary leave of absence he took from his sportswriting job to go to Florida became a permanent break with his profession, and the rupture with his previous life was confirmed by the extension of his "fugue" (25)[2] beyond Florida, to France, where he was joined by Catherine Flaherty. Frank was seeking a "temporary refuge" where he might feel "revived, less anxious, possibly even happy and at peace", which he more or less achieved by liberating himself from the "suspenseful perturbations" (92) of his agitated womanizing period following his divorce from X. When boredom eventually set in, Frank and Catherine went their separate ways, with Frank returning to Haddam, but fired now with an urgency to take possession of, rather than avoid, his "middle life" (93).[3] Everything in

---

[1] Richard Ford, *Independence Day*, New York: Knopf, 1995, 25. Further references to the novel will be included parenthetically in the text.

[2] Continuing the psychological view of the post-Easter 1983 period, Frank uses a term here from psychiatry, and one that specifically addresses problems of identity. The *OED* defines a "fugue" as a "flight from or loss of the awareness of one's own identity, sometimes involving wandering away from home, and often occurring as a reaction to shock or emotional stress".

[3] This raises the question of Frank's age. Frank speaks of living "in a forty-four-year-old bachelor's way" (7) and of having "observed my forty-fourth birthday" (42)

the passages recounting his flight to France, his psychological and emotional repose and his turning realistically towards the future is consistent with the language of resurrection and renewal in the epilogue to *The Sportswriter*. A new period of Frank's life beckons, and a new energy to seize it courses through him.

It was a matter of some surprise to Frank that it was to Haddam that he "instinctively and in a heat came charging back". Despite the homage to Haddam in *The Sportswriter* the town no longer seemed able to accommodate Frank by the end of that novel, and it could also conceivably have been too intimately linked with the period of his life that Frank now wishes to relinquish. But it is the town's very lack of personality that allows him to slip easily back into its unimposing ways and even to feel "a homey connectedness" to it: Frank notes that Haddam is less "a true *place*" than "a simple *setting*" (93). Haddam offered Frank on his return a reassuring sense of familiarity and even a temporal continuity available to someone who "can remember how things used to be before something else happened and as a result feels right at home".

Frank's revised notion of his life as a temporal unity has a definite ring of MacIntyre and Taylor to it: he speaks now of his new projects having the sense of being what his "whole life was all about" (94). Frank even speaks of his "responsibilities" (98) towards his two children, a moral response to his having "flown the coop for a while" (94). And his "responsibility to a somewhat larger world", announced at the end of *The Sportswriter*,[4] has Frank return to Haddam envisaging a certain civic engagement, conscious now that he had contributed little to the town in his fifteen years there. Apart from reading stories for the blind on a local radio station, he ultimately

---

sometime between March and the Independence Day weekend on which *Independence Day* is set. There are several references to the novel being set in 1988, most of them relating to the presidential election campaign of that year. This would mean that Frank was born in 1944, but this contradicts the year of birth recorded in *The Sportswriter*: "I was born into an ordinary, modern existence in 1945" (24), which would make Frank forty-three years old by the summer of 1988. One can sympathize with the author, who has spoken about the "complex and involved clerical process" of writing a long novel which is "related to another book", a relation that creates a "clerical morass" (*Conversations with Richard Ford*, 166). The error is corrected by *The Lay of the Land*, where Frank is recorded as being fifty-five in November 2000 (117).

[4] Ford, *The Sportswriter*, 366.

combined his own and others' interests a few years after his return by purchasing two houses in the black area of Haddam,[5] thus allowing him the opportunity to invest his money, but also to "[reinvest] in my community". In this way Frank hoped to maintain "a neighborhood integrity" he admired, and to achieve for himself a "greater sense of connectedness" (27) to his community. The causality, temporality and wholeness of the narrative view of life rejected by Frank in the first novel, but tentatively embraced by the end of it, seem fully acknowledged in the trajectory of Frank's life since Florida: life now appears to have a unity and a *telos*, and Frank seems ready to assume his historical and social identity, and to recognize a moral dimension attending that commitment..

One of Frank's other goals upon his return is to try to persuade his ex-wife, now named as Ann Dykstra, to remarry him. But a year after his return Ann announces her marriage to successful architect, Charley O'Dell, and her intention to move herself and the children up to his expensive home in Connecticut. Frank's reaction indicates that he is not the fully reformed character his narrative had been suggesting: he felt "bitterly, scaldingly betrayed" just as he was preparing himself, with "all sins forgiven", for "life's gentle amelioration" (100), a reaction that echoes the solipsistic attitude that pervades *The Sportswriter*. Frank's embracing of the past, then, is revealed to be selective and, typically, somewhat self-serving. It involved "Certain crucial jettisonings", most notably "all you did and surrendered to and failed at and fought and didn't like" (95). Frank's view amounts to little more than wanting to forget anything that is problematic and as seeing his past failings as merely an unhelpful encumbrance on the present. He advocates a simple forget-so-forgive policy, but Ann, unlike Frank, could not forget, so does not forgive.

---

[5] As we will see, the issue of race is very prominent in *Independence Day*. This raises the question of nomenclature, and specifically the terminology to describe people belonging to different races. This has quite properly become an important and sensitive issue, and is so for African Americans. Commentators on Ford's Frank Bascombe novels are faced with a specific problem of designation, and particularly where *Independence Day* is concerned, as race is an important issue in the novel. Ford uses the term "black" throughout, and occasionally "Negro", the latter used as both noun and adjective. It seems to me to be desirable to use the term "black" in my discussion, in accordance with Ford's usage. To do otherwise (that is, to use the term "African American") would have introduced a vital nuance of meaning absent from the novel, which would be to take a liberty not sanctioned by the text.

All that Frank can do in the wake of Ann's departure is to buy her house, feeling that his own is too associated with an unhappy past and is therefore an unpropitious location from which to construct his new life. But once installed there, Frank feels "lonely and inessential" (108) without Ann and his children and sees himself turning into the depressing cliché of the "suspicious bachelor" figure. Nor have any of his vague professional ambitions come to fruition. It is in this isolated condition, "having parted with or been departed from by most everything", and feeling "almost devoid of all expectation" (109), that he takes up the offer to become a "Residential Specialist" (91), or realtor, with a Haddam real estate agency. He also does so to protect himself. Richard Ford has noted that Frank in *Independence Day* is in a "moment of transition" and is, as a consequence, "terrifically exposed".[6] Frank is seeking to pass from a period of crisis to a stage in life where he can be "as close to day-to-day happy" (111) as possible. He also considers that this is his due, having paid the price for his "various rash acts and bad decisions" (110), yet he found himself slipping into a crabby existence of solitude, fretfulness and eccentricity.

Frank's change of profession has had the desired effect. As he begins his Independence Day weekend, he is able to say that becoming a realtor was the right choice, professionally and personally – he is content, is glad to be "earning a living by the sweat of my brow" (115), yet does not have to work hard or worry about making a lot of money, financially secure as he is from the profitable deal he made on the sale of his house. But he has also been buffeted by the arbitrary gusts of contingency and chance: the teleological momentum that brought him from Haddam to Florida, and then to France and back to Haddam, driven as it was by the fervour of atonement and renewal, had been stalled, and then diverted, by forces over which he had no control. Frank's narrative analepsis to explain how he became a realtor has anticipated a dilemma that informs much of *Independence Day*, the dilemma that achieving independence involves a delicate negotiation with others, with one's own needs and expectations, and with uncontrollable events.

---

[6] *Heat Magazine*, 169.

The titles of the first two Frank Bascombe novels point towards their different centres of gravity. *The Sportswriter* designates a person and directs our attention towards the protagonist of the novel; *Independence Day* designates a national holiday but also alludes to a potential theme. Both novels are faithful to the nucleus of concern suggested in their titles. The personal nature of the narrative in *The Sportswriter* was signalled in its opening words, and while Frank's life and existence are also at the heart of *Independence Day*, he is nonetheless presented to us in the context of the specific theme of independence. The opening passages of the novel present the prevailing mood in Haddam as it awakens into the Friday morning of the Independence Day weekend, and they announce discreetly that the theme of independence will be applied to more than just Frank, that it will apply to his wider community, and, on this national holiday, to America itself. In the case of both Frank and the United States, their respective identities will be explored and evaluated: the novel will expose the pressure points and frailties of Frank as he settles into middle age, and those of America as it celebrates its independence and recalls its founding principles.

The plotlines that facilitate these investigations are varied – Frank's efforts to sell a house to a difficult couple, the Markhams; his journey with his troubled adolescent son to the basketball and baseball halls of fame; his relationships with Ann and his new girlfriend, Sally; and his encounters with a variety of characters, including the tenants of one of the houses he owns and his stepbrother, whom he meets by chance while on his trip with his son. The national and personal dimensions of the novel's overall theme of independence weave in and out of each other, and sometimes even coincide. We will abide by the initial resonance of the novel's title, and indeed by the example of the novel itself in the opening chapter, by first examining Richard Ford's portrayal of his country, before moving on, in the next chapter, to consider the fate of Frank himself over Independence Day weekend, 1988.

The tranquil opening paragraphs of the novel, depicting the sounds and smells and slow emergence into a peaceful early summer morning of suburban America, are anything but a harbinger of things to come, as the novel quickly turns to the more ominous news of how the ills of the wider world, a source of only distant anxiety in *The Sportswriter*, have finally found their way to Haddam. Frank had noted in *The Sportswriter* that the town's quiet isolation did not perhaps "fit with the way the world works now" (51), but recently, in quick succession, Frank had been mugged near his house, two neighbours' homes were burgled and, most shockingly, a black female colleague of Frank was murdered while showing a property. But it is particularly in the economic sphere that Haddam has been unable to maintain its isolation from the world, as the long tentacles of economic recession enveloped and then squeezed the business community, and thus the whole town. *Independence Day* is quick to situate its characters within the specific context of economic conditions and to indicate that personal well-being is inseparable from economic well-being. Falling property values in Haddam are attributed the characteristics of a noxious gas that the population breathes in, affecting moods and demeanours, and leaving the inhabitants of the town with "an untallied apprehension" and "a new sense of a wild world being just beyond our perimeter" (5). The town's physical and psychological landscapes have been inexorably transformed – once-thriving businesses now stand empty, leaving debts unpaid, while takeovers, postponed investment and sudden collapses are the new commercial reality. And the day-trippers to Haddam are no longer the "suave New Yorkers" (23) of the early eighties, having been replaced by less affluent New Jersey visitors who make more noise and spend less.

The profound impact of economic conditions on personal life in America is developed in the novel through the venture of real estate, Frank's new professional occupation. Indeed, the complex dynamics of acquisition and relinquishment, of exhilaration and disappointment, along with the financial and personal investment in a house and the subtle interactions between occupants and home, contribute to the function of real estate as a metaphor for the hazardous negotiations and choices of adult life. The real estate process acquaints one with transition and adaptation, and also determines, to some extent – as will be seen – one's sense of self. But the impact on identity is economically as well as emotionally dictated. Frank submits that personal recognition and sanction from one's community derive from "the only way communities ever recognize anything: financially" (51-52), euphemistically expressed as "compatibility" (52). In modern America, we are to understand, one's public identity and the formation of communities are determined, not by one's moral worth, but by the crude laws of capitalism. It is no coincidence that it was these same laws that allowed Frank to realize some of his objectives upon returning to Haddam: his investment in the two rental houses, and particularly in a root beer stand (where he bailed out the near-bankrupt owner), provided the "chance to help another, do a good deed well and diversify in a way that would pay dividends" (135). In other words, Frank's new found sense of social responsibility and his new civic identity are functions of the market economy, and made possible by his financial independence.

The economic imperatives of the real estate market are brought to bear in extended fashion in the efforts of Frank to find a house for Joe and Phyllis Markham. Their arrival from the far reaches of north-east Vermont to central New Jersey parallels their sudden relocation from the sixties to the late eighties, and their spatial and temporal disorientation serves to illustrate how personal development is subservient to economic values. The Markhams' story contains a potted social history of the sixties' generation's grasp at freedom and its culmination in banal disappointments. The Markhams' respective first marriages ended in divorce, with children in detox or no longer in touch with their parents. Joe and Phyllis found each other at the second attempt and settled down to produce a child, build their own house and establish a successful small-scale pottery business. Their desire for a better education for their daughter brought them to Haddam, but their exile in Vermont had disconnected them from economic realities: the 148,000 dollars they have to spend would have bought them what they wanted in 1976, but not in 1988. They have looked at forty-five houses since March, liked none of them, and have used up whatever goodwill Frank may have had for people "who wander back to civilization from piddly-ass Vermont with emaciated wallets and not a clue about what makes the world go around" (86).

The Markhams' biggest sin as citizens of a capitalist society is economic ignorance and financial naiveté. They sold their own house without appreciating the intricacies of the real estate market, and are now facing financial and personal implosion. Market forces dictate their destiny, provoking in both a deep fear and loss of self-worth and self-assurance, and pushing them towards, as Joe articulates it, being "trapped in some shitty life I'll never get out of except by dying" (52). More profoundly still, their dilemma has occasioned a crisis of identity that causes both to re-evaluate the choices they have made and those they might have made, and to feel less sure about their place in the world. Joe tells Frank how, in a symbolic moment of self-illumination, he looked at himself in the mirror and felt less certain now that his life was "leading someplace" (49), reaching the conclusion he now confides to Frank: "I've completely quit becoming" (50). Joe and Phyllis are now transfixed by indecision and apprehension, "caught in the real estate crunch" (89), the prey of "cannibalistic financial forces" (54).

The Markhams' house-buying episode everywhere proclaims the hegemony of the market and the subservience of the personal to economic laws. This is hardly unexpected news in a ruthlessly free-market society like that of the United States, but what is noteworthy in *Independence Day* is not simply that the effects of market economics on personal welfare and freedom receive such extended treatment, but that the harsh personal effects are depicted by way of a couple as easy to dislike as the Markhams (essentially Joe). The novel stacks the deck resolutely against them, in a manner designed to cast them as the sole authors of their own misery. Responsibility for their predicament lies as much with, as Frank puts it, their "staying in the mountains and becoming smug casualties of their own idiotic miscues" (90) as with the pitiless laws of a capitalist economy.

The Markhams' predicament allows Ford to propose an initial interpretation of a very American view on independence, by demonstrating that, tough market realities notwithstanding, the Markhams can still control their own destiny. To do so, however, they must stop seeing themselves as victims of outside forces. The novel, through Frank, advocates two clear strategies to achieve this independence: first, they must indulge in "a certain self-viewing" (89) and "self-seeing", and, second, they must begin to "think about themselves and most everything else *differently*" (90). Underpinning Frank's strategy for his clients' attainment of independence is the Emersonian notion of self-reliance. Richard Ford has noted that Ralph Waldo Emerson is his "great influence",[7] and he has had Frank already announce that he intends to bring Emerson's essay, "Self-Reliance", on his weekend trip to help him communicate with his son, Paul. When Joe and Phyllis are indecisive about yet another house shown to them, Frank decides to "set [them] adrift" in the hope that

---

[7] *Conversations with Richard Ford*, 146.

they will fall back, in Emersonian fashion, on their own resources. Frank is contemptuous of the Markhams' compliance with "Vermont's spiritual mandate" (89) of painstakingly avoiding self-seeing and, instead, of looking outwards, of looking to society, for sanction. But society, for Emerson, in its conformity, imitation and general spiritual feebleness, "everywhere is in conspiracy against the manhood of every one of its members".[8] And Frank's notion of "self-seeing" as a turn towards the inner self equally displays an Emersonian influence: in "Self-Reliance" Emerson advocates a turn inward to find the "self-sufficing, and therefore self-relying soul".[9]

Emerson is also the guiding light for Frank's remedy for the Markhams' inertia. His view that they need new perspectives, "fresh understandings based on the faith that for new fires to kindle, old ones have to be dashed" (90), surely has its spiritual provenance in Emerson's advocacy of change in "Self-Reliance": "Power ceases in the instant of repose; it resides in the moment of transition from a past to a new state, in the shooting of the gulf, in the darting to an aim." In this launching into the future and change, observes Emerson, "the soul *becomes*",[10] an insight so precisely calibrated to respond to Joe's earlier remark that one senses that Ford worked directly backwards from the Emersonian cure to Joe's ontological malaise of stalled becoming.

The specifically American understanding of independence developed in these passages draws deeply on the American notion of the primacy of the individual, on the belief that the individual represents the basis and potency of society, but also on the American faith in individual freedom, be it the freedom to fail or the freedom to succeed. If the Markhams are seen to fail in these early passages, it may be said that they do so because they have failed to understand or adapt to the fundamental values of their own culture, one reason, perhaps, they are treated less than sympathetically. Independence understood as individualism and freedom will be recurring themes in *Independence Day*, as Frank leaves the Markhams to reflect on their cultural naïveté and "miscues", and as he moves on to take the pulse of the heartland of the original colonies.

---

[8] Ralph Waldo Emerson, *Self-Reliance and Other Essays*, New York: Dover, 1993, 21.
[9] *Ibid.*, 30.
[10] *Ibid.*, 29.

Richard Ford has said about *Independence Day* that "There's no doubt that I was trying to write a book about America".[11] From this perspective the novel's concern with economic matters is understandable, as the 1980s were, after all, the years when Ronald Reagan and Margaret Thatcher together succeeded in bringing about a definitive reorientation in economic and social values: they imposed economics as the decisive discourse in their respective societies, a new order that other Western countries were quick to adopt. Another major national theme addressed in *Independence Day*, however, has a much longer genealogy and did not derive its legitimacy as a subject for discussion from a newly established topicality. A book with the ambition to be about America could hardly ignore the race issue, and Richard Ford, as a Mississippian, was deeply aware of this: "in particular, I wanted *Independence Day* to be about race. I really wanted it to be about race." He continues:

> ... too many people have too much invested, in America, in races not being reconciled. There's too much of society built on this rickety structure that separates the races. Too many people have careers; too many people have institutions. Too much money is involved. Too much ego is involved for things to be reconcilable, or for conversations to go on except in highly stratified and formalised ways. This all leads to the truism that race is only going to be reconciled in America by human beings getting beyond it in a personal way.

Ford also notes in this interview "how absolutely impossible in American culture it is for whites to talk about race", or to have what he calls "a public conversation" about it.[12] Ford attempts such a public discussion in *Independence Day* by developing three distinct race-related plotlines: the purchase by Frank of two houses in an "established black neighborhood" (24) in Haddam; his encounter with Mr Tanks, a black truck-driver; and his romantic relationship with Clair Devane, a black real estate agent in his office.

If Frank's purchase of the two houses was facilitated by his financial independence, his altruistic motives were also informed by economic pragmatism. The Wallace Hill neighbourhood was mostly populated by "blue-collar professionals" and retirees, although it was

---

[11] *Heat Magazine*, 171.
[12] *Ibid.*, 172.

becoming gentrified by the arrival of "a few black dentists and internists and three trial lawyer couples". Frank's investment was predicated on the neighbourhood becoming further "gentrified by incoming whites and rich blacks" as limited "in-town property becomes more valuable" (25), another instance of social arrangements being dictated by economic and market factors. Yet Frank has been unable to find a tenant for one of the houses for six months now, and it is noteworthy that the only prospective tenants have been black. And the renting of the other house, occupied by "a mixed race family" (28), the McLeods, has not allowed Frank to display the qualities of "the perfect modern landlord" (27) to which he had aspired. On his first contact with "former black militant" Larry McLeod, Frank's eye had immediately fallen on the vulgar and violent slogan on Larry's tee-shirt and on the "big automatic pistol" (28) lying on the hall table. Ford underlines the difficulties of "getting beyond" racial barriers "in a personal way" by having his own remedy founder against the accumulated mistrust of centuries of inequality and resentment – Frank's relationship with Larry is marked by an utter inability to connect with each other.

The one extended scene between them is characterized by the failure of a conversation to take place, partly a consequence, one senses, of the inequality in the economic and power relations between them: Frank is the white landlord and Larry the black tenant, but Frank is also a white landlord in a black neighbourhood, surely a source of resentment to his former black-militant tenant. Likewise, the mixing of the races in the McLeod family unit generates its own tensions and fears: the couple are reclusive, the house is heavily locked and bolted, Frank has restricted access, and he has the disturbing sense that the McLeods could "someday go paranoid and barricade themselves" (122) in the house, with the usual violent outcome. As a portrayal of racial contact and cohabitation in America, the McLeod episode could scarcely be more pessimistic. The difficulty of achieving harmony in black and white relations is symbolized by the arrival of a heavily armed police officer (called by a confused elderly neighbour when Frank calls to the McLeods to collect the rent) to act as ostensible mediator, or law enforcer, in the encounter between white man and black man, between two members of the same country, society and generation who are condemned to function within their oppositional historical identities.

The two other racial plotlines are free from this level of personal tension, yet these encounters between the races are also marked by a certain wariness, and, symbolically again, are both attended by violence and a police presence. Outside the motel room he has taken on his way up to Connecticut to collect his son, Frank meets and has a conversation with Mr Tanks, a black truck-driver. It is another significant contact between the races in the novel, as much for the setting as the content of the conversation. A motel guest has been murdered during a robbery of his room, and Frank's conversation with Mr Tanks takes place in the garish and tragic aftermath of violent death, conferring on the scene "the backlit, half-speed unreality of a movie set" (197). Richard Ford has said that he presented this scene with "lights flashing, just to let you know that something's going on here",[13] meaning the troubled contact between black and white America. Yet the entire *mise-en-scène* (state troopers, local police, blue flashers, ambulance strobe lights, headlights, crackling radios), highly familiar from cinema and television drama, is also specific to the site of violence and death in America, as if Ford wanted the setting of the conversation to epitomize the sometimes-violent contact between the races in America.

The subsequent conversation between white man and black man, which turns around the possibility of Mr Tanks buying a house somewhere on the East Coast, confirms this difficult cohabitation. Despite Frank's desire to help Mr Tanks and his strong antipathy to "the idea of raising the drawbridge" (206) to keep unwanted people out, their encounter is permeated with an unspoken but palpable racial sensitivity: Frank is concerned that Mr Tanks might feel that he (Frank) is "amused by him" (203) and his ambition, and he feels obliged to mention Rev Jesse Jackson as a potential winner of the upcoming presidential election, although silently intoning a "fat chance" (206) to that possibility. Mr Tanks, for his part, seems keen to test Frank's liberal credentials and indicates he might ask Frank to find a house for him in Haddam, asking him provocatively: "You got any niggers down there in your part of New Jersey?" Frank immediately regrets his fatigue-induced "Plenty of 'em" response, and their conversation ends with Mr Tanks asserting that he "wouldn't care to be the only pea in the pod down there" (209).

---

[13] *Ibid.*, 167.

This random contact of two American travellers in the night, in the quintessential American setting of a motel lot, and whose topic of conversation is belonging and compatibility in one's own country, is unable to free itself from the burden of America's past. The potential personal affinities between Frank and Mr Tanks cannot overcome the meanings that history has attached to their different skin colours. Frank is deeply sympathetic to the latter's "seeking, with hope, to emerge from a condition he's grown weary of in pursuit of something better" (204), a formulation that resonates with the faith and aspirations that inspired millions of immigrants to seek a better life in America. Both men are Americans, yet their group identities prevail over their ostensible shared national identity, leaving Frank to regret that "Mr. Tanks and I have not shared much, in spite of my wishing we could" (209).

It is significant that it is in the disappointing aftermath of Frank and Mr Tank's failure to "utter a convincingly encouraging word to the other" (216) that Frank recalls his amorous relationship with Clair Devane, his black real estate colleague. And, again, this human contact between Americans is framed in terms of race, as if to emphasize that America has not yet evolved to the point where a person's individual or moral identity matters more than his or her racial or group identity. Although Clair insisted that the seventeen-year age difference between them excluded any possibility of "a real future" (212), Frank knows that race was also a major factor. For her, their relationship bore a "tinge", and she insisted that their affair be conducted clandestinely. Frank was aware of – although indifferent to – how "crabby small-town" prejudices would view a "divorced white man" being involved with a "black woman with kids" (211).

The racial, cultural and political contexts of their relationship are emphasized in Frank's remark that he and Clair were "impersonating the very complexly ethical, culturally diverse family unit that millions of liberal white Americans were burning to validate" (212). But Frank and Clair's relationship, too, is condemned to remain aspirational only. Clair finally ended it, having met and started to date a "somewhat older" black attorney (143), and she tells Frank that her mother had told her "to get as far away from [Frank] as possible" (214). The races separate, and racial segregation is restored: Clair and her black lawyer become "a nice, viable, single-race item in town" (215-16). Until, that is, she is raped and murdered and has her throat slashed in the condo she was about to show, with indications that the crime was committed by "white" men (143), a detail that, in a narrative about race relations in America, carries obvious and cruel historical echoes of white violence inflicted on the black population.

Frank's three exchanges with black characters share significant features: violence or the potential for violence attend all of them; consciousness of colour difference in each case blocks the possibility of a less anxious contact; and the three encounters ultimately fail at "getting beyond" the race barrier "in a personal way". Richard Ford, then, obeys the logic of his own insight that "too much of society [is] built on this rickety structure that separates the races". The final racial image in the novel is emblematic of this national failure. At one point, late in the weekend, Frank glances at a television set where a presidential election interview with black candidate Jesse Jackson is being broadcast: "Reverend Jackson in an opened-collared brown safari shirt is being interviewed by a panel of white men in business suits, who're beaming prudish self-confidence at him, as if they found him amusing; though the Reverend is exhibiting his own brand of self-satisfied smugness plus utter disdain, all of it particularly noticeable because the sound's off" (373). The television debate is one forum where the "public conversation" should be taking place. But both parties in this television image seem entrenched in their own camps, their historical divisions and relations of power underlined by dress codes and the courtroom connotations of the interview setting, and by the inability or unwillingness of the races to speak to each other, symbolized by the muted television.

Since the Civil War, official ideology and rhetoric has promoted an assimilationist, one-people American national-identity narrative, whereby individual identities prevail over group identities based on race, ethnicity or national background. Historians debate whether this "melting-pot" unity has actually been achieved. A recent contribution to the debate strongly contests the assimilationist account. According to Desmond King, "American nationhood is built on a community of groups more than individuals in spite of the national ideology of one people".[14] Where race is concerned, Richard Ford's novel endorses this view. Ford has said that he wanted *Independence Day* to "reach out" to Americans and tell them that "We share something. We share

---

[14] Desmond King, *The Liberty of Strangers: Making the American Nation*, New York: Oxford UP, 2005, 174.

a national experience."[15] He brings the races together in his novel in the personal ways he advocates, keen to show Americans where that common experience may be found and fostered. It is all the more significant, then, that he has these strategies fail in the face of the obdurate structural, cultural and historical forces ranged against them, leaving one with the strong sense that the shared national experience of which Ford speaks is close to being an illusion, a conclusion for which one finds much support in American history and contemporary society.

Independence Day's focus on economic hegemony and race relations contributes to the wider picture that Richard Ford is painting of the condition of contemporary America. There is a great deal of narrative reflection and commentary by Frank on his country, facilitated structurally by Ford sending Frank out on the road and into America on the holiday weekend. Frank's grand sweep takes him from central New Jersey to the Jersey Shore, on up to Connecticut and then to Massachusetts, across to upstate New York, before the long descent back to Haddam. Frank's journey, to visit his girlfriend and then to collect his son on the way to the halls of fame, provides Ford with a form of road-movie opportunity to present scenes from American life, and to reflect on his country's understanding of its independence and the relevance of the national narrative of the founding of the republic.

As Frank savours the Friday morning of the holiday weekend, he interprets the prevailing mood: "Independence Day is the mounting spirit of the weekend, and all outward signs of life mean to rise with it" (22). The surging spirit invoked here is that of optimism and a sense of promise, palpable not only in the "outward signs" but in Frank's attachment to this public holiday, which, he considers, "[leaves] us only as it found us: free" (7). Freedom, then, the cherished promise and abiding value of America, is the implicit interpretation of independence against which one may measure the expression of national character and identity as the weekend unfolds. Much is permitted, of course, in the name of freedom, and the elasticity of the concept is revealed in contrasting behaviours that Frank encounters, two of which are illustrative and instructive.

---

[15] *Heat Magazine*, 171.

As Frank and Paul arrive at the entrance to the Baseball Hall of
Fame in Cooperstown, they are confronted by a group of protestors
circling with placards in front of the building, blocking their entry.
Like the other onlookers Frank reacts magnanimously to the
inconvenience, without even knowing the reasons for the protest,
reassured that a spirit of peaceful contestation "can be alive still"
(346) and respectful of the protestors' right to disagree. It is notable
that his reaction is explicitly informed by his awareness of the lessons
from America's history, that of "our nation's early days, in which
legitimate grievances were ignored and a crisis followed" (346-47).
Freedom, in this instance, means freedom of expression and a
generous respect for that principle when reasonably invoked, as it is
by the Cooperstown protestors. The scene is also, of course, a
celebration of the rights enshrined in the First Amendment to the
Constitution, which is also the first of the ten Amendments that
constitute America's Bill of Rights. But this manifestation of national
freedom is also presented as a form of wisdom available to Americans
with a sense of their country's history and with the capacity, which
Ford has accorded his character, to understand that a nation's present
identity emerges out of its past errors and tribulations.[16]

A less palatable interpretation of freedom is displayed in the
dining-room of Frank and Paul's Cooperstown hotel when they come
down for breakfast:

> Several munching breakfasters ... have raised wintry eyes up from
> their plates to where Paul and I are standing .... Their guarded eyes
> say, "Hey, we won't be hurried." "We've paid for this." "We're
> entitled to our own pace." "It's our vacation." "Waitchyerturn." (339)

---

[16] One might record here that Frank is selective in his gleanings from Emerson, as he
would not find sanction in "Self-Reliance" for his return to America's history to guide
his behaviour. In his essay Emerson asks: "Whence, then, this worship of the past?
The centuries are conspirators against the sanity and authority of the soul" (*Self-
Reliance*, 28). Emerson rails against memory, consistency in utterance and deed, and
is resolutely committed to the present and the future, the ontological temporality of,
respectively, being and becoming (the temporality to which Frank is instinctively
attracted). For a discussion of Emerson and *Independence Day*, and of Americans'
relationship with the past in general, see William G. Chernecky, "'Nostalgia Isn't
What It Used To Be': Isolation and Alienation in the Frank Bascombe Novels", in
Perspectives on Richard Ford.

The scene is noteworthy for its portrayal of a strain of American independence distasteful to Ford:

> ... it's just part of our American heritage to exclude. White people came to the American continent to exclude ourselves, and as soon as we got here we started excluding everybody else. It's this whole spurious idea of independence. The American practice of independence is premised on the notion of "get away from me, because I'm better off when I'm here by myself and can be seen; or, my independence or my worth is more easily proven when I'm not somehow diluted by you."[17]

Freedom, in this case, is articulated as uncompromising individualism, and is part of an exclusionary culture already identified in the novel through the impact of laissez-faire economics and the social politics that would "[raise] the drawbridge" on the Mr Tanks of the world. These instances also contribute to a theme in the novel that Ford himself has identified: he has noted that *Independence Day* is about "people wanting to find shelter from something",[18] a reaction to their sense that, as Frank has already put it, there is "a wild world ... just beyond our perimeter". The aggressiveness of Larry McLeod, the distress of the Markhams and the sensitivity of Mr Tanks are all related to these characters' need for shelter. Ford's "wild world" image suggests a kind of frontier territorialism where everyone looks out for oneself, exemplified in its own small way by the provocative individualism of the "breakfasters". Such an attitude, in turn, generates a climate of defensiveness and mistrust, reactions particularly evident in Larry McLeod and Mr Tanks. Ford gives concrete expression in *Independence Day* to this threatening world. One is struck by how much violence, reported and intuited, there is in the novel. In addition to the two murders, Frank's mugging and his

---

[17] *Conversations with Richard Ford*, 139. The exclusionist tendency was indeed manifested soon after the establishment of the Plymouth colony by the English Puritans in 1620. The Native American inhabitants who had lived in the south-eastern part of Massachusetts for over 12,000 years, the Wampanoag, soon found themselves driven away from their lands by the settlers' desire for more territory. And within the colonist communities themselves, the settlement of New England was greatly facilitated by the constant schisms and expulsions as a result of newer colonists coming into conflict with the religious rigour of the Massachusetts colony.

[18] *Ibid.*, 130.

apprehensions about Larry and his gun, we learn that Frank's root-beer-stand partner, Karl, is readying his "sawed-off twelve-gauge pump" (219) to deal with the "Mexicans" or "Hondurans" (139) he believes are preparing to rob him; Frank receives an anonymous threatening phone call on his answering machine; he expresses concern on several occasions about being the victim of random murder (195, 197, 263); and there is, in general, an ominous police presence throughout the novel.

It is the exclusionary, individualistic notion of freedom that is seen to be a significant factor in creating the segregated America that Frank discovers on his trip with Paul. Their first taste of Connecticut is the village of Ridgefield, portrayed as affluent, pretty, artificial and pretentious, and as "a town that invites no one to linger, where the services contemplate residents only", an affront to Frank's democratic (and Democratic) beliefs, making Ridgefield, for him, a "piss-poor place to live" (197). Apart from its intimidatingly exclusive appearance, the wealthy inhabitants of Ridgefield's "lush-lawned, deep-pocketed mansion district" protect themselves from unwanted outsiders by "big-time security" (196). This stockade mentality is equally in evidence when Frank lands amidst the "sylvan purlieus of the rich" (230) of Deep River, the new domicile of Ann and their children. Here, the "Endowed law profs", "moneyed shysters" and "moneyed pensioners" have sought a haven within "the usual enclave of self-contented, pseudo-reclusive richies", a class of people whose backs are "resolutely turned to how the other half lives" (229). The self-segregation and self-protection of these wealthy Americans are assured by a private security force, one of whom edgily accosts Frank and threatens to call a state trooper, without the excuse of even the slightest provocation from Frank. The inhabitants of the enclave, the security guard advises Frank, "really don't like being harassed" (234).

Frank likes to think of himself as an "arch-ordinary American" (141-42), but, on successive days, he finds that this identity has limited currency in his own country: by straying out of his allotted territory, a notionally vast space for this ostensibly national citizen, and into contrasting socio-economic landscapes, he has been unable to associate with his fellow Americans without the intervention and vetting of uniformed law-enforcers. Frank will have yet another experience of being an outsider in his own country, making it one for every day of his weekend journey through America. His weekend trip concludes in Oneonta, in upstate New York, and a walk through the town with his step-brother, Irv Orstein. They drift into a part of town where Frank begins to feel out of place, although "it's our own country" and a "common language alone *should* assure us entry-level acceptance anywhere within a two-thousand-mile radius of Kansas City". However, "pushing your luck" here, concludes Frank, "could mean trouble" (384).

There is, however, an important distinction to be made between, on the one hand, Ridgefield and Deep River, and, on the other, Oneonta and Wallace Hill. In all four locations Frank experiences America as separated and disunited, the effects of either economic status or racial membership. The inhabitants of the wealthy enclosures of Ridgefield and Deep River wilfully decline to participate fully in the American republic (Frank observes that there is little "4th of July street regalia" on display in either town, [293]), and they have the financial means to take the necessary measures to separate and isolate themselves. The isolation of the residents of the Oneonta and Wallace Hill areas, however, is essentially imposed, a function of either economic or racial dynamics they do not control. The parts of Oneonta traversed by Frank are run-down, with the houses either badly maintained or deserted, a witness to economic neglect; it is a landscape where everything speaks "the downward-tending lingo of loss" (383). Wallace Hill, by contrast, is a respectable neighbourhood, but its identity is nonetheless that of a respectable black neighbourhood, and it is contrasted in the text with the "white sections" and "white demesnes" (24) of Haddam. Racial difference means separate neighbourhoods, or, as Martyn Bone puts it, "Haddam's social geography has been defined by racial segregation".[19]

---

[19] Martyn Bone, "New Jersey Real Estate and the Postsouthern 'Sense of Place': Richard Ford's *Independence Day*", *American Studies in Scandinavia*, XXXIII/2 (2001), 113. One might record here that a contributory factor to the growing segregation of American society is suburbanization. As people came to live in the suburbs from both metropolitan and non-metropolitan locations (small towns and rural areas), the suburbs, as Robert D. Putnam observes, "fragmented into a sociological mosaic". In other words, people congregated in the suburbs in "lifestyle enclaves" according to finely tuned demographics and became "segregated by race, class, education, life stage, and so on" (Robert D. Putnam, *Bowling Alone: The Collapse and Revival of American Community*, New York: Simon and Schuster, 2000, 209). Desmond King draws upon different scholarship for his observation that "Americans have become residentially more segregated in the 1990s than in the previous post-1964 decades" (*The Liberty of Strangers*, 210).

And then there are the areas that suffer the double blight of economic and racial exclusion: Frank gets lost when he arrives in Springfield and ends up in a poor black neighbourhood where the only sign of how the other half lives is a billboard of Democratic presidential candidate Michael Dukakis. His image beams down on streets where "No garbage has been picked up ... for several days" and where "a conspicuous number of vehicles are abandoned or pillaged along the streetside" (263). Frank is further reminded of the exclusion and "displacement woes of other Americans" (281) when he is out on the road, noting that "it's that time of the month—when leases expire, contracts are up, payments come due", before continuing: "Car windows ... reveal drawn faces behind steering wheels, frowns of concern over whether a certain check's cleared or if someone left behind is calling the law" (175). These are the victims of an essentially laissez-faire economic system, those who have lost their independence entirely and whose only freedom, apart from flight, is the freedom to fail, and to fall to a lower rung on the socio-economic ladder.

Inspired by the original colonies' efforts at nation building, Frank has situated his trip with Paul under the heading, "Reconciling Past and Present: From Fragmentation to Unity and Independence" (259), in an attempt to show his son that the nation's history is relevant to personal dilemmas. However, the colonies' achievement and legacy of unity seems scarcely sustainable in the face of Frank's weekend experiences, and the trajectory proposed in his journey theme seems, if anything, to have suffered a reverse movement since 1776, going from unity to fragmentation. As for the other accomplishment of the colonies, that of national independence, Frank's experiences suggest that segregation and isolation must now be added to the exclusionary understanding of independence in contemporary America already on display in the novel.

Frank's road trip provides some of the novel's quintessential images of America, yet these hardly authenticate the comforting view of the national condition suggested by the theme of Frank's journey. Frank has left Sally's house on the Jersey Shore on Friday night and is trying to get as near to Connecticut as possible in order to pick up Paul early on Saturday morning. But he becomes ensnarled in the night-time car frenzy of America on the road, furiously asserting its freedom and mobility. Ford presents an apocalyptic vision of flight and escape as a lumbering herd of metal monsters ("U-Hauls, trailers, step vans, station wagons, tow dollies, land yachts"), with passengers "belted in so tight that an easy breath can't be drawn", battle their way to "someplace that can't wait till morning" (175). As Frank seeks a way out of this almost-science-fiction vision of hell, he succeeds only in getting further sucked in, enveloped in a "hot mechanical foreboding that the entire seaboard might simply explode". In a car-obsessed country it is perhaps unsurprising that Frank has regularly recorded the make and size of people's cars, a witness to the cycle of production and consumption upon which the market economy depends and to its place in the national psyche. These are the very cars that are now "stacked before, beyond, around and out of sight toward the George Washington Bridge" (195) as encaged, individualistic, mobile America ensconces itself in its second homes, "everyone with kids on board and screaming" (175), glorying in this ostensible affirmation of personal freedom.[20]

Vehicles and voyagers need refuelling, so the Vince Lombardi Rest Area allows a close-up view of Frank's "adversaries from the turnpike". In everything he sees, Frank records that "Nothing suggests the 4th of July". He has had little evidence thus far, in fact, that his fellow Americans share the Independence Day values he would like to celebrate; whatever his compatriots are so aggressively seeking this weekend, it does not appear to have anything to do with learning the lessons that history may impart, or with reviewing or questioning their understanding of independence. The Independence Day weekend seems, rather, a useful opportunity to do in more concerted fashion what is done throughout the rest of the year, namely buying and consuming: "passengers and drivers [troop] dazedly inside … toting diaper bags, thermoses and in-car trash receptacles, their minds fixed on sacks of Roy Rogers burgers, Giants novelty items, joke condoms." The road warriors' sense of history does not even extend as far back as Vince Lombardi, whose memorabilia collection will receive only a "quick exit peep".[21] These modern-day pilgrims are doggedly focused on the present and on the satisfaction of present needs in Ford's

---

[20] Americans' dependence on the car is yet another topic that a book about America can scarcely avoid – Putnam notes that "By 1990 America had more cars than drivers" (*Bowling Alone*, 212).
[21] Vince Lombardi (1913-1970) remains one of the most successful coaches in American Football history.

nightmarish image of robotic twenty-four-hour consumerism: "it's as chaotic as a department store at Christmas ... with its dark video arcade bing-jinging, long lines at the Roy's and Nathan's Famous and families walking around semi-catatonically eating, or else sitting arguing at plastic tables full of paper trash" (178).

These images of mobile Americans trundling voraciously and aggressively across the land represent the antithesis of genuine forms of independence that the novel is exploring. The absence of an Independence Day sensibility that Frank observes among his compatriots is in all likelihood due to their complacent sense that the promise of the founding republic has already been delivered. In one sense, we may indeed view them as united and free, but only in the degraded sense of their being in thrall to the enticements of the free market and the lure of the consumerist liberty it dangles in front of them. They do not see the holiday, as Frank does, as "an observance of human possibility" and as an opportunity "to contemplate what we're dependent on" (288-89). Indeed, if there is a common thread running through the experiences and observations of Frank's symbolic journey, it is that the notional celebration of the ideals of the Declaration of Independence has metamorphosed into a celebration of American commerce and economic freedom. The wealthy Connecticut towns of Ridgefield and Deep River display little or no holiday spirit, but everywhere display, through the variety of their shops, their allegiance to the free market. Cooperstown, home of the Baseball Hall of Fame, may well have draped itself in holiday regalia, yet the town functions ultimately as little more than an artificial and contrived "period backdrop to the Hall of Fame"; it is full of "baseball vacationers" and its shops are "full of baseball *everything*". It is a town trading on a commercial spin-off, "with nothing authentic ... really going on" (293). And if there is a theme to the sounds and images of Frank's road movie as they drive through America, it is provided by the radio spots selling anything that can be traded and by the images of the commercial American landscape that flash by.

America's past has little chance of competing with the consumerist present. There are few human activities more clinically concentrated on the present and more essentially indifferent to the past than commerce. The market exists to meet present needs and to create future desires; it must, indeed, actively induce forgetting, a weaning away from tradition, and incite interest in novelty, in the not-yet acquired. It is here, *Independence Day* seems to be saying, that one will find the true legacy of the Revolution: the citizen has resolved into a consumer, and independence has resolved into the freedom of the market. It is probably no coincidence that, in the midst of Frank's entanglement with his voracious fellow citizens at the Vince Lombardi Rest Area, he concludes that "The best all-around Americans, in my view, are Canadians" (191).

However, this will not be Frank's definitive judgment on his country. Just as much as he wants now to distance himself from the highway hordes he will later in the weekend experience a glow of pleasure when he wanders into Doubleday Field in Cooperstown and momentarily yearn to be part of a scene of happy Americans, of men and women united in a communal celebration of team spirit, companionship and past achievement. Frank's weekend will indeed have brought him into contact with faces of America that displease and disturb him, and with which he could scarcely find any common ground, any sense of a shared national belonging or identity. But the weekend is not yet over and the dominant national understandings of independence conveyed to him thus far – those of freedom as exclusion, as individualism, as isolation and separation – have yet to commingle with the personal experience and exploration of independence that the weekend will facilitate. It is now time to turn to this aspect of the novel, to the condition of Frank Bascombe himself on Independence Day weekend.

CHAPTER 4

INDEPENDENCE DAY

II: LAISSEZ-FAIRE AND ISOLATION

As he looks forward to his Independence Day weekend Frank can reflect that his life, "at least frontally, is simplicity's model". He is "happily if slightly bemusedly" settling into middle age, dealing with limited success with his role as a distant parent and easing his way through an existence that essentially "goes unnoticed" (7). Frank, philosopher and historian *par excellence* of his own existence, is firmly installed in a definitive new phase of his life, for which he has found the expression, "the Existence Period". The most immediately striking feature of the term "existence" in this context is its modesty and restraint: it suggests a certain lack of ambition when set beside the term "life", with which it is often contrasted. Where "existence" has an undoubted ontological weight, it lacks the corporeal heft of "life"; "existence" seems thin in its minimum condition of being when set beside the activities and commotions, the dramas and sheer physicality of a "life". In its understated way, existence is to life somewhat as setting is to place, which might explain why Haddam was the ideal location for Frank to live this new phase of his life.

The thinness of being implicit in the term "existence" translates into a neutral mode of living, the goal of which is to find a balance in one's engagements: "it is one of the themes of the Existence Period that interest can mingle successfully with uninterest in this way, intimacy with transience, caring with the obdurate uncaring" (76). The Existence Period, therefore, is not merely a descriptive term; it is also a self-conscious strategy for achieving a "balancing of urgent forces" (94) in Frank's life. It represents an ostensibly safe middle ground and is Frank's version of seeking shelter from the storm, which for him was his dreaminess phase of self-disconnection, followed by his separation and divorce from Ann. It is indeed the mode of living of someone who has been scarred by the harsh consequences of extreme behaviour and who now seeks refuge in an innocuous zone of self-containment. The Existence Period informs Frank's life in very specific ways, most notably in his adopting a neutral attitude and a non-interventionist mode. He no longer worries if his life is "leading someplace" (49); he aims to "ignore much of what I don't like or that seems worrisome and embroiling" (10); he is happy to let things drift along as they are, particularly in the hope that what is worrisome will simply go away; and, in the acceptance that we control little enough in life, he advocates a general policy of letting go in the face of the "unfixable crises [that] cruise past" us, a philosophy that he considers "a useful coping skill of the Existence Period" (14).

Such a philosophy has consequences, of course. It leads to life as a form of hovering around one's engagements, to a holding mode of existence; it demands an attitude of passivity and non-commitment; and it leads to lowered ambitions and expectations: Frank is no longer aiming for the "*best*", but for what is "*fine* in the eternity of the here and now" (145). This slipping back into the primacy of the present has an obvious affinity with a similar tendency evident in *The Sportswriter*. Here, it is the necessary temporality of a life that functions in a mode of permanent suspension, where the strict minimum is undertaken in the interest of maintaining balance, distance and non-intervention. Frank is entirely conscious that this period of his life is marked by a lessening, by a settling for smaller gains: "to the old taunt that says, 'Get a life,' I can say, 'I already have an existence, thanks'" (117).

This brand of quietism may constitute a feasible life philosophy if one lives alone at the top of a mountain; it is much less sustainable when one is entangled down in the world of aggravating clients, accusing ex-wives, unhappy children, disappointed lovers and threatening tenants. Frank, in other words, is treading yet again the dangerous ground of seeking to live life according to a theory while paying too little attention to the practical consequences of the deficiencies of his theory. It is precisely in the area of relations with others that the Existence Period philosophy is most subject to strain. Frank had returned from France with a "deep-beating urgency having to do with me and me only, not me *and* somebody" (92), an instinct that was confirmed for him when he realized that "intimacy had begun to matter less" (96) to him. The great advantage of this was a newly won sense of independence: Frank was no longer prey to his womanizing urges, was content in his bachelor's life and was more self-reliant.

The price of his independence, however, is the distance that has opened up between him and other people, one that looks very much like self-isolation. Yet Frank's life is necessarily entwined with those of others, and although he may wish to distance himself from people, they may need or want a closer relationship with him. And Frank has indeed begun to notice that his philosophy is not working, and that it has brought him to where "more things seem to need sorting out now" (76): he has not shaken himself free emotionally from Ann, which prevents him from fully inhabiting "the eternity of the here and now"; he has just had an uneasy midnight phone call from his girlfriend, Sally; and his son, perhaps suffering the consequences of an absent father, has fallen into mildly delinquent ways. The individualist self-withholding of the Existence Period philosophy, and Frank's understanding of independence as self-isolation, are being tested by the continuing, and inevitable, emotional relationships with others.

Frank's descriptive phrase for the current period of his life is well chosen, as the word "existence" has another connotation, beyond that of his non-committal mode of living his life. The term directs us to the philosophical focus on the condition of being itself. It is also the origin of the term "existential", an adjective with precise philosophical meanings, but that is also used more loosely to describe a certain anxiety about the condition of existence. It comes as something of a surprise to learn that Frank Bascombe, living the ordinary, conventional life of a white middle-aged professional American in the materiality of the New Jersey suburbs, is prey to a recurrent and disturbing existential anguish. If Frank is living out a reduced form of life, it is partly because he has come to see the actions of his life, including his daily routines, not as a drive to fulfilment but as so many ways of shielding himself from an existential abyss that threatens to engulf him: "I try ... to keep something finite and acceptably doable on my mind and not disappear. Though it's true that sometimes ... I sense I myself am afloat and cannot always feel the sides of where I am" (117). There is a certain insubstantiality to Frank's sense of his own being, a nagging hollowness that obliges him to fabricate meaning and purpose rather than being able simply to experience, without thought or effort, a fullness of meaning.

Frank's existential angst receives different articulations in the novel. Some of these are prompted by a "wince", a powerful stab that sets his heart pounding as his being registers a penetration of its defences. One of these occurs as he arrives at Sally's house and takes in the view of the sea and people on the beach. Frank becomes suddenly emotional at the sensation that he has been here before and at the fleeting conjunction of his past and present selves, causing him to ponder the relation of self to place. He will brusquely discount his sentimental reaction by concluding that one should never look to place to sanction either our existence or our life: "Best just to swallow back your tear ... and shove off to whatever's next, not whatever was. Place means nothing" (152). Yet Frank is shaken by this insight that places do not bear witness to our passage through time: "there is now no sign of you, no mention in the air's breath that you were there or that you were ever, importantly you, or that you even *were*" (151). Frank may routinely recommend turning one's gaze to the future, but he is nonetheless disturbed to find one's past life so casually obliterated by place and time.

A short time later, as he awaits Sally's return, he experiences another wince, as place again hardens itself against a human presence. Frank's sensation is more prosaic than the earlier moment – he suddenly wonders "what exactly in the hell I'm doing here" (155) – but this sensation of being somewhere he should not be produces another existential sting of emptiness, as he cannot imagine anywhere else he could be, and is confronted by a sense of existential "Nullity". His defences against these attacks of angst are slender, and, once breached, a tenuous bond between existence and meaning is revealed: "You simply reach a point at which everything looks the same but nothing matters much. There's no evidence you're dead, but you act that way" (156).

The two registers of the Existence Period – the thinness of life and the thinness of existence – are seen ultimately to be connected. As Frank heaves his way through the night-time traffic on his way to Connecticut, alone and "bound for an empty set of sheets in who knows what motel in who knows what state", he reflects that, due to the personal "flexibility" of time and place that he has contrived for himself in his life, it could "take days, possibly weeks, for serious personal dust to be raised" if one day he simply were not to turn up where he was supposed to be. Frank's limp commitment to his own life and the reduced impact he makes on the lives of those around him have had the effect that neither his presence nor his absence would be "noticed that much". The Existence Period, then, is ultimately a question of the degree to which Frank inhabits both his life and existence, and it is his failure to fully inhabit his life that leads to his sense that he does not fully inhabit his existence: "It's not exactly as if I didn't exist, but that I don't exist *as much*" (176).

At this moment of insight into what is wrong with his life Frank begins to makes another vital connection. He had understood his isolation from others as a form of independence, as a freedom from his dependency on them and their dependency on him. Now he is less sure of these benefits; his diminishing impact in other people's lives "may also imply that laissez-faire is not precisely the same as independence" (177). The two understandings of Frank's Existence Period have finally converged. At one end, Frank's withholding in his life – his passivity, non-intervention and absence of commitment – is being confronted by the claims of others; at the other, his diminished presence in others' lives is leading to an extreme form of isolation, and to a desiccated form of independence. Five years after the Easter weekend events described in *The Sportswriter*, Frank has fallen back into a habitual isolation.[1] He must now make a choice between solitude and society, and, in that choice, also find a bearable and fruitful mode of independence.

Frank's Independence Day weekend brings him into direct and long-deferred serious engagement with three important people in his life (Sally, Ann and Paul) and, in so doing, into confrontation with his

---

[1] To an interviewer's question as to whether he felt Frank's character had "evolved" between *The Sportswriter* and *Independence Day*, Richard Ford replied: "I didn't, but other people did" (*Conversations with Richard Ford*, 196). One is inclined to agree with the author here, simply because, in both novels, Frank's character is heavily defined through his relationships with others, and it is clear that, in *Independence Day*, he is continuing to keep a distance from others, most notably from women with whom he is involved.

Existence Period identity and understanding of independence. As was the case in the period of his life described in *The Sportswriter*, Frank's current identity has important moral implications, in that it regulates his relationship and conduct with others, but it also has an increasingly important social dimension, in that it informs his wider relationship with people, society and his community. Out of the articulation and redefinition of Frank's moral and social identities over the weekend, there will emerge, by way of his engagement with those closest to him, revised understandings of dependence and independence.

Frank has been involved in a relationship for ten months with Sally Caldwell, the weekly highlight of which is a "Friday evening rendezvous". Their relationship, however, is more of an arrangement conducted within clearly understood parameters, within which a certain freedom is allowed and "generous portions of companionship" and pleasure supplied, without the illusion that this amounts to love. Frank is content with this "laissez-faire" (8) understanding, as it responds precisely to the Existence Period exigency of pleasure without pain or commitment. Sally's night-time phone call to Frank, however, in which she intimates that she was "missing something" (9) and that it had to do with the two of them, alerts Frank that "trouble may be brewing" (8). He knows that her untypically distant manner to him when he visits her on the Friday evening is due to his own uncommitted attitude: Frank likes the "tintinnabulation of early romance" (10) but prefers, in good Existence Period fashion, to ignore the signs that more is being asked for and to let things drift along.

Sally's disquiet comes out in her question to Frank about love: "What does it mean to you to tell somebody you love them? Or her?" In his womanizing, post-separation phase from Ann, Frank found himself regularly telling women he loved them; now he is more cautious, and his "provisional" (168) and less than convincing response to Sally's question casts a shadow over their evening, compounded by Frank letting himself be caught saying that "Trust's for the birds". This latter moment is a familiar Frank gesture of heedlessly grasping for the pleasure of the moment and, in so doing, wildly misreading a person and a situation: as he half-jokingly discounts the importance of trust he is grasping Sally into his arms, anxious to experience the thus-far withheld "froth of a moment's pseudo-intimacy and pleasure". In its timing, this is a lesser version of his tactless invitations to Vicki and Ann in *The Sportswriter*, and it produces a corresponding reaction: Sally pushes Frank's "cloying arms off in a testy way" (169) and walks away from him. The evening cannot be recuperated and ends with Frank's departure and the unspoken mutual understanding that they will "not ... see each other anymore" (172).

While on his trip with Paul, Frank attempts to retrieve the situation with Sally. In a mode of communication symbolic of the nature and state of their relationship, they speak to each other through answering-machine messages and phone calls, juggling distance and proximity, absence and presence, as a mobile Frank orbits around a fixed and steadfast Sally. But they fail to connect with each other because they are trying to communicate from different perspectives and with a different relationship to language, to the point that they barely seem to speak the same language at all, in either a literal or metaphorical sense. It is telling and appropriate, then, that it is indeed language that sabotages their efforts to connect with each other. In their first phone conversation Sally reproaches Frank with being "too smooth from one thing to the next" and complains that she "can't keep up with [him] very well" (272). Their second phone conversation is remarkable for its focus on language itself. Sally repeatedly comes back to what Frank said during his visit and first phone call, inviting him to clarify what he said and what he meant. Sally puts her faith in the solemn language of stability, permanence and commitment as she seeks in Frank's words a solid ground upon which to build a long-term relationship. Frank, however, uses language as a tactical weapon, ducking and weaving around Sally as he tries to evade the weight of permanent meanings, and as he strives only to salvage the original expectation of a weekend of pleasure by trying to convince her – irresponsibly, given the goal of his trip – to come join him and Paul. And when Frank does not like the direction of a conversation, or when he feels cornered by something he said, as happens now, he does what he typically does – he says something else: in a conversation about the responsibility of meaning and the gravity of language, Frank blurts out that he loves Sally. Invited by her, inevitably, to explain what he means, Frank replies: "I just realized I wanted to say it to you. And so I said it. I don't know everything it means ... but I know it doesn't mean nothing" (307).

Not surprisingly, their conversation ends unsatisfactorily, as Sally tells Frank in her disappointment that he is "not really very easy to fix on" and that "Everything isn't just about how you say it" (311). The relationship between men and women is the fundamental human connection in Richard Ford's fiction, through which Ford explores the moral implications of how men and women abide by their commitment to love each other. Language, the words of love or estrangement that are spoken, is at the centre of that relationship in Ford's fiction, in which one is a moral being as much through what one says as through what one does. In his unforthcoming, flitting way Frank has failed to assume the moral responsibility of his own words, and, in so doing, has estranged Sally and has estranged himself from the truth. He will also, in due course, become aware that his Existence Period philosophy has not been equal to the task of helping him make a choice between freedom and commitment, and between isolation and intimacy.

Seven years after his divorce from Ann, Frank has still not accepted the full implications of their separation, a state of mind that is partly responsible for his unsatisfactory relationships with women. Rather than seeing divorce as a conclusive act, he speaks of "divorce's shaky unfinality" (161) and has preferred to see his post-divorce life more as a revised arrangement, one setting Ann and himself in a "different equipoise" (104), yet still in vital ways inextricably connected to each other. That Frank so clings to this fundamental relationship in his life is a measure of how, as he quickly came to realize, his very identity was dependent upon it. The moment Ann announced her remarriage, Frank was invaded by an image of her death and his own subsequent drift into futility and non-identity, into, in other words, his own metaphorical death.

Frank formulates his visceral connectedness to Ann according to four dependencies. First, he lived for Ann: using a theatrical metaphor Frank speaks of how his "life was (and to some vague extent still is) played out on a stage in which she's continually in the audience" (105), a form of being-for-another that is credited by Frank with developing all that was morally good in him. This reminds us of Charles Taylor's premise that "one cannot be a self on one's own" and that our moral identity develops within "webs of interlocution",[2] among which he includes the "intimate relations to the ones [we] love".[3] Second, Ann invested herself in Frank: this took the form of a vital existential caring for him, which continues in the manner in which she "still superintends everything about me just by being alive and sharing ineluctable history" (177). Third, Frank's self image is influenced by how he thinks Ann views him: this is rather less agreeable, as "Your life, because of this, can become goddamned awful and decline into being a 'function' of your view of *her* view" (247-48). And, finally, Frank saw that his and Ann's identities had merged into a single identity, entailing the loss of Frank's independent identity, but having the immense benefit to Frank of his not needing to be "responsible for everything that had me in it" (177). As in *The Sportswriter*, one of Frank's greatest flaws is his fear of responsibility. In one vital area of his life, then, he is far from having achieved a necessary independence, "necessary" because what is holding him back is founded on the illusion that there is still, or still can be, a meaningful relationship between them.

That illusion is to be ended when Frank arrives to collect Paul, as Ann feels provoked by Frank into performing an autopsy on their marriage. This, we sense, is the conversation that should have taken place long ago but never did, and only takes place now because Frank suggests that they might "Get married to each other again" (251). Apart from Frank's emotional absence in their life together (Ann tells Frank that he was "never entirely there" [254]), Ann identifies an absence of trust as the profound cause of their divorce: "I divorced you ... because I didn't like you. And I didn't like you because I didn't trust you. Do you think you ever told me the truth once, the whole truth?" (252-53). Ann and Sally both turn away from Frank for essentially the same reason, his failure to recognize that our words are also our deeds, that language is nothing less than moral action. The significant feature of Ann's conversation with Frank is that she touches on the philosophical flaw at the core of Frank's world-view. In a phone call the previous evening with Frank she had told him that he was "willing to let *seem* equal *be*", which is one way of saying that

---

[2] Taylor, *Sources of the Self*, 36.
[3] *Ibid.*, 35.

Frank took his wishes and fantasies for reality. The surface of things, we recall from *The Sportswriter*, has always mattered more to Frank than any depth they might have; appearance attracts him more than substance. And one of the ways Frank has cultivated this perspective is through language. During their phone call Ann also said to Frank that fiction had been his ideal medium as "You could have everybody saying what you wanted them to ... and everything would work out perfectly—for you anyway" (184). In other words, "seem" could be made into "be" at will, and wishes turned into reality. Frank's only justification for his remarriage idea was that "If you can say it you can do it, I guess" (251).

From one perspective Frank's philosophy is exceedingly contemporary, and even postmodern, in its privileging of the signifier over the signified, in revelling in the play of appearances at the expense of reality, and in blurring the boundaries between the two. It is indeed Frank's dissatisfaction with reality that lies at the heart of his philosophical and moral world-view. More precisely, Frank intuits that reality is not the reliable bedrock we credit it with being, in so far as there is always a disconcerting contingency at work in human affairs. For Frank, the end result that we credit with the name and weight of reality might just as easily have turned out differently. Thinking about a Volvo car that Ann and he had almost bought in their early days together, Frank muses:

> I'm often struck with a heart's pang of *What if?* What if our life had gone in that direction ... some direction a *car* could've led us and now be emblem for? Different house, different town, different sum total of kids, on and on. Would it all be better? .... And it can be paralyzing to think an insignificant decision, a switch thrown this way, not that, could make many things turn out better, even be saved. (My greatest human flaw and strength, not surprisingly, is that I can always imagine anything—a marriage, a conversation, a government—as being different from how it is, a trait that ... seems to produce a somewhat less than reliable and morally feasible human being.) (225-26)

Exactly so. And it was as a writer of fiction, as Ann points out, that Frank could glory in contingency, in the fabrication of reality, and in juggling with the different ontological orders of seeming and being.

As Frank puts it: "Writers ... understand that almost everything—e-v-e-r-y-t-h-i-n-g—is not really made up of 'views' but words, which, should you not like them, you can change" (248).

In *The Sportswriter*, and now in *Independence Day*, Frank has danced on the surface of things and has functioned morally in seeming and in fantasy, and in the assumed evanescence of language. This has brought him in both novels to the brink of a drastic isolation. In the real world of people, expectations, responsibility and trust Frank's order is unsustainable, practically and morally. Vicki and Ann turned away from him in the first novel, and now Ann, following hard on Sally's rejection of him, has pronounced the definitive end of any personal, complicit relationship that might have remained between them. In the latter two cases the central issue was one of trust. We are witnessing again in Richard Ford's fiction the elaboration of the moral vision of personal responsibility, through the creation of characters "who bear the consequences of action as fully as it can be borne".[4] An immediate consequence of Ann's judgement is that one of the most enduring attachments that connected Frank to others has been severed. It remains to be determined whether the severing of a dependence is the prelude to the attainment of a healthy independence.

Frank's Existence Period philosophy and his notions of independence and dependence will be sorely tested during his trip with Paul, just as they have been in his contacts with Sally and Ann. Frank's fifteen-year-old son, in addition no doubt to being in the throes of adolescent rebellion and anxiety, is struggling to deal with debilitating childhood memories, which has culminated in sporadic delinquent behaviour. He has been arrested for shoplifting condoms and is due in court after the holiday weekend. Frank recognizes guiltily that he has not been as "vigilant" (140) a parent as he should have been and has undertaken the weekend trip in an attempt to help his son liberate himself from his anxieties. Paul traces his problems back to the death of the family dog, run over by a car when Paul was six: "It seems like it ruined everything that was fixed back then", he tells Frank (292). But beyond the trauma of the violent death of the beloved family pet and Paul's brutal introduction to life's random cruelties, it seems clear that his

---

[4] *Conversations with Richard Ford*, 116.

sense of loss is also associated with the unravelling of his secure family life. He is now in the grip of severe self-monitoring, a self-conscious surveillance of his own thinking processes as he tries and fails to control his memories and thoughts and make everything fit together. He is ill at ease in his own body, makes barking and *"eeeck-eeecking"* sounds (13) and generally feels miserable and morbid.

Frank's strategy for helping his son is to situate their trip within the themes of the Independence Day holiday. In what seems a highly idealistic and optimistic plan he intends to use the Declaration of Independence and Emerson's "Self-Reliance" as texts for launching thematic discussions with Paul, whom Frank sees as needing "independence from whatever holds him captive" (16), including memory and personal history. This liberation can be facilitated over the Independence Day weekend, in Frank's view, through a reflection on America's past and an appreciation of the correspondences between national and personal histories. The colonies' success in overcoming internal divisions to achieve unity and independence is, as Frank sees it, a lesson that is "totally relevant" to "Paul's difficulty in integrating his fractured past with his hectic present so that the two connect up in a commonsense way and make him free and independent". For Frank, "History's lessons are subtle lessons, inviting us to remember and forget selectively" (259).

It comes as little surprise that Paul is bored by Frank's pedagogical approach. Historical figures mentioned by Frank mean nothing to him ("Who's John Adams?" [259]), and history cannot break into his contemporary, personal world. Indeed Paul practises his own forms of exclusion, isolating himself from Frank through listening to his Walkman and inuring himself from history through his fidelity to the present alone. He is a walking endorsement of the market and the marketing idiom: everything is personal statement, be it the slogans on his t-shirts and gym bag, or the slavishly fashionable clothes he wears. While Paul is indeed, in his distress, partly captive to the past, he is also, like the other consumers met in the journey through America, even more captive to the present. It is only when Frank departs from the complex lessons of history and translates them into Paul's modern idiom – personal, coarse, slogan-like and of the present – that he succeeds in communicating with him: "I fuck up a lot. But I try" (295), says Frank in exasperation at one point, but that momentarily breaks through Paul's defences and allows a small contact, and a little progress, to be made.

Yet, for all Frank's talk about the value of the lessons of the past, he, too, is captive to the present, and the attitude displayed by his compatriots to their nation's past is much the same as Frank's attitude to his own personal past. While counselling Paul to heed the lessons of history, it is noticeable that Frank understands history as an invitation to forget as much as to remember. He acknowledges that he sometimes regrets no longer being a writer of fiction, as fiction, like history, allows a self-serving selection, and would have also, had he continued as a writer, allowed him to consign unwanted memories and meanings to the controllable space of a story. We noted earlier Frank's very selective "jettisonings" of awkward memories in relation to Ann's decision to remarry, and an important aspect in general of his Existence Period philosophy is a willed forgetting. Frank is ultimately afraid of his past. He knows that an important part of who he is lies dormant there, but fears what he might discover were he ever to look. At one point Sally asks him if his mother had been frustrated in her life, a topic that Frank wishes immediately to avoid for fear of what it might tell him about himself: "[I am] made uncomfortable by thinking of my guileless parents in some revisionist's way, a way that were I only briefly to pursue it would no doubt explain my whole life to now. Better to write a story about it" (163). Elsewhere, despite what he might say about the selective lessons of history, he proclaims his philosophy of forgetting to himself and Paul, hardened into a mantra: "Forget, forget, forget" (320). In this respect the Frank of *Independence Day* is utterly consistent with the Frank of *The Sportswriter*.

Their trip has two climactic moments, both of which deeply undermine Frank's certainties. In their Cooperstown hotel Frank comes across a copy of his twenty-year-old book of short stories. His initial pleasure at this serendipitous discovery dissipates when he reads the inscriptions written by the book's one-time owners, announcing love found, then lost in bitterness. A "totally unexpected, sickening void" opens up in Frank's stomach as the inscriptions trigger a surge of grief: "Ann, and the end of Ann and me and everything associated with us, comes fuming up in my nostrils suddenly like a thick poison and in a way it never has." Frank's systematic evasion of his past and the lessons his past might contain, including the fact that Ann has long been lost to him, leaves him defenceless now as the festering boil of unattended emotions is lanced. Most destabilizing for him is the "chasm" that suddenly opens up between "our long-ago time and this very moment" (322). Frank is unable to reconcile past and present (something he preaches to Paul but has never practised himself) because, as he demonstrated forcefully in *The Sportswriter*, he has always eschewed narrative causality and the narrative preservation of past meaning. Frank simply abandoned his past by refusing to attend to it, and now, seven years after his divorce, the full force of what he ignored confronts him, and all he can do is suffer the tears of sadness that well up in his eyes.

The second moment is even more devastating. The intermittent tension between Frank and Paul has Frank taunt his son to follow his example by hitting a few pitches in an automatic baseball batting cage in Cooperstown. Paul angrily storms into the high-speed-pitch cage without any protective equipment (following Frank's example) and receives a pitch full in the eye. The holiday trip comes to a brutal end with Paul being urgently evacuated to hospital in Oneonta.

The accident is the sadly apt culmination of years of insufficient attention by Frank, an unreliability that had continued the previous evening through an emblematic act of negligence: engaged by the attractions of a woman he flirted with, he was unaware of, and not terribly concerned about, Paul's whereabouts for several hours. But that act of negligence was emblematic equally of his entire approach to others. His Existence Period philosophy of low-level involvement in his own and others' lives, of mingling interest with uninterest and caring with uncaring, has patently failed those closest to him. In close succession Sally, Ann and Paul have had to deal with the consequences of Frank's absent mode of being with others. But by the Sunday morning of the Independence Day weekend, it is Frank who finds himself radically alone.

In this moment of extreme isolation, and following a series of painful personal encounters precipitated by his remoteness from the lives of others and from his own life and past, it is highly symbolic that Frank is rescued by a once-familiar presence from his distant family past: Paul's accident was witnessed by Frank's step-brother, Irv Ornstein, the son of Frank's mother's second husband. Irv takes

Frank in hand, drives him to the hospital and attends to Frank as they
await the arrival of Ann and her eye-specialist friend.

In their conversation it soon becomes clear that Irv will play the
role of Frank's *alter ego*, in whom certain conflicts, similar to Frank's,
are being worked through. The function of Irv as Frank's mirror image
is subtly suggested in the text when Frank sees his and Irv's reflection
in a store window as they walk around the streets of Oneonta: in a
moment of self-seeing, Frank is shocked at his hunched, semi-stooped
posture beside the upright Irv. Significantly, Irv is "oblivious to his
reflection" (385), and is so, we may conclude, because Irv does not
need to look at himself, as, metaphorically, he already does so through
the process of self-questioning to which he is subjecting himself. Irv is
going through an important period of stocktaking and self-reflection,
and is looking closely at his past and present in a search for continuity
in his life. The decisive themes of the whole novel now begin to
crystallize in the step-brothers' conversation: the personal, the
national and the historical all find expression and weave through each
other as Irv ruminates on his desire for continuity in a fragmented
personal and national life, concerns with obvious relevance to Frank's
atomized temporal and social existence.

Irv's earnest search for continuity is prompted by his sense of
being "detached from his own personal history" (388), a feeling that
leads him to fear a form of spiritual diminishment. In this frame of
mind the chance meeting with Frank has great significance for him
and he becomes slightly emotional at the opportunity of establishing a
vital connection to his life of twenty-five years previously, as he tells
Frank: "you're my only link to that time. I'm not gonna get all worked
up over it, but you're as close to family as anyone there is for me"
(387). Frank sees the link between Irv's fear of spiritual diminishment
and his own existential "fear of disappearance" (388), yet their
responses to what are crises of identity are utterly contrasting,
particularly in relation to their respective personal histories. Irv, in
thoroughly Ricoeurean fashion, is actively scrutinizing his past in
order to get "a clearer sense of where I've come from before I try to
find out where I'm going" (390). Frank's confrontation with his past,
however, when he came across his old book, highlighted his conscious
rupture with the past and his life-long refusal to draw upon its lessons.

One moment encapsulates their different attitudes to the past. Irv shows Frank a laminated photograph he has carried around for five years, containing an image that has become the icon for his solemn quest for continuity. Frank looks blankly at the photograph, recognizing neither his mother nor himself (standing beside Irv and Irv's father) from twenty-five years earlier, a response that bespeaks more than a literal failure of self-recognition: Frank's failure to recognize his own image from the past is emblematic of his failure to recognize his previous selves throughout his life. For Frank, instruction and the past meet only in History, and not in his personal life.

If Irv and Frank's responses to sustaining an identity over time are different, they nonetheless share certain dilemmas. Irv, too, is struggling to balance independence and isolation. He has had two marriages and two unhappy divorces, and must now decide whether marriage to Erma, whom he loves, means "losing" (389) himself and his independence, or whether it will bring an end to isolation. Irv, in fact, appears as isolated as Frank, both admitting that they do not have many friends (meaning none, no doubt, as Irv, like Frank, takes off on his own rather than socialize – in Irv's case for "a long walk in the desert alone" [385]). Both of them are having to deal with an increasing atomization in their lives and with the wider disengagement of individuals from each other in their society, a condition that, as the evidence mounts, is seen to be the defining malaise in the novel: Frank and Irv have three divorces between them, are wary about committing themselves again and are essentially friendless; Frank has irregular contact with his children; the Markhams have both been divorced, while Joe has lost contact with one of his children; and Sally's husband simply disappeared out of her life and the lives of her two children.

To the estrangement sorrows of the principal characters may be added those of secondary characters: Mr Tanks is divorced and, nomadic and rootless in his truck, is seeking a neighbourhood that will find him acceptable; Clair Devane's first husband left her for another woman; and Char, the hotel chef with whom Frank flirts, has a husband who is no longer around. Americans, it would seem, have lost the fidelity and patience to stay with those they once thought they loved, or at least claimed to love. In *Independence Day* it is fragmentation rather than unity that defines the personal life of contemporary America.

It is precisely Irv's quest for continuity amidst this fragmentation that has him solicit Frank's views on the subject, in the latter's professional capacity as realtor. Troubled by the pattern of remoteness in his personal life, Irv looks to his wider society to provide a sense of community and, thus, a sense of continuity. He receives no comfort from Frank, for whom communities are "isolated, contingent groups" whose only link to continuity is the "illusion of permanence" they live with and try to improve on, while being fully aware that it is an illusion. And where Irv would seek to posit continuity as a spiritual force in the construction and maintenance of communities, Frank, in his job, sees only the economic reality of "Buying power" (386). Frank and Irv's conversation gathers together the threads of several of the novel's important themes and plotlines relating to the condition of community life in America: set against Irv's communal ideal is the reality of the segregation of Haddam on racial lines, the self-segregation of the wealthy enclaves of Ridgefield and Deep River, and the "displacement woes" of the Markhams and Mr Tanks, who both find it difficult to stake out their place in suburban America. Community life in America is portrayed as atomized and exclusionary, with Americans cutting themselves off, or being cut off, from each other. And in this, Ford's novel has proved to be perspicacious, as the major study on American community life published since *Independence Day* has confirmed.

Robert D. Putnam's *Bowling Alone: The Collapse and Revival of American Community* brings a vast amount of quantitative and qualitative survey information to bear on the nature of American community life in the twentieth century. Drawing on the social science concept of "social capital", which he defines as "connections among individuals—social networks and the norms of reciprocity and trustworthiness that arise from them",[5] Putnam charts the decline in community involvement by Americans in the last third of the twentieth century. Using various measures of participation in communities (political, civic, religious, work-based and a range of informal relationships), he shows that, by the end of the century,

---

[5] Putnam, *Bowling Alone*, 19.

Americans had radically disengaged from their communities and neighbourhoods, and even from their immediate neighbours. Putnam presents a vista of a disturbingly individualistic and atomized society. He proposes that the suburbanization of America has been an important factor in the collapse of community life, of particular relevance to the suburban world of Haddam and to the suburban-realtor view of Frank Bascombe.[6]

The most dramatic change in the configuration of communities in America has been the shift to the suburbs in the second half of the twentieth century. The proportion of Americans living in the suburbs grew from 23% in 1950 to 49% in 1996.[7] This vast migration to the suburbs led to a greater fragmentation of society as residents began to cluster together according to homogeneous demographic groups – of class, race, education, lifestyle, and so on. This accentuated sense of group identity often led to "gated communities" that physically separate different communities from each other. Putnam quotes an ethnographer who lived in a suburban New Jersey community in the 1980s and who found a "culture of atomized isolation, self-restraint, and 'moral minimalism'", recording that "suburbanites kept to themselves, asking little of their neighbors and expecting little in return" (210).[8] Putnam also cites Kenneth T. Jackson, the "preeminent historian of the American suburb", for whom the important change in suburban living is "the way in which our lives are now centered inside the house, rather than on the neighborhood or the community" (211). The car, of course, facilitated the massive migration to the suburbs and now contributes to the isolation endemic to suburban life. Putnam offers a striking image of the "symbiosis between the automobile and the suburb" that encapsulates the wider self-isolation in American society that his study delineates: "we spend measurably more of every day shuttling alone in metal boxes among the vertices of our private triangles."[9] It is an image that brings us back to, and finds its

---

[6] The other major factors in the collapse of community life cited by Putnam are pressures of time and money, the impact of electronic media and entertainment, and the simple replacement of engaged generations by less engaged generations.
[7] Putnam, *Bowling Alone*, 206-207.
[8] *Ibid.*, 210.
[9] *Ibid.*, 212.

corroboration in, *Independence Day*: Frank never walks anywhere in Haddam, but always drives through it.

The further one travels with Frank on his weekend journey through America, the more a coherence of theme emerges in Ford's novel. Ford has explored his major theme of independence through the national narrative of America and the personal narrative of Frank. These parallel narratives converge in the similarity of vision that is offered of both. We recall that the working theme of Frank's trip was the colonies' achievement of unity and independence from the threat of internal fragmentation. In *Independence Day*, however, modern American society is portrayed as having followed something of a reverse trajectory. At both the personal and national level, unity is succumbing to fragmentation, and independence is leading to isolation: "arch-ordinary American" Frank is isolated from those closest to him and from his own self and personal history, while American society has adhered to the nation's enduring myths of freedom and individualism to the point where Americans are turning away from each other, isolated as individuals and segregated as groups. Richard Ford's words about the "American heritage to exclude" come back to us: "The American practice of independence is premised on the notion of 'get away from me, because I'm better off when I'm here by myself'."

That Ford's exploration of the theme of independence at both a personal and national level concludes on the diagnosis of a shared condition of isolation prompts one to consider potential affinities. Independence in America, in Ford's novel, is understood as freedom, and particularly as individualism. To that may be added the shared *modus operandi* of a laissez-faire approach, which functions as an economic doctrine at a national level and as a personal philosophy where Frank is concerned. The term "laissez-faire" is used on several occasions in the novel. As an economic theory, laissez-faire preaches the minimum government or regulatory intervention necessary to allow an economy to function efficiently according to its own economic laws. The general spirit of laissez-faire economics as faith in free-market liberalism was, and continues to be, highly influential in America. It also became a philosophy of individualism and freedom, encouraging individual well-being as the path to the general good, and allowing economic values to dictate the worth and value of the individual.

Ford's novel takes place towards the end of a decade in which, in Ronald Reagan's America, deregulation of the economy was actively promoted and laissez-faire economic principles triumphed. Economic power and value allow some Americans to isolate themselves from others (the wealthy residents of Deep River and Ridgefield), while distributing others within the hierarchy of the socio-economic order, separating and isolating individuals and groups from each other (the Markhams and the residents of the run-down neighbourhoods of Oneonta and Springfield discover to their personal cost how their place in society is dictated by laissez-faire economic doctrine). The ruthless logic of laissez-faire economics, its place in the national psyche and its relation to individual freedom are summed up by Frank at one point as he ponders the broken promise of a seller to give him the exclusive listing of his house: "And who can be surprised in a free country? It's laissez-faire: serve your granny to the neighbors for brunch" (335).

There is a visceral link between economic values and American identity. As Calvin Coolidge, American president in the 1920s, once famously remarked: "The business of America is business", and American business values have penetrated the entire national value system. The origins of these values can be traced back to pre-Revolutionary and pre-Independence days. The inequalities that so ravaged the lives of poorer white Americans in the second half of the eighteenth century were perpetuated and codified by the conservative elitist classes intent on dampening any over-republican sentiments engendered by the Revolution. As Gary B. Nash comments in his book, *The Unknown American Revolution*, the wealthy classes and the landowners, gaining the upper hand in Congress, moved quickly in the latter years of the war for independence to impose a harsh policy of fiscal stability, hammering home the mantra that "Only sound money, taxation to retire discredited paper currency, and a laissez-faire posture toward merchant activity could salvage the struggling republic".[10]

---

[10] Gary B. Nash, *The Unknown American Revolution: The Unruly Birth of Democracy and the Struggle to Create America*, New York: Viking, 2005, 367.

From one perspective it is possible to read America's post-Revolution history as a breakneck rush towards the future as the country threw itself into territorial conquest and economic expansion, leading to the attainment of great wealth and influence, the *sine qua non* of which was the relatively unquestioned primacy of economic freedom and the unfettered approach to economic practice and activity. It is little wonder, then, that modern America puts its faith so zealously in laissez-faire economic principles. And it is, in part, the fruits of such a philosophy on social configuration and human relations that is depicted in *Independence Day*.

In his profession as realtor Frank sees at first hand how "Buying power is the instrumentality" in society, and, by a process of osmosis, one suspects, he has adopted the modality of laissez-faire in his own life. It is indeed a fitting metaphor to describe the most important aspects of his Existence Period doctrine, and it sits easily with his own brand of individualism. The definitive feature of laissez-faire is non-intervention, the very core, as we have seen, of Frank's philosophy, but the metaphor also functions for Frank's attitude of passivity and neutrality, for his not seeking to exercise control over events. It is as if the competing forces in human interaction constituted a kind of economy where individual relationships find their own most efficient mode of operation, independent of his intervention. Frank conceives his relationship with Sally in these terms. He observes at the outset that their ten-month relationship is based on the principle of mutual freedom and "the complete presumption of laissez-faire" (8). Significantly, he also uses the expression when he comes to realize that his remoteness and putative independence cause him to weigh little in the lives of others, having him ruminate, as we have already noted, that "laissez-faire is not precisely the same as independence". And he might well have used the term to describe the event that has come to dominate the weekend and stand as an indictment of his non-interventionist approach, namely his negligence in allowing Paul to enter the batting cage without any protective equipment.

At both a personal and national level, then, laissez-faire manifests itself in *Independence Day* as a doctrine of indifference to others, as a kind of selfish Darwinist creed of the survival of the fittest. It functions in the clear knowledge that there is a hierarchy of power, be it economic or emotional, and that some individuals will be protected and will survive, while others will be cast aside and forgotten. It is by definition, therefore, an exclusionary doctrine, and a mechanism of separation and, inevitably, isolation. The doctrine of laissez-faire and the rugged individualism of Emerson dominate the economic and social world in *Independence Day*, and articulate the dominant understanding of independence. It is precisely independence so understood that, by the eve of Independence Day itself, has produced a generally dismaying portrait of contemporary America in Richard Ford's novel.

Independence Day

Where the previous chapters received a simple numerical identification, the last chapter is accorded a title, "Independence Day", Richard Ford's way of signalling, one senses, the need for reflection on the purpose of the national holiday – there is an obligation on Americans to think about, and not simply celebrate, their independence. Independence Day morning finds all the main characters undergoing their moments of transition. Frank, Sally, Ann and the Markhams are all now on the other side of confrontation and crisis, soberly reflecting that one is never always right, and that making peace with people and circumstances is one form of independence, allowing one to move beyond impasse and towards the possibility of something better. In Ford's moral novel, compromise and a little humility will bring amelioration. It is this concatenation of individual epiphanies that gives the final chapter its mood of post-crisis weariness, relief and optimism. The chapter will also return to some of the novel's important themes, and will seek, here too, to reach an accommodation with pressures and tensions, and so find ways of moving profitably on.

The dominant motif is now transition, a return, in other words, to the Emersonian spirit at work in the novel. The events of the weekend and the events of Independence Day itself function, respectively, according to the twin principles underpinning Emerson's notion of transition: the stagnation of the weekend events represent the repose when "Power ceases", while the Independence Day epiphanies and personal evolutions represent "the darting to an aim", the vital moment of transition and becoming. And the mechanism that Ford adopts to move his characters forward is that of finding a new perspective. The message here is that, if circumstances blocking progress cannot be changed, then a new perspective on these circumstances can reconfigure the terms of the problem, thus uncovering new possibilities. The remedy that Frank originally advocated for the Markhams alone is now applied to all the principal characters as the means to their renewed becoming and renewed independence.

The Markhams' transition takes the form of an "almost equable acceptance" (416) that their original goal is unrealizable in the short term and that obduracy will bring them only further grief. The solution Ford contrives for them allows him to return to the race issue, and to his advocacy of small, personal steps as the means to deal with the intractable national race problem. The Markhams' need for a new perspective on their situation has them decide to rent Frank's vacant rental house in Wallace Hill, and to begin to come to terms with the fact that a good number of their fellow Americans are black. Joe's language of acceptance, however, exposes a dormant racism that has had to be overcome, revealed notably in his patronizing recollection of the acceptable "colored family" (406) they know in Vermont and in his would-be ironic reference to the "darky section" (421) of Haddam. His original caustic refusal to consider Frank's rental house has been replaced by a capacity to convince himself that Wallace Hill is a "completely stable neighborhood", even if Frank understands this to mean that there are "no Negroes in evidence" (415).[11]

Richard Ford, as social historian, demands implicitly that the promise of the 1960s quest for an alternative lifestyle and politics, which originally inspired the Markhams, become a reality in a genuinely radical personal commitment to racial coexistence: Frank hopes that that "which always made the Markhams see themselves as out-of-the-ordinary white folks" will translate now into "letting little dark-skinned kids sleep over" (423). The Markhams' moment of transition to a new perspective, then, presents them with an opportunity to seize a particular form of independence: by embracing racial coexistence they can regain an important measure of control

---

[11] Ford's forceful confrontation of widespread racism in America extends to making Joe a Democrat, whose father was "a Socialist" with "a wide streak of social conscience" (421). Much as Ford likes to satirize Republicans, they are clearly not the only culprits when it comes to an America divided on colour lines.

over their lives and can free themselves from a debilitating national (that is, white) prejudice. On Independence Day it would be a highly symbolic, if belated, observance of the "self-evident" Truths of the Declaration of Independence.

Sally and Frank must also find new perspectives if they are to find a way out of their own personal impasse. Paul's accident has jolted Frank out of the undemanding zone of appearances: "There is no *seeming* now. All is *is*" (369). He now has the opportunity to rejoin the moral world of trust and responsibility. He is filled with remorse and guilt as he recognizes how he has failed in his responsibility to his son. The long hours after the accident have allowed him to reflect on his ways, free of the self-flattering and self-protective carapace of his Existence Period neutrality: "I feel a change is now in motion, a facing of fact long overdue" (400). Alert and attentive to Frank's post-accident solemnity in their Sunday night phone call, Sally encourages the direction of their conversation towards the possibility of a future together. For Sally, this means "looking for good sides" (434) in Frank by way of constructing a new narrative about him. In a generous act of faith she chooses to reconfigure Frank as a "good guy" and as someone who is "pretty sympathetic" (433). Her commitment is uniquely the outcome of a desire to see the positive traits of another person, another moral note in a chapter about the claims of reciprocity and responsibility.

Their conversation also contains an important echo of one of their previous conversations. Sally, like Ann (and like Ann and Vicki in *The Sportswriter*), has painful experience of Frank's facile use of language to configure the world to suit himself and to deflect commitment and responsibility; it was this untrustworthiness that had them all turn away from Frank on different occasions. For the time being Sally's narrative of a new Frank exists purely in words, but the personal investment in the meaning of her words is unquestionable, as she is prepared to commit herself on the basis of the truth that her words have called into being. And it is Sally's generous act of faith and commitment that saves Frank from the barrenness of his Existence Period and encourages reciprocity, as he now finds the right words to convince her that they should continue on together. It is clear that Frank is finally learning the lesson about the moral implications of the language of commitment: he notes pointedly that he does not tell Sally that he loves her, but simply that he "wasn't beyond affection" (436), something he had said to her in one of his evasive and defensive moments.

Frank remarks with regard to the Markhams that "real independence must sometimes be shoved down your throat" (423). His comment could now equally apply to himself. It is to others, and specifically to women, that Frank owes his nascent independence from his sterile existence. While Paul's accident created the psychological and moral frame of mind in Frank to accept change, the transition to a new perspective would not have been possible without the honesty, loyalty and moral force of Ann and Sally. Ann has liberated both Frank and herself in a way he was unable to do himself, and, unburdened now of Frank's hopeless illusion (and relieved at Paul's successful eye surgery), they can speak calmly to each other from a new space of healthy independence from each other. For her part, Sally's commitment to Frank has rescued him from isolation and reveals to him that freedom as remoteness is a barren form of independence. Together, Ann and Sally have offered Frank a glimpse at a new phase in his life, which he now terms the "Permanent Period", that "long, stretching-out time" between now and "oblivion" (450), a phase of transition and a period of stability he seems inclined to embrace. Frank has never been able to survive without women. This, too, of course, is a form of dependence, but he seems to realize now that assent, rather than resistance, to this dependence will ultimately produce a fruitful independence from isolation.

The Puritan settlement of New England is synonymous with the origins of modern America.[12] The Pilgrims, as they would eventually

---

[12] The symbolic importance of the Puritan settlement at Plymouth tends to overshadow America's "pre-history". There had been a human presence – the ancestors of today's Native Americans – in what became North America for at least 25,000 years before the European settlers began to arrive. Moreover, the Spanish and French had settled vast areas of the New World before the Separatists and Puritans arrived in 1620. And it would be more logical to associate the birth of modern America with the first English settlement, at Jamestown, Virginia, in 1607. Yet the story of the "Pilgrim" settlement has prevailed (the Plymouth settlers were not then known as "Pilgrims"), with its rich associations – and rich narrative possibilities – of flight from persecution, a grasp at freedom and the heady symbolism of the first Thanksgiving.

be called, were a community in search of a home, an aspiration that was to be replicated and realized in the following centuries as the American nation was built, with the arrival of new communities of immigrants seeking a new home and a better life. But, in modern America, particularly since the 1960s, the umbilical chord uniting home and community has been fraying, and may even have snapped. Emerson's notion of personal self-sufficiency has mutated into a national atomization: Putnam's study everywhere proclaims the decline of community and the privatization of American society as families and individuals wall themselves off from each other in their own homes. *Independence Day*, in its own way, is also preoccupied with growing isolation in America, so it is not surprising to find the final chapter of the novel reflecting on the implications of its earlier insights into community, home and place. On Independence Day morning Frank takes his annual drive through Haddam, a tour that, for him, "embodies its own quiet participation" in the "civic good" (424). Frank's first journey, through New England, confronted him with fragmentation and isolation; his second journey, through Haddam, presents the opportunity to check the health of his own, smaller community. A distinguishing feature of these passages, indeed, is the tension between, on the one hand, a desire for community and permanence, and, on the other, the inevitability of transition and progress.

This conflict is accorded an existential weight through the recurrence of Frank's anxiety about the depthlessness of his own being. As he stops and looks across at his old Hoving Road house, he experiences a pang of disquiet, similar to the earlier one in Sally's house, as he instinctively seeks sanction for his existence from a place he once inhabited. Frank's weekend journey has, among other things, been a powerful metaphor for his own rootlessness; this native of the Mississippi Gulf Coast has led the nomadic existence of many Americans, an uprooting that, in Frank's case, carries an existential cost.[13] Frank will fight off his melancholy, will robustly declare that only "other humans" (442) can provide existential sanction and will announce that he has decided, "in a mood of transition and progress"

---

[13] Putnam quotes a study that records that, on average, Americans "change residences about every 5 years" (*Bowling Alone*, 477, n.4).

(439), to be buried far from Haddam, not wishing to fall for, as he sees it, the illusion of permanence that communities offer.

Yet these blustering declarations sit uneasily with a desire for a more active community spirit expressed elsewhere in his post-weekend mood: Frank ardently hopes that the Markhams will throw themselves into their new community, imagining possible community activities for them (416) that constitute the very stuff of Putnam's social capital; he would prefer to see "our merchants in town" favoured over bigger outside retail chains in town development plans, or else have undeveloped land turned into people's parks instead of shopping malls (425); he envies the life that he imagined for a man he observed in another town the previous evening, a life of civic engagement and easy contact with friends in his community (431); and he is "happy", following the "near disaster" (438) of the weekend, to be back in the reassuring familiarity of his own town. Moreover, the cheerful and optimistic tone of the final chapter is due in part to the preparations for the town's parade. For this one day in the year the community has come together to celebrate the national holiday, bringing citizens out of their houses, onto the streets and into contact with each other. The emblematic moment when these individuals become a community occurs when parachute jumpers descend on the town, clad, significantly, in the "stars 'n' stripes": "Then the crowd—as random minglers, they have not precisely *been* a crowd—makes a hushed, suspiring 'Ohh' like an assent to a single telepathic message" (437).

Pragmatism, however, will win out over idealism in Frank's inner conflict, but not without self-denial and a certain abrogation of responsibility on his part. The hard-nosed realtor will conclude that home is essentially an economic unit ("home's where you pay the mortgage" [449]) and will yield to the market-led realities of economic progress: it "never [happens]" that parks get built instead of malls (425). In a passage full of metaphors of rootlessness and instability, the historical American search for, and discovery of, home and community has dissolved into a forlorn nurturing of an illusion of permanence and a quotidian struggle for spiritual survival:

> We want to *feel* our community as a fixed, continuous entity, the way Irv said, as being anchored into the rock of permanence; but we know

it's not, that in fact beneath the surface (or rankly all over the surface) it's anything but. We and it are anchored only to contingency like a bottle on a wave, seeking a quiet eddy. The very effort of maintenance can pull you under. (439)

Frank relents to the powerful forces that overwhelm the individual's desire to be part of a community. Yet his own individualism, itself a modern expression of a founding national myth, plays its part in undermining community. On Independence Day he seems to miss the irony of his driving around, as opposed to walking through, town, and that his "own quiet participation" takes the form of "being a bystander" (424); he takes instant evasive action to avoid contact with a man who waves at him and wishes to speak to him (427); and he gets fidgety when his Independence Day conversation with Carter Knott, "arguably my best friend in town" (443), extends beyond the ninety seconds of badinage they normally exchange on the rare occasions they meet. Communities will not be built on such desultory human contact. Putnam's injunction about the need for Americans' personal investment in their communities is a salutary response to Frank's hand-wringing: "Americans are *right* that the bonds of our communities have withered, and we are *right* to fear that this transformation has very real costs. The challenge for us, however … is not to grieve over social change, but to guide it."[14]

Richard Ford has adeptly constructed his novel around the idea of independence, and on the tensions and choices that attend the achievement of independence in contemporary America. From its initial resonance in the national celebration of the founding of the republic, the concept has found its profound relevance in the novel at a personal level in the choices that individuals make between being alone or being together – in the choice between exclusion and inclusion, segregation and integration, individualism and community, fragmentation and union, isolation and affiliation. Ford had a clear idea of what he wanted his exploration of the theme of independence to achieve:

---

[14] *Ibid.*, 402.

I hadn't ever realized that independence in the most conventional sense means leavetaking, putting distance between yourself and other people .... so I thought I'd write about it and see if I couldn't make it mean something else, if independence could in fact mean a freedom to make contact with others, rather than just the freedom to sever oneself from others.[15]

Always the moral writer, and always deeply committed to communicating with his readers, Ford does not shirk from having his own preference prevail in the novel's two final scenes. As Frank sleeps after his return to Haddam, his phone rings. No one speaks – Frank hears only the breathing of someone he senses he might know, possibly Paul. Frank offers some words of comfort and encouragement, happy now, with the "reemergence of some small hope" in his life, to connect with another. It is a small moment of altruism, and serves, when linked with the anxious Thursday night phone call from Sally that also woke him, to frame the weekend's events and to map Frank's spiritual journey. In the first call Frank was uneasy and defensive; now he is open and at peace.

The final image confirms Frank's emergence from the self-protective shell of his Existence Period. The Independence Day parade has begun, the bands are passing along and people move in to view the spectacle. No longer detached from others, Frank is in amongst the crowd. And the crowd is now the community of Haddam, come together to celebrate independence. Frank savours the atmosphere and assents to be part of this union: "My heartbeat quickens. I feel the push, pull, the weave and sway of others" (451). Frank's self-exile from others seems ended, and the transition to a period of serenity seems to have begun.

Powerful and moving though this final image may be, the personal salvation is not necessarily a national one. Drawing back from the scene of Frank amidst the crowd to a panorama of the wider society, the counter-images of isolation and fragmentation that pervade the novel are not so easily ignored. The prevailing spirit throughout has been Emersonian individualism and self-sufficiency. In "Self-Reliance" crowds and communities are synonymous with a detested conformity. One would do better, according to Emerson, to cultivate

---

[15] *Conversations with Richard Ford*, 122-23.

an individual independence. The final scene of *Independence Day*, then, with its uplifting images of independence in union, must compete for our acceptance with the Emersonian vision of independence everywhere evident in the novel, and articulated thus in "Self-Reliance": "the great man is he who in the midst of the crowd keeps with perfect sweetness the independence of solitude."[16]

---

[16] Emerson, *Self-Reliance*, 23.

CHAPTER 5

THE LAY OF THE LAND

I: AMERICA DIVIDED

Twelve years have passed. Ronald Reagan's era – which was also the era of *The Sportswriter* and *Independence Day* – came to an end and gave way to the one-term George Bush presidency. But the 1990s were to belong to President Bill Clinton, and he led America to the end of that decade, to the millennial year 2000. We rejoin Frank in November of that year, in the final months of the Clinton administration, but, more pertinently, in the strange, suspended aftermath of the disputed outcome of the presidential election between Republican George W. Bush and Democrat Al Gore a few weeks earlier.

The twelve years since *Independence Day* have brought immense changes to Frank's life. He married Sally Caldwell, his girlfriend in *Independence Day*, left Haddam, having lived there for twenty years, and set up home with Sally on the Jersey Shore, and now, aged fifty-five, has fallen victim to the malady that awaits many men in late middle age, prostate cancer. And in a novel much concerned with time, the passing of the years has contrived to play another trick on Frank: out of the long-lost past emerged Sally's first husband, Wally, believed dead and officially declared so. Wally's return prompted Sally to leave Frank in search of answers to the enigma of the man who is the father of her two children and in search of the life she had begun thirty years earlier. Ironically, as Sally's first marriage reconstituted itself, the passage of time has seen the final atomization of Frank's first family, with its four members now dispersed over four separate locations: Frank lives in his beach-front house in Sea-Clift; his ex-wife, Ann, is back living in Haddam following the death of her second husband; their son Paul works in Kansas City, while their daughter Clarissa lives in New York.

If the end of *Independence Day* portended an end to the willed isolation and remoteness from others that had served Frank ill during the Existence Period of his life, time has managed to unravel the bonds between Frank and those of his two families, leaving him, in November 2000, perched alone on the edge of America, on the thin sliver of earth that divides the Atlantic Ocean to the east and Barnegat Bay to the west. The one thread of continuity in Frank's life that has survived the buffeting of time and change is his profession as realtor, which Frank now practises in Sea-Clift, although the fact that he does so there, and not in Haddam, had much to do with unpalatable changes in that area of his life as well.

Frank's altered and more austere personal circumstances are appropriate to the temporal setting of the novel. Autumn is ending, winter approaches, and the stocktaking of one's life sometimes occasioned by the end of a year is hastened by the arrival of Thanksgiving, the national holiday that asks Americans to consider the origins and evolution of their country and to give thanks for the opportunities and munificence it bestows. Frank's native optimism found easeful expression in the lengthening spring days of *The Sportswriter* and in the high-summer light and heat of *Independence Day*. In late November 2000, however, the colder, darker days pervade the atmosphere like a baleful spirit, constricting existence and infecting moods. Frank likens the period between Thanksgiving and Christmas to a "vale of aching hearts and unreal hopes, when more suicide successes, abandonments, spousal thumpings, car thefts, firearm discharges and emergency surgeries take place per twenty-four-hour period than any other time of year except the day after the Super Bowl".[1] It would seem that not everyone in the darkness of winter finds sufficient cause to express their gratitude to God for the gifts of the republic.

This sombre and discordant mood is reflected in the weather. In the three days in which most of the events of *The Lay of the Land* take place – the two days preceding Thanksgiving Day and Thanksgiving Day itself – the text never fails to emphasize the cheerless weather and darkening days. On the Tuesday morning, as Frank is visiting Haddam

---

[1] Richard Ford, *The Lay of the Land*, New York: Knopf, 2006, 26. Further references to the novel will be included parenthetically in the text.

and as he watches people sweeping up the last of the late-autumn leaves, he anticipates a "front, maybe cold New Jersey rain, true harbinger of winter" (43). The day turns increasingly unpleasant and gloomy, dropping the midday temperature to thirty-six degrees, leaving Frank, as he stands outside in conversation, feeling cold and anxious to be away. Thanksgiving Eve finds Frank on the road again, up to Asbury Park and back, and although there is a brief period of warm midday sun, it is preceded by the morning's "cold seaside air" (275) and "cold November sun" (293) and is followed by the cold drizzle and rain of the afternoon and evening, with the day ending on a night-time storm. Thanksgiving Day itself goes from "cold and damp" (418) to "wintry" (441), leaving Frank to "shiver ... from the accumulating cold" (450).

The failing light and penetrating cold partly reflect the prevailing mood of the novel, and partly induce it. They also contribute to a fertile paradox that Richard Ford adroitly mines, that of the solitary life and threatened existence of a character, unprepared and often inadequately clothed, bracing himself against the approaching winter, yet a character solicited by the tradition and custom of his country to give thanks for all that life in this land has brought him. Once again – it was also profoundly the case in *Independence Day* – man and landscape, citizen and nation, individual and society, are bound to each other: Frank's experiences and emotions at Thanksgiving, although often determined by family contact and personal circumstances, are also decisively influenced by his interaction with the wider culture and his fellow Americans. The third act of the trilogy, then, continues in the vein of its predecessor as it takes stock of a character and his country, or, to avail of the deep resonances of the novel's title, as it surveys the physical and spiritual lay of the land of a man and a nation.

In structuring the two previous Frank Bascombe novels Richard Ford drew on little more than the succession of days that constituted the Easter and Independence Day holidays: in both cases the action unfolds at a leisurely pace as Frank deals with the business of his daily life, interrupted occasionally by the recollection of earlier experiences that bear upon his account. In both cases, too, Frank goes on a major trip within America, to Detroit in the first novel and through New England in the second, although in *Independence Day* the travelling is more explicitly directed at allowing Frank take the pulse of the nation. Frank is on the road again on all three days of the Thanksgiving holiday, but this time his itinerary, in keeping with his straitened circumstances, has him range within a more limited territory and has him return to Sea-Clift at night. Yet the horseshoe section of mid-New Jersey that is the terrain of Frank's excursions is rich in encounters with his fellow citizens and again offers Ford the opportunity to ponder the state of contemporary America.

If the Independence Day holiday allowed Frank to witness Americans' understanding and practice of independence, the all-embracing nature of the Thanksgiving concept affords the opportunity to consider American culture and society from a variety of perspectives. As in *Independence Day*, national and personal themes interweave throughout. In choosing to examine first the national dimension of the novel, it is not simply to provide a manageable structure for the discussion, nor merely to align the discussion of *The Lay of the Land* with that of *Independence Day*; it is also to acknowledge the structure and content of the novel itself, which each day sends Frank out into America before bringing him home at the end of the day with the new knowledge gained about his country and himself on his journeying. Our discussion, then, will begin with America before moving on to Frank himself in the next chapter. However, nation and citizen, society and individual, cannot be long held apart in these novels, and *The Lay of the Land* will sweep America and Frank together towards Thanksgiving Day, and towards the setting for a dramatic confrontation between national cultural predilection and the life of an ordinary American.

The initial articulation of the novel's title occurs during Frank's Tuesday morning drive inland from Sea-Clift to Haddam. Frank is the great cartographer of the American physical and cultural landscape, assiduously recording the nature and designation of the highways and roads he takes, their complex interconnections and directions, the human and physical geography of towns, villages, and countryside, the booming malls and ubiquitous franchises, the declining shopping sectors of town centres, the strident onslaught of commercial exhortations, the place names, the clothes, the noise, the activities, the general dizzying aggressiveness of the cultural cacophony of contemporary America. If the public expression of American culture is unruly and intrusive, it is surely because its dominant voice is that of the salesman, the merchant clamouring to be heard over the voices of his competitors. It is a mating call to which Americans are susceptible, and heartily so in Ford's novel in the days before Thanksgiving. No sooner have Frank and his real estate associate, Mike Mahoney, crossed the bridge linking Sea-Clift to the mainland than they find themselves ensnarled in a traffic jam: "Route 37 ... is already jammed at 9.30 with shopper vehicles moving into and out of every conceivable second-tier factory outlet lot, franchise and big-box store, until we're mostly stalled in intersection tie-ups under screaming signage and horn cacophony" (18).

Ford is returning here to a theme explored in *Independence Day*, particularly through the apocalyptic scenes in which Frank is trapped in night-time traffic jams, confronted with heaving masses of Americans, cooped up in their vehicles, crunching their way through New England. If the freedom of mobility was sufficient cause for those Americans to exercise the right to be in night-time holiday traffic jams, now it is addictive consumerism and the lure of pre-Thanksgiving "'gigantic' Black Tuesday and Black Wednesday Sales Days" (18) that herd them into gridlock and send them scurrying ant-like from store to store. Commerce, one may conclude from these scenes in *The Lay of the Land*, allows the public expression of the true contemporary meaning of Thanksgiving, which is less a matter of giving thanks to God and bounteous nature than of glorying in the benefits of the market economy. Consumerist culture, indeed, in creating devoted attachments, commanding icons and regular worship has more than a superficial resemblance to the religious disposition, although it displays little affinity in these scenes with either the religiosity of the first Puritans or the humble gratitude that suffused President Lincoln's declaration of a national Thanksgiving Day during the Civil War.

Consumerism has people buy because they enjoy buying and shop for the sake of shopping, acquiring possessions and consuming goods well beyond their needs. As Frank remarks: "when we shop, we no longer really shop *for* anything" (19). When Frank and Mike return to Sea-Clift on Tuesday night they find that Route 37 is "not a bit less crowded" than it was that morning. It seems to Frank "as if everyone we passed this morning is still out here, wandering parking lot to parking lot, ready to buy if they just knew what, yet are finally wearing down, but have no impulse to go home". Like a church that remains permanently open to enable believers to commune with and seek solace from God, the local mall is "staying open 24/7" (193) during Thanksgiving week, allowing the consumer faithful to worship in the cathedral of the market economy and to pay homage to the munificence of the high priests – the global brands – of capitalism.

Commerce, the free market and consumerism are, of course, the pistons of the American economic machine, and represent the foundations of American wealth-creation and material prosperity. It is a measure of the importance accorded to commerce in Ford's novel that he has Frank conceive of it as an essential American cultural expression. One might expect, of course, that realtor Frank, whose own prosperity directly depends on buying and selling, would indulge in intuitive promotion of commerce, but that he does so while suffering from a serious illness, and possessed of the heightened awareness of true significance that only a potentially fatal illness can bring, serves to sanctify his award to commerce as definitive American, and indeed personal, value. Ensnared in shopping traffic though he may be, the commercial vista of Route 37 holds a visceral appeal for him:

> Yet frankly it all thrills me and sets my stomach tingling. Unbridled commerce isn't generally pretty, but it's always forward-thinking. And since nowadays with my life out of sync and most things in the culture not affecting me much—politics, news, sports, everything but the weather—it feels good that at least commerce keeps me interested like a scientist. Commerce, after all, is basic to my belief system. (19)

In *Independence Day* Frank characterized himself as "an arch-ordinary American", and the portrait of Frank that emerges over the three novels allows us to conclude that his opinions are not untypically American, certainly with regard to his commitment to the free market and in his conviction that this attachment is fundamental to American identity. Commercial culture now receives the further, crowning accolade of definitive means of orientation in the American landscape: Frank's exposure to the "commercial-ethnic-residential zeitgeist of a complex republic" produces in him a "specialized well-being" that deserves the singular title of "Culture comfort", while the commercial outlets and aggressive brand promotion that fill the

American landscape constitute a reassuring mapping of the land that Frank calls "cultural literacy" – he experiences an inner glow of well-being and locatedness from "knowing by inner gyroscope where the next McDonald's or Borders, or the next old-fashioned Italian shoe repair or tuxedo rental or lobster dock is going to show up on the horizon" (289). In these various identifications of citizen and culture, commerce is proposed as being as fundamental to American identity as religion, representing in its own way an adequate source of spiritual and practical guidance.

Yet it does not escape Frank's attention, "citizen scientist" (22) that he is, that a pervasive commercial ethic has created a commodification culture. As he attends the funeral of a friend in Haddam and observes the smooth operation of the funeral home as it moves one funeral out to the cemetery and prepares for the next, it strikes him that the "funeral business is not so different from running a restaurant" (65). He records, too, a subtle expression of corpse commodification and hierarchy of value: the funeral home "always uses SUVs for unattended interments" (61). Frank's sweep through his patch of America provides irrefutable evidence that everything can be commodified into a marketable product and economic value. The business of dying is just that, and, whether death is arrived at naturally or through suicide, there is a commercial service at hand to ease death, or indeed its survival, into the familiar cultural shape of a commodity: "WELCOME SUICIDE SURVIVORS" (19) shouts a roadside sign to passing motorists, while a *New York Times* article that Frank reads explains that, "from a purely financial perspective, doing away with oneself's probably a good investment" (20). Elsewhere, signs promoting a "HEALTHY MATE DATING SERVICE" and a "DOLLAR UNIVERSITY INSTITUTE FOR HIGHER EARNING" (22) reassure the troubled traveller that commerce caters for all conditions and ambitions, as does the Custom Condom Shoppe ("We build 'em to your specs" [270]), which promises to combine old-world quaintness and new-world frankness.

A commodification culture reduces whatever it touches to an economic value and to the exchangeable and marketable status of a measurable economic unit. This extends, in *The Lay of the Land*, to American history itself. The Haddam town fathers have decided in this Millennium Year to re-enact the Battle of Haddam from the

Revolutionary War "in an effort to rev up sidewalk appeal" over Thanksgiving. But that utilitarian goal has met with resistance from some of the town's "merchants", who are "already sensing retail disaster, and have retained counsel and are computing lost revenue as damages" (49). The re-enactors will carry out their routines regardless, gambolling about on the former battle sites, occupied now – in an apt compression of the evolution of the republic – by Frenchy's Gulf, Benetton, and Hulbert's Classic Shoes, taking cover behind the SUV hearse, and conducting the Battle of Willow Street in under two minutes. The town's merchants are more tolerant of the other Thanksgiving historical product on offer, the Pilgrim Village Interpretive Center, where the young Pilgrim re-enactors – an assortment of black, Jewish, Japanese and wheelchair-bound performers chosen for modern political statement rather than historical accuracy – explain, when not "chattering to themselves about rock videos", "how our American stock was cured by tough times, blab, blab, blab, blab". The merchants hope that the touching sight of the "paraplegic" Pilgrim might somehow move citizens to spend their money on a "Donegal plaid vest" or "half a case of Johnnie Walker Red".

Here is American history and heritage as cynical commodity, as easily consumable product and commercial inducement, and, certainly in the case of the recreation of the early Pilgrim settlements, as soft-focus myth-making. In a nice turn of vengeful comedy – but with a solid basis in historical fact – Ford populates the Pilgrim scene with a group of "New Jersey's own redskins" with placards protesting "THE TERRIBLE LIE OF THANKSGIVING". These Native Americans dare challenge one of the palliative myths of American nationhood, and in the process – the inexcusable anti-American outrage – disrupt commercial activity and stir up a "bad-for-business backlash" (50).

In a novel much concerned with taking stock, both of an individual life and a society, Frank is led to wonder what "real scientists, decades on" (45), might conclude about this era of American cultural life. It is here that the detrimental effects of consumerism and commodification are explored: Frank sees the instant assuaging by the market of every consumerist whim as creating a society of passive and indolent risk-avoiders, drained of vigour and enterprise, dedicated to no more than docile pleasure and self-protection:

... future delvers will ... think .... how little we ourselves *invented*! And ... how little we *had* to invent, since you could get anything you wanted—from old records to young boys—just by giving a number and an expiration date to an electronic voice, then sitting back and waiting for the friendly brown truck. Our inventions, it'll be clear, were only to say yes or no .... Future scholars might also conclude that if we ever did think of trying something different ... we must've realized that we risked desolation and the world looking at us with menace, knew we couldn't stand that for long, and so declined. (46)

In the context of the Thanksgiving holiday and, ultimately, of the great expansionary drive west to conquer the American continent, the suburban version of New Millennium *homo americanus* has evolved into a being who is timid and self-indulgent from over-consumption and who has little affinity with the pioneering spirit and ferocious ambitions of the first and later settlers of the New World. Given enough time, of course, societies evolve out of all recognition from their origins, yet there is undoubtedly an intentional irony in Ford's Thanksgiving portrait of suburban American society enervated by excessive consumerism to the point of decadence.

Frank's unfavourable conclusions about modern Americans arise from his speculation about the evidence that the latter's existence on "our own patch of suburban real estate" (45) would yield to the scrutiny of future generations. He is aware that "real estate's a profession both spawned by and grown cozy with our present and very odd state of human development" (46-47), and that it is complicit with grasping developers in satisfying an endemic restlessness and avidity in American society, the less benign face of a natural desire for self-improvement. On the Tuesday morning drive to Haddam Frank records the panorama with the gimlet eye of the realtor, constitutionally alert to the transformations of the landscape wrought by real estate development. He wonders at good houses that are now abandoned, and at others that were built "to last only five years or less" (46), and he passes by once-sought-after sites that were half-developed, then left to ruin. At this stage Frank will allow no more than a doubt that the "basic formula" (47) of satisfying the market's every desire is as positive a factor as he once thought it was. His disquiet is due, of course, to his own implication as a real estate practitioner in land development, but also to professional dilemmas where philosophical choices need to made about issues such as the morality of the free market, the value and implications of economic growth, and the identity and integrity of communities.

This Tuesday morning Frank is accompanying Mike as advisor in response to the invitation to Mike by a developer to join a partnership to turn one hundred and fifty acres of farmland into expensive houses, a prospect that causes Frank, realtor though he is, to reflect that "Someone should draw the line somewhere" (44) to contain unnecessary development. He will later conclude, somewhat lamely, that "There's nothing wrong with development if the right people do the developing" (419), despite the evidence presented by the development-scarred New Jersey landscape, and despite having conceded earlier that "Your typical developer, Jersey to Oregon" is "in cahoots with the cement trade, the Teamsters, the building inspectors and city hall" (280) to concrete over the land with criminal disregard for anything but their own interests.

Richard Ford acknowledges that he discovered the "way in which real estate connects to our national spirit in America ... entirely fortuitously", but he put this discovery to fruitful use in *Independence Day* by exploring the subservience of personal well-being to the economic imperatives of free-market capitalism, explored in particular through the efforts of the Markhams to buy a house. And, based on his belief that "We calculate our spiritual condition, in part, in terms of how and where we live",[2] Ford uses the real estate process in *The Lay of the Land* to investigate the spiritual and moral condition of contemporary America. He does so by representing a society that has ceded important powers of social intervention and transformation to the vagaries of the economy and the free market, and to the value-free configurations of the economy, a vision of the country that is in keeping with a deep-rooted and historical American resistance to government regulation. If there is a value attached to the economic vision of society, it is that – in the most forceful prosecution of this ideology – the management of the economy is sufficient for the management of society.

The doleful consequences of the free market on wider society became clear to Frank in the early 1990s while he was still living in

[2] Deborah Treisman, Interview with Richard Ford, "Frankly Speaking", http://www.newyorker.com/archive/2006/08/28/060828on_onlineonly02 (12/01/2008).

Haddam. As property prices began to rise, the ethics governing Frank's profession quickly vanished, replaced, in a gold-rush-like frenzy, by ruthless exploitation by both sellers and the real estate industry of the market demand for valuable properties. The upshot, among others, was, first, the white gentrification of the black neighbourhoods of Haddam; second, the enormous disjunction between property and value; and, third, an almost community-wide departure from civic spirit and moral behaviour. Frank began to perceive the dynamic that was deeply distorting human values as "a malign force", and was able to identify it: "this force, I realized, was the economy." Society organized solely according to the imperatives of the economy and the greed that this engenders "was holding property hostage and away from the very people who wanted and often badly needed it" (85). Frank found himself rebelling against the realtors' amoral take-the-money-and-run mantra: surely, he wondered, "everyone's entitled to some glimmering *sense of right* in his (or her) own heart" (86). And it was indeed Frank's moral sense, along with – in an irruption of nineteenth-century American frontier gun-law – the violent outcome to two real estate transactions in Haddam, that convinced him he needed to work and live in a less greed-ridden community.

The ideological issue concerning the degree of influence that economic forces should be allowed to exert on both the nature and development of communities is a recurring theme in *The Lay of the Land*, particularly in the contrast between the two communities Frank inhabits in the book, those of Haddam (a phase of his life narrated retrospectively) and Sea-Clift. Republican Haddam was managed like a branded product positioned in a particular niche in the market, a brand whose appeal and unique selling propositions had to be obsessively protected. As Frank puts it: "Housing is Haddam's commerce." Successive Republican councils severely restricted in-town commercial development and limited the supply of new residential properties, thus preserving the quality of its suburban appeal and keeping "prices fat" (32), an approach that Frank had supported. This manipulation of supply paid dividends when demand began to increase, sparking the astronomical price inflation and immoral practices that ultimately contributed to Frank's departure. Marked by that experience, and coming from a town where "*gasping increase* was the sacred article of faith" (399), Frank is more conscious now of the link between economic factors and a community's quality of life.

The issue facing the inhabitants of Sea-Clift is one of the very desirability of economic growth. Frank came to live there because he liked its modest view of itself as a town offering seasonal attractions that generated adequate economic revenues, yet being happy to settle back afterwards into an off-season low-level existence. The town's economic cycle and attitude to development created a community identity that Frank describes as "seasonal, insular, commuter-less, stable, aspirant within limits". Sea-Clift's lack of ambition with regard to growth, however, is now considered a problem by its business community, particularly after a disappointing summer season. In opposition to Frank's ideal of achieving a level of commercial activity "with no likelihood of significant growth or sky-rocketing appreciation" of property values, the "Dollars For Doers" business group have a plan to "'transition' Sea-Clift into the 'next phase,' from under-used asset to vitality pocket and full-service lifestyle provider". Frank notes that "we all like it fine here" the way it is, so he is inclined to see the urge to develop as another expression of Americans' visceral but questionable attachment to change: "Permanence has once again been perceived as death" (399), he notes.

The terms of this confrontation of values as understood by Frank are quite simple: should a community develop and grow organically, letting its character evolve slowly over time, allowing, as Frank puts it, "population growth do its job the way it always has" (400), or should marketing and economic factors dictate a dramatic transformation of the town's identity and character from a "seasonal concept" to a "year-round" (399) brand? In the wider context of the novel's concerns about the role and impact of commerce in American life, the Sea-Clift dilemma states the terms of the debate as a choice between community integrity and loss of its traditional identity, between quality of life and commercial gain, and, ultimately, between a vision of society whose primary concern is the greater good of all its citizens and one that views society as essentially an economic entity that can be most efficiently regulated by the exigencies of the free market. It is significant that it is Frank himself who has gone on to undermine this latter vision, despite his initial qualified advocacy of "unbridled commerce": the novel demonstrates that, given free rein, commercial and economic mechanisms applied without checks and balances will transform citizens into servile consumers, commodify cultural life, encourage avarice and convert communities into marketable brands.

Frank's initial tolerance of hardnosed commerce suffers fitting rebuke when, through professional conditioning, he attempts to make a hefty profit through exploiting several angles of the sale of a house in Sea-Clift, a scheme, however, which ends in ignominious failure, leaving him to rue his violation of a neighbourhood's and a street's "sense of integrity" (405). That Frank, for all his experience in and lucidity about real estate, could so err is explained by the portrait of the wider cultural context offered by Ford's novel – that of a society with a deeply ingrained commercial instinct and with an unshakeable faith that, whatever the failures, corruptions and excesses of commerce, commercial health is equivalent to national health, and that an active economy means a prosperous nation. It is precisely this cultural symbiosis that has Frank read the *Shore Home Buyer's Guide*: this record of the local real estate market – its offers, transactions, price trends, lists of new developments, signs of failing and thriving businesses – gives him "some sense of how we're all basically doing" in the wider sense of societal well-being and provides what he terms significantly "spiritual sign-pointers" (341).

This symbiotic relationship between commerce and society is a national cultural value transmitted though the generations and is one that finds special resonance in real estate. In Richard Ford's novel, characters routinely buy and sell houses, with the slightest excuse making them "itchy to buy" (26) – Frank notes that, in one neighbourhood of Sea-Clift in the "moderate bracket", most of the forty-year-old houses "have changed hands ten times" (404). Here, the innate commercial reflex of Americans meets the nation's supreme value of freedom, and offers perhaps the most obvious reason why, according to Frank, "Houses sell whether you want them to or not" (26): Americans "move so much", observes Frank, "because they can" (21). In this – in the enthusiastic indulgence in the freedom of commerce, the freedom to move and resettle, to seek out a shelter and a piece of land where person and place harmoniously conjoin – America at Thanksgiving is, after all, paying appropriate homage to the first Puritan settlers, to that original burning quest for a haven and freedom, and for a new place to be oneself.

If America is a nation founded upon and devoted to the strong values of individualism and personal freedom, it has paid the price for this at the level of community: *Independence Day* depicted a segregated and atomized society, a consequence of what Ford calls the "American heritage to exclude", an "American practice of independence" that is "premised on the notion of 'get away from me, because I'm better off when I'm here by myself'".[3] Ford did not intend initially to set *The Lay of the Land* in 2000,[4] but was perhaps persuaded to do so, in part, when he appreciated the metaphorical possibilities offered by the disputed result of the November 2000 presidential election, which added an extra layer of resonance to his decision (already taken) to set the book at Thanksgiving. The Bush/Gore Florida vote-count stand-off became a metaphor for a deeply divided America, as the sharply opposing visions of society proposed by Democrats and Republicans during the campaign (particularly in the area of what Republicans liked to call morality) were crystallized in the acrimonious month-long dispute over voting irregularities and the counting of ballot papers.

Whatever the influence of the Florida stand-off on Ford's decision about the year in which to set his novel, in setting it in 2000 he found a perfect backdrop against which to explore divisions in American society. He exploits this context to the full, initially through depicting the entrenched political divide itself. There are recurring references to the continuing count machinations in Florida, and Frank constantly records the inscription of political division on the American landscape itself through banners, stickers and signs proclaiming fidelity to one or other of the candidates. The lay of the land, in this context, is a political one: Frank classifies areas and towns by political affiliation,

---

[3] *Conversations with Richard Ford*, 139.
[4] In an interview published in a journal dated 2000 Ford was asked in what year the new novel would be set. He replied: "I can't decide. I don't want to have it be set in the year 2000, because I think that's just asking for trouble, so I'll probably have it set in 1999" (*Heat Magazine*, 167). The choice of year had to be carefully weighed: 1999 would inevitably have drawn him into end-of-Millennium and Y2K considerations, while the post-9/11 emotions of Thanksgiving 2001 would have overshadowed the book he wished to write. The year 2000 obviously came to be seen by Ford as the one least likely to be overshadowed by historical events.

most notably the town he left, Republican Haddam, and the one to which he moved, moderately Democratic Sea-Clift. Frank consistently associates acquisition and expensive real estate with Republicans, be they the residents of the "New Jersey wealth belt" (16), or "old-monied southerners" (99) now living in New Jersey.

Frank, indeed, correlates increasing personal prosperity with political apostasy: most of his "Haddam acquaintances are Republicans ... even if they started out on the other side years back" (60), a topic, Frank notes, that these former Democrats do not wish to discuss. The political, in other words, has become personal: the always-liberal Frank now categorizes his interlocutors, virtually without exception, as either Democratic or Republican supporters, and often not indifferently or benignly, aware that the strength of the political affiliation may well be an important measure of his affinity with that person. Although burdened with prostate cancer and his wife's desertion, Frank is still exercised enough to speak of the "election hijacking" (269) by the Republicans and to give vent to his opinions on "devious" [vice-presidential candidate] Dick Cheney (252) and on "numbskull Bush" (16) and "dumb-ass Bush" (297), the "smirking Texas frat boy" (117). And, in what is a thoroughly political novel in its own way, the most egregious characters are Republicans, be they the two grubby small-town racists Frank meets in a Haddam bar, or the gun-toting, pseudo-vigilante fascist (and religious fundamentalist, Frank reckons) with whom Frank is obliged to exchange a few words in Asbury Park.

It transpires, however, that political division is merely the topical expression of a more widespread fragmentation of American society into individual and group identities. The phenomenon of disconnectedness begins in the family unit itself. The four members of the first Bascombe family now live in four different locations, but, more to the point, each one of them has a difficult relationship with at least one other member of the family – Clarissa with both her brother and her mother, Paul with his sister and his father, Ann with both of her children, and Frank with Paul, not to mention the unease between Ann and Frank. The anxiety that attends this familial contact is encapsulated in Frank's damage-control Thanksgiving Day dinner plans, to which Ann is not invited (at least initially), and in which everything is geared to ward off the "apprehension, dismay and rage" (26) that threatens family implosion.

Things are even worse in Sally's first family, where her two children refuse to have any contact with her, or, indeed, with either of the parents when Wally returns, lost as the adult children are to religiosity. Other telling indications of family disintegration are the absence of either the wife or son at the funeral of an old friend of Frank's; the desire of another acquaintance of his, Detective Marinara, to stay away from the family "fighting" (449) at Thanksgiving; the squabbling between husband and wife of Frank's neighbours; the marriage break-up of another old friend of Frank's, Wade Arsenault; the marital problems of one of his clients, Clare Suddruth; the break-up of Mike's marriage and his living apart from his wife and children; and, of course, the departure of Frank's own second wife, Sally.

The breakdown of supportive personal networks is evident also in Frank's Sponsoring duties, a network formed to offer low-level advice to people "who have no friends they can ask sound advice from" (13). According to the newspaper story that triggered the setting up of the Sponsoring network, "many functioning, genial" people "had *no* friends" (91) at all. Frank noticed the changing spirit while still in Haddam, where people he had "known for a generation and sold homes to … now refused to meet my eyes, just set their gaze at my hairline and kept trudging" (89). Frank's experience during the one Sponsoring visit he makes epitomizes the potential for isolation in middle-class suburbia (an isolation that is heartily satirized). He has to get beyond the security of a chain lock, a peephole and a dead bolt before he is allowed entry to his Sponsoree's home. The expensively dressed hostess leads him into an almost-empty living-room of hard surfaces, harsh light and clinical white, the windows of which have been "sheathed with shiny white lacquered paneling", presenting "no evidence of prior human habitation" (100). Even the dying are not immune to the meaner spirit that stalks the land: Sally gave up her business of organizing social outings for the terminally ill because of the latter's endless complaints and the tension between the dying and the staff who looked after them..

The novel does not attempt to offer a systematic explanation for this malaise in interpersonal relationships. The anecdotal evidence provided, however, suggests a variety of reasons: generational differences, individualism, selfishness, discontentment, a sense of lostness, and a general cultural restlessness and yearning that have people run after sex or religion in the quest for new meaning. To these may be added the American practice of exclusionary independence that Ford developed in *Independence Day*. It is notable, indeed, that Ford feels obliged to return to this vision of an individualistic American society in *The Lay of the Land*. It is noteworthy, too, that greater personal isolation is seen to deprive Americans of traditional points of reference. Frank has come to understand the Sponsoring program as a response to the spiritual and moral vacuum in which isolation has imprisoned people. Cut off from an orientating contact with "the world at large", they look to their Sponsor for an answer to the great existential and moral question: "Am I good? Am I bad? Or am I somewhere lost in the foggy middle?" (94)

Although the novel does not make the connection, the early scenes of teeming masses converging on and swarming through the out-of-town shopping malls further suggest a society in which endemic consumerism, in its appeal to individual and private gratification, actively encourages a self-centeredness, an identification with brands and services and a corresponding lesser attention to other people. As Robert D. Putnam observes:

> Rather than at the grocery store or five-and-dime on Main Street, where faces were familiar, today's suburbanites shop in large, impersonal malls. Although malls constitute America's most distinctive contemporary public space, they are carefully designed for one primary, public purpose—to direct consumers to buy. Despite the aspirations of some developers, mall culture is not about overcoming isolation and connecting with others, but about privately surfing from store to store—in the presence of others, but not in their company. The suburban shopping experience does not consist of interaction with people embedded in a common social network.[5]

If there is a common denominator in all of this anecdotal evidence, it is surely that of a greater concern with self, the corollary of which, of course, is a lesser interest in others, a cultural state of affairs that inevitably poses the question about the condition of love itself in *The*

---

[5] Putnam, *Bowling Alone*, 211. See the chapters on *Independence Day* for a fuller discussion of the relevance of Putnam's findings to Ford's novels.

Lay of the Land (and indeed in the entire trilogy). One feels inclined to speak of a systematic inattention to love, and particularly in this third novel where Frank's second marriage lies in ruins and he is alone, and where many of the characters are living solitary lives. (The sixty-year marriage of Sally's parents-in-law is an exception, but they are from another generation, while Paul's promising relationship with Jill is still in its early stages.) The inattention to – and betrayal of – love is a theme explicitly addressed by Ford elsewhere in his fiction, notably in *Women with Men* and *A Multitude of Sins*. The vista of disunion and personal isolation on display in Ford's fiction, and no less so here (Frank finds himself thinking at one point about "how much protection we need from others" [376]), indeed suggests a greater self-absorption as the profound cause of love's neglect, a condition that seems to be the very repudiation of the notion of love, in its lessening of the place of the other as the object of love and in its corresponding focus on one's own desires, gratification and well-being.

The flight from marriage and relationships, and the turn towards individualism and self-gratification, are paralleled in *The Lay of the Land* by the forceful affirmation of group identities. Ford has Frank remark at one point that "In-depth communication with smaller and smaller like-minded groups is the disease of the suburbs" (145). Ford's analysis is remarkably close to that of Putnam, who observes that the migration to the suburbs in the second half of the twentieth century allowed American society to reconstitute itself as a "sociological mosaic": "people fleeing the city sorted themselves into more and more finely distinguished 'lifestyle enclaves,' segregated by race, class, education, life stage, and so on."[6] Frank recalls how, towards the end of his time in Haddam, organizations sprung up "whose mission was to help groups who didn't know they comprised a group become one" (89).

One like-minded group of people, of course, can quickly become hostile to another, and such indeed is the wider picture of special-interest exclusionism and mutual antagonism in Ford's novel. Confrontations, lawsuits and police intervention mark the disagreement between animal-protection staffers of the Haddam De Tocqueville Academy and suburban dwellers worried about the integrity of their gardens; Sally's two children are, in Frank's

---

[6] *Ibid.,* 209.

formulation, "neck-high in charismatic Mormon doings", reserved for "whites only" (219); Frank notes how the adolescent members of the "Haddam gang element" (162), who hang around the town square and taunt a group of Presbyterian crèche assemblers,[7] give each other the attention not available to them in their families; driving through Sea-Clift in his car, Frank feels the hostile glare of the Thanksgiving Day 5-K road-race runners, people who "cut themselves off from friend, foe and family—everyone except their 'running friends'" (400); and the Sea-Clift cemetery lies empty because the fifteen white families with family members buried there could not reach agreement with the black descendants of the freed slave also buried there who wished to erect a monument to commemorate a "black trailblazer" (438), with the result that all the deceased – black and white – were disinterred and buried elsewhere.

Overall, the novel lays bare a latent intolerance that has its source in sectionalism, in a taking refuge in group identifications that can quickly translate into antagonism to the otherness of different groups and individuals. In conjunction with the troubled personal relationships already mentioned and the general abrasiveness that characterizes relations and contacts between individuals – notably in the case of Frank's paranoid neighbour who blares ear-piercing music in his direction (the Thanksgiving Day message of which is, Frank knows, "Fuck you" [442]) – the overall atmosphere of the novel is edgy, ominous and sombre.

The turn towards the self, expressed in the inattention to love and the manifestation of self through assertive group identifications, receives very public and calculated articulation through people's dress, in a riot of statement-making that runs from the ridiculous to the sinister. Identity-projection is pervasive, be it to reinforce one's sense of self or to make a strong statement of one's affiliations to others. Frank does not quite know what to make of the old-fashioned suit that makes Paul "look like a burlesque comedian" (442), although it has something to do with Paul's new identity as zany comedy-meister; Mike, in his slightly confused Tibetan-American identity, appears in a series of inharmonious ensembles designed to project easy and complete cultural assimilation; Frank's neighbours, the paranoid, self-

---

[7] "Crèche" here refers to a model of the Bethlehem manger scene.

isolating Feensters, parade their difference by dressing up in garish
Lycra bodysuits; his other neighbour, Terry Farlow, in his only
appearance in the novel, exits his house on his Harley, in an explosion
of attention-seeking throttle, "black-suited, black-helmeted as an evil
knight, an identically dressed Harley babe on the bitch seat" (448),
pointedly ignoring everyone watching; the Haddam male adolescents
wear the uniform and strike the pose of studied disaffection, "baggy
jeans cut off at the calves, long white athletic jerseys and combat
boots" (162); and the road runners make their identity statement with
all the rituals and paraphernalia – the stretchings and contortions, the
shorts and shoes, the bibs and bottles – of modern, media-influenced
athletic display.

Dress in the novel is calculated public exhibition of both difference
and identity. In contrast to Frank, who has always been content with
his middle-of-the-road national identity as "arch-ordinary American",[8]
and who clothes himself accordingly in non-assertive mail-order
attire, these other characters are deserting the middle ground and
turning to individualized, sometimes extreme, expressions of personal
identity, in a conspicuous distancing of self from both others and the
amorphous middle, in what becomes a very public manifestation of a
fragmented society.

Divided America receives its harshest expression when Frank visits
one of his favourite old haunts, the "safe haven" (170) of the bar in
Haddam's August Inn. Entering it suffuses Frank with a glow of
gratitude to a place where he used to find comfort in the lonely days
after his divorce and that contributed to a harmonious sense of
belonging to his life in Haddam. This sustaining sense of temporal
endurance by way of personal history is paralleled by the bar's
decorative reminders of a spirited national history, through its
resemblance to a "Revolutionary War roadhouse tavern" (170) and a
wall-sized mural of Johnny Appleseed. Frank's fight with one of the
customers and his verbal confrontation with the barman are in ironic
contrast to the setting: the spirit of the hard-earned unity needed to
achieve independence and establish the republic, and the celebration
of the peaceable generosity of one of the nation's much-loved iconic
figures, are thoroughly betrayed in the contemporary American scene
that takes place in the bar.

---

[8] Ford, *Independence Day*, 141-42.

The physical and verbal clashes, triggered by the Democratic-Republican face-off in Florida, separate America into two radically opposed camps, presenting two irreconcilable visions of the country. On one side, there is the inclusive vision of Frank, proud to be a Democrat and a liberal of the kind bilious Bob Butts would characterize (as Frank imagines it) as "nigger-lovin', tax-and-spend, pro-health-care, abortion-rights, gay-rights, consumer-rights, tree-hugging" (174). Against that is the ur-Republican "vision" of the repugnant Butts and barman Lester, founded on racist, xenophobic venom against non-white, and particularly immigrant, America. The scene is a disconsolate commentary on the extreme form that the exclusionist, isolationist American view of independence can take. The August Inn episode will seal Frank's definitive rupture with the Haddam era of his life, which is a painful personal separation, for, as Frank observes, a "town you used to live in signifies something—possibly interesting—about you: what you were once" (13).

But it is also a scene that insists on the changing spirit and mood of a country. Frank's sense of well-being as he enters the bar is recalled after the fight when he is obliged to consign "a homey town and a bar I used to dream sweet dreams in" (178) to an irretrievable past. The scene becomes a lament for a lost time and represents a certain loss of innocence for an optimistic American. The novel on occasions adopts an elegiac tone when Frank regrets an impoverishment of spirit in American life, as the passage of time breeds values inimical to an American tradition that is dear to him. The incarnation of these old and better ways is Frank's friend, Lloyd Mangum, "a man not much made in America now, though once there were plenty" (66). In a passage as heavy with nostalgia as the scent of Lloyd's Old Spice, Frank mythologizes Lloyd as an archetypal American family man, solid as a rock and going quietly and simply about life's duties, leading the exemplary "normal applauseless life" exalted by Frank in *The Sportswriter* (10). And after his Sponsoring visit Frank slips into prelapsarian nostalgia for a time "in our grateful and unlitigious village past" when "this kind of good deed happened every day and all involved took it for granted" (111). But, as he notes elsewhere, in a comment that alludes to the wider climate of suspicion and unfriendliness portrayed in the novel, "Those innocent days are behind us now" (435).

Frank's demoralized mood on leaving the August Inn is merely another instance of a general pessimism that prevails in the novel, a mood whose most recurrent form is fear. Frank's cancer becomes the dominant metaphor for the quiet feeling of dread that has infiltrated the lives of many of the characters. While Frank has to confront cancer in all its unpleasant reality, the lives of others are contaminated by an enervating spiritual malaise that saps their will and has them recoil from a full commitment to their own lives. So recurrent is the evocation of fear in the novel that one senses a resolve in Richard Ford to depict American society as afflicted by a debilitating form of cultural insecurity and lack of self-confidence. Speaking in an interview about what he calls the "sense of menace lurking around the edge of every scene" in the novel, Ford goes on:

> One of my points in writing this book is that everything that happened in 9/11 was already happening in America before 9/11. The magnitude was just not there. But there was the passivity of government, entropy, fear of the other, violence around the periphery of life, a quiet sense of unease.[9]

Frank understands his Sponsoring visits in part as an antidote to this malaise, as it offers "a rare optimism" and "[renders] Sponsorees less risk-averse" (96). He sees Clarissa as living in a mode of "crucial avoidance" (123), as if she had stalled her life in a holding mode for fear of "*making the big mistake*" and out of fear of "unbearable pain" (123). The fear of making a ruinous mistake, and a pre-9/11 dread about the vigour of the country and its ability to withstand catastrophe, along with an awareness of his mortality, all paralyse Frank's otherwise-dynamic client, Clare Suddruth, into uncertainty about committing himself to buying a house. More generally, an increasing consciousness of death inhabits the characters in late middle age. Ann thinks she wants to live with Frank again partly out of fear of an early death for both of them (the consequence, as she sees it, of having had a child die and of their living alone); Sally puts her pessimism down to an end-of-millennium fear of death; and Frank sees the middle-aged 5-K runners' frenetic exertions as an attempt to ward of their own fear of death.

---

[9] "Ford assesses America's house", Interview with Richard Ford, *Toronto Star*, 29 October 2006, Section C, 7.

Frank finds confirmation of a wider cultural malaise when he consults the notice board at the De Tocqueville Academy. He makes a point of checking such announcements as they allow him take the pulse of a place, to "sense its inner shifts and seismic fidgets": "Real life writ small is here, etched with our wishes, losses and dismays." The fear-filled notices in the De Tocqueville Academy mostly catalogue the ills of the times (rape, sexual harassment, hate crimes, grieving, disease detection, aloneness) and communicate a "careworn and fatigued" spirit (147). They are entirely in keeping with the general atmosphere of disunity and self-centredness that scars human relations in the novel, causing Frank to think at one stage, after yet another disagreeable exchange: "What's the matter with the world all of a sudden?" (320) Frank, of course, is better placed than anyone to stand above "the world's woe and clatter" (286) and to survey the spiritual lay of the land. Cancer has brought him the sense of perspective that proximity to death inevitably brings and has allowed him to measure the legitimacy of fear. He has come to understand that there is a certain "sweet satisfaction" (290) in having finally arrived in the inescapable reality of his own mortality. The anguished other characters continue to live in fear of life itself; for them, the irrevocable confirmation of mortality is still something "out there to dread" (290). When this undercurrent of fear is added to the other scenes from American life in the novel – the decadent consumerism, the spiritual enervation, the distant human relations, the lessening of solidarity – there emerges a portrait of a culture and a society ill at ease with itself, sapped of its vital energy, glorying in its freedom and wealth, but seeming no longer quite to know what the point of it all is. It is a depiction of a society in crisis, what Ford sees as representing "part of the book's moral vision", and that represents a call to his country to "pay attention" to what it has become.[10]

There is an ironic footnote to the nation-building mythology and iconography of the Haddam bar-scene setting, as the first thing Frank sees when he leaves the August Inn is the Pilgrim Interpretive Center. This Thanksgiving reminder of modern America's first settlers and of

---

[10] Michael Ross, Interview with Richard Ford, "The final chapter", *Sunday Times*, 1 October 2006, Features Section, 12.

a country built on immigration is in keeping with a novel where the increasing diversity of America is constantly highlighted, be it in the new reality of globalization (on several occasions Frank notes the presence of foreign corporate economic power in New Jersey), in the more traditional manner of new immigrants arriving in pursuit of a better life, or, finally, in the increasing visibility of immigrants from recent generations who have become successful in private enterprise. Turks, Pakistanis, Filipinos, South Koreans, Sri Lankans, Arabs, Hindus, Somalians, Hondurans, Sudanese, Russians and, of course, Mexicans, all feature in the mosaic of multicultural America presented by the novel, the new cultural diversity that so enrages barman Lester.[11]

If multicultural America is presented in the background as the changing face of the country, the immigrant experience is thoroughly foregrounded in the novel through the character of Mike Mahoney, Frank's associate in his Sea-Clift real estate agency. Forty-three-year-old Mike is a cultural hybrid of the sort that would give Lester nightmares. He is Tibetan by origin, Tibetan-American by experience, carries an Irish-American name given to him by his first American colleagues, yet is a "full-blooded, naturalized American" (15). In the choice imposed on every immigrant between assimilating into the culture of arrival or clinging to one's native culture, Mike has chosen the former (although his Buddhist beliefs, flexible as they are, are a reminder that assimilation in its deeper reaches is never complete for an immigrant already conditioned by the native culture). He has embraced American identity in some of its most recognizable external features – clothes, accent, children in a private school, big mortgage, flashy car, separation from his wife, and, in an ultimate act of assimilationist desire, voting Republican.

Yet, for all that Mike would wish to assimilate and be accepted as fully American, and for all that Frank willingly accords him that

[11] In a report in its 18 September 2000 issue (coinciding precisely with the setting of Ford's novel), *Newsweek* noted that New Jersey was one of the six "most popular states for immigrants" (48). 68% of its population was classified as "White, non-Hispanic", while the most populous other groups were "African-American" at 15%, "White Hispanic" at 11%, and "Asian, Pacific Islander" at 6%. With regard to the changing profile of the national population, the report recorded that, while there had been a 4% increase in the "White, non-Hispanic" population in the previous ten years, the corresponding increase for "Hispanic (of any race)" was 45%, and for "Asian and Pacific Islander", 50%.

identity ("He's just as American as I am" [192]), Mike remains in a space of indeterminate, interjacent identity, aware that the melting-pot, assimilationist ideal of American identity is still withheld from him, both from within and without. In other words, neither Mike himself nor others find him a fully suitable candidate for irrefutable American identity. From without, Mike's otherness is perceived variously, running from a low-level, unspoken awareness of Mike's non-American appearance to overt racist bigotry. Mike's "standard Tibetan's flat, bony-cheeked, beamy Chinaman's face, gun-slit eyes" (14) and tiny size produce behind-the-back smirks from real estate competitors and some puzzlement from clients, reactions that are entirely race-related. Frank sees, too, that Mike's value to his potential business partner lies in his status as a "bona fide and highly prized minority", one capable of attracting "big federal subsidy dollars" (17); otherwise, Frank knows, Mike would be frozen out on racial grounds. The withholding of American identity from Mike by others finds its worst and fully racist expression in liberal-hating Lester, when he calls Mike a "midget" and a "coolie" (184).

But even within himself Mike often seems uncertain about his own identity, his incongruous, exaggeratedly American clothes – Frank remarks at one point that he looks "like a pint-sized mafioso on his way to a golf outing" (22) – being one indication of his need to convince himself that he is no longer an immigrant. In *The Liberty of Strangers: Making the American Nation* Desmond King explores the prevailing and opposing versions of America nationhood. There is the one-people, or one-nation, assimilationist ideology of national identity based on shared cultural traditions, values, beliefs and practices, and, at the same time, a nationhood constructed upon, and that must take account of, strong group identities based on race, ethnicity or national background. Discussing the manner in which some Asian immigrants feel themselves excluded from American identity, King quotes a middle-aged Vietnamese woman:

> [H]ow can I feel I am American? If you say you are American, you must look American .... That means being white .... Even if I get citizenship, I cannot say I am American. I am still Vietnamese with American citizenship.[12]

---

[12] King, *The Liberty of Strangers*, 144.

It is through this internalization of external physical difference that Mike withholds American identity from himself. It is Frank who acts as the interpreter of Mike's uncertainties, which stem from his inability, despite his strivings, to fully think, act and be like a native-born American. In Mike's hesitation over accepting developer Benivalle's proposition, Frank discerns a wavering in Mike about trading in "his minority innocence" for a shot at the big time, something "any natural-born American wouldn't think twice about" (25). Nor can Mike read the cultural codes and co-ordinates that would allow him to establish his position on the road to full realization of the American Dream. He has already been successful, "an impressive climb most Americans would think was great" (33), observes Frank, but he simply does not possess the innate American cultural knowledge to let him know if this is enough to represent full assimilation and success: as Frank points out, "there's much about America that baffles him still" (21). And when he comes back from his meeting with Benivalle, Frank sees him returning as "an immigrant vanquished by uncertainty" (200), and suspects that he is even relieved – in his "errors, failures and uncertainties" of cultural misprision – at being able to "feel momentarily less American" (202).

It is as if Mike is striving too hard to be a "useful, purposeful" immigrant (16), but uniquely according to the assimilationist model of citizenship. He is wearing himself out in an effort to conform to a notion of one-nation, homogenized American identity, but at the expense of his own native cultural identity. Seeing himself still as an outsider, he understands his situation in utterly binary terms, as one in which he must choose between outside and inside, between otherness and a common identity, between being an immigrant and being an American. His acceptance of the ideology of a one-people model of a single common American identity has him disregard the reality and truth of his own hybridized identity. It also, indeed, has him go against the grain of his own moral identity. That the concept of American identity ought not to be considered in terms of commonality, as part of a simple binarism, is evident not only from the historical reality of the country's multi-national and multi-ethnic immigrant background, but also from the moral choice that Mike sees being presented to him in his zeal to be fully American: in the divided America encapsulated in the election stand-off, Mike's vote for Republicans over Democrats, as well as his interest in becoming an aggressive developer, represent a moral choice he is making between the two highly polarized visions of America on offer, between, in his case (as Frank sees it), "Flattening pretty cornfields for seven-figure mega-mansions", or continuing to do what he does now in working with Frank, "really *helping* people ... find a modest home they want" (198).

There are many ways to be American, but Mike has mistakenly concluded that the extreme mercantile, plutocrat Republican version is the only path to true American identity. That he has indeed conceived of Americanness in this homogeneous and mercantile manner, and that he has been mistaken in so doing, emerges as the novel progresses and as he weighs up his professional future. He tells Frank that he "[feels] regret" (200) for having voted for Bush, and later accuses himself, as his native morality reasserts itself, of "covetousness" (253). When he finally announces his decision not to become a developer, he does so by saying that he has "tamed" himself (421) of his desire to be excessively rich. Mike's acceptance of his present condition – although he continues to nurture a quintessential American individualism and ambition to improve himself materially (to the point of offering to buy Frank out) – is an acceptance both of a less rapacious and less limited form of American identity, and an acceptance, too, of his own hybridized identity. He has concluded that there are different ways to be American and that achieving this does not oblige him to jettison an essential part of who he is. Just before Mike announces his decision to refuse the Benivalle offer, Frank notes Mike's relieved demeanour as he speaks to a client, an Indian-American. The two men are chatting and laughing about "the dog's breakfast the Bills were making of the regular season", causing Frank to observe: "They are both Americans and acted like nothing else" (417). In this political novel about a divided country, and that depicts the general state of the American spirit at a highly symbolic national holiday, the xenophobic bigotry of Lester is firmly counteracted by Frank's liberalism, and by the pluralist tradition and vision of America.

CHAPTER 6

THE LAY OF THE LAND

II: THE RETURN OF THE PAST

If Richard Ford's vision of America at Thanksgiving in the year 2000 is essentially pessimistic, the predicament of his protagonist does not promise to lighten the mood of the novel. In the space of a few months earlier in the year Frank's second wife, Sally, had left him for her first husband, and Frank had discovered that he had prostate cancer. It is now, however, laid low by the worst news that life could bring, that Frank, for the first time in the trilogy, proves himself equal to the occasion. In the past, Frank's dogmatic optimism left him ill-equipped to deal with the circumstances of his life and with the responsibility of living with others. But alone and threatened by death, his native optimism is now his most important resource.

Frank's altered relationship with life is the theme of the novel's Prologue, set a week before Thanksgiving. Reading a newspaper report about a disturbed nursing student who entered his classroom, pointed a gun at the head of his teacher, then asked her if she was ready to meet her "Maker" (before shooting her dead), Frank is astonished and moved that the teacher was able to answer in the affirmative. Stalked by death himself, but allowed more time to consider a response, Frank is galvanized to seek his own answer to the same question. A "self-actualizing dip" in the cold Atlantic, feeling himself in ruddy contact with the elements, invigorates his body sufficiently to tell him that he is not yet ready to meet his Maker, "because there was still something I needed to know and didn't ... and that could make me happy" (7). He swims back to land and back to his life.

If Frank returns to land from the non-human element of the sea, his home nonetheless stands as a permanent metaphor for his more tenuous hold on life. His house is surrounded by water on both sides and joined to the mainland by a bridge, the thin metaphorical line connecting Frank to the fullness of life. The view of the ocean through the floor-to-ceiling windows of his house is a reminder of his living now at the edge of the earth and, as he waits to find out if his treatment is working, at the edge of life. Yet this proximity to death brings a new clarity, an absoluteness and a sense of necessity to his life that gives him new resolve. In discovering that he is still committed to his own existence, the way is opened for his account to be a narrative about life, and not about death. And not in the sense of life winding its sad, inexorable way to death, but rather about life lived lucidly in order to adjust to changed circumstances, yet lived with the conviction that life still represents the enduring possibility of worthwhile experience. In late middle age, Frank's optimism has found the perfect circumstance, the ideal opponent. Cometh the time, cometh the man.

The passage of time and the dramatic upheavals in Frank's life have contrived to produce a realignment in Frank's relationship to others. Where before, in both *The Sportswriter* and *Independence Day*, the forces of attraction and avoidance that governed his relationships with others had Frank orbiting around the fixed physical and moral points represented by other people (and women in particular), now it is Frank who is the nucleus around which others hover, coming to or drawing away from him depending on the person and circumstances. Time and experience have transformed Frank into the steadfast centre, and this, too, in a moral sense. He was motivated to became a Sponsor by the altruistic urge to help those who had difficulty making friends, displaying a new, committed and sympathetic form of interaction with others. His cancer, too, played a role, supplying an empathy with "other people's woes".

Frank the avoider has become Frank the contributor, finding himself "*more* interested in life—any life—not less" (96). He had mused at the end of *The Sportswriter* that Walter Luckett's death had "had the effect on me that death means to have; of reminding me of my responsibility to a somewhat larger world".[1] That effect had not endured, but the doleful reminder of his own mortality has indeed awakened a sense of responsibility. His new sensibility receives

---

[1] Ford, *The Sportswriter*, 366.

authenticating witness from his ex-wife, Ann, who commends Frank as "a kind man" (153) in recalling how he sat with her dying second husband, Charley, afflicted by cancer and Alzheimer's (when his friends were nowhere to be seen). Frank finds Ann's testimonial ironic in its belatedness, but it has all the greater force coming from someone who, in the previous novels, had found little good to say about Frank.

The transformation and realignment are such that it is Frank who becomes the person wronged in *The Lay of the Land*, and ironically by women, the historical victims of Frank's vacillations and evasions: now it is Frank who suffers the consequences of mistakes by women to whom he is, or has been, close – abandonment by his wife, and the emotional misjudgements of his ex-wife. His new status as injured party extends to his wider experiences in the novel. He has to submit to the boorishness of an old acquaintance, Bud Sloat; the aggressive paranoia of his neighbour, Nick Feenster; the violence of Bob Butts; the bigoted slurs of Lester the barman; the fretfulness of Mike; the insults of Wade Arsenault; the suspicions of the police; and the wacky unpredictability of his son. In the sombre, abrasive atmosphere of the novel it is Frank who emerges as the beacon of light and as the standard-bearer for stoicism, steadfastness and decency. Alone and with cancer he might have hoped for sympathy and support from his family and friends, and from life in general. But, in love's absence, he will find only aggravation. Steadfast and available as he is, people and events will pick and pull at him over Thanksgiving, testing his new commitment to life and leaving him with less and less for which to feel thankful.

As far as the personal lay of the land is concerned, it is Frank's solitude that most distinguishes the third novel from the previous two. Above all, Frank no longer has a close relationship with a woman. At different levels of intimacy, he was involved variously with Ann, Vicki and Sally in the first two novels; now he rarely sees Ann, and Sally is gone. His children, moreover, lead independent lives far from Sea-Clift. The huge emotional and intimate hollow in his life, however, is due to Sally's absence. Whatever occurs in the novel in terms of Frank's emotional state takes place in the melancholy shadow of her abandonment of Frank. In keeping with the structure and content of many of Richard Ford's stories, Frank's account will grapple with the consequences of acts already committed. Although

Sally is already almost six months gone when the novel begins, this momentous event needs to be narrated and understood by Frank. It is notable that the retrospective narration of her departure occurs in the centre of the novel, an indication of the continuing pivotal role of the event in Frank's life.

In the spirit of compromise and reconciliation that permeated the end of *Independence Day*, Sally Caldwell, Frank's girlfriend at the time, chose to see Frank as a "good guy" and as someone who was "pretty sympathetic",[2] a judgement that rang true but that could have been countered by evidence of less admirable traits. In committing herself to Frank she offered him a path out of his sterile isolation and released him into a promising future. Four years would pass before they married, in 1992, and set up home in Sea-Clift. Frank considered their eight-year marriage to have been "much more than satisfying-fulfilling" (217). It was a second marriage built on the lessons learned from previous failures and disappointments, and guided by a lucidity about the emotions and expectations that brought and kept them together. The present was given precedence over the past, promise over regret, and affinity, which they agreed was their form of love, over passion. Frank allows no doubt about the quality of their affections: "In the simplest terms, we really, really loved each other", and insists now, in the light of events, that "We *were* happy" (230).

If Sally's subsequent decision to leave Frank for Wally is in itself devastating for Frank, it is all the more so because of Sally's reasoning: she left Frank because she decided "it was worse to be with someone who didn't need you than to let someone who maybe did be alone" (137). Frank's distress has its source in his failure to understand how Sally could transform a choice to leave him for Wally into an imperative: it had always been something of an article of faith for Frank that obligations arose merely from a provisional failure to recognize that there was always a choice in any given situation. Above all, though, it is love's impermanence that is Frank's undoing: "I thought life isn't supposed to be like this when you love someone and they love you" (240), he confesses to his daughter. Sally, and his love for her, had been the foundation upon which he had consciously constructed the rest of his life. Although he is certain that he still loves her, her departure has transformed mutual love into an unrequited

---

[2] Ford, *Independence Day*, 433.

experience and caused a thinness of affection in Frank's existence, and Sally's continued absence contributes to the general moroseness that pervades the book as Thanksgiving approaches.

One of the felicities of the Frank Bascombe trilogy has been the emergence of a philosophical voice whose raw material is the mundane offerings of quotidian existence. Richard Ford has always been anxious to render in his fiction what he calls "lived life".[3] Frank's reflective nature and his embeddedness in regular life prove to be a rewarding blend, as his continual contact with the world provokes him to constant assessment of his own condition. Frank's philosophizing is his great merit; it is also, however, his greatest flaw in that he over-conceptualizes his life, categorizing his experience into theories and principles that, more often than not, originate in his instincts and desires rather than in neutral inquiry.

There is no dimming of his conceptualizing zeal in *The Lay of the Land*. In a tradition that began with the notions of dreaminess, mystery, factualism and literalism in *The Sportswriter*, and continued with the Existence Period of *Independence Day*, Frank now understands the shape and evolution of his life through what he calls the Permanent Period. The designation and provenance of this new classification of his life are ironic: Frank's entire behaviour in *The Sportswriter* phase of his life was determined by his fear of permanence, by his glorying, indeed, in what he called then the "frothiest kind of impermanence",[4] part of a strategy for evading a fixity of identity and, thus, responsibility. Frank cultivated difference at the expense of sameness in his identity, or non-permanence at the expense of permanence, the effect of which, at the end of *The Sportswriter*, was a curious absence of wholeness or coherence of self.

In the Haddam of the early nineties, however, Frank began to suffer a crisis of identity. He began to conceive of his life in terms of incompleteness, insufficiency, absence, a sense of perpetual becoming that never became anything. The new commanding metaphors were "*the need for an extra beat*" (52) and "feeling *offshore*" (52), coined

---

[3] *Conversations with Richard Ford*, 28.
[4] Ford, *The Sportswriter*, 224.

to convey the sense of a life that had become naggingly peripheral and ephemeral:

> ... very little about me, I realized—except what I'd *already* done, said, eaten, etc.—seemed written in stone, and all of that meant almost nothing about what I *might* do. I had my history, okay, but not really much of a regular character, at least not an inner essence I or anyone could use as a predictor. And something, I felt, needed to be done about that. I needed to go out and find myself a recognizable and persuasive semblance of a character. (53)

After a life of calculated impermanence, of wallowing in choice, possibility and self-avoidance, Frank found himself experiencing a wanness of being and a yearning for a recognizable self, an identity of substance and permanence: "Here, for a man with no calculable character, was a hunger for *necessity*, for something solid, the thing 'character' stands in for" (54). Instead of difference and becoming, Frank wanted consistency and self-actualization, and to bring his whole existence into sharper relief. If, as Frank acknowledges, a character or a self is not something you pluck out of the air, there were nonetheless new arrangements and resolutions that could give one's life a sharper configuration and a recognizable identity. Leaving Haddam, moving to Sea-Clift and marrying Sally accomplished the physical and symbolic realization of the transition to the time and selfhood of permanency.

It is indeed a question of time, as it has so often been with Frank's grandiose concepts. Instead of a drifting, featureless becoming, there would be resolute being in the present, a corollary of which would be a lessening concern with the past: "we try to *be* what we *are* in the present" (31) is one of Frank's Permanent Period formulations; "nose-down and invisible to yourself as an actualized unchangeable non-becomer" (75) is another. The Permanent Period means taking a stand – and taking responsibility – for what you are now, accepting that this is both all and the best you will be, and then getting on with the realization of the self that this condition is to bring into being. It is also the acceptance that this is your final self, the identity that you will take to the grave, and for which you will be remembered. It is life as arrival and final destination, offering the permanent, daily opportunity to live up to the gravestone inscription you have already composed for yourself.

Successfully negotiating the Permanent Period, as suggested by the formulation itself, meant coming to terms with its particular temporality. The future threatened to close down into an ongoing sameness of the present, rendering "possibility small and remote" (76); the disadvantage of final destination, in other words, was that the story of Frank's life was already written, and the future promised little in the way of innovation or stimulation. Happiness with Sally, however, promised to be the antidote to this deficit of new meaning.

As for the past, it seemed to offer no difficulty: if the "blunt break with the past" (54) and the Permanent Period imperative to view the past as "more generic than specific" (46) seem familiar, it is because Frank's new life-concept has much in common with his earlier life-concepts. His notions of literalism and mystery in *The Sportswriter* privileged the present moment and future anticipation over the claims of the past, while in *Independence Day* the Existence Period emphasized the "eternity of the here and now".[5] As Frank advises Mike at one point, translating his views about the past into a practical philosophy: "If I were you, I wouldn't think so much about causes. I'd think more about results" (202). Causes draw you back to the chronological unfolding of events in the past, whereas results allow a less fretful existence in the present and an opening towards the future. Frank is an old hand at seeking to evade the pull of the past and to make "the present brighten with its present-ness" (95). His cancer has accorded a new validation and urgency to that challenge: it has removed his dread of the future and intensified his being in the present, and has stripped him of the false promise of hope as an unwarranted dispersal of his being beyond the present.

The corroboration of the Permanent Period view of human temporality provided by the experience of cancer was simply further evidence, in Frank's eyes, of an obvious truth already soundly demonstrated by the episode of Sally's departure. Sally's failed attempts to be reconciled with her children had proved to Frank that "Too much unredeemed loss can be fatal", a truth he passed on to Sally as "one of the early glittering tenets of the Permanent Period". In what was one of Frank's more tenable opinions about the past, he advised her that, at some point and in some circumstances, one must

---

[5] Ford, *Independence Day*, 145.

"consign the past to its midden" (219): if her children would not forgive Sally for having Wally declared dead, then so be it. This was part of Frank's attempt to build his marriage on the rock of the present, through "permanently [renouncing] melancholy and nostalgia" (230). Frank puts the unravelling of their marriage down to Sally's critical error of seeking an impossible return to the past in order to "put right" a "misfeasance of a large and historical nature" (226), namely Wally's disappearance from their marriage thirty years earlier. Frank's antidote to Sally's dilemma is drawn from "what the Permanent Period teaches us: If you can't truly forget something, you can at least ignore it" (227).

However, for all that Sally is responsible for leaving him, Frank makes his own critical error in continuing to see Wally's return as a lesson directed only at Sally about the futility of seeking to return to the past. Wally's return also demonstrated that the past is not always "more generic than specific", that it does not always allow itself to be minimalized and "generalized" (250) into the mute amorphousness to which Frank would reduce it. There *was* an unresolved burden from the past that weighed on Sally's present that no amount of wilful forgetting or grand conceptualizing could relieve. In failing to see that the very specificity of the return of Sally's past might have some bearing on the immutable certainties of his Permanent Period concepts, Frank is committing an error he has often committed in the past, that of living his life according to doctrinaire, self-protective theories that make little allowance for either the legitimate claims of others, the uncontrollable course of human emotions, or the illimitable domain of human temporality.[6] Convinced that the Permanent Period has "proved durable" after being put to "its sternest test" (55) by Sally's abandonment and his dramatic confrontation with mortality,

---

[6] The "legitimate claims of others" recalls Frank's various relationships with women in the past, in particular with Ann, Vicki and Sally, all of whom had to suffer the consequences of Frank's conceptualizing. An example of the "uncontrollable course of human emotions" would be Frank's own drift into dreaminess in *The Sportswriter*, or the unexpected irruption of his distress at his realization in *Independence Day* of "the end of Ann and me" (322). And Frank should be aware of the "illimitable domain of human temporality" by virtue of his rediscovery of his own family past at the end of *The Sportswriter* (thanks to the Florida Bascombes), his son Paul's continuing adolescent trauma in *Independence Day* nine years after seeing the family dog run over by a car, the sudden reappearance of Frank's step-brother Irv Orstein after Paul's accident, and even the continuing presence in Frank's mind of his dead son.

Frank faces into pre-Thanksgiving with a certain degree of serenity and buoyed by his native optimism that tells him that Sally might not be permanently lost to him.

Frank's Thanksgiving contact with his first family begins the process that will ultimately lead to the unravelling of his Permanent Period demarcations and to a direct confrontation with a past that he seeks at every turn to elude. In *Independence Day* Ann had stripped away Frank's illusion that divorce did not mean what it was supposed to mean, the illusion that Ann and he had merely entered a new phase of their relationship, one held together now in a "different equipoise".[7] The harsh autopsy carried out by Ann on their marriage in *Independence Day* and Frank's subsequent painful acceptance that Ann was indeed gone from his life released him into independence and handed him back his future. Now, following her second husband's death, Ann is back living in Haddam, and, although their contact is infrequent, time, diminished passions and their shared role as parents to "our two grown and worrisome children" (12) allow a less strained relationship than before, to the point that Frank even detects on Ann's part a "form of interest" (30) in him since Sally's departure.

Ann's acting upon that interest, however, will have an unhappy end: regret, frustration, loss and old remembered grievances will mark the final important contacts between them as Ann disappears definitively from Frank's life. Telling Frank now that she loves him, although unsure "if it's again, or still" (154), and that she is willing to live with him again, before then going on to retract her declaration two days later, is the sign of the deep confusion engendered by a relationship in which love was never allowed to run its natural course. Ann now sees qualities in Frank that she had not been able to see before, occasioned by Frank's selfless sitting with Charley in the final stages of his illness. Her awareness of these qualities attach themselves to old affections, which, when added to old regrets, her present solitude and vivid reminders of her own mortality, produce her impossible declaration of love. All of Frank's old resentments at Ann flare up in the wake of her expression of love – his sense of always being unfavourably judged by her, his memory of her disapproval of

---

[7] Ford, *Independence Day*, 104.

his abandoning a promising literary career, her failure to appreciate his qualities when they were married, and her indifference to Frank's marriage and to Sally herself. His ultimate reaction is one of cynicism about Ann's motives.

Yet what lingers from this episode is less the high moral ground that one or other may occupy than the sense of unfinished emotional business between them, one that writes a melancholy epilogue to their thirty-year relationship. As Frank recognizes, the great burden carried by both of them was the death of their son. From that moment, "Death became all we had in common, a common jail" (344). Frank will also come to the final conclusion that they "didn't even love each other all that much" (377), although that is a contradiction of all he expressed in the two previous novels. But Frank has always had a very personal notion of what love means and was not averse to declaring his love to women when he never meant it, as Ann and Sally had reason to know. And, as he himself reflects, "For every different person, loves means something different" (376). On both their parts, one senses a lament for love that was blocked, frustrated, then failed because of the intervention of tragedy. Its unrealized potential and its premature end came back to trouble both of them at different times since Ralph's death, depending on personal moods and vulnerabilities and on particular circumstances, but the resurgence of feeling for the other never coincided. Now it happens to be Ann's turn to feel the power of a stunted emotion, which she expresses with much affection to Frank, who, however, is no longer disposed to receive it. Their chance to love each other is long past, and Ann's failure to recognize this brings their relationship to a sorry close.

Beyond this emotional upheaval, however, the episode has other troubling consequences for Frank. Ann's expression of love comes at the end of a day (Tuesday) in which the "Permanent Period and its indemnifying sureties are in scattered retreat" (156). Frank's refuge in the temporal cocoon of the present has failed as a self-protective strategy against a return of the past. Ann has a healthier and more stoical view of human temporality, as a phone message she leaves on Frank's answering machines conveys: "I just want to say that I can't get over the long transit we all make in our lives. The strangest thing we'll ever know is just life itself, isn't it?" (254). Ann's very being is registering normal human awe at the accumulation of time and experience, at unexpected change, and at the configurations through which time and our sensibilities will present our lives to us. The past has come back to Ann and Frank in an unexpected and melancholy manner. Yet again, the generic past has become a specific past.

Where Frank's children are concerned, the past continues to press in on the present. The astute, precocious Clarissa of *Independence Day* has become the sympathetic, intelligent but somewhat lost twenty-five-year-old in the third novel, unsure whether she will choose from men or women for her partners. Frank blames his and Ann's distracted past, their love that was "too finely diced and served", for his daughter's "distrustful temper and pervasive uncertainties" (115). He believes, too, that he has passed on to Clarissa her "instinct for crucial avoidance" (123), a defence mechanism that she is employing now to deflect these uncertainties and the fear of her life being shapeless and peripheral. Clarissa's gift of "sympathy to excess" (117) brought her to Frank's side to look after him after his cancer procedure, where she has remained. In return, she has found provisional shelter and a non-judgemental adult against whom she can take the measure of her life. The antithesis of permanence – Sally's departure, Frank's illness, Clarissa's confusions – has offered them a space where mutual affection may be expressed, and offers Clarissa, as Frank puts it, "her last chance to have a father experiencing his last chance to have the daughter he loves" (116). In the generally bleak human landscape of the novel, Clarissa's ministrations represent the one restorative human presence in Frank's life.

The third member of what has to be considered the generally failed Bascombe family unit is Paul, the source of Frank's greatest family stress. His son's arrival for Thanksgiving from his life as a greeting-card writer in Kansas City fills Frank with apprehension. Mutual incomprehension is their only common ground, apart from the conviction that the other is lacking in the qualities necessary to be a normal human being. For Frank, Paul is resentful, affected, has "become an asshole" and is a huge disappointment to him. In Paul's case, adolescent hostility has not been mellowed by adulthood: he sees Frank as repressed, as living at arm's length from life and as "stupid" (120). In this relationship, too, past experience dictates present behaviour, or, at least, present behaviour appears not to have been able to move beyond old antagonisms, or to extricate itself from the consequences of earlier traumas and turmoil. Frank recalls the effect on Paul of Ralph's death, how, as "a troubled boy of tender years", Paul behaved "as if the left-behind brother of a dead boy had to be two boys" (391-92). Frank acknowledged in *Independence Day*, moreover, that he had not been vigilant enough as a parent where his son was concerned. The family break-up, too, shifted Paul about, having him live for a time with Ann and her second husband in Deep River before he moved back to Haddam to live with Frank.

It is striking, indeed, how the present exchanges between father and son replicate in significant ways their exchanges of twelve years earlier. Frank complains as much now as he did then about Paul's appearance. And in *Independence Day* Frank and Paul's essential medium of exchange was jokes and puns, with both of them unable to find a direct and less dissimulative language of communication. Nothing has changed. Neither of them has the self-confidence nor the courage to break out of their evasive coded language, which succeeds only in maintaining the distance between them, prevents each of them from showing the person they truly are to the other and acts as a very thin defence against the unspoken emotions bubbling under the surface.

When Paul's forced jokiness, in a would-be comical bear-hug of Frank, fails to observe the emotional and physical boundaries of their code, father and son end up repeating the scene from twelve years earlier outside the Cooperstown batting cage where they angrily wrestled with each other. The outcome of the earlier incident was Paul's eye injury; now, their physical altercation leads to a scene of confrontation, where, provoked by anger, they finally speak the truth to each other in a welter of accusation and personal abuse. Although it is never made explicit, Paul's anger at his father stems from ancient anguishes and grievances that have festered as the years have passed, while Frank is animated by his disapproval of the man his son has turned out to be. In their inability either to speak to or behave naturally with each other, outside their well-practised codes of dissimulation or surges of anger (we learn that Frank and Paul's previous meeting also ended in recrimination), it is left to Paul's girlfriend, Jill, to act as intermediary and to draw out what is surely the underlying truth about father and son that neither can speak to the other. Jill tells Frank that Paul is "really a big fan of yours" (388), to which Frank replies: "I'm a big fan of his" (389).

Frank and Paul have spent most of their lives hiding themselves from each other. Both have given up on the other, although it is undoubtedly the father who bears the greater burden of responsibility. That the son has all the time been seeking the father's approval emerges clearly from a later scene contrived by Paul in which he hopes to have Frank grant public approval – by way of a positive reaction to one of his greeting-cards – to his new role and identity as a self-styled "comic figure" (120). And that Frank does indeed love his son is ultimately expressed twice by Frank, although in both cases he blurts it out after an angry exchange with Paul, thus stripping the sentiment of the context and emotion needed to overcome years of inadequately expressed love. In a novel in which Frank emerges with much greater credit than in the previous two, his severe judgement of Paul neglects nonetheless to take account of his responsibility as an often-absent parent in Paul's childhood and adolescence, yet another failure by Frank to understand that the past, whether he likes it or not, cannot simply be willed into silence.

If Frank attempts to circumvent human temporality through his Permanent Period demarcations, and if his conflicts with Sally, Ann and Paul conceal from him the true operations and effects of time, his experiences elsewhere confront him with the consequences of the "long transit we all make in our lives". In late middle age he is everywhere exposed to change and to the challenges and confusing emotions it engenders. In Frank's professional life Mike represents the modern world and is a reminder to Frank that old ways are eventually pushed out by the new. Mike favours the new "realty psychology" (33) approach to selling houses, in contrast to Frank's straightforward traditional style. Despite Mike's disapproval Frank does not have a company website and has resisted acquiring a computer or a cell phone. He likes, too, the simple lettering on his office window, which recalls "an old-time shirtsleeve lawyer's office" (199).

But Frank's old ways are everywhere yielding to the values and needs of later generations. Clarissa and her girlfriend employ a new vocabulary that situates Frank firmly as a man from an earlier age, while change is inscribed on the landscape itself through relentless development – Frank records the changing face of his old town where newer tastes have brought new commercial outlets to replace those from his time in Haddam. His trip to Haddam, indeed, unexpectedly becomes a trip back in time in another way, back to his dead son and to a defining memory preserved in time, cementing Frank's inescapable relationship with the past. Frank finds himself at a now-abandoned vegetable stand outside the town that Ann, Ralph and he used to visit on Saturday mornings. Frank's "Memory rockets to that ... gilded time" (41), his mind filled with the colours, lights and smells of happier days when his family was joyful and his son still alive. But the vegetable stand sits beside the cornfield to be developed by Benivalle, a now-hallowed piece of ground that will soon disappear, leaving Frank in wistful mood as he leaves: "I say silent adieu to the ground my son trod and will no more. The old lay of the land" (44).

The disappearance of the old lay of the land, and the old ways it supported, receive an emblematic set-piece scene in the novel through the controlled destruction of the Queen Regent Arms hotel in Asbury Park, which Frank attends with old friend, Wade Arsenault (father of Vicki from *The Sportswriter*).[8] While Frank purports to appreciate, in the staged destruction of an old building, the "orderly succession manifesting our universal need to remain adaptable through time", his cancer has him align himself more with the view he attributes to the elderly Wade, for whom, Frank believes, it is evidence that "the past crumbles and that staring loss in the face is the main requirement for living out our allotment". The destruction of the "elegant old Queen Regent Arms" – to make way for "a high-end condo development" (251) – and the way of life it epitomized come to stand as a metaphor for human transience for the two men there to witness its disappearance: Frank personifies the old hotel into the figure of a condemned man awaiting the hail of firing-squad bullets, a confrontation he understands as a "[tilt] between man's hold on permanence and the Reaper" (300), exactly the struggle in which both the failing Wade and he are engaged.

If Frank has always welcomed change in the present, as he continues to do in *The Lay of the Land* – he talks about how his "natural habit would be to consider most all things as mutable" (323) – and even if he allows change within the Permanent Period – the latter is conceived essentially in terms of the finally unchanging self –

---

[8] For some reason, "Arcenault" of *The Sportswriter* has become "Arsenault" in *The Lay of the Land*.

it is change at the historical level, evident in inexorable personal decline and in growing estrangement from the ways of the world, with which he must come to terms. This distinction between present and historical change seems to be in his mind at one point: "I'm always more at home with chance and transition than with the steady course, since the steady course leads quickly, I've found, to the rim of the earth" (416). Life, the long transit through time, can only lead to the "rim of the earth", yet Frank has always sought to thwart time's arrow through distractions, change, new possibilities and the ecstasy of choice. But the steady course of time inevitably prevails, leaving Frank's old ways on the rim as well: "One hardly knows how or when or by what subtle mechanics the old values give way to new. It just happens" (423).

The "rim of the earth", of course, is a metaphor for proximity to death. In a trilogy of novels in which Frank's passage through time has been meticulously charted, it is fitting that, in his late middle age, mortality and actual death intrude into the consciousness and lives of his generation. Several deaths – natural, accidental and violently inflicted – are reported in the book, and Frank attends the funeral of an old friend in Haddam, an event he understands as a "*Memento mori*" (56). And when death is not pressing in on Frank, it is the pre-death antechamber of decrepit old age that announces human mortality. This is indeed the effect that an afternoon in the company of Wade Arsenault has on Frank, and is also the reason he dislikes being with men of his own age. Death is already written on the bodies of these men: "We all emanate a sense of youth lost and tragedy-on-the-horizon" (71), laments Frank.

If Frank's illness has had the positive consequences already noted – he is less fearful, feels a new sense of necessity, is more responsible, has greater empathy with others and has had the opportunity to get to know his daughter better – this latest stop in his journey of "graduated obsolescence" (161) requires of him continual readjustments and a response to the challenge of having to live life "like a man being followed by an assassin" (112). How can he, as he puts it, "maintain a supportable existence that resembles actual life" (290), or, to extend the range of the challenge, how is he to deal with death as "big-D *and* little-d"? (73). Yet again, Frank comes into his own. His philosophical nature and happy immersion in ordinary life equip him well to deal

with both metaphysical Death and physical death. Frank copes with
the existential anguish of Death through a greater intensity of
appreciation of life, through a newly discovered "low-wattage
wonder" (140) at human originality and through a concentrated
attention to the momentary "random sensations" (304) that human
existence has to offer, those textures of unremarkable experience that
would otherwise be ignored, and that were ignored by Frank in the
"*before*" (457) of cancer.

Overcoming the threat of "little-d" death involves dealing with the
immediate effects of his cancer – seeing beyond the mortifications and
obsessions of the continual urge to urinate and the manifold signs of a
failing body. Frank's natural enthusiasm for sensation and his
commitment to work are natural antidotes to defeatism: hours after the
biopsy results confirmed the presence of cancer Frank was out selling
a house and was soon back in the Permanent Period mode of "doin'
and bein'" (73). In a novel that reflects on the wonder of being and the
fragility of life, existence in the shadow of abstract Death and literal
death act powerfully upon Frank – in another manifestation of the
novel's moral vision – as a *memento vivere*.

Throughout his adult life Frank has sought to delimit the temporality
of his existence – through his concepts and demarcations – to the
experience of the present. Were he not so blinkered in this he would
have noticed that Sally's departure gave the lie to the attempt to ignore
the past, as did, in the days before Thanksgiving, Ann's renewed
affections, his continuing problems with Paul and his encounter with a
former lover on his Sponsoring visit. To these might be added his
recurring thoughts about Ralph, whose death, nineteen years earlier,
Frank believes he has accepted, although this acceptance is tinged
with a dreamy ambivalence. When, at one point, Clarissa forgets that
she is a third, and not a second, child, Frank quickly corrects her,
fulfilling the role he has assumed as "Ralph's earthly ombudsman".
This is a role to which he grants the title of "my secret self", surely the
ultimate, if unacknowledged, testimony of a personal investment in
the past and of an indissoluble connection between past and present.

Frank's role of "[giving] ... silent witness" (239) to Ralph's short
existence also exposes the contradiction at the heart of the Permanent
Period conception of time. And it is indeed Ralph who is the catalyst
for Frank's emotional breakdown in *The Lay of the Land*. A chance

reading of an article describing the grief and recovery of a fellow realtor, Fred Frantal, following the death of his twenty-year-old son has the effect of plunging Frank back into his own grief at Ralph's death. Despite Frank's lifelong awareness that he would carry Ralph with him "forever and ever after" (343), he is racked with tears of newly experienced sorrow. He recognizes that his distress has its origin in the Frantals' acceptance of their unbearable loss, but is puzzled nonetheless at the intensity of his own grief, given his ostensible acceptance of the worst that life had thrown at him. He comes very slowly, therefore, to the acknowledgement of the wound at the core of his existence – that his life "is founded on a lie" and to the realization that he knows "what the lie is and won't admit it, maybe can't" (350). In a moment of life- and self-convulsing significance Frank identifies his lie as that of the non-acceptance of Ralph's death:

> All these years and modes of accommodation, of coping, of living with, of negotiating the world in order to fit into it—my post-divorce dreaminess, the long period of existence in the early middle passage, the states of acceptable longing, of being a variabilist, even the Permanent Period itself—these now seem *not* to be forms of acceptance the way I thought, but forms of fearful nonacceptance, the laughing/grimacing masks of denial turned to the fact that … my son … would never *be* again in this life ….
>
> *That* was my lie, my big fear, the great pain I couldn't fathom even the thought of surviving, and so didn't fathom it; fathomed instead life as a series of lives, variations on a theme that sheltered me. The lie being: It's not Ralph's death that's woven into everything like a secret key, it's his *not death*, the *not* permanence—the extra beat awaited, the mutability of every fact, the grinning, eyebrows-raised chance that something's waiting even if it's not. These were my sly ruses and slick tricks, my surface intrigues and wire-pulls, all played *against* permanence, not *to* it. (357)

Frank's epiphany – a notion he had always disdained as a lie of literary contrivance and narrative manipulation – is a moment of enormous significance in the trilogy. Frank is doing nothing less here than dismantling the entire conceptual foundations of his adult life and revealing the fault-lines in his personal identity. The past, and Frank's lifelong suppression of it, have finally come back with a vengeance, exposing a fundamental aspect of his emotional life as an exercise in self-deception. The entire conceptual apparatus of the previous two novels is named and denounced as so many strategies to avoid the truth of Ralph's absolute disappearance and the harsh fact that his son can exist only in the ethereal element of Frank's memory. And at the core of Frank's crisis and epiphany lie his flawed notions of human temporality and conceptions of character and self.

From the outset Frank has fled self-definition. At the end of the chapter on *The Sportswriter* it was remarked how ungraspable Frank's identity was, how he seemed to be "constituted more by difference than by sameness, or by non-permanence more than permanence", a consequence of his systematic cultivation of impermanence. By *The Lay of the Land*, however, he is noting in himself a lack of "inner essence", and a need to find a "recognizable and persuasive semblance of a character", the remedy to which was his decree that the Permanent Period had inaugurated a new substantiality of self. This self was to come into existence through a willed intensity of being in the present, in other words through exactly the same strategy employed by Frank ever since *The Sportswriter* days.

But, as Frank now discovers in his epiphany, life as a succession of presents, as "a series of lives" (and, therefore, identities), did not constitute – did not institute – permanence, but, rather, "played *against*" it. The Permanent Period had changed nothing, left Frank's self as ephemeral and dispersed as it always was and let him continue to nurture his unacknowledged ambivalence about Ralph's death. And this is so because the one dimension where permanence of character, a recognizable self, is to be constructed, and where, crucially, the truth of the absoluteness of Ralph's death is located, is the past, the very temporal dimension to which Frank's adult life has been dedicated to avoiding. In straining to live in the present he has been running away from his past.

The great irony of this flight is that Frank, unknowingly, became profoundly stuck in the past of Ralph's unaccepted death, while all the time convinced that he was living life resoundingly in the present. He simply abandoned his past in his flight from the unbearable truths it enclosed, thus avoiding the slow accommodation with grief and the slow evolution into a post-loss self. Frank's understanding of time and identity are nicely captured in his advice to his Sponsoree, Marguerite, when he tells her that what passes for character are "memories, presents, futures, desires, hatreds, et cetera. And it's our job to govern those as much as we can" (106). Frank scrupulously avoids using the word "past" here, yet he acknowledges through the term "memories" that the past has an inevitable role to play in the construction of self. But, true to his philosophy of past-avoidance, he counsels Marguerite to "govern" the emergence of self through ignoring the past: "Sometimes we think that before we can go on with life we have to get the past all settled .... But that's not true. We'd never get anyplace if it was" (107). It is precisely the contrary that now proves to be true: in not "settling" his own past, including the past of his son's death, he has led a life of avoidance and delusion, culminating now in his crushing distress.[9]

In the aftermath of the collapse of his Permanent Period philosophy, and in words that echo the theories of identity of MacIntyre, Taylor and Ricoeur, Frank is able to answer the question he had set himself in the prologue about his readiness to meet his Maker: "When I asked what it was I had to do before I was sixty, maybe it's just to accept my whole life and my whole self in it" (358). With his abandonment of the demarcated, present-only temporality of the Permanent Period, Frank now inscribes his life and identity within the unity of a whole life. Alasdair MacIntyre, we recall, insists that temporal atomization in the construction of self – as practised by Frank through isolating his present from his past – inevitably leads to a form of unintelligibility, and that the narrative gathering together of past, present and future is the only means through which a wholeness of character, or self, can emerge – "a concept of a self whose unity resides in the unity of a narrative which links birth to life to death as narrative beginning to middle to end".[10] MacIntyre everywhere insists on our embeddedness in history at the level of individual actions, of our own lived lives and at the level of the society and traditions into

---

[9] Marguerite's living room provides the perfect visual metaphor for Frank's counsel to forget the past. Frank is sure that Marguerite is actually Betty "Dusty" Barksdale, with whom he once had a sexual liaison. Former wife of Fincher Barksdale (from *The Sportswriter*), Betty is now reincarnated as Marguerite Purcell, widow of a wealthy second husband, and with virtually every trace of her past effaced. Her clinically white living room gives no indication of "prior human habitation" (100), just as her entire self-presentation seeks to give no evidence of her previous identity.

[10] MacIntyre, *After Virtue*, 205. See the second chapter on *The Sportswriter* for a fuller discussion of the theories of selfhood of MacIntyre and Charles Taylor.

which we are born: "I am born with a past; and to try to cut myself off from that past ... is to deform my present relationships."[11] Charles Taylor, too, emphasizes the temporal wholeness of a life as the prerequisite to identity: "In order to have a sense of who we are, we have to have a notion of how we have become, and of where we are going."[12] For Taylor, time, history and narrative are the inseparable components of our becoming into selfhood: "I can only know myself through the history of my maturations and regressions, overcomings and defeats. My self-understanding necessarily has temporal depth and incorporates narrative."[13]

For all his talk at the beginning of the Permanent Period of seeking a substantiality of self, Frank has been content to understand selfhood as a form of "self-actualizing invisibility" (275), a simple "doin' and bein'" in the present that actually conceals time and self. Elsewhere, he mocks the "hallowed concept of character" (231) and prefers to conceive the mind as metaphor rather than manager. Yet, at the moment of crisis, when his Permanent Period defences crumble, Frank is exposed to the full fury of pure "present-ness", a state free of temporal context that reduces experience to what he can only call "*be-ness*" (349) in the present moment, a quasi-Beckettian clamourousness of unmediated being and feeling. Frank's life "as a series of lives, variations on a theme", has led merely to what he now terms "self-extinguishment" (402), his contemporary version of the much sought-after impermanence of self of *The Sportswriter*.

The disconnection and fragmentation associated with Frank's absence of coherent selfhood is actually quite perceptible in the novel, beyond anything that Frank specifically has to say about it: his days seem without structure or shape, an accumulation of independent comings and goings that create a palpable sense of disjointedness and purposelessness. Mere succession seems to be the only structure available to Frank as he bounces from one duty to the next, an effect, it often seems, of the absence of the managing and configuring interventions of self.

Richard Ford has very deliberately placed the question of identity at the centre of his novel's concerns, as is clear in an interview he gave to coincide with the book's launch:

---

[11] *Ibid.*, 221.
[12] Taylor, *Sources of the Self*, 47.
[13] *Ibid.*, 50.

Western religious culture is founded on the notion of a soul, and then after that a character. Much of literature presumes that there are such things as characters, that is to say, we have an essence which is solid, and which is persistent. And what I found is that it just ain't so. We have histories, we have expectations, we have our pasts, we have our days, and we create this notion of character to forcibly assert that that means essence, that that means a wholeness about ourselves, to ... fight off those qualities of inessentialness, to fight off those qualities of insubstantiality.[14]

Ford poses the problem of identity – as he does for Frank – in terms of a substantial self, an essence. These are indeed the terms one sometimes encounters, particularly in the discourse of analytical philosophy. Yet it is the narrative construction of identity, and the creation of a narrated, not substantial, self that is best placed to respond to the predicament described above by Richard Ford – our "histories", our "expectations" and our "pasts" are indeed the non-substantial constituents from which we seek to construct a sense of self that will counter dispersal and disconnection, "inessentialness" and "insubstantiality".

Like Richard Ford, Paul Ricoeur also emphasizes personal history in the construction of selfhood, but does so to counter the notion of a substantial self, insisting that personal identity "can be articulated only in the temporal dimension of human existence".[15] Wresting the concept of identity away from its meaning as "sameness", in which certain philosophical traditions proposing a substantial self have imprisoned it, and understanding identity rather as "selfhood", Ricoeur investigates personal identity as "a form of permanence in time which can be connected to the question 'who?' inasmuch as it is irreducible to any question of 'what?'"[16] Is it possible, in other words, asks Ricoeur, that the answer to the question "who?" might be other than the "what" of a substantial self? In replying affirmatively Ricoeur insists that personal identity, the raw material of which is embedded inescapably in time, can only be understood as a dialectic, as a constant exchange between the existence of permanent features – what

---

[14] Gabriel Gbadamosi, Interview with Richard Ford, *Night Waves*, BBC Radio 3, 27 September 2006.
[15] Ricoeur, *Oneself as Another*, 114.
[16] *Ibid.*, 118.

he calls "character", by which he means "the set of distinctive marks which permit the reidentification of a human individual as being the same" – and the change to which a human existence in time is inevitably exposed.

Ricoeur's articulation of identity as a dynamic evolution over time finds a privileged mediation through narrative, specifically through the operation of emplotment in the stories we narrate about our lives: narrative is the "specific mediator between the pole of character, where *idem* [sameness] and *ipse* [selfhood] tend to coincide, and the pole of self-maintenance, where selfhood frees itself from sameness".[17] The self to which one has access through the mediation of narrative is never fixed, or permanent; it is configured, then endlessly refigured as it passes through the filters of revised self-tellings. Agreeing with MacIntyre and Taylor, Ricoeur insists that it is only narrative that is capable of accounting for the temporal condition of the self and for the exchange between permanence and change over a whole life (Sally's departure, Frank's cancer and Ann's revived affections for Frank represent the kind of change that undermine the immutability of permanence).

Frank's great error has been to seek to conjure up a self within the present alone, a strategy that produced only a "series of lives", a succession of disconnected self-imaginings that cut him off from the defining event of his adult life, the death of his son. Ultimately, Frank oscillated in his life between sheer difference (in *The Sportswriter*) and contrived permanence (the Permanent Period), but never found a balance between the two, never understood personal identity as a necessary exchange between permanence and change, and between past, present and future. Nor did he fully accept Ralph's death; he did not carry the grief with him as part of his evolving story, to be configured and reconfigured as his life progressed, gradually to be woven into the wider story of his whole life and experience, a more propitious terrain for true acceptance finally to be earned.

In the early hours of Thanksgiving Day Frank resolves to embrace the implication of his epiphany. But old habits die hard, and Frank has found a new concept through which to understand his post-Permanent Period existence – the Next Level. The neutrality of the new title, however, indicates a greater circumspection in that it does not seek to

---

[17] *Ibid.*, 119. "Emplotment", with its emphasis on a dynamic operation, is Ricoeur's preferred term for "plot".

corral life and human temporality into a rigid dogma, and denotes merely the existence of a new phase in his life. If the nature of the new era has yet to be fully understood, acceptance nonetheless will be at its core, and Ralph's death is the first great meaning to be accepted.

Beyond that, Frank's anecdotal articulations of the Next Level seem to have a lot to do with a simple desire to say "yes" to as much in life as possible. Accepting Ralph's death, of course, means consenting to its wider implication, namely "that things, both good and sour, have to be accounted for" (379). This is the moral burden of acceptance, which is an acceptance of responsibility, and that extends, moreover – above all, even – to accepting the moral responsibility for himself. The Permanent Period phase of "self-extinguishment" is to be followed by self-acceptance: in the spirit of accepting his "whole life" and his "whole self", Frank says "yes" to the person he has become, and remains: "I am this thing, seller of used and cast-off houses, and I am not other .... gone in a gulp are all the roles I might still inhabit but won't" (402). Frank the evader, the one-time fantasist, the avoider of history and self-definition, has come to rest in his own inescapable identity.

In the novel's Prologue Frank discovered that he still had a taste for life, that there was something "still there to be found out and that could make me happy" (7). In other words, life held important and as-yet unknown meanings, the thirst for which his cancer had not quenched. The novel goes on to thematize Frank's quest for meaning by way of the recurring opposition between the examined and unexamined life, and by the continuous and urgent reflection on the meaning and value of life by a man threatened with the imminent loss of his own life. In one sense it could be said that the defining quality of the three Frank Bascombe novels is the manner in which life is so microscopically examined: drawing on unexceptional daily life in its slow unfolding rather than on compressed dramatic events, these lengthy novels focus on short periods of time, the better to examine the moment-to-moment sensations and significance of human existence.

This is another aspect of the novels' moral vision, in that life so depicted confronts us with the moral imperative to – as Richard Ford would put it – pay attention to our lives. Frank and his friends and acquaintanceships are mostly in late middle age; they have accumulated, as is pointed out on several occasions, much life experience, and are now prone to reflect on life in a more existential manner, particularly as death is more present in their lives. The refrain in *The Lay of the Land* that "life is strange" is just one indication of lives being seriously examined. In that context, the events and experiences of the Tuesday and Wednesday of pre-Thanksgiving may be understood as life's offerings to Frank in his quest for new meaning.

However, if life is still valued by Frank, living it is proving arduous. From the Tuesday morning traffic jam onwards, he has found himself undergoing events rather than directing them – in the space of two days he has been the victim of Ann's declaration of love and its retraction, Bob Butts's assault, Lester's insults, Mike's vacillations, Wade's hostility, police suspicion, has had his car window smashed and has experienced the overwhelming return of grief at his son's death. And all of this while still undergoing the consequences of Sally's departure and the diagnosis of his cancer. It is these experiences that create the growing sense of events gathering momentum and sweeping Frank along, provoking a mood of instability and the impression of a society and an individual spinning out of control. This sensation is intensified on Thanksgiving Day morning when events accelerate further, precipitating Frank on a headlong rush towards the disaster that the novel has announced since its beginning in a violent act.

The single event he manages to initiate himself on Thanksgiving Day – an attempt to get together with a woman friend to find some consolation amidst the growing agitation of events – ends in failure. In a scene that recalls the desolate Ground Zero Burg scene on Easter Sunday evening in *The Sportswriter*, Frank now finds himself alone in closed-up Ortley Beach on Thanksgiving Day morning, unable to find Bernice, not wanting to go home and feeling generally frazzled by events. Noticing an X traced in the sky by two jet contrails, which he interprets as a signal to locate his own position in the wider scheme of life's unfolding, Frank considers where events have brought him, and can only record that his latest, and last, defence, the acceptance mode of the Next Level, is no barrier against life's clamour. Frank reaches an end-point here, finds himself without resource, confronted finally with the futility of his conceptualizations. He had conceived and embraced the Next Level – much as he had with the Permanent Period – as (in an interesting nod to narrative identity) his final "story, what the audience would know once my curtain closed—my, so-to-speak, character". But the Next Level must go the way of his other pointless conceptualized attempts to manipulate time and control meaning:

> Except now there's *more*? Just when you think you've been admitted to the boy-king's burial chamber and can breathe the rich, ancient captured air with somber satisfaction, you find out it's just another anteroom? That there's more that bears watching, more signs requiring interpretation, that what you thought was all, isn't? That this isn't *it*? That there's no *it*, only *is*. (436)

Acceptance of Ralph's death has not proved to be the foundation of an easeful new phase in his life. Conceptually modest as it may have been, the Next Level was nonetheless conceived as a final attempt to lock down Frank's sense of self and his place in the world. But, as he acknowledges here, meaning proliferates in all directions, and there is always more of it. There can be no fixed "it" of meaning or identity; there can only be a continuing "is" of being and becoming, and thus of identity – Frank's "story" cannot yet be fixed. With the Next Level dead in the water, with both meaning and events beyond control, and feeling remote from all his family members, Frank drives home on the afternoon of Thanksgiving Day prey to dread and feeling exposed: "events have left life and my grasp on the future in as fucked-up a shape as I can imagine them" (440).

In a final ominous rush of events at his house involving a visit from a detective, tension with Paul and unsettling news about Sally and Clarissa, Frank is propelled towards the denouement of a particularly American drama, one prefigured as far back as *Independence Day* and foreshadowed everywhere in *The Lay of the Land* in the depiction of unstable American society. The "fear of the other, [the] violence around the periphery of life" that Ford wished to evoke in the novel, and that is enacted in its own way at the highest level of the land in the division and hostility on display at the election recounts, culminate in gun violence, with the shooting dead of the Feensters and the wounding of Frank by two young Russians.

In a country born in violence, and expanded and conquered through the violence of the descendents of its new immigrant population, and in a country that elevates freedom above all other values,[18] it is fitting that the national holiday conceived as a celebration of the nation's heritage – and at the end of a trilogy of novels deeply concerned with American culture and identity – should culminate in gun violence perpetrated on the native population by newly arrived immigrants. The celebration of Thanksgiving in *The Lay of the Land*, no more than Frank himself, will not be allowed to escape the past.

Thanksgiving
The Wampanoag Native people had inhabited south-eastern Massachusetts for over 12,000 years when English traders began to arrive there in the early seventeenth century, carrying and spreading disease and often kidnapping Wampanoag men and bringing them back to England. When the *Mayflower* Separatists and Puritans[19] arrived in New Plymouth (Patuxet to the Wampanoag) in December 1620, the Wampanoag village was empty, the population decimated by disease brought earlier by English traders. While exploring the territory before finally settling in New Plymouth, the Puritans discovered and stole Wampanoag supplies. They also considered that the land was theirs for the taking, believing the Native people incapable of proper stewardship of the land as, visibly, it was not exploited in the only way it should be – the European way.

In early 1621 an alliance between the Puritans and the Wampanoag was concluded, allowing a Wampanoag man, Tisquantum (also known

---

[18] One of the most cherished freedoms in America is the right to bear arms, to the extent that this right is protected by the Bill of Rights. The American Constitution was written in 1787 and ratified a year later, and emerged out of a battle between the proponents of a strong central government and the advocates of states' rights. The goal of the Bill of Rights was to rectify what many saw as inadequate protection in the Constitution of individual freedoms from the potential tyranny of the federal government. The Bill of Rights, in the form of the first ten amendments to the Constitution, placed explicit limitations on federal power and introduced explicit protections of individual rights. The second of these amendments runs as follows: "A well regulated Militia, being necessary to the security of a free State, the right of the people to keep and bear Arms, shall not be infringed" (*The Declaration of Independence and The Constitution of the United States*, New York: Bantam, 1998, 78).
[19] Separatists and Puritans were actually different groups, and members of both groups were among the *Mayflower* settlers. The latter term, however, has come to designate both groups of settlers.

as Squanto), previously kidnapped and taken to England but back home now and speaking English, to live among the English settlers. He advised them on what to grow and how to fertilize the land. The first successful harvest was celebrated by the settlers over three days in autumn 1621, attended by Wampanoag leader, Massasoit, and ninety of his men, a secular event erroneously labelled the "First Thanksgiving" (the Wampanoag had long celebrated the gathering of the harvest). It was not until 1623 that the first religious giving of thanks was offered by the Puritans to mark the ending of a two-month drought that threatened that year's crops.

The peace between Native peoples and the colonists lasted a mere fifteen years and ended in savage violence during the massacre by the colonists (assisted by rival Native tribes) of Pequot natives in Mystic in 1637. Worsening relations between the colonists and Native peoples, stemming from expansionist demands for land among the colonists and resentment among Native tribes at their treatment by the colonists, led to the bloody "King Philip's War" in 1675-76. The Native peoples were defeated and many of them sold into slavery in the West Indies. The colonists declared a special Thanksgiving to celebrate their victory. The subsequent violence inflicted upon Native Americans by colonizing white immigrants in the building of the American nation has been amply recorded.

The Thanksgiving holiday is surrounded by myth, but the least that may be said about it is that it is a celebration not easily dissociated from violence, and that, in the popular evocation of the origins of the tradition, the presence and fate of the Native peoples are often expunged. Both of these tendencies are visible in the Presidential Proclamation of Thanksgiving Day 2006.[20] President George W. Bush spoke only of the "early settlers [giving] thanks for their safe arrival and pilgrims [enjoying] a harvest feast to thank God for allowing them to survive a harsh winter in the New World". He then moved quickly on to invoke the Revolutionary War and the Civil War, before switching to the "freedoms ... defended by our Armed Forces throughout the generations", up to the present day.[21] In a very short

---

[20] The most recent at the time of writing.
[21] http://www.whitehouse.gov/news/releases/2006/11/20061116-8.html (7/12/2006). Frank's view is that the annual Presidential Proclamation of Thanksgiving is

proclamation the essential messages are the celebration of the Pilgrim myth and the association of Thanksgiving with armed force. As a consequence of the routine effacement of the Native peoples from the Thanksgiving story and the oppression they suffered since the arrival of the English colonists in 1621, Native Americans, since 1970, observe Thanksgiving Day as a National Day of Mourning.

Richard Slotkin, in his landmark study on the power of the frontier myth on the American imagination, and on the violence celebrated in this mythology, associates the origins of the myth firmly with the arrival of the colonists in 1620: "The first colonists saw in America an opportunity to regenerate their fortunes, their spirits, and the power of their church and nation; but the means to that regeneration ultimately became the means of violence, and the myth of regeneration through violence became the structuring metaphor of the American experience."[22] The colonists were indeed the first systematic violent oppressors of the Native peoples. Unable to convert them to Christianity, and blocked by them in their drive to expand their territory, the "Puritans", notes Slotkin, adopted "a policy of exterminating the Indians or, at best, reducing them to a semicaptive status",[23] and "came to define their relationship to the New World in terms of violence and warfare".[24]

The Thanksgiving celebration, then, has inescapable violent associations, fully realized in Richard Ford's novel. Frank's Thanksgiving Day ends in violence and murder, an event that, along with the newspaper report of the classroom killing that had so animated him a week earlier, frames the entire narrative. In between, the gun violence attending two property transactions when he lived in Haddam is remembered, and the Columbine School massacre of 1999 is also evoked; in addition, a bomb attack at the Haddam hospital kills a man, and there is a regular police presence in the novel. The simmering menace of violence (also present in *Independence Day*) and the volatile mood encountered by Frank in his contacts with American society combine to thoroughly undermine the ostensible

---

"generally full of platitudes and horseshit" (466). Be that as it may, the platitudes are revealing.

[22] Richard Slotkin, *Regeneration Through Violence: The Mythology of the American Frontier, 1600-1860*, Hanover, NH: Wesleyan UP, 1973, 5.

[23] *Ibid.*, 42.

[24] *Ibid.*, 56.

spirit of the national celebration, as does the generally critical evocation in the novel of the origins and meaning of Thanksgiving. The Pilgrims, or Puritans, are caustically referred to by Frank on a number of occasions; the Pilgrim Village Interpretive Center is satirized; and the fate of the Wampanoag is recalled, for whom Thanksgiving, as Frank puts it, "celebrates deceit, genocide and man's indifference to who owns what" (26).[25] Elsewhere, Frank's unhappy pre-shooting experience of Thanksgiving, as well as his general view of the celebration, has him refer to it as "bullshit" (348) and as the "recapitulative, Puritan and thus most treacherous of holidays" (349).

At a national level the holiday is presented as an opportunity for a consumerist binge, one, moreover, that distracts Americans from reflecting on the state of their country. It is given to one of Frank's clients, Clare Suddruth, to highlight explicitly the country's pre-9/11 frailties, the portrayal of which was one of Ford's "points in writing this book". For Clare, America has "foundation problems" (283), with enemies abroad and a loss of purpose at home, while continuing nonetheless to live under the illusion of invincibility. It is an image consistent with the mood and spirit of the country that prevails in the novel: there is a palpable sense of a society in a state of flux, a society that is fidgety and casting around for meaning, and whose members seem to be out of place, in search of an identity and spiritual peace. It is this agitation, no doubt, that has Frank speak of America at one point as "our frail, unruly union" (470). The self-absorption, the refuge in sectional identifications, the assertive group identities, the undercurrent of fear, the general enervation and the instinctive recourse to violence coalesce to portray a country pulsing with a nervous but ill-focused energy, internally divided, and no longer seeming to know where its own next level is to be found.

As Frank is transported by ambulance to hospital, he resolves to write to the President to tell him that it is important that the country's leaders, with special responsibility for "the life span of a whole republic", move on "to the Next Level but never give up the Forever Concept" (466). The American republic, too, has its myths, the stories

---

[25] The connection of the novel's events to the Thanksgiving celebration of 1623 is subtly evoked through the repeated references to the drought in New Jersey in 2000. On Thanksgiving morning Frank is able to record, Pilgrim-like, "last night's drought-ending rain" (367).

that inaugurated, constitute and narrate its identity. Yet narratives from and about the past need to be opened out to embrace a changing world and different circumstances. The myth of the frontier is one mired in violence, yet is still being played out in contemporary America – the myth of the frontier survives, except that the frontier itself does not. As Slotkin points out: "A people unaware of its myths is likely to continue living by them."[26] Frank observes that "Violence, that imposter, foreshortens our expectancies, our logics, our next days, our afternoons, our sweet evenings, our whole story" (469). America has let a defining feature of its identity become fossilized into an inflexible and self-destructive narrative glorifying freedom, individualism and violence, to the point that it often seems to constitute its "whole story". As Frank's and the nation's dilemmas finally coincide, the need in both for a regeneration of identity, for an evolving narrative and mythology, is one of the compelling messages of *The Lay of the Land*.

The temporal structure at the end of *The Lay of the Land* replicates that of *The Sportswriter* and *Independence Day*, just as it has done throughout: in all three novels there is a final, titled chapter that functions as an epilogue, a time for taking retrospective stock of experiences, examining consciences and drawing conclusions. The "Thanksgiving" chapter at the end of *The Lay of the Land* moves forward in time to late December as Frank and Sally fly to the Mayo Clinic in Minnesota for Frank's first post-treatment check-up.

As in the two previous novels, events have had a cathartic effect. The conspicuous disjunction throughout the novel between the spirit of Thanksgiving and the spirit of the nation has given way now to a truer spirit of Thanksgiving – here, in the airplane, Americans are happy to be together, gaining strength from the knowledge of a shared experience and destiny. The empathy, vulnerability and fatalism of the clinic-bound passengers, accompanied by their spouses and partners, produce a certain serenity and a kinder contact between people. All these "veterans of this life" (483), as Frank calls them, are obliged to deal with either the possibility or certainty of imminent death and have, as a consequence, a transformed relationship to life. They have already arrived at their own next level, where there is no time for the

---

[26] Slotkin, *Regeneration Through Violence*, 4.

delusions of life lived as if death were not its only outcome. Frank's post-epiphany mood of acceptance finds its natural environment here, and the chapter is imbued with a dignified awareness of human transience and the knowledge that acceptance makes a better companion for mortality than resistance. Proximity to death, moreover, is a powerful inducement to examine one's life – we learn now that Frank and those closest to him have emerged from recent events with a revised sense of what is important in their lives.

In the wake of the shooting, Frank and Paul have extricated themselves from the anachronistic father-adolescent-son mode in which they had become stuck, and have moved beyond their quick anger and mutual incomprehension. Paul is "not as furious as he was before" (471), and Frank, if still not quite able to understand his son, can accept that he is a "different kind of good man from most" (482). Having accepted the death of his dead son, Frank seems better able now to accept the life of his living son.

And Sally is back living with Frank, although, as she said in her letter to him, she was unsure whether she wanted "to be married to [him] anymore" (383). Nonetheless, she has seemed to Frank to be "unaccountably happy" (471) since her return. Like Frank, she has had her bruising experience with the past. Sally was unable to heed another of the novel's repeated temporal injunctions, that – as Frank's friend Lloyd put it – "You can't enter the same stream twice" (72). Frank and Sally failed in a similar way to deal with a traumatic past event. Both tried to ignore and defeat time by leaping beyond it: Frank ran away from loss and leaped towards the future, and thus failed to fully accept the reality of his son's death, while Sally tried to leap backwards into the past, as if the past could simply be relived. Time, however, this novel tells us, is the inescapable human element, and will not be by-passed. Frank and Sally have learned that true healing after loss will be achieved only through the slow release of earned acceptance in time. The serenity of acceptance, however, has had to be won the hard way by both of them, through experiencing a form of double death of a loved one: Frank experienced the actual death of Ralph and then its return through the irruption of suppressed grief, while Sally experienced the disappearance and then the actual death of Wally.

In the healing mood of this post-catharsis period the two important troubled relationships in Frank's life, with Paul and Sally, have moved back into their proper orbit, and, in so doing, counterbalance to some extent the emotional disequilibrium seen to be at the heart of the fretful human contact in the novel. Love, in other words, now gets its due and receives its proper expression. Frank can now say without misgiving that he loves Paul, and, in response to Sally's search in her letter for the word that would speak the truth of the "human state" (384, 471) that exists between them, Frank concludes: "*Ideal* probably wouldn't be the right word; sympathy and necessity might be important components. Though truthfully, love seems to cover the ground best of all" (471). Here again is the expression of the moral vision of Ford's novel, the obligation both to pay attention to those we purport to love and to examine the lives we lead. The self-absorption and extreme individualism depicted in the novel are the antithesis of these imperatives. If love has been associated with failure in the novel, it is not so much that love fails people as people fail love.

Much of the final chapter is given over to Frank's own self-examination. The Next Level is mentioned but seems to attach itself to nothing more than a commitment to an acceptance already conceded. Events, in any case, took over and moved Frank into a different, lower-case, next level. The changes now deemed necessary by Frank are of a very personal nature, small improvements as opposed to the grandiose contrivances of his conceptualizing days. Notably, he sees the need to become "more intuitive" (476), which would represent a true liberation from the old inflexibilities of mystery, the Existence Period and the Permanent Period.

The three Frank Bascombe novels are all structured to allow a moral reflection at their conclusion, and the moral tone is evident here in Frank's talk about "Self-improvement" (477), but also in his musing about the concept of "good". The reader is reminded of the concluding passages of Ford's novella, "The Womanizer". There, in another conclusion devoted to an examination of conscience, the male protagonist, Martin Austin, accepts that he has been deceived by his fixed view of himself and that he had also lost his orientation to the "good", represented by his wife and their marriage. Morality and identity are also the deep concerns of Frank's final ruminations. In seeking to be more intuitive, he wishes now to move away from the fixed identities of his conceptualized phases. Like Martin Austin, he is examining his identity as a moral identity, checking, as Charles Taylor would put it, his orientation in relation to the good: "Do I see good as even a possibility?", Frank asks himself (476). In his affirmative response, and in a further gesture of acceptance and responsibility (he blames himself for the melancholy tone of his relationship with Clarissa), Frank makes the moral adjustments that he hopes will prepare him for what lies ahead. Although he has been more sinned against than sinner in the novel, his new reckoning with the past brings his whole life back into play, and demands a settling of the past he had once abjured.

Among the important themes of *The Lay of the Land* are time and the human struggle to cope with the changes it brings over a lifetime. Fittingly, Frank's final thoughts are concerned with the entirety of a human life. And Richard Ford finds a grandeur of imagery equal to the magnitude of the moment. As Frank's plane descends towards the earth, he sees the snowy landscape spread wide and white beneath him. The vastness of the view reminds us of the new wholeness of vision now available to Frank, just as its wintry aspect reminds us that time has carried him to the later stages in his pilgrim's journey through life. In the same way that Frank returned to land after his self-actualizing swim at the beginning of the novel, sure of his continued commitment to life, now he comes back to land again at its close, not so much with the answer to the great existential question posed in the Prologue, but with the knowledge that any such answers are provisional. The apparent immutability of his post-epiphany state, the ostensible condition of ultimate necessity, has itself had to yield to time and change: "get shot in the heart and live, and you'll learn some things about necessity—and quick" (484). For a man who talked a lot about change but who spent his life trying to defeat it by manipulating and fixing time, Frank now lets time carry him along. Having first determined after the shooting to have the ashes of his cremated body dispersed at sea off the Jersey Shore, he has finally decided to leave his body to science, to the future. Here, too, the final imagery of the vastness of the earth, of the larger perspective on life, is in keeping with Frank's wish to "[make] a contribution": his "death and life" is "a small event", and life will go on after his death. Another contact with the sea when he came out of hospital, standing at the absolute edge of land and life, had communicated to Frank the extra beat, the only necessity available to us on our "human scale": "to live, to live, to live it out" (485).

In this novel committed to the contemplation of being and time and human transience, the commanding symbol is Paul's time capsule, which is "buried" behind Frank's house at the ocean's edge, in a "quiet ceremony" (482) the day Frank leaves hospital after the shooting. This is the moment of ultimate acceptance and of peace finally achieved: the burial of the "coffin-shaped" capsule (386) in "a hole the size of a small grave" (365) represents the symbolic, final burial of Ralph, just as it also reminds Frank of his own mortality. And in entrusting objects to discovery and scrutiny by unknown future generations, the time capsule also symbolizes, and underlines again, the smallness of the human scale of things, the value of the examined life and the human passage through time. Symbolic, too, is the rediscovered harmony in human affairs, testified at the ceremony by the presence of the reunited Frank and Sally, the reunited Clarissa and old girlfriend, Cookie, and by the presence of Paul with Jill. The time-capsule burial ceremony has a legitimacy that the planned but uncelebrated Thanksgiving Day family meal did not have. Now is a proper time for celebration and to give thanks, at least at a personal level: the novel allows only personal reconciliation, leaving the direction and destiny of the "frail, unruly union" unresolved, but a cause for great anxiety.

The plane descends to earth, to a vast and open and white expanse ready to welcome Frank back to life after his brush with death. It is up to him now to write the rest of his life on the palimpsest of the surface of the earth, to leave his own small and transient trace on the ever-changing lay of the land.

CHAPTER 7

"THE WOMANIZER"

IDENTITY AND THE GOOD

"The Womanizer", one of the two novellas in the three-story collection, *Women with Men*, is, in both its structural features and moral thematic focus, something of a modern parable: the story outlines a situation and circumstances from everyday life, confronts the protagonist with a moral dilemma and makes clear the consequences of his choice. As a modern tale, however, "The Womanizer" is much more complex than the brief narratives of the New Testament parables, the best-known examples of the form. In Ford's story the wider circumstances of the protagonist's life, as well as the particular situation he finds himself in, are presented as the complex causes of the moral dilemma confronting him; the options open to him in the choice he faces – what may be gained and what may be lost – are made clear; and the protagonist's reflections, as he weighs up his present life and considers his future, receive extensive treatment. But for all its complexity and modernity, the story remains a simple moral tale, as the bluntly explicit title suggests, and is constructed according to a moral dilemma in which unambiguous choices must be made, and where the consequences of making the wrong moral choice are powerfully portrayed. In these features, it resembles the non-allegorical parables of the New Testament, and specifically those that offer a model, either positive or negative, as an example.[1]

Martin Austin is a forty-four-year-old Chicago-based sales representative for a company that sells expensive printing paper. He is married, has no children, and his wife, Barbara, has a successful career

---

[1] The narrative of the Good Samaritan is an example of the New Testament parable as a model, while that of the Sheep and the Goats is an allegorical parable.

in real estate. He has responsibility for European sales, so frequently visits major European cities. The story deals with a sales trip Austin[2] makes to Paris during which he meets a French woman, Joséphine Belliard, to whom he is attracted. He extends his stay in Paris by a few days to spend time with her, although they do not sleep with each other. He finally goes back home to Oak Grove, Illinois, feels unsettled in the days after his return, has a row with Barbara and takes a flight back to Paris to be with Joséphine. The story concludes in a dramatic event that destroys any chance of a relationship with Joséphine, an event precipitated by the moral failing in Austin that occasioned the wider moral predicament in which he finds himself in the first place.

That predicament resolves itself into a stark choice for Austin between continuing in his marriage with Barbara, whom he has been with for twenty-two years, or leaving her to develop a possible relationship with Joséphine. The story is very precisely structured according to the evolution of Austin's unfolding moral dilemma. It is divided into eight sections: the first four recount the nature of the moral dilemma as understood and articulated by Austin and explore the grounds upon which he makes his decision; sections five and six represent a space of transition and suspension between his leaving Barbara and his returning to Joséphine; and the final two sections deal with the events surrounding the renewal of his relationship with Joséphine and the consequences of these events, which portend an uncertain future for Austin and a sober period of reflection by him on his character and moral identity. The discussion in this chapter will align itself with this very deliberate structure, the better to understand a story deeply concerned with the notion of becoming, in this case with Austin's departure from the person he has been and his becoming a person whose moral transformation he is left anxiously contemplating at the conclusion of the story.

---

[2] The author's view of his character is subtly communicated to us in the manner in which he refers to him. Martin Austin is referred to by his second name, as is Charley Matthews in "Occidentals". These characters, Ford has remarked, "are not admirable—even to me" (*Conversations with Richard Ford* [202]). Ford has clearly more affection for Frank Bascombe, and the latter is always referred to by his first name. The sense of distance from Austin – for both author and reader – is accentuated by the third-person narration.

Austin meets Joséphine at a cocktail party given by one of his clients, a publishing company in which she is a sub-editor. They have dinner that evening, after which he leaves her home in a taxi and goes back to his hotel. The first indication of Austin's character and intentions occurs when he makes "an aimless, angling call" to her the next day. It is not completely aimless, however: "Maybe he could sleep with her—not that he even thought that. It was just a possibility, an inevitable thought."[3] We have already seen, in the first chapter on *The Sportswriter*, that Richard Ford "never believed we really sin in thought, only in our deeds", so one might see Austin as simply having the "inevitable thought" that might occur to a man like him when alone in a foreign city. But Austin sins in deed as well – he has had affairs, or sexual encounters at least, with women while on his trips abroad. As he has dinner with Joséphine on the second evening he speculates that:

> Probably, if he wanted to press the matter of intimacy, he could take her back to his room—a thing he'd done before on business trips, and even if not so many times, enough times that to do so now wouldn't be extraordinary or meaningful, at least not to him. (7)

This is the casual, practised voice of experience. In this past behaviour, which for Austin is without consequence or moral stain, he earns the identity accorded him in the story's title.

A defining feature of Austin's attitude is the contrast between his initially nonchalant and even uncommitted attitude to a relationship with Joséphine and the persistence of his subsequent pursuit of her, particularly in the face of her general unresponsiveness to him. Austin finds certain of Joséphine's characteristics attractive, and specifically her attitude of not feigning an interest he would not expect her to feel "after one harmless encounter" (5). He thinks, too, as they have dinner together on the second evening, that perhaps neither of them was interested in intimacy with the other, and that although she "appealed to him in a surprising way ... he was not physically attracted to her". Yet he is bothered that he does not manage to elicit a more enthusiastic response from her during their second evening together. Austin "felt ready to begin a discourse on his own life" (7) and to

---

[3] Ford, *Women with Men*, 5. See note 8 in the Introduction for publication details. Further references to "The Womanizer" will be indicated parenthetically in the text.

speak intimately about certain discontents that had been troubling him in his middle age, but he does not have the opportunity to tell his story as Joséphine shows no interest in his personal life. He finds her "not very responsive, which he felt was unusual", although he also finds this appealing in her, in a way she was not "when he was only thinking about how she looked and whether he wanted to sleep with her" (8).

Austin's frame of mind, then, as they leave the restaurant on their second evening together, is a curious mixture of ambivalence and insistence. He seems uncommitted to any particular course of action and is prepared to see how things turn out, be it a sexual encounter or something else that Joséphine might initiate. Yet he believes that something should emerge from this time spent with her – it is important to him that something significant occurs to make these two evenings with her more than simply two pleasant dinners a man and a woman had together, but that both will quickly forget.

The immediate aftermath of their departure from the restaurant on the second evening reveals all of Austin's limp yearning and moral ambivalence. These are important scenes as it is here that Austin will deal with the competing calls on his conscience and decide on the course of action that will point him towards his definitive moral choice. As they walk to her car Joséphine surprisingly takes Austin's arm and pulls herself closer to him, saying that everything was "all confusion" to her (9), a gesture to which he readily responds by putting his arm around her shoulder and pulling her closer. But when they arrive at his hotel it is clear that, from Joséphine's perspective, the time they have spent together has come to an end: "Obviously she was waiting for him to get out, and he was in a quandary about what to do" (10). Even after Joséphine's linking of his arm in the street Austin had "decided" that his role would be that of "a good-intentioned escort for her" (9). But his own desire for a meaningful encounter has him persist, and he uses Joséphine, who has asked for nothing, to pursue his ostensibly noble train of thought: "he wanted to do *something* good, something unusual that would please her and make them both know an occurrence slightly out of the ordinary had taken place tonight" (9-10).

Yet all that guides him in his search for meaning is a primitive sense of wanting something, and a need to get something from this woman, knowing that he cannot make love to her. This "extraordinary something" (10) can be had in only two ways – either with or through Joséphine. He attempts first to elicit a co-authored pronouncement of shared meaning, a mutual promise that will move them on to deeper future meaning together, by taking Joséphine's hand and telling her, "in a sincere voice", that he would like to make her "happy somehow". Joséphine may well be going through a divorce and be unhappy at being the thinly-veiled protagonist of her husband's recently published tacky novel, but Austin's attempt to achieve meaning is entirely about his desires, only contingently about the two of them, and certainly not about her or her happiness. Joséphine ultimately responds "in a cold voice" by putting the moral argument to Austin he has weakly chosen to forget, and by piling on practical arguments that make his attempt to find a shared meaning almost absurd: "You are married. You have a wife. You live far away. In two days, three days, I don't know, you will leave" (11).

This is the moment to withdraw, where a certain dignity is still available and where Austin could manage to convince himself of the integrity of his original noble intentions. But in a single gesture he crosses a moral line and assumes a new moral identity: from being merely incongruous and histrionic, he becomes patriarchal and aggressive as he announces to Joséphine: "I'm at least going to kiss you. I feel like I'm entitled to do that, and I'm going to." The notion of sexual entitlement, if only for a kiss, amounts to a modern form of what the French in earlier times called *droit de cuissage*, a form of sexual obligation that Austin knows he is now guilty of: "She let herself be kissed, and Austin was immediately, cruelly aware of it. This is what was taking place: he was forcing himself on this woman." However, Austin's immediate reaction to the awareness of what he has done – he sees himself as "delusionary and foolish and pathetic" and wants to forget "the idiotic things he had just an instant before been thinking" (12) – does not deter him, and indeed conforms to the pattern in his behaviour of persisting in the face of evidence that his attentions are not sought after. He announces "very resolutely" to Joséphine that he would like to see her the next day, to which she agrees in the same way she had ended up kissing him – compliantly.

But Austin has nonetheless found his meaning: "Things were mostly as they had been before he'd kissed her, only he *had* kissed her—*they* had kissed—and that made all the difference in the world" (13). Yet, when set against the indignity of his behaviour, his momentary but piercing sense of shame, the palpable indifference of Joséphine and – the wider but unacknowledged context – the betrayal of his wife, Austin's sense of achievement indeed seems pathetic and his behaviour infantile. It is precisely this incongruity, the incommensurability of trivial achievement with his moral responsibility to himself and others, that is so striking and puzzling in Austin's behaviour, and that resolves itself into a simple question: what exactly does Martin Austin want?

At the heart of Austin's ill-defined quest for meaning lies a dissatisfaction with his life in middle age. Yet the person to whom he is most intimately bound, and with whom he has built this life, is nothing but a source of well-being and fulfilment:

> Barbara, in fact, was the most interesting and beautiful woman he'd ever known, the person he admired most. He wasn't looking for a better life. He wasn't looking for anything. He loved his wife. (8)

This love and admiration for his wife notwithstanding, the meaning that has sustained his adult life up to now will not, he now senses, be adequate to fulfil him for the rest of his life: he is bothered by an "uneasy, unanchored sensation he'd had lately of not knowing exactly how to make the next twenty-five years of life as eventful and important as the previous twenty-five" (7). Austin finds himself taking stock of his life in middle age and discovering that something is lacking, and that this lack concerns his future. He recognizes that he has much that is valuable in his life, wants to keep what he has, but wants something more as well. In his more pessimistic moments he finds that "very little pleased him at all" (36), that "ordinary life had the potential to grind you into dust", and that, in such circumstances, "unusual measures were called for" (33).

This is the unsettled and contradictory frame of mind he brings to Paris, one that allows him to affirm his love for and commitment to his wife, but that at the same time has him search for extra meaning in a relationship with another woman. The problem for Austin – and he recognizes it as a moral one – is to balance these competing demands of responsibility to his wife and his desire for experiences and meaning outside of their relationship. He cannot afford to conceive of his relationship with Joséphine as tawdry womanizing. It is this awareness that has him assemble a moral justification of his behaviour, which takes several forms: he decides that the eventual remedy for his dissatisfaction will require courage and the taking of responsibility for his life; he believes that what he is doing will have no impact on him, or on his life with Barbara; and he convinces himself that his interest in Joséphine is essentially altruistic and good, and is indeed quite moral – he understands his kiss ultimately as a satisfactory expression of his desire "to do right" in his contact with Joséphine (13).

This philosophy is expressed by Austin at the end of his first trip to Paris, as he contentedly anticipates his return home, satisfied that his "contact" with Joséphine left "No damage to control" (26). In a moment of self-conscious self-evaluation, lying on his bed and looking at his reflection in the hotel-room mirror, Austin smugly asks himself a great philosophical question about life, and finds the perfect self-serving answer:

> What does one want in the world? …. What does one want most of all, when one has experienced much, suffered some, persevered, tried to do good when good was within reach? What does this experience teach us that we can profit from? That the memory of pain, Austin thought, mounts up and lays a significant weight upon the present—a sobering weight—and the truth one has to discover is: exactly what's possible but also valuable and desirable between human beings, on a low level of event. (26-27)

Austin's notion of entitlement returns here, in this case the conviction that, having long and nobly borne the human existential burden, he has earned the right to lighten the load of his future years. Set against the universal and ostensibly objective terms of his question, his response, although highly equivocal, could represent a commendable enough doctrine. Yet the question is neither universal nor objective, despite the subject and object personal pronouns used – this is all about "I" and "me", and not about an impersonal or universal "one". And, in these personal terms, Austin's articulation of his moral philosophy allows a great deal of freedom to a man in his relationship with women.

The immediate context of Austin's musings underlines their purely personal nature and motivation. He holds off ringing Barbara on the chance that Joséphine might ring him and he could tell her he wished she was with him in his hotel room. Yet he notes how happy he felt to be returning home, and "to have not just a wife to come home to but this wife—Barbara, whom he both loved and revered" (26). When Joséphine does not ring, he rings Barbara, and has a rather tense conversation with her, after which he tries again, at two o'clock in the morning, to ring Joséphine. This, then, is how Austin's grand philosophical aspiration is to realized: "what's possible but also valuable and desirable between human beings" amounts to little more than wanting everything women have to offer while insisting that one's investment represents a "low level" involvement of minor consequences and no responsibility.

The great irony is that the very condition Austin wishes to assuage, the "unanchored sensation" he had been experiencing, is intensified as he seeks to put his philosophical conclusion into practice. As the story progresses Austin is physically and emotionally uprooted, flying from Paris to Chicago, then back to Paris, feeling increasingly homeless, unstable and out of place, no longer knowing, indeed, where home or his place is. He vacillates as he attempts to establish exactly where he belongs. On the last evening of his first stay in Paris he tells Joséphine that his interest in her "isn't a sidetrack" for him and that it is "real life" (24). Yet, back in Oak Grove, he wants to "take straight aim on his regular existence" (32) and lists the pleasurable components of the life he has built with Barbara. Lying in bed with her he dismisses his being "infatuated" with Joséphine and pronounces that that was "not real life—at least not the bedrock, real*est* life, the one everything depended on" (34).

If Austin vacillates, he nonetheless begins to see his life, and his mid-life malaise, in terms of a simple contrast between what Barbara and Joséphine represent. Life with Barbara is the "realest" one, solid, secure but somewhat routine, while his relationship with Joséphine becomes his fantasy life, novel and exciting. In the opening paragraph of the story we learn that Austin is taking Joséphine out "for a romantic dinner" (3) and, when he is back home, his mind attaches itself to the thrilling details of his contact with her – her way of walking, her soft arms, her whispered voice. And as he anticipates a confrontational conversation with Barbara he takes refuge immediately in the "Ebullience" he had felt after speaking to Joséphine on the phone. In Austin's male, middle-age mindset she seems to represent the frothy exhilaration of seduction and renewal, leaving him feeling "fiercely alive". Austin claims to be aware of the "illusory quality" of this, but longs for it "achingly" as it offers him "a break" from his life as a "[realist]" (41).

Martin Austin is a recognizable character in Richard Ford's fiction, which is full of male fantasists, dissatisfied, desirous men who want something they cannot have, but who persist in their futile quests, leaving disappointment and unhappiness in their wake.[4] Austin's vacillation is the confusion of a man who wants two people when he can only have one, but whose covetousness has stripped him of the moral co-ordinates that would allow him to know where true value lies. And if his condition represents an emotional crisis, it is one that is precipitated by a moral crisis. Yet again Ford brings us back to moral issues, to the moral vision in his fiction. We have seen the predicament into which Austin is slipping as he seeks to balance competing desires and to reconcile moral and emotional claims on him. What remains to be understood, if we are to appreciate fully the moral vision in "The Womanizer", are both the causes and effects of Austin's behaviour. While these could be explored on the basis of the text alone, the analysis will be enriched by drawing upon Charles Taylor's work on selfhood and morality as developed in *Sources of the Self.*

Taylor sets himself the task of writing a history of our modern notions of identity, of various understandings of "what it is to be a human agent"[5] in the modern western world. This obliges him to consider the relation between the self and morality, or, as he puts it, "between identity and the good".[6] Taylor begins his argument in support of this vital link through his use of the concept of "strong evaluations",[7] or the discriminations we make between right and wrong, between what is morally higher and lower, better or worse. He sees these as involving claims about "the nature and status of human

---

[4] The Frank Bascombe of *The Sportswriter* certainly falls into the category of "fantasist", as does Charley Matthews of "Occidentals". Austin and Matthews are both "dissatisfied" and "desirous", and Howard Cameron of "Abyss" becomes consumed with desire. For a discussion of the fantasist in Charley Matthews (and the role of self-narrativization in this), see Brian Duffy, "The Story as Cure in Richard Ford's 'Occidentals'", *Mississippi Quarterly*, LIX/1, 2 (Winter 2005-2006, Spring 2006), 225-41.
[5] Taylor, *Sources of the Self*, ix.
[6] *Ibid.*, x.
[7] *Ibid.*, 4.

beings", as opposed to simply being a set of aversions based on gut instincts, such as our "fear of falling", or our "love of sweet things".[8] It is this ontological dimension that compels us to articulate an account of these strong moral reactions – we feel that something intrinsic to the human condition is involved in these moral reactions that calls for formal articulation. The articulation of these evaluations becomes the background we draw upon and against which we measure ourselves, at the level both of moral action and of assessing the "fulness or emptiness" (16) of our lives. Taylor moves on to call these ontological accounts "frameworks", and defines them more precisely as follows:

> What I have been calling a framework incorporates a crucial set of qualitative distinctions. To think, feel, judge within such a framework is to function with the sense that some action, or mode of life, or mode of feeling is incomparably higher than the others which are more readily available to us.[9]

These frameworks are incomparable because they exist for us on a higher plane than other sets of values we might draw upon to gauge our actions or the value of our lives. They are not simply more valuable, but exist in a category all of their own, and have the status of near-absoluteness for us. They are not absolute, of course, the proof of which is, as Taylor allows, that "no framework is shared by everyone".[10] Yet he also insists that "doing without frameworks is utterly impossible for us": their ontological status, their ineradicable constitutiveness of our notion of the human, means that to step outside the boundaries of these moral co-ordinates would be "tantamount to stepping outside what we would recognize as integral, that is, undamaged human personhood".[11] And, crucially, these evaluations "stand independent of our own desires, inclinations, or choices"; they represent, rather, the "standards by which these desires and choices are judged".[12]

Having discussed the "morality" part of his equation Taylor moves on to establish its relation to selfhood and identity. For Taylor, the

---

[8] *Ibid.*, 5.
[9] *Ibid.*, 19.
[10] *Ibid.*, 17.
[11] *Ibid.*, 27.
[12] *Ibid.*, 20.

answer to the question, "Who am I?", is furnished only in a superficial sense by a name, but profoundly so by an expression of "where I stand", in other words by "the commitments and identifications which provide the frame or horizon within which I can try to determine ... what is good, or valuable, or what ought to be done, or what I endorse or oppose".[13] The self as understood by Taylor is deeply a moral self. We know who we are by knowing where we stand, and our determination of what is good or bad, right or wrong, what we judge to be meaningful or trivial, is what determines our identity. Equally, our identity, so defined, is what allows us, Taylor states, "to define what is important to us and what is not",[14] which quite obviously embraces the strong evaluations about how we live our lives, and the nature of our moral obligations and responses to others. It follows that if one is unable to make these determinations, if one does not have this moral orientation, one does "not ... know who one is".[15]

The manner in which Ford's fiction and Taylor's thesis complement each other is remarkable. For both, identity cannot be detached from morality, and the loss of moral orientation in one's life is ultimately a loss of identity. The first indication in "The Womanizer" that self-knowledge may be an important issue occurs when Austin rings Barbara on the eve of his return home from the sales trip where he had met Joséphine. Despite Barbara's welcoming tone he detects a "small edge" in her voice, which he feels may be due to something in his own voice as he tells her about having taken "a woman to dinner" and to something "she'd heard before over the years and that couldn't be hidden" (28). To Barbara's question about whether he might "just possibly have taken [her] for granted tonight" (30) Austin gets irritated, a reaction that continues on his return home where he feels "bewildered" at the sense, emanating from Barbara, that "something was wrong" (32). Austin has so little reflected on himself, and therefore so little understood himself, that he has never, for example, considered a possible connection between his mid-life discontent and his womanizing. And, if he did so, he would probably conclude, in a simple solution-to-problem mode, that it represented merely a "break" from the dull routine of settled life and that, as he felt was the case

---

[13] *Ibid.*, 27.
[14] *Ibid.*, 30.
[15] *Ibid.*, 29.

with Joséphine, "there were no bad consequences to rue" (26). It is clear that he has never considered other, less self-oriented connections between his dissatisfaction and his behaviour. Nor has it occurred to him that his sexual and romantic adventures abroad might have effects on either himself or Barbara. Back home he feels in full control, "with everything in his life arrayed in place and going forward" (36). In his eyes, his womanizing has changed nothing: he knows it has meant little, so that is fine, and Barbara knows nothing about it, so that is fine, too.

It transpires, however, that while Austin was blithely unaware of what was happening to him, Barbara was not. A pre-dinner drink too many liberates the verdict on the change in his character that only Barbara's loyalty and forbearance had previously censured:

> … you think—about yourself—that you can't be changed, as if you're *fixed* …. You think of yourself as a given, that what you go off to some foreign country and do won't have any effect on you, won't leave you different. But that isn't true, Martin. Because you *are* different. In fact, you're unreachable, and you've been becoming that way for a long time …. I've just tried to get along with you and make you happy, because making you happy has always made me happy. But now it doesn't, because you've changed and I don't feel like I can reach you or that you're even aware of what you've become. (42-43)

Barbara's judgement makes an explicit link between Austin's identity and his moral behaviour, and makes clear that it is this behaviour that has changed him from the person he used to be to the person he has become. And, exactly as Taylor does, she identifies that, at the heart of this issue of identity, lies a profound moral confusion – Austin knows neither who he is nor what he has become because he no longer knows what is right or wrong, what is important or trivial, what has greater or lesser value in his life, or what he ought or ought not to do. He no longer knows, in Taylor's terms, where he stands in relation to the strong moral evaluations that a person must make, as his direct response to his wife's devastating verdict reveals: "He didn't exactly know what this meant or what could've brought it about, since he didn't think he'd been doing anything wrong" (43). And, unable to see that he may have done something wrong, he can only tell Barbara that there is nothing he can do to address the moral and identity questions she has raised.

This reaction has its source in Austin's self-conscious moment of self-reflection in his Paris hotel room, when he asked himself his big philosophical, and ostensible moral, question. Taylor insists that the frameworks we draw upon to guide our actions and determine the value of our lives are "not rendered valid by our own desires, inclinations, or choices, but ... offer standards by which [these] can be judged".[16] Austin's would-be moral framework, however, is entirely constituted by his desires, as the opening sentence of his hotel-room question indicated: "What does one want in the world?" Had he asked himself the question, "Where do I stand?", in the sense understood by Taylor, he would not have arrived at his self-serving answer, which functioned only as a justification of his womanizing in the guise of a moral perspective on human contact.

It is also possible to connect Austin's "unanchored sensation" with Taylor's notion of an identity crisis. When Austin delivers his response to Barbara, she tells him that she no longer wishes to be married to a "womanizer" and a "creep" (44), and walks out of the restaurant, making it clear that this represents a definitive break with him. Austin immediately packs a bag and flies back to Paris, a mere few days after flying from Paris to Chicago. He no longer has a stable, rooted hold on his life and is oscillating between the two poles of Barbara and Joséphine, Chicago and Paris, and between present dependability and future stimulation in a search for where he feels he belongs. This oscillation is the perfect metaphor for Taylor's notion of an identity crisis, a condition in which people "lack a frame or horizon within which things can take on a stable significance, within which some life possibilities can be seen as good or meaningful, others as bad or trivial".[17] This is precisely the moral identity crisis afflicting Austin: he is no longer capable of making this kind of strong moral evaluation, so has no moral framework to help him determine where he should be, or where he belongs. This moral vacuum and oscillation finds another telling metaphor in the story when Austin, in his half-sleep, fears that he has betrayed himself to Barbara by mumbling something from the two conversations he is conducting in his mind, "one with Barbara, his wife, and one with himself about Joséphine Belliard" (35).

---

[16] *Ibid.*, 4.
[17] *Ibid.*, 27-28

Taylor makes an important distinction between the self constituted by a moral identity and the use of the term "self" in the notion of self-image as used in the disciplines of psychology and sociology. He insists that self-image is not the same as identity in the moral sense in which he uses the latter term. Self-image has more to do with people's concern that "their image matches up to certain standards, generally socially induced"; what is important for people here is that they "appear in a good light in the eyes of those they come in contact with as well as in their own". Self-image has more to do with esteem than morality, and is not seen, as Taylor points out, "as something which is essential to human personhood".[18]

The concept of self-image is raised here because, yet again, Taylor's discussion proves to be remarkably relevant to Ford's story. Austin has a highly developed sense of self-image, which manifests itself in three important ways. First, it serves to nourish his ego on those occasions when, contemplating his thoughts and actions, he finds himself admirable. Reflecting on his views of the range and complexity of feelings that Joséphine and he might have for each other, "It made him feel pleased even to entertain such a multilayered view" (7). And having left Joséphine at the end of the first stay in Paris without – as he sees it – having complicated their lives, he felt "quite good about everything. Even virtuous. He almost raised his glass to himself in the mirror" (27). The scene of Austin gazing at his literal image in the mirror emphasizes the importance to him – and the importance in the text – of his moral self-image.

Austin's image of himself here is a form of self-flattery and encourages his conceitedness, a trait that is very evident in the second important manifestation and function of self-image, namely the positive idea he has of himself and of the role he plays in his relationship with Joséphine. Austin offers different perspectives on his relationship with her and different reasons to explain why he persists in his pursuit of her when he receives no encouragement. He sees himself above all as someone who can enrich her life – he believes he can offer her "a different human perspective from the ones she might be used to" (8), although admitting elsewhere that he knows virtually nothing about her; he decides he will be "a good-intentioned escort for her", although he would also like to sleep with her; he wants to make

---

[18] *Ibid.*, 33.

her "happy somehow", even though she has asked him for nothing; and, taking her hand on one occasion, he decides he "would be protective of her, guard her from some as yet unnamed harm or from her own concealed urges" (10). His self-image as altruist serves to conceal the truth from Austin about his true motives in pursuing Joséphine and about Barbara's charge, borne out by his own past, that he is a womanizer. This self-image also occupies the space that should be occupied by Taylor's concept of an identity, thus allowing Austin to confuse the two. He does not behave with Joséphine on the altruistic basis of a selfless concern for her welfare; if he did so, he would not be involved with her in the first place. Austin's "altruism" is merely an exercise in self-esteem, filling him with a warm glow emanating from a sense of his own goodness and allowing him to consider this to be a cornerstone of his moral identity.

The third function of Austin's self-image is indeed that of substitute for an identity – the person Austin believes himself to be replaces and obscures what he actually stands for through his behaviour. We recall that Taylor noted that self-image was concerned with appearing in a good light to others, but also to oneself. It is clear that Austin's self is not one brought into being through fidelity to a moral framework, but is, rather, one that emerges from the flattering image he has of himself. He gives much thought to the kind of man he perceives himself to be and often evaluates himself, indeed, as if he were speaking objectively of someone else. Ford's use of free indirect style allows us to hear Austin's verdicts on himself. Although betraying his wife, "He was not the conventionally desperate man on the way out of a marriage that had grown tiresome" (8). Nor would he risk his "real*est*" life with Barbara as "He wasn't a fool" (34) and because "He was a survivor, he thought, and survivors always knew which direction the ground was" (35). And in a long, unctuous passage full of self-regarding statements on his version of an identity, he contrasts himself with his college classmates, the conventional "cowardly leavers" who had walked away from their marriages, something only "weak people did". In his case, though, "his love for Barbara was simply worth more. Some life force was in him too strongly, too fully, to leave". Austin's self-image tips into full-blown self-delusion as he puts the final touches to the portrait of his identity as a moral man – loyal, responsible and exceptional:

> He was a stayer. He was a man who didn't have to do the obvious
> thing. He would be there to preside over the messy consequences of
> life's turmoils. This was, he thought, his one innate strength of
> character. (48)

With this thought, he leaves his home and twenty-two years of shared
life with Barbara and takes a plane to Paris to be with Joséphine.

One final question remains to be answered before moving on to
Austin's return to Paris and the dramatic consequences of his flight:
why is he so persistent in his pursuit of Joséphine? Many of the more
obvious reasons allowed by the text are explicable as much by
conducive circumstances as by explicit, direct causes. These reasons
include Austin's dissatisfaction with his life, certain features in
Joséphine that he finds attractive, his desire to sleep with her, the
romantic aspect of a Parisian affair, the simple fact that he was alone
abroad and therefore free to conduct an affair, and, of course, the
absence of a moral framework that allows him to think this way in the
first place. The absence of a moral framework would certainly explain
his womanizing while abroad, but does not explain the persistence of
his pursuit of Joséphine – while he does find her "appealing", he "was
not physically attracted to her" and he acknowledges that "He did not
for an instant think that he loved her, or that keeping each other's
company would lead him or her to anything important" (18). The real
reason is never acknowledged by Austin, but a vital clue to it is
revealed by him when he returns to Paris and is pondering Joséphine's
continued "reluctance" (80):

> That was an attitude he could overcome, given time. He was good at
> overcoming reluctances in others. He was a persuasive man, with the
> heart of a salesman, and knew it. From time to time, this fact even
> bothered him, since given the right circumstances he felt he could
> persuade anybody of anything—no matter what. He had no clear idea
> what this persuasive quality was, though Barbara had occasionally
> remarked on it, often with the unflattering implication that he didn't
> believe in very much, or at least not in enough. (80-81)

Conducive circumstances aside – and these are indeed relevant –
the direct cause of Austin's persistence with Joséphine is that her very
reluctance begins to take on the allure of a challenge for him, and his
efforts to provoke a response from her become part of a game he gets

drawn into, in which her unresponsiveness stirs his desire to persuade. It is as if his self-image is offended by his inability to break down her resistance. He remarks on her unresponsiveness on several occasions during his first stay in Paris, yet finds "this very reluctance in her ... compelling, attractive. And it caused him to woo her in a way that made him admire his own intensity" (18-19). When he succeeds to some extent in occupying her life – by being in her apartment, meeting her son and child-minder, and seeing into her private life – he feels "as though he'd accomplished something, something that was not easy or ordinary" (19). On their last evening together, when Austin wants to speak to her about things "with some future built in" for them, it is as much in order to see what his words "called forth" from her as for any genuine interest in planning such a joint future (22). And when they sit in the car in their last moments together Austin finds her silence and distance "annoying and stupid". It is his frustration and growing anger at her continued imperviousness to his efforts to win a positive response that has him raise the stakes, as if stiff resistance demanded extreme measures to keep the game alive: "'You know,' he said, more irritably than he wanted to sound, 'we could be lovers. We're interested in each other. This isn't a sidetrack for me. This is real life'" (24).

Austin, in fact, does not know what he wants, a deficiency of character no doubt related to what Barbara had identified as his not "[believing] in very much". The challenge of drawing Joséphine out of her apparent indifference to him has become the ultimate goal in these first few days, a vain little game he could play, safe in the knowledge that he had a real life back home. Barbara and home represent his fallback position, allowing him to pursue his romantic diversion long enough to see what it would produce. But he had indeed taken his wife for granted, and when she walks away from him, and when he decides after all that he would prefer not to "be there to preside over the messy consequences of life's turmoils", he flees to a woman who has asked him for nothing and has promised him nothing.

Place is important in Richard Ford's fiction. In particular, the relationship between character and place is a rich source of meaning, and has given rise to much critical commentary about a sense of place in his work. Ford has observed that "anything you feel about a place" is something that "you have authored and ascribed to some piece of geography".[19] A sense of place, for Ford, is not something that is offered to us by a specific location, that is somehow objectively, innately there, but is rather something that we construct – we accord meaning to place rather than it imposing its meaning on us. The attribution of meaning to place comes to play an important role in "The Womanizer" through Austin's awareness that the Paris of his first stay is not the same Paris to which he returns a few days later. It is not the city that has changed, of course, but rather the circumstances of Austin's presence there, and these dictate his view of the city.

During his first stay in Paris, Austin's sense of freedom, his insouciant disregard for consequences and the brief period of his sojourn allowed him to discount important warning signs of cultural difference. Feeling in control and enjoying the challenge of seducing a French woman, it does not have to matter to Austin that he "didn't know anything" about the French (7). Nor does he absorb the lessons of his own insight that this cultural ignorance extended to Joséphine. He finds her "completely opaque" (14), and all the indications are that this is an intercultural rather than an interpersonal obstacle. He regards her "pessimism" as a reproach to him, an attitude he finds "very French", and would prefer that she display instead a "more hopeful, American point of view" (21). Cultural stereotyping also helps him explain her silence and distance, which he takes as a form of being "closed to the world", one he finds "annoying and stupid and French" (24). Misunderstanding stalks their conversations, and they occasionally seem to be speaking at cross purposes: Austin notes of one of Joséphine's silences that it "was as if what he'd said didn't mean anything" (11). Both have difficulty in communicating their meanings to the other, not simply the meaning of words and sentences, but the meanings expressed through attitudes and even gestures (Austin is irritated by the typically French shrug of the shoulders, a gesture he does not understand but that is more expressive than any word in the dictionary). They do not appear to be able to read each other because they do not understand the codes of the other's culture, yet it is only Joséphine who has absorbed the profound lesson that may have to be drawn from this. Referring back to an unhappy few months she had once spent living with a man in America, she tells Austin, in what will come to stand as one of the commanding truths of

---

[19] *Conversations with Richard Ford*, 142.

the entire story: "You cannot live a long time where you don't belong" (19).

Back in Paris, Austin no longer feels in control of things, and what had seemed exciting and without consequence the previous week now seems threatening and destabilizing. There have been unexpected consequences to his first stay in Paris, and, now that Barbara has walked out on him, what happens this time around is bound to have important implications for his future. These middle sections of the story ostensibly narrate Austin's transition from one life to another, but, in fact, for most of the time in these passages, Austin occupies a psychological state of suspension and in-betweenness, cut off from his life and past with Barbara and without any guarantee of a future life with Joséphine. Austin's evolving vision of his life had contained only the poles represented by the two women and the two spaces of home and Paris. Now he has to contend with this unexpected interjacent space of exile and exclusion, which becomes the space of non-belonging alluded to by Joséphine.

He is burdened above all with a deep sense of cultural lostness, one that finds its appropriate metaphor in his physical disorientation in Paris. He is frustrated that his instincts about spatial orientation "seemed all wrong" (55): "He couldn't keep straight which arrondissement was which, what direction anything was from anything else, how to take the metro, or even how to leave town, except by airplane" (15). He tries to adopt the demeanour of the self-confident cosmopolitan, but the fantasy of drinking coffee in a Parisian café while reading *Le Monde* cannot be realized: he grows "discouraged as the words he didn't understand piled up" (56). During these first two days back in Paris, when he is too disoriented to contact Joséphine, Austin feels both excluded and out of place. Secluded behind the window of his café, he envies the passing tourists' sense of knowing "precisely where they were going and precisely why they were here" (57), in contrast to himself who does not know "what he was in Paris for" (56).

The Paris of his second stay has become Austin's limbo, an intermediate space of abeyance between the two poles of his existence, both of which, however, are now a source of disquiet. Walking through Paris, Austin carries on a silent conversation with Barbara in his mind, noticing things he might buy her and storing up things he might tell her. She occupied, he recognizes, the "place of final consequence—the destination for practically everything he cared about or noticed or imagined" (58). And when Austin eventually telephones Joséphine, one of the sources of disquiet in the phone call is his sense that she "seemed much more French than he remembered". In his idealized recollection of her back in Oak Grove she had been "almost an American, only with a French accent" (60). Austin had suppressed her cultural difference in his fantasized evocations of her, just as he does with the French and Americans he observes on the streets of Paris, whose cultural particularities he seeks to flatten out: in what seems an attempt to convince himself that he will have little difficulty in integrating into French culture, he "decided" that the French and the Americans "looked basically like each other" (56). Austin did not have to bother with cultural difference during his first stay, but now that it is beginning to manifest itself his only defence is to seek to minimize it, as he does here. There is no going back for him now; he has made his choice to be in Paris, and in these circumstances. Feeling out of place though he does, all that is left for him is to push on in the attempt to make the transition to whatever life Joséphine may have to offer.

The final two sections of the novella cover Austin's renewal of his relationship with Joséphine and his catastrophic lack of attention that leads to his losing Joséphine's four-year-old son in the Jardin du Luxembourg and the subsequent sexual assault on the child. This latter part of the story is structured according to a "before" and "after" of the events in the park – Léo's abduction is the pivotal moment, the turning point, the event that crystallizes Austin's moral decline and shocks him into a realization of what he has become. Ford carefully traces the stages of Austin's decline and fall through this before-and-after structure, exposing the manner in which his protagonist's behaviour, disconnected from the imperatives of a moral framework, is governed only by his needs and desires, and by the stimuli of immediate experience. It is also the phase of the story where its parabolic nature and intent are most evident.

Austin's literal and spiritual journey, which culminates now in his return to Joséphine, had its origins in the double dynamic of fantasy and self-image, bolstered by a teleological self-narrative of becoming. The illusory nature of these constructions are now confronted with reality. Austin immediately finds Joséphine "slightly fat and a little sloppy", and her son makes him feel "awkward and reluctant" (68). He realizes now that he does not belong here. Nothing conforms to his fantasy. The disagreeable details of another's private life repel him, from the child's bad-tempered screaming to Joséphine's toilet noises. Above all, Joséphine does not hide her lack of interest, and even unease, at Austin's return. His attempt to instigate the "love" (70) that might be possible between them takes the form of another imposed kiss, another grotesque indication of how he has at every step misread the culture he is in and the woman he has tried to seduce. His waning interest in Joséphine is renewed only by the sexual thrill of wandering through the intimate space of her apartment (after she leaves him to look after her son while she visits her lawyer to finalize her divorce), and by looking through her ex-husband's novel where the fictionalized Joséphine is performing a sexual act.

It is in moments such as these that the full meaning of the story's title reveals itself. Austin's view of women is essentially instrumental. Joséphine's attraction lay, in large part, in the role accorded her in Austin's game of seduction. But in the changed circumstances of his renewed contact with her, only the sexual dimension manages to keep his interest in her alive. And before his involvement with Joséphine, his relations with women in his various affairs abroad could have been little more than sexual in nature. As for the most important relationship in his life with a woman, the intense expressions of his love and reverence for Barbara seem hollow in the light of his womanizing, and also in his reaction to her distress at his infidelity. He is surprised at Barbara's walk-out because, in the past, "when he'd gotten temporarily distracted by some woman he met far from home", a talk and apologies had, as far as he was concerned, sorted out the problem – a thoroughly reasonable outcome, in his view, to what he considered to be "Ordinary goings-on" (45). Sexual infidelity is something that Austin expects women to accept, including the woman he "loves", and seems to be part of the implicit terms of his contract with women. And although appreciating their undoubted charms, he finds that the personal investment in women, particularly within the enduring intimacy of a marriage, produces an emotional entanglement that is not adequately rewarded:

> ... women were sometimes a kind of problem. He enjoyed their company, enjoyed hearing their voices, knowing about their semi-intimate lives and daily dramas. But his attempts at knowing them

often created a peculiar feeling, as if on the one hand he'd come into
the possession of secrets he didn't want to keep, while on the other,
some other vital portion of life—his life with Barbara, for instance—
was left not fully appreciated, gone somewhat to waste. (45-46)

It is difficult to avoid the conclusion that the common denominator
in Austin's love for his wife, his various relationships with women
and his pursuit of Joséphine is the instrumental one of getting and
enjoying – at the least cost to himself – what women have to offer,
particularly the passion and physical pleasures, but also the stability of
a "real life" to which he can return after one of his affairs abroad. His
attitude is one in which it is difficult to discern a place for the love of
which Austin so easily speaks, but that goes a long way to elucidating
the mindset of a womanizer.

Austin brings Léo to the Jardin du Luxembourg to distract him, and
begins to take stock of his situation while the boy amuses himself. The
let-down of finding himself back with a woman in whom he is no
longer interested has him construct a new narrative of becoming, one
that will relegate his miscalculation over Joséphine to an unimportant
sub-plot in the greater story of his taking control of his life and of
moving resolutely forward to an exciting future. Charles Taylor notes
how important it is for us to have a sense that our lives have a
direction, which arises from our instinct that our lives are not static:
"our lives move …. The issue of our condition can never be exhausted
for us by what we *are*, because we are always also changing and
becoming."[20] Austin's midlife anxiety, the symptom of which is his
"unanchored sensation", was provoked, we recall, by his uncertainty
over how to make "the next twenty-five years of life as eventful and
important as the previous twenty-five". The future, therefore, is what
preoccupies Austin, a sense that he is moving towards self-fulfilment
and new meaning. As Taylor puts it (in a way that chimes perfectly
with Austin's concern): "the issue for us has to be not only where we
are, but where we're *going*."[21] For Taylor, as for MacIntyre and
Ricoeur, we attend to the direction of our lives – as we have seen in
earlier chapters – through narrative. The dynamics of narrative
emplotment allow us to configure and reconfigure the shape and

---

[20] Taylor, *Sources of the Self*, 46-47 (italics in the original).
[21] *Ibid.*, 47 (italics in the original).

direction of our lives, tracing its trajectory from past to present and setting the course into the future.

Austin begins the construction of his new teleological narrative by consigning Joséphine to his past, a space already inhabited by Barbara, with whom, in his marriage, he was just "playing out the end of an old thing" (81). Joséphine's appeal did not survive the glimpse into what daily life with her would be like. He now shores up his case against her through a mix of personal criticism and cultural stereotyping. Her annoying personal faults, and her being a "typical bourgeois little Frenchwoman", are individual manifestations of the wider problem with French women, who "all talked like children: in high-pitched, rapid-paced, displeasingly insistent voices, which most of the time said, "*Non, non, non, non, non,*" to something someone wanted" (82). Having to deal with French female inflexibility has no place in Austin's revised self-narrative, one informed essentially by his self-image. All it took to improve one's life was to be the kind of man he understands himself to be, a man who had "the courage to take control of things and to live with the consequences" (75). Deciding that Joséphine took her life too seriously, Austin casts himself now as one who believes that life "had to be more lighthearted" (82), and he retrospectively accords this insight the status of an irrefutable causality: "[This] was why he'd come here, why he'd cut himself loose—to enjoy life more. He admired himself for it" (82-83). Austin has now reconfigured his personal story, narrated a defeat as a victory, buttressed his self-image and opened up his future to whatever pleasurable possibilities might present themselves. The apogee of this delusionary self-narrative is reached when Austin decides that he will not assume the role of "savior in Joséphine's life" (83), a part he had assumed but that she had never asked him to play. Reality, then, has not succeeded in holding Austin down for long; fancy and fantasy have restored him to the idealized roles of his self-image.

Austin's self-absorption causes him to lose sight of Léo. When he looks for him, the child is nowhere to be found. Austin now enters the time and mode of nightmare as he frantically searches for the boy, clawing his way helplessly through intractable space and unresponsive onlookers, convulsed by panic. He finds Léo in undergrowth, naked, dirty and white-faced. At the sight of Austin, Léo screams, a piercing cry that resounds like an alarm siren in Austin's world, indicating the occurrence of ruinous behaviour and foreshadowing a dramatic turn in the direction of his life.

In a story with affinities to New Testament parables, Austin will be punished with Old Testament severity. His lack of attention and responsibility have led to a terrible event, for which Austin's guilt is only the beginning of his punishment. Ford's vision of his novella as a parable is realized through the scale of the punishment he visits on Austin and through establishing clearly that his character's moral failings, so carefully exposed in the story, are the direct cause of the catastrophe that now befalls him – his neglect of Léo is merely one manifestation of his wider moral failure to be respectful of and responsible to others. Austin brings about his own fall and is set to reap what he has sown.[22] In an instant he is transformed from the vainglorious paragon of his self-narrative to self-flagellating sinner, a metamorphosis witnessed in the free-indirect-style reproduction of his thoughts:

> ... he had ruined everything now .... He would go to jail, and he *should* go to jail. He was an awful man. A careless man. He brought mayhem and suffering to the lives of innocent, unsuspecting people who trusted him. No punishment could be too severe. (86)

Austin had become caught up in the sense of his own omniscience; he felt he had access to superior truths about himself and life not available to Barbara and Joséphine. And as is the case with Frank Bascombe in *The Sportswriter* and *Independence Day*, it falls to women to speak the uncomfortable truth to Austin about his moral failings. Barbara had seen the effect of Austin's womanizing on him when he was unable to do so himself, going so far as to imply in her comments that he no longer knew who he was. Now Austin must face Joséphine's wrath and judgement.

The scene between them is striking in its elaboration of opposing moral orders, one inhabited by Joséphine, the other by Austin. As far

---

[22] The expression "to reap what one has sown" has indeed come to us from the New Testament, but not from one of the parables. It is contained in the Epistle of St Paul to the Galatians, and reads as follows: "Be not deceived, God is not mocked. For whatsoever a man soweth, that shall he reap" (Galatians 6:7). As demanded by a parable, there is a meticulous causality at work in Ford's story.

as Joséphine is concerned, she and Austin no longer inhabit a common moral space in which mutually understood meanings may be exchanged. It is likely that their earlier misunderstandings were already a manifestation of their different moral codes – Joséphine had not responded to Austin because she simply did not understand the moral plane he was operating on, and therefore did not understand what he was looking for in pursuing her. Her doubts about him have been appallingly realized, and now she lays out the basis of their different moral visions of human relationships: "It is not a game. You know? Maybe to you it is a game." And in her powerful judgement of Austin's moral worth she makes the same connection as Barbara did between identity and morality, and makes explicit what Barbara implied: "You don't know who you are …. Who are you? …. Who do you think you are? You're nothing." Joséphine's verdict also bears out the link between morality and identity proposed by Charles Taylor – Austin does not know what he stands for, therefore he does not know who he is. Joséphine's "nothing" is a moral nothing,[23] a judgement that also accords with Taylor's thesis that moral frameworks represent an affirmation of "a given ontology of the human" (5),[24] and that for someone to step outside the limits of strong moral discriminations is "tantamount to stepping outside … undamaged human personhood". In pronouncing her final judgement on Austin, Joséphine makes the same ontological connection between an absence of moral frameworks and personhood: "I don't care what happens to you. You are dead" (89). Barbara pronounced the death of Austin's old self when she told him how radically he had changed; now Joséphine pronounces the death of his moral self, which she equates with the death of all that is of fundamental value in a person.

In the days that follow Léo's abduction, Austin's mind is full of thoughts of death, be it the fear of Barbara's death, or the death of something vital in his life with which she is associated. He comes to understand this as a metaphor for a great loss he has suffered, and one that has led to his exclusion from the society of others, a punishment akin to a biblical banishment from one's community. It is in this sense

---

[23] Paul's Epistle to the Galatians finds an interesting echo in Ford's story through Joséphine's verdict on Austin as "nothing". The following passage could well be applied to Austin: "For if a man think himself to be something, when he is nothing, he deceiveth himself" (Galatians 6:3).

[24] Taylor, *Sources of the Self*, 5.

that he feels the need to "repatriate" himself, particularly where Barbara is concerned. Charles Taylor's work on morality, identity and narrative continues to be highly relevant to Austin as he contemplates the cause of his near-perdition.[25] Austin understands clearly that he has failed morally:

> Not to know what that something [lost] was, though, meant that he was out of control, perhaps meant something worse about him. So that he began to think of his life, in those succeeding days, almost entirely in terms of what was wrong with him, of his problem, his failure—in particular his failure as a husband, but also in terms of his unhappiness, his predicament, his ruin, which he wanted to repair. (90)

Taylor identifies "three axes of what can be called, in the most general sense, moral thinking". First, there is "our sense of respect for and obligation to others";[26] second, there are the understandings we have of "what kind of life is worth living",[27] what constitutes a meaningful or full life; and, finally, there is the issue of dignity, by which he means our command, or failure to command, the "respect of those around us". One's sense of dignity can be grounded in the awareness of how one fulfils important functions in one's life, in one's roles, for instance, "as a householder, father of a family, holding down a job, providing for my dependents".[28] Our sense of dignity, of commanding the respect of others, is also closely connected to our feeling of self-worth.

Measured against all three of Taylor's axes of what constitutes a moral life, Austin has failed. On the first criterion, he has failed in his obligation to others – to Barbara, Joséphine and Léo. On the second criterion, he has failed himself. Taylor notes significantly that one can, in the quest to lead a worthwhile, fulfilling life, "take a wrong turn"

---

[25] In its articulation of irrevocable loss, the biblical term seems appropriate in Austin's case. In the Bible the term signifies loss and ruin, terms that Austin specifically uses to describe his condition. Depending on the context, "perdition" in the Bible can signify, *inter alia*, spiritual death, the fate of the sinner, or eternal death. Perdition, however, is a final state of ruin, where salvation is no longer possible. "The Womanizer" allows Austin a chance at redemption.

[26] Taylor, *Sources of the Self*, 15.

[27] *Ibid.*, 14.

[28] *Ibid.*, 15.

by "following one's immediate wishes and desires".[29] Austin has indeed drastically veered off the moral path by allowing self-gratification to become his guiding principle in achieving a meaningful life. He acknowledges his guilt in this regard when he speaks of being "out of control", of "what was wrong with him" and of his "failure". And, finally, we have seen how Austin no longer commands the respect of those around him: he has failed "as a husband" in the most important relationship in his life, and, for Barbara, has become a "womanizer" and a "creep", while for Joséphine he is "dead". His self-judgment as being "an awful man" indicates also the dramatic reversal that has occurred in his own feeling of self-worth.

In his remorseful state Austin seeks now to "repair" the damage he has committed. Shocked out of his previously impenetrable solipsism by an appalling event, he recognizing the moral value of the two women he has wronged. He now appreciates Joséphine because of the way she had felt a "greater sense of responsibility than he had; a greater apprehension of life's importance, its weight and permanence" (91). But Austin sees that he has done most harm to Barbara, and, stripped now of his fantasies and conceit, can fully appreciate what he had known before he had begun to take her, his own life and moral worth for granted:

> He recognized again and even more plainly that his entire destination, everything he'd ever done or presumed or thought, had been directed toward Barbara, that everything good was there. And it was there he would need eventually to go (91).

The original meaning of what had become empty words of love and reverence for Barbara are being recovered; his life with her is surely the "something important in his life" that he had lost. Charles Taylor's insights are again useful to us here. He has established the relationship between selfhood and morality, between identity and the good. But what is good or moral is decided within "a space in which questions arise about what is good or bad, what is worth doing and what not".[30] In other words, our moral frameworks are constituted within a context of possible choices about what is important or unimportant,

---

[29] *Ibid.,* 14.
[30] *Ibid.,* 28.

meaningful or trivial, and so forth. This means that our identity is constantly defined by our orientation in relation to the good, which in turn poses the problem of the direction of our lives and the movement of our lives in relation to the good. We understand and articulate this movement through narrative, which is what Austin did in caricatured fashion in his Jardin du Luxembourg self-narrative as he sought to reorient his future towards a self-serving good when he decided he was no longer interested in Joséphine. But he had by that stage long lost his orientation in relation to the good, because he had lost the knowledge of what was important and worthwhile. Now he rediscovers both – what is good, and his need to reconnect with this good. The good lies with Barbara and in his relationship with her, and he articulates the need to redirect his life in terms of Taylor's notion of orientation: "it was there he would need eventually to go."

The vital relationship between morality and identity proposed by Taylor continues to resonate in Austin's final thoughts. He returns to the question he had first asked himself in his Paris hotel room, but does so now from a different perspective, less focused on the self-centred concern of what "one" wants in the world:

> ... he wondered again ... what was ever possible between human beings. How could you regulate life, do little harm and still be attached to others? And in that context, he wondered if being *fixed* could be a misunderstanding, and ... if he had changed slightly, somehow altered the important linkages that guaranteed his happiness and become detached, unreachable. Could you *become* that? (91-92)

There are two preoccupations in Austin's final reflections: our relationships and behaviour with others, and our understanding of ourselves and our lives. The first deals with issues of moral behaviour, the second with identity, but they are indissociable. Austin, we are to understand, once knew what was important in his life, once knew where the good lay. However, in a prolonged lack of attention to his own life, as catastrophic as his lack of attention to Léo in the Jardin du Luxembourg, he had stopped thinking about this good. He began, as Barbara had pointed out, to take both her and himself, and their life together – this good – for granted. He continued to see himself as morally "fixed", as a "given", not noticing how his womanizing was changing him. This change, his moral loss, represents his loss of identity.

Austin now sees the change that occurred in him in terms of a failure to preserve the "important linkages" in his life (earlier he had spoken of "the crucial linkages of a good life" [57]). Austin does not explain what he means by the term "linkages", but, through Taylor's concept of a moral identity as an orientation to the good, and through both Taylor's and Austin's (and indeed Barbara's) emphasis on becoming, we may understand Austin's linkages as narrative linkages. Taylor, MacIntyre and Ricoeur all remind us that we grasp the movement of our lives through narrative, through the connections, or plotted linkages, that we establish from among the disparate material of our lives. It is Ricoeur who elaborates a full theory of the synthesizing function of narrative that is accomplished through the operation of emplotment. Ricoeur defines emplotment as a "synthesis of heterogeneous elements", one aspect of which is its capacity to transform a multiplicity of events and incidents into the unity of a story, into an intelligible whole. As Ricoeur puts it, an event so narrated becomes "more than just an occurrence, I mean more than something that just happens; it is what contributes to the progress of the narrative".[31]

The single, isolated event is now defined and transformed by its function in the development of an unfolding network of relationships effected by the act of configuration carried out by the narrator. By way of these configured, or narrated, connections, these imaginative linkages, our lives assume a temporal and moral shape, and are given a direction. Austin sought most visibly and most blatantly to reconfigure his life story in his Jardin du Luxembourg narrative. There, his self-serving narrative linkages eliminated Barbara from his life, dismissed Joséphine as more trouble than she was worth and reconfigured himself as a man on the threshold of a bright new future.

Now, in his condition of moral ruin, and in a life that has taken many wrong turns, Austin is in need of a new self-narrative, a new life-story with linkages that will reconnect him to Barbara and his life with her, that will reorient him towards the good. He has made an important start – he has rediscovered where the good resides. In a story about loss of bearings, wandering and exile, he has rediscovered where he belongs.

---

[31] Paul Ricoeur, "Life in Quest of Narrative", in *On Paul Ricoeur: Narrative and Interpretation*, ed. David Wood, London: Routledge, 1991, 21.

Chapter 8

"Occidentals"

Americans in Paris

The geographical settings of Richard Ford's fiction never function as contingent background presence, or as mere perfunctory locale. Nowhere is the significance of place more evident than in "Occidentals", the second of the two novellas in *Women with Men*. The Paris setting of the story becomes much more than the tourist site it initially represents for the protagonists, and is ultimately revealed to be a polysemous space of multiple identities and competing meanings – artists' mythological *terre d'asile*, city of contested difference, historical site of oppression and conflict, clichéd location of guide books and enigmatic space to be decoded.

The relationship between character and place is particularly relevant to the understanding of what is at stake in "Occidentals". Ford's protagonist, Charley Matthews, may spend no more than a few days in Paris, but it is undeniably his presence there that dictates the nature of the decisive experience he undergoes in the city, which is nothing less than an important transformation in his sense of self.[1] But beyond this, and beyond the story of Matthews' relationship with his girlfriend, Helen, who accompanies him on his trip, Ford draws decisively upon the setting of his story to develop an entirely separate set of themes. Ford's story brings Americans and the French into contact and confrontation, and explores an intercultural contact held captive by history and burdened with prejudice and crude chauvinism, in which cultural stereotyping is often the ready, atavistic response to the perceived threat of cultural difference.

---

[1] For a full discussion of this aspect of Matthews' experience in Paris, and in particular the function of narrative in his self-transformation, see my article in the *Mississippi Quarterly* (see note 4 in the previous chapter on "The Womanizer").

That Ford wished his story to be a vehicle for exploring the theme of interculturalism and the attitudes that inform the construction of cultural perceptions is evident from his systematic return to these issues throughout the story, and from his use of different characters to represent different perceptions of native and other cultures: both Matthews and Helen are accorded views on France and the French, while two boorish American friends of Helen whom they meet exemplify a form of attachment to one's native culture that quickly tips into racism and xenophobia. But Ford also gives the French a voice to express their views of Americans, and he extends the scope of his depiction of cultural perceptions by having Matthews reflect on his own culture in the light of his exposure to France and the French, and by having his characters also come into contact with German and Japanese tourists.

The discourse of image studies (known also as imagology) concerns itself with the images one culture holds of another, as well as those it holds of its own culture, and provides a useful context within which to approach the issues of interculturalism and national identity in Ford's story. Joep Leerssen, one of the leading theorists of image studies, defines the preoccupations of image studies as follows:

> ... image studies ... is specifically designed to deal with the discursive manifestation of cultural difference and national identification patterns. Image studies analyses its source materials (encompassing literary artworks and other forms of discourse) for the formulation of notions of domestic and foreign, and of the character of national-cultural "selves" and "others". Its central preoccupation is with the dichotomy between the images of the other and the self-image.[2]

Image studies, then, concerns itself with the expression of national attitudes to native and other cultures. The images referred to are characteristics or qualities attributed to a native or foreign culture; they are not the truth about this or that nation or culture, but tell us rather how these cultures are represented or perceived through a given set of images held about them. This attribution of qualities to both native and other cultures engenders an intricate and dynamic

---

[2] Joep Leerssen, *Remembrance and Imagination: Patterns in the Historical and Literary Representation of Ireland in the Nineteenth Century*, Field Day Monographs 4, Cork: Cork UP in association with Field Day, 1996, 6.

interaction of self-images (termed "auto-images" in image studies) and images of the other (or "hetero-images"). Within this exchange, there also circulates the self-images that are influenced by the images of one's own culture held by another culture.

Leerssen gives us a flavour of this reciprocal assimilation through the complex and centuries-long image transactions between England and Ireland: "the imagologist must study, not just the substance, but also the mutual interaction and interdependence of the English image of 'Ireland', of the Irish image of 'England' and of the English and Irish auto-images of themselves as related to both those hetero-images."[3] Image studies is appropriate to "Occidentals" in that the core cultural interaction in the text is between two cultures, American and French, whose relationship, particularly in the modern era, has often been blighted by mutual incomprehension and antagonism. Richard Ford is far from indifferent to the issue of intercultural understanding, as we learn from an article he wrote a few years before the publication of "Occidentals":

> To me this is what multiculturalism is worth ... in writing short stories and novels: it's an invitation to imagine more meticulously the distinctions and similarities which make us able to share the planet together; it's an opportunity to challenge and if need be break the hold of conventional wisdom, of history, and to complicate our responses on behalf of extending the benefice of sympathy to others who aren't just like us but may be more like us than we know.[4]

Ford uses the term "multiculturalism" here, which is to be distinguished from "interculturalism". Multiculturalism refers to the existence of cultural diversity within a given country or society, and is currently a lively subject of debate in America. Multiculturalism demands the full acceptance and respect of group identities based on racial, ethnic or national identity. It stands in opposition to the one-nation, assimilationist ideology that has been considered, since about the beginning of the twentieth century, the most effective ideological

---

[3] Joep Leerssen, *Mere Irish and Fíor-Ghael: Studies in the Idea of Irish Nationality, its Development and Literary Expression prior to the Nineteenth Century*, 2nd edn, Field Day Monographs 3, Cork: Cork UP in association with Field Day, 1996, 12.

[4] Richard Ford, "What We Write, Why We Write It, and Who Cares", *Michigan Quarterly Review*, XXXI/3 (Summer 1992), 379-80.

means of uniting the diverse immigrant communities arriving in America into a single, unified nation.

Interculturalism, on the other hand, refers to the meeting of different cultures, to the various relationships and contacts that characterize the exchanges between them. The latter term is the appropriate one in the case of "Occidentals", as it is precisely the contact between different national groups that is at the heart of the story. Nonetheless, Ford's articulation in his essay of the ethos and benefits of multiculturalism are equally relevant to intercultural contact, when different cultures are brought together and must find ways of achieving harmonious coexistence. In "Occidentals", however, Ford will portray an intercultural contact in which the empathy, re-imagining and self-interrogation that he associates with multiculturalism are the qualities most dramatically absent. Ford's story investigates – in addition to the personal narrative of Matthews and Helen – aggressive notions of American national identity and exclusionism, thus complementing the exploration of these issues in *Independence Day* and *The Lay of the Land*. Americans at home cut themselves off from others; Americans abroad, as we will see in "Occidentals", are no less inclined to self-segregation and self-isolation.

The failure of intercultural understanding receives its sharpest expression through the characters of Rex and Bea, American friends of Helen whom Matthews and Helen run into while they are all doing the obligatory visit to the Eiffel Tower. These loud, obtuse Americans, complacent and untouchable in their bubble of jingoistic cultural superiority, seem to be Ford's worst nightmare of his compatriots abroad. "We're American",[5] announces Bea, as she introduces Rex and herself to Matthews. What seems at first a merely fatuous proclamation of national belonging is in fact a symptom of an aggressive and cultivated sense of their American identity in the face of their unwanted but unavoidable presence in France. Where Matthews and Helen have at least some notions about the history and culture of the country they are visiting, the motivations and incentives accorded to the character of Rex, who lives in France, are crudely mercantile and portrayed in terms that evoke a hawkish and

---

[5] Ford, *Women with Men*, 184. See note 8 in the Introduction for publication details. Further references to "Occidentals" will be indicated parenthetically in the text.

unscrupulous Wild West frontier spirit, the lucrative outcome of which is all that retains him in France. From his unremarkable position in a machine parts company back home, "Rex had spied an opening where a smart gunslinger type could pick up refurbished parts in the States, sell them directly into the infant retail implement market here in France, and come away with a bundle". Rex attributes some of his success to a deficiency he finds in the French, one hardened into the simplistic mantra of a stereotype, the reassuring blunt instrument through which negative cultural attributions are most readily and efficiently transmitted: "The French all hate to work. It's that simple", he declares.

Rex had thought he would get two or three profitable years out of his business venture before "some bureaucrat up in Brussels tailor-made a regulation to embargo exactly what he was doing" (199). Rex has transposed his American faith in laissez-faire economics to France, and resents government, or, even worse, pan-European, intervention in the marketplace, just one instance of his inability to appreciate the notion of cultural difference. But Ford is also keen to draw our attention here to a strain of paranoia and anti-government sentiment associated with right-wing sensibilities in America. These sentiments are exacerbated in the multi-national context of Europe, where the opinions of numerous governments and cultures have to be accommodated. Both Bea and Rex warn Matthews not to get Rex "started on the UN", "*Or* the EU", institutions that either directly hinder Rex's zealous moneymaking, or, in the case of the UN, promote values that are irrelevant and possibly inimical to that enterprise: "The UN's a loada crap", proclaims Rex in a response to a remark by Helen about "different nationalities needing to get along better" (202).

Living in France is the unfortunate price that Rex and Bea have to pay for making money out of the French. In these unavoidable circumstances, everything they do is geared to ensuring that the France in which they are obliged to live is as little like France as possible. Rex and Bea, in fact, live in France as if they were still living in America. So it is that the principal scene involving Rex and Bea takes place in Clancy's, an American restaurant opened by "a couple of guys named Joe from Kansas City" for "people like themselves, who were stranded here with similar needs and tastes" (198). The antidote to this enforced exile is a "big, noisy, brassily lit"

(197) American restaurant where customers feel they are actually back home, thanks to "a lot of vintage black-and-white photographs—Babe Ruth hitting a homer, Rocky Marciano KO'ing some black guy". The atmosphere is one of an overwrought, good-ol'-boy celebration of all things American.

Clancy's, indeed, is less a restaurant than a stronghold, and in both senses of the term: it is a bastion where the cause of certain American values are celebrated, "a place where you could relax, be yourself and get shit-faced in peace, just like back home", but is equally a fortified place of defence against the surrounding hordes, the enemy in this case being the French. The exclusionary and isolationist instincts on display in *Independence Day* and *The Lay of the Land* have been exported to France. But despite the attempt to preserve a segregation policy, "Regrettably, it was beginning to get crowded, and even some French people were showing up, though they were always given the worst tables" (198). The term "segregation", notorious as it is to American ears, is more than invited here. Following an explanation by Helen to Rex and Bea that Matthews had once taught African-American studies in college, Helen teases Matthews with the rhetorical question, "He doesn't *look* black, does he?", to which Bea responds: "You can't always tell .... They're not like the French—visible for miles in every direction." Things would be better in Rex and Bea's white American world-view if those who did not belong to their exclusive group remained less visible in their respective homelands. When the French do have the audacity to manifest their presence in Clancy's, Rex switches immediately into enemy-spotting mode: "'Yep, yep, there they are,' he said. 'I see 'em. Four of 'em with their fuckin' pooch'" (202).

Ford's consciousness of the race issue – although the prejudice here is mostly directed at the French – is no doubt connected to his unsettling exposure to racism in his childhood and adolescence in Mississippi.[6] For all that, this does not cause him to lose his satirical or comic edge, as when, for example, he tinges Rex and Bea's Francophobia with a bovine intuition of the prestige of Gallic exotica:

---

[6] In the *Paris Review* interview, Ford, speaking of his growing up in Mississippi, evokes the racism and segregation he witnessed: "the race part was bad. The cynicism of the whites, me included .... I simply didn't understand some very fundamental things in Mississippi in the early sixties and fifties: why it was we went to separate schools, why all this violence" ("Richard Ford: The Art of Fiction CXLVII", 58-59).

Rex gloats, in his typically essentialist view of cultural otherness, that Clancy's is located in the "Frenchiest part of Paris" (197), and we learn that Rex and Bea visit the Eiffel Tower once a year, otherwise, Rex "solemnly" pronounces, "you could forget you're in Paris" (184). Ford completes his portrayal of the refusal to engage with French culture through the defining cultural expressions of food and clothes. *Nouvelle cuisine* has no place in Clancy's. Enormous quantities of food are served up and consumed – "big iceberg salads with beefsteak tomatoes and onion slabs drenched in white vinegar, continent-sized sirloins". And more food is available, Rex announces, "just as long as it isn't *poulet* and *haricots verts*". Rex, too, has remained happily untainted by French dress codes and notions of elegance, no doubt reasonably enough in his eyes, as it is the French who are the foreigners in Clancy's, and Rex who is at home: "He was dressed like somebody headed for a college football game, a big red crewneck sweater over a green plaid sport shirt and a pair of brown corduroys" (200), in contrast to the French diners, "all small men and women in pastel sweaters and nice jackets" (204). In all of these aggressive expressions of cultural difference and ostensible superiority, there is a sulphurous whiff of the colonizing demeanour – Rex is contemptuous of the French and their culture, and reduces both to immutable stereotypes;[7] Rex and Bea, culturally, inhabit a colonizer's stockade, protecting themselves from the unbearable natives and refusing to have anything to do with them; and Rex glories in the spoils of his brand of capitalist neo-colonialism, exploiting the French economically for all he is worth.

A sense of cultural superiority is one element in the nexus of relations between cultures codified by image studies. The French theorist, Daniel-Henri Pageaux, distinguishes the three dominant levels of exchange that "govern the representation of the Other" within this nexus:[8]

---

[7] The assertive display of attachment by Rex and Bea to their native culture through food and clothes has its corollary in the denigration of French culture and, in good colonizing fashion, of the French language. A brand of French wine, Pouilly-Fuissé, which they deign to drink, is nicknamed "foolish pussy" by Bea (199), a "translation" inspired no doubt by the stereotype of the French obsession with sex and of the reputed effeminacy of the French language.

[8] Daniel-Henri Pageaux, "De l'imagerie culturelle à l'imaginaire", in *Précis de littérature comparée*, ed. Pierre Brunel and Yves Chevrel, Paris: Presses

In the first case, the reality of the foreign culture is considered ... to be absolutely superior to the "national" culture, the culture of origin .... The consequence for this observing culture of origin is that its own is considered to be inferior .... This gives rise to "mania" ... and the representation of the foreign(er) has more to do with a "mirage" than an "image" ....

The second case is the reverse of the first: the reality of the foreign culture is considered to be inferior and negative with respect to the culture of origin: this gives rise to "phobia", an attitude that produces in return a positive valorization, a "mirage", of all or part of the culture of origin ....

In the third case, the reality of the foreign culture is considered to be positive and will take its place within the observing culture, which is a welcoming culture, and is itself considered as positive. This mutual esteem ... goes by the name of "philia", and is the only case of real, bilateral exchange.[9]

Rex exemplifies the second level of intercultural exchange: he is Francophobic, and displays equally the traits that are a corollary of that attitude, among which a vainglorious pride in his own culture. Indeed, there is no possibility of exchange in the phobic, even xenophobic, mode in which Rex functions. As Pageaux notes, in such cases "the Other is not only 'observed', but is obliged to be silent".[10] Rex and Bea demand of the French a literal silence in the restaurant and the metaphorical silence of an inferior culture in the presence of an obviously superior one.

Universitaires de France, 1989, 151: "qui régissent la représentation de l'Autre" (my translation, as are all quotations in English from Pageaux's article).

[9] "Premier cas: la réalité culturelle étrangère est tenue ... comme absolument supérieure à la culture 'nationale', d'origine .... La conséquence pour la culture d'origine, regardante, est qu'elle est tenue pour inférieure .... Il y a, dans ce cas, 'manie' ... et la représentation de l'étranger relève plus du 'mirage' que de l'image ....

Second cas, inverse du premier: la réalité culturelle étrangère est tenue pour inférieure et négative par rapport à la culture d'origine: il y a 'phobie' et cette attitude développe en retour une valorisation positive, un 'mirage' de tout ou partie de la culture d'origine ....

Troisième cas: la réalité culturelle étrangère est tenue pour positive et elle vient prendre sa place dans une culture regardante qui est une culture d'accueil, tenue également pour positive. Cette mutuelle estime ... [a] un nom: 'philie'. La philie est le seul cas d'échange réel, bilatéral" (Pageaux, "De l'imagerie culturelle à l'imaginaire", 152).

[10] "l'Autre sera non seulement 'regardé', mais obligé de se taire" (Pageaux, "De l'imagerie culturelle à l'imaginaire", 151).

The characters of Matthews and Helen allow Ford to broaden his exploration of the theme of intercultural exchange and expressions of national identity, and to counterbalance to some extent the scathing portrait of his compatriots abroad provided through Rex and Bea. From the beginning of the story Ford takes care to establish the cultural sensibility and attitudes to Paris and France that Matthews and Helen bring with them, which range from Matthews' lazy unawareness and confused idealization to Helen's somewhat arcane historical knowledge and tourist-lore clichés.

Matthews is highly educated – he is a former college professor – and has written a novel, yet, despite having set part of the novel in Paris, he is surprisingly ignorant of the city and country where he hopes to have his novel published (he is in Paris to discuss its publication in France). His surprise at the cold, wet Parisian weather is due to his having understood Paris to be situated "closer to the Riviera" (156), and it transpires that, for the Parisian settings of his novel, he had "researched everything out of library books, tourist guides and subway maps". His intellectually incurious attitude serves him badly upon his arrival, as he has the deflating and disorienting sense that Paris "seemed baffling. It might as well have been East Berlin". Matthews' perception of France, indeed, has its own tourist-cliché tinge to it: his idea of Parisian verisimilitude in his novel took the form of having "important events take place near famous sites like the Eiffel Tower, the Bastille and the Luxembourg Gardens" (154). Moreover, whatever Matthews has actually retained about Paris has fossilized into an idealistic and exotic image informed by the mythology of post-war Paris and embellished with the clichés of these narratives to which he is susceptible: "In the past, when he'd imagined Paris, he imagined jazz, Dom Pérignon corks flying into the bright, crisp night air, wide shining streets, laughter. Fun" (153).

In all of this, Ford is subtle but unsparing in his delineation of the cultural unawareness and lack of curiosity of an educated American mind. It is surely no coincidence that Ford has created characters that represent different strata of American society. One senses a clear desire not to restrict his indictment of American insularity to the easy target of lumpen, ill-informed Rex but, rather, to broaden it to represent American society in general. Rex's racism, nasty and stupid as it is, could be put down to simple lack of exposure in insular

America to the cosmopolitan notion of a world of cultural moral equals; Matthews' cultural ignorance and national complacency, however, are more disturbing in so far as his education and professional experience gave him every opportunity to extend his cultural awareness and appreciation beyond his country's borders.

Opposed to these remnants of Matthews' unhelpful bookish knowledge is Helen's autodidacticism, stimulated by her late father's fascination with Napoleon. Matthews is surprised to discover that Helen can make a reasonable attempt to speak French, something he cannot do, and to realize that Helen "seemed to know a lot about absolutely everything having to do with Napoleon, Louis XIV, the Domed Church and all the buildings" (176). Yet one senses that this knowledge is sentimental and vaguely fetishistic, and that the visits to the Napoleonic sites represent for Helen a form of pilgrimage to honour the memory of her dead father. And, elsewhere, it is the tourist itinerary dictated by their indispensable Fodor's guidebook that is Helen's reference for her discovery of French culture, which is to consist of his-and-hers Fodor's-plotted tours, a "romantic boat ride" (179) on the Seine, "long walks through the Bois de Boulogne", and that is to culminate in the eating of "a couple of incomparable meals" (149).

If Rex and Bea's exchange with the culture of the "Other" conforms to Pageaux's concept of a unilateral, phobic relationship, that of Matthews and Helen displays symptoms of all three of the dominant types of cultural exchange of Pageaux's model. Matthews' initial intercultural apathy quickly slides into petulant animosity when confronted by unavoidable and bothersome quotidian contact with French life, particularly where the French language is concerned. He becomes irritated, for example, with French numbers, "which the French purposefully complicated" (224), and is capable of falling back on the stereotype of the difficult French, as when he decides against ordering a meal in French: "His French wouldn't hold up, and lunch would degenerate into bad-willed bickering and misunderstanding— the horror stories people talked about" (242). And German tourists he comes across at the Eiffel Tower are equally reduced to the immutable identity of stereotype and cliché. On hearing them use the German noun *die Bedienung*, the imperialist fantasies of the Third Reich of fifty years previously are Matthews' only reference point: "He imagined it meant something admiring: the recognition of a paradise lost for the fatherland" (182).[11]

Along with these tangible manifestations of Pageaux's "phobia" intercultural mode in Matthews, there are also tentative indications of his potential to evolve towards the genuine cultural exchange of the "philia" mode. For the most part, however, Matthews' exchange with French culture belongs to the one-sided "mania" level of overvaluation of the other culture. In both the "mania" and "phobia" modes of Pageaux's scheme, the perception of either the native or other culture is founded on a "mirage" rather than an image. It is important to note here that the mirage is not a "false" image, to be contrasted with a "true" one. Leerssen insists on the "important epistemological shift"[12] from essentialism to constructivism that has taken place in image studies, whereby the analysis of supposed objective characteristics of native and other cultures has been replaced by the study of the subjective images and stereotypes that one constructs of these cultures. The mirage in Pageaux's scheme, then, is a willed, or required, perception, producing an overvaluation of either the native or other culture.

We can best understand the "mania" mode of Matthews' interaction with France precisely through this metaphor of "mirage", and specifically through an understanding of how this willed, necessary perception evolves out of Matthews' personal quest in Paris. Matthews arrives in Paris carrying the burden of sadness and disappointment that has marked his personal and professional life in recent years. His wife has left him for another man, taking their daughter with her, and is now seeking a divorce. Matthews' academic career, too, had been a source of frustration and disenchantment, leading him to resign his college post. And his novel, upon publication, "had gone immediately and completely out of sight"

---

[11] The German noun *Bedienung* means, in fact, "service", and has no connotation that could be made fit with Matthews' stereotyping of the German tourists. A possible explanation for his erroneous speculation may be that he picks up on the stressed "dien" in *Bedienung*, and links this to the noun *Dienst* or the verb *dienen*, both of which apply to military service. The "service" of *Bedienung*, however, has more to do with serving a customer, in, for instance, a restaurant.

[12] Joep Leerssen, "The Allochronic Periphery: Towards a Grammar of Cross-Cultural Representation", in *Beyond Pug's Tour: National and Ethnic Stereotyping in Theory and Literary Practice*, ed. C.C. Barfoot, Amsterdam: Rodopi, 1997, 285.

(161). As the days pass by in Paris in which Matthews waits to meet with his translator, he begins to envisage the possibility of a dramatic change in his life. His presence in Paris inspires a very precise and highly teleological self-narrative that sows the seeds of a potential new identity, that of the exiled American writer living in Paris. Matthews' self-narrative draws upon the idealized historical figure of the self-exiled American artist welcomed by the French, as well as upon the mythology of the café culture of late-1940s Saint-Germain-des-Prés.[13] His exchange with French culture, then, is largely based on his fantasy of a future life in that culture and on his speculations about his capacity to function and survive in it. This potential relationship with Paris, therefore, is one that he needs, that is willed; it is the "mirage" at the heart of his view of France. It is in this context that Matthews' desire to embrace French culture is to be understood: it is less a desire for the real, equal exchange of Pageaux's "philia" mode than a manifestation of expedient, self-interested acculturation. At one point, in a giddy flush of the fantasizing to which he is prone, he purrs to himself:

> … he could operate in [Paris] more or less on his own, just as he thought he'd be able to, even though it annoyed him not to know enough words to ask directions, or to understand if any were offered. He would need to stick to the simple, familiar touristic objectives (buying a newspaper, ordering coffee, reading a taxi meter). (226)

This is a good illustration of the dandyism that Pageaux identifies as one of the defining features of the "mania" mode of cultural exchange, namely a one-sided borrowing from another culture (of ideas, manners, attitudes, clothes, habits), which, although at the opposite end of the spectrum to Rex's xenophobia, has ultimately the same

---

[13] Matthews evokes the self-exile of American writers and artists to France on several occasions (153, 223, 227). It is interesting to record that Matthews specifically remembers the "black artists" (223) who had made Paris their home. He surely has in mind the 1920s, when black artists such as Josephine Baker and Sidney Bechet (mentioned by Matthews) made a name for themselves in Paris. Desmond King observes that "The failure to find acceptance in American society and bitterness at the daily routine of segregationist racism encouraged individual African Americans to leave [America] either permanently or temporarily". Many of them ended up in Paris, where, King notes, they enjoyed "Parisian society's openness to and interest in their work" (*The Liberty of Strangers*, 57-58).

consequence as the latter in so far as it does not initiate an equal exchange with that culture. Matthews at this moment may genuinely believe that he wishes to integrate into French culture and society, but seems not to understand that the height of his ambition is to be able to adopt the external signs and imitate the gestures of participation in French life. His desire for integration through superficial borrowing has him at one point imitate "a little gasping sound" followed by a "quick, shallow intake of breath" (150) that his French publisher makes, and that a former French colleague used to make. In so doing, Matthews is quick to make the leap – his ignorance of French culture notwithstanding – from the particular to the general, from the anecdotal to the stereotype: "All French people must make this noise, Matthews believed .... He had no idea what it meant" (151).

Ford returns elsewhere in the story to this notion of dandyish performance at the point of intercultural contact. Matthews observes at one stage that "there were a lot of Americans on the street, trying to act as if they spoke the language—his grad school French was too poor to even try". The Americans who are trying to pretend they speak French are guilty of the mimicry of which Matthews himself is guilty. It is dandyism as appropriation, as facile impersonation, the goal of which is to create the impression of an easy, natural adaptation to the foreign culture, but that, in reality, has more to do with dissimulation than assimilation.

This notion of performance and self-projection at the point of intercultural contact is an implicit theme throughout the story. Matthews concludes that the French, too, in the above scene, are guilty of performing: "They were like amateur actors playing French people but trying too hard" (179). Just as Rex and Bea seem to consider it insufficient simply to be American, and consider it necessary to play out their roles as Americans for the benefit of their French audience, Ford is suggesting here that the French are also self-consciously parading their idiosyncratic cultural repertoire in front of the Americans. Both nationalities are guilty of peacockish displays of, at once, cultural assertiveness and cultural defensiveness, and both drawing upon self-images and perceived national characteristics.

Nor is Helen, the remaining American character, immune to acting out her cultural identity. Upon meeting Rex and Bea by chance at the Eiffel Tower she becomes loud and ostentatious, lapsing, in an instance of cultural atavism, into a mode and performance she takes to be quintessentially American. It is significant too that, at the moment Helen, Rex and Bea are over-performing the rituals of unexpected reunion, they are mingling with German and Japanese tourists. The performance of elemental Americanness seems directed at this precise audience – the Germans stare at them, and the text makes clear that neither Helen nor Rex appreciate the presence of the Japanese tourists. The latter's presence has Helen remark that "You might think you're in Tokyo up here", and the language used to describe the Japanese tourists – attributed to Helen's thoughts – has racist overtones: they are in "clusters" and are "jabbering" (184). The German and Japanese tourists are both portrayed as invading armies of tourists pushing others aside: the Germans are "shouldering in" (182) to have a better view of the city, while the Japanese are "pressing toward" the observation windows. And both are explicitly condemned to the burden of their Second World War identities: the text describes them, from Matthews' perspective, as "Axis-power tourists" (184).

Many of these instances of uneasy intercultural contact can be elucidated by Leerssen's model of the auto-image/hetero-image interplay, whereby cultures, at the point of intercultural confrontation, react to the manner in which they perceive the other culture to be perceiving them. Thus, Rex and Bea's affirmation of their national identity in Clancy's is influenced by their impression of how the French perceive them at that moment: Rex becomes unmistakably more hostile and vulgar in his manner the more the French presence in Clancy's is manifested, as if in reaction to the disapproval he feels emanating from the French.

It is also the case, however, that the perceived disapproval may well be due to more than simple over-sensitivity on behalf of the American characters. In Clancy's the Americans overhear a snippet of conversation from a nearby table at which, presumably, non-Americans are seated: "It was Egyptian turkwoz—that's the very best. Better than that American garbage" (206).[14] And in extended scenes in the story the two French characters who are given a voice to express their views of Americans are supercilious and insulting. Matthews' French translator explains to Matthews "how [the French] see Americans", and, when he asks for clarification, she replies: "As

---

[14] It is likely that the French word they heard was *turquoise*, hence its rendering in the text, as heard by Anglophone ears, as "turkwoz".

silly ... as not understanding very much. But, for that reason, interesting" (254). The attitude of Blumberg, Matthews' publisher, while also no doubt rooted in condescension, is more directly informed by history. Rudely cancelling his appointment with Matthews at the last minute to go on a Christmas holiday, he lays bare a long-nurtured wounded national pride:

> Now is, of course, a perfect time to be in Paris. We all go away where it's warm. You have it all to yourselves, you and your friends the Germans. We'll take it back when you're finished. (152)

A moment of mild personal friction is immediately recontextualized, situated now within the historical tensions of political and ideological conflicts and relationships. It is clear that Blumberg has wartime and post-war occupation on his mind, and his conflation of the two utterly different forms of historical military presence in Paris is impressive proof of the obstinate resistance of cultural prejudice to time and historical truth.

Overall, indeed, the French do not emerge with greater credit than the Americans. Despite Helen speaking French to shop personnel, she is the victim of a snooty superiority, with "small aproned Frenchmen" looking at her "in annoyance, often before simply turning around and ignoring her" (179). It might be too generous to offer this background hum of disdainful anti-Americanism as a defence of Rex and Bea's Francophobia – the "turkwoz" incident in Clancy's takes place at the end of the scene, in other words after Rex had already given full vent to his Francophobia – and the text itself does not seek to do so. Yet it is also the case that anti-American sentiment is quite widespread in France, a phenomenon that is quickly perceptible through observation of daily cultural life in France. It is, indeed, a subject that is regularly debated in France itself, which was the case in the aftermath of the disagreement between the French and US governments over the war in Iraq. Ford's story predates these events but nonetheless taps into a latent historical tension between the two cultures that continues to the present day.

There is another important political and historical dimension running through the story, one consistent with the paradigm of intercultural perceptions generated by the presence of a non-native, be it colonizer or traveller, in foreign space: "Occidentals" is permeated with the spirit of the historical representation of the relationship between the Occident and the Orient. Richard Ford seems to insist on this wider ideological context by the very title of his story, the meaning of which is not immediately clear. The term "the Occident" is now more or less obsolescent, having being superseded by "the West". But the use of the term "Oriental" by Matthews' publisher when he promises to show Matthews "secret Oriental gardens" (150), provides an interpretive key to the story's title. In *Orientalism*, Edward Said establishes from the outset both the indissociable relationship between the concepts of "Occident" and "Orient" and the binary opposition inherent in what he terms the "general meaning for Orientalism": "Orientalism is a style of thought based upon an ontological and epistemological distinction made between 'the Orient' and (most of the time) 'the Occident'."[15]

"Occidentals" seems to tap into this historical binary relationship. It is impossible to ignore Ford's intriguing title, his use of the loaded coupling of "Occident" and "Orient" and his precise attribution of these terms to specific characters in the story – Blumberg uses the term "Oriental", while Helen refers to the Eiffel Tower as "the miracle of the Occident" (178). This distribution of the terms, and the fact that the title can refer only to the two protagonists (and to Rex and Bea, the other principal characters), identify the Americans as "Occidentals" and the French as the inhabitants of "the Orient", a relationship of identities supported by the countries' geographical relationship: France lies to America as the Orient does to the Occident. The text supports this figuration of space, as it does the identities that attend these designations. Leerssen identifies a typical and, he asserts, structural representation of foreign space into centre and periphery in "metropolitan" discourse (a representation consistent with colonialist discourse in general).[16] All four American characters leave the centre, America, to come to the periphery, France, a foreign space that is, by definition, somewhat remote, particularly in the colonial imagination. Rex spots the business opportunity in France when back home in America, "From thousands of miles across the ocean" (199), while Helen seems truly to imagine France as a distant and unexplored land: when she gazes upon the Eiffel Tower for the

---

[15] Edward Said, *Orientalism*, London: Penguin, 2003, 2.
[16] Leerssen, "The Allochronic Periphery", 293-94.

first time, she marvels: "Well, oh my .... There it is. I'm so happy to see it. I wondered if I would" (178). And almost a quarter of the entire story is devoted to an exhilarated vagabondage by Matthews through Paris, as if the city were indeed a newly discovered, exotic and virgin territory to be explored.

The historical relationship of Occident to Orient is also, of course, a deeply political one, and the power relationship implied by the centre/periphery organization of space is mirrored in the text in the assumed identities and postures of Rex, Bea and Blumberg. Rex and Bea consider France to be, on their American terms, less than civilized, and display a typical centre-to-periphery colonizer's attitude to France and the French, while Blumberg seems ossified in his identity as the colonized native, seeing the Americans as occupiers, resenting their presence and resorting to the guerrilla tactics of discourtesy and disdain to undermine the foreign occupants of his city, which he intends to "take back" when they are "finished".

It is through the Occident/Orient paradigm that one may understand another American attitude to France on display in the story, one that partakes of a structural feature of the imperial view of the periphery, and one typical of the Occidental attitude to the Orient: Matthews is drawn to Paris and led to envisage a life there as a writer partly because of the mysteries and possibilities kindled by his sense of French exoticism. Exoticism, in accordance with its etymology in the Greek term *exo*, meaning "outside (of)", connotes a foreign space, a space, therefore, of difference and otherness. But also attached to the word are the powerful suggestions of the alluring, the desirable, the mysterious. Said reminds us of the "entire range of pre-Romantic and Romantic representations of the Orient as exotic locale".[17] The possible significance of the theme of exoticism in "Occidentals" is hinted at in the opening paragraphs when Matthews recalls Blumberg's tantalizing promise (in another example of the latter slipping into the Oriental identity) to act as his guide to Paris and to show him "special parts tourists would never be lucky enough to see", including the "secret Oriental gardens in Montparnasse" (150). Matthews needs no encouragement to exoticize France: his Paris is a romantic city of alluring otherness, a writer's *terre d'asile* and a

---

[17] Said, *Orientalism*, 118.

bacchanal location of laughter, fun and Dom Pérignon. And based on nothing more than his correspondence with Blumberg, Matthews' fantasizing imagination had conceived of his publisher as "an old man, a kindly keeper of an ancient flame, overseer of a rich and storied culture that only a few were permitted to share" (152).[18] These are the idealizations and reveries of the exoticist. As is Matthews' intention, when he sets out on his exploration of Paris and is thinking about a Christmas present for his daughter, to find a toy store "where there were precious objects unimaginable to American children" (220).[19] And, as already noted, even Rex and Bea, entrenched as they are in their surly monoculturalism, have a primitive sense of the exotic allure of Paris.

It is, however, in the sexual domain that the exotic view of the oriental space of France is most intriguingly depicted. In *Orientalism* Said describes the importance in the Western mind of the sexual identity of the Orient. He surveys the work of several writers on the Orient, culminating with the writings of Gustave Flaubert:

> Woven through all of Flaubert's Oriental experiences, exciting or disappointing, is an almost uniform association between the Orient and sex. In making this association Flaubert was neither the first nor the most exaggerated instance of a remarkably persistent motif in Western attitudes to the Orient .... The Orient seems still to suggest not only fecundity but sexual promise (and threat), untiring sensuality, unlimited desire, deep generative energies.[20]

Matthews does not have an exotic sexual experience while in Paris, but he does display a sharpened awareness of romantic or sexual possibility, an anticipation linked to his presence in a city that, from the outset, he considers exotic and that has attached to it the typical exoticist's associations of freedom and adventure in sexual matters. On his peregrination through Paris, Matthews – alone in the city for

---

[18] Matthews lurches from one stereotype to another. When Blumberg cancels their meeting, Matthews instantly re-imagines him as "small, pale, balding, pimply, possibly a second-rate academic making ends meet by working in publishing, someone in a shiny black suit and cheap shoes" (152).

[19] Despite finding a toy store with "a bewildering variety of wonderful possibilities" (224), Matthews ends up buying his daughter a wall tablet (for written messages) covered in the usual clichéd images of Paris.

[20] Said, *Orientalism*, 188.

the first time, having left Helen sleeping back at the hotel – chances upon his publisher's building. He immediately fantasizes, in his publisher's absence, that a "young secretary" or "pretty" assistant editor, although "not recognizing him", might "bring him up to the offices" where she would be "charmed by him" and would "eye him provocatively" (232), leading to a dinner date later in the evening.

A little further on in his wandering Matthews decides to allow himself "a flight of fancy, a single indulgence" for which he had not thought he would "have the chance". Now that he is alone, however, he is free to pursue a possible sexual opportunity. He decides to ring a woman with whom he had an affair while he was a college professor and who now lives, he believes, alone in Paris. Margie McDermott had written to Matthews from Paris, but he had never bothered to reply. Now, however, he recalls their sexual "careenings" (233). Matthews' renewed interest in Margie is essentially sexual and is instigated by his temporary freedom in the exotic foreign space of Paris: "His only thought was that he wanted to see her simply because he could, and because this was Paris" (236). While Paris, at the precise moment this thought comes into his mind, might represent nothing more for Matthews than a sense of heady freedom and romantic possibility, there can be no ambiguity regarding his intentions, nor about the role of Paris, as he lets himself be drawn into his sexual fantasy:

> Margie could be different now. What he'd finally found uninteresting and going-nowhere about her in an Ohio college town ... might be changed in Paris. Something locked away due to circumstance, that inhibited everyone's view of everything and everybody, might have opened up here. All kinds of things were now possible .... in five minutes she could appear, breathless, expectant, wearing little other than a green cloth coat. After which they could hurry back to her "poor flat," and he wouldn't return to the [Hotel] Nouvelle Métropole until after dark, and possibly never. (238)[21]

---

[21] It seems more than coincidence that Ford should so name Matthews' hotel. "Metropole" is another term used in the representation of space as centre and periphery, designating the parent state in relation to a colony. Nor is one surprised to discover that the hotel manager and staff are either Indian or Pakistani. The term "métropole" is also one still widely used in France to distinguish the France of the European continent from French territories such as Guadeloupe and Martinique.

Said notes the association "between the Orient and the freedom of licentious sex". And he continues: "We may as well recognize that for nineteenth-century Europe, with its increasing *embourgeoisement*, sex had been institutionalized to a very considerable degree."[22] Several associations of the exotic locale with sex described by Said are present in Matthews' fantasy of his meeting up with Margie – his sexual encounters with her in Ohio took place in a restricted institutionalized context, in so far as both of them were married and had children; the exotic locale of Paris represents the freedom to have a purely sexual encounter, as well as the possibility of a new, more licentious sexual experience, now that Margie may be "different" and "changed", emancipated by the sexual freedom of libertine Paris; and, finally, there is the chance of a greater sexual appetite in Margie, as she may no longer be "inhibited" and he will be the willing recipient of whatever has been "locked away": perhaps Margie will arrive "breathless, expectant" and scantily dressed, unequivocal signs, in Matthews' exoticized Paris, of sexual availability and desire.[23]

Situated within the wider context of the story, Matthews' sense of the exotic is another manifestation of his essentially utilitarian attitude to France and Paris: they are of interest to him only in so far as they contribute to the achievement of personal goals and the realization of personal fantasies. He is keen to assume the demeanour of the *habitué* in Paris and to display the external signs of participation in French life, but does not generally seek to understand French culture, nor let himself be changed by contact with it. He does not generally participate in what Pageaux calls the true intercultural exchange, "the dialogue on equal terms with the Other".[24] Matthews' relationship to France is non-reciprocal and unbalanced. His attitude, despite an apparent openness to some of its external (though usually exotic) features, has in common with the stereotype – and indeed with Rex's attitude – the reduction of the other culture to a set of immutable perceptions that refuse to acknowledge that culture's diversity and difference and that condemn it to submission and silence.

Matthews is generally unavailable to grapple with the difference of

---

[22] Said, *Orientalism*, 190.
[23] Matthews also fantasizes that the young secretary or pretty assistant editor in his publisher's office will arrive "a little out of breath" (232).
[24] "le dialogue d'égal à égal avec l'Autre" (Pageaux, "De l'imagerie culturelle à l'imaginaire", 152-53).

French culture. Yet, as suggested earlier, there are indications of an incipient recognition of a cultural parity, hinting at the potential for evolution to a fully bilateral exchange with French culture. This takes the form of occasional insights, triggered by an instance of an unfamiliar cultural practice, into the differences between his own and French culture. Confronted, for example, with the entry-code panel at the door of his publisher's building, he observes:

> No names were listed, as there would've been in the States. You needed a code even to gain entry. France was a much more private place than America, he thought, but also strangely freer. The French knew the difference between privacy and intimacy. (231)

Similarly, he pulls himself up when he finds himself wondering where "downtown" Paris is, suddenly conscious that "downtown" might be "an American idea" (237). And there is great symbolic significance at the end of the story in his having lost the Fodor's guide and in beginning to find his way around from experience and local knowledge alone. Helen, too, is allowed her own insight into the French, saying to Matthews: "The French are more serious than we are. They care more. They have a perspective on importance and unimportance" (177-78). This nascent appreciation of French cultural values even occasions an instance of the self-reflection and re-evaluation that signifies, for Pageaux, the bilateral, "philia" mode of genuine intercultural exchange. Matthews talks of Paris henceforth "coloring" his views, before continuing: "He would never, for instance, think of Christmas again in the crude, gaudy American way. Paris had been added" (244).

Through his American characters in "Occidentals" Richard Ford seems intent on depicting a variety of modes of intercultural exchange, and it is striking how neatly these match up with Pageaux's model. So, if there is the unilateral, "phobia" mode of Rex and Bea and the fantasies and mirages of the one-sided "mania" mode of Matthews, there is also the example of Margie, who, although a minor American character, quietly yet tellingly exemplifies an evolution towards the "philia" mode – she has come to France, has studied French and now lives and works in Paris. But for all of Margie's unobtrusive cultural integration, it is nonetheless the difficulties and misunderstandings attending intercultural contact that Ford's story highlights. While "Occidentals" is neither ideological (it was natural for an American writer to choose American protagonists and to choose France, a country and a culture Ford knows well) nor didactic (the story is illuminating but infused throughout with humour and satire), its broad themes and preoccupations allow the reader to discern the obstacles to more harmonious and balanced intercultural contact. Ford specifically addresses the question of intercultural misunderstanding in two scenes dealing with the translation of Matthews' book into French, in which Ford applies and extensively develops the metaphor of translation.[25] Appropriately, the use of the metaphor is granted to the two principal French characters, in other words to the representatives of the culture that is seen in the text to be the victim of cultural misunderstanding by Americans. Matthews' publisher, Blumberg, speaking about the translation of Matthews' book, situates the task, perhaps unknowingly, into its wider context:

> Translation is not a matter merely of converting your book into French; it is a matter of *inventing* your book into the French mind. So it is necessary to have the translation absolutely perfect, for people to know it correctly. We don't want you or your book to be misunderstood .... People spend too much time misunderstanding each other. (151)

Blumberg's notion of "the French mind" supports the view – one implied throughout the story – that understanding a culture means understanding an entire way of life, embracing history, traditions, beliefs and practices, as well as the moral, social, political and economic structures of a culture. Cultural difference runs deep, in other words, as must translation from one culture to another. It is hardly surprising, then, that both the artist Ford and the theorist Pageaux concur that equal, bilateral intercultural exchange, characterized by "mutual esteem", is the exception rather than the rule. Matthews' translator, Madame de Grenelle, is even more exacting in her view of what is needed in the translation from one

---

[25] The translation metaphor has a second application in the story. Matthews' trip to Paris coincides with a personal crisis in his life. He hopes, and needs, to break with his past of failure and disappointment and to find a new direction and goal in his life. He articulates this to Helen at one point by saying: "I'm hoping to be translated into something better than I was" (166).

culture to another. She considers that Matthews' book "is not quite finished in English" and "is not entirely understandable" in certain ways, by which she means, among other things, that it would not, without proper translation, be understood by a French audience. Her intention is to render the book's "logic" (253) into French. Understanding the "logic" or "mind" of another culture are different ways of formulating the challenge of achieving greater intercultural understanding, a task that appears, at least at the level of the personal intercultural contact depicted in Richard Ford's story, extremely difficult.

At a national level, "Occidentals" has proved to be prescient in its depiction of cultural misunderstanding between Americans and the French. The story, even allowing for its satirical undercurrent, is quietly instructive in the manner in which it draws attention to the risks involved in cultural misunderstanding and in the excessive attachment to one's native culture. One need look no further than the mutual incomprehension that afflicts relations between the Christian and Muslim worlds (the Occident/Orient relationship again) to find evidence of the critical importance of auto- and hetero-images in the construction of the self and the other. Prejudice, cultural stereotyping and clichés are too often the depressing currency in the exchange between cultures and countries that routinely fail to understand each other. Prejudice and stereotyping, of course, have deep and vigorous roots in history, as "Occidentals" reminds us: the story may well take place in late-twentieth-century Paris, but the cultural attitudes are often informed by events that took place there fifty years earlier.

From a purely American perspective "Occidentals" may be viewed as the continuation of Ford's reflection on his own country begun in *The Sportswriter* and developed extensively in *Independence Day* and *The Lay of the Land*. There are important consistencies in the depiction of Americans at home and abroad. The racism and xenophobia on display in the latter two novels of the trilogy is exported to France. So, too, is the emphasis on commerce, through Rex's hawkish exploitation of the French market. Above all, though, one discovers in "Occidentals" the isolationist and exclusionary tendencies so prevalent in *Independence Day* and *The Lay of the Land*. Clancy's is the site of self-segregation, where Americans "stranded" in Paris band together as a homogeneous group and seek to exclude the other, just as the inhabitants of Ridgefield and Deep River do in *Independence Day*.

But the exportation to France of the physical self-isolation at home breeds a new form of exclusion, that of an entire culture. Together, the four American characters of the story, with their different backgrounds, are seen to be representative of American society in general and to articulate typical understandings of American national identity. At the better end of the range Matthews' and Helen's knowledge of and interest in France is nourished mostly by stereotype and cliché, and, although there are positive notes struck by both (particularly by Helen), there is no sustained opening out to the other culture on their part. As for Rex and Bea, they are overtly and proudly exclusionary and treat France and the French as a form of malady, the only sane response to which is self-quarantine. Underpinning these views is the cultural ignorance that defines the "phobia" mode of intercultural contact described by Pageaux. But this mode is also typical of the imperialist and colonizing mindset that is born of the certainty of one's cultural superiority and that takes the form, when exported, of insisting that the cultural Other should conform to the values, cultural practices and – to a certain extent – identity of the superior culture.

The depictions of America and Americans in the Frank Bascombe trilogy and in "Occidentals" are complementary, and combine to portray the national and international effects of American cultural values. Richard Ford himself establishes the parallel between American attitudes and behaviour at home and abroad. Speaking of the trilogy portrait of American society in the interview at the end of this book, he says: "There is a force in America that wants to identify the other as your adversary. There's no doubt about that. The person different from you is your adversary."[26] "Occidentals" demonstrates Ford's view that this national characteristic on display at home is equally and abundantly on display when Americans are abroad. And Ford sees these national cultural values being manifested in a highly detrimental manner when they are exported to the rest of the world: in the same interview he speaks of America "doing irreparable harm to the globe, irreparable harm to other countries", and of "the outsized effect that we have on the rest of the world".[27] If the notion of identity

---

[26] Interview, 329.
[27] *Ibid.*, 326.

in Ford's stories has its most obvious expression in the portrayals of his characters, it is equally employed in his fiction to explore the values and self-understandings of his country, and the consequences of the expression of that identity in America and the wider world.

CHAPTER 9

A MULTITUDE OF SINS

ACTS AND CONSEQUENCES

In an interview given by Richard Ford to coincide with the publication of *A Multitude of Sins* he explained the genesis of the ten thematically linked stories that constitute his collection:

> I wrote "Privacy" first, "Crèche" second and "Quality Time" third. Then I thought, "Oh, I see where this taking me." [*sic*] So I'm going to exclude stories that didn't go into what I thought this was going to be about.[1]

Ford's awareness of both the thematic affinities in the stories he was writing and the narrative potential of the subject area he was beginning to explore did more than provide a general focus and direction to the stories he subsequently wrote: he also noted that these first three stories "prefigured the rest of the book".[2] The significance of two of these stories, "Privacy" and "Quality Time", is acknowledged in the collection by placing them at the beginning. It is here, we might well conclude, that the inspiration of the remaining stories is to be found and where the vital themes are first developed. One immediately understands the seminal status of "Privacy" and the reason it is accorded its privileged position in the collection – the story that begins the book is itself a story about beginnings. It is the shortest of the ten stories, yet the four-page text is as long as it needs to be to evoke the first loosenings and slippages – thoughtlessly set in motion

---

[1] "Richard Ford", *identity theory: the narrative thread*, 2.
[2] Ellen Kanner, Interview with Richard Ford, "A Multitude of Sins: Errors of omission are the stuff of real life", http://www.bookpage.com/0202bp/richard_ford. html (26/06/2006).

and barely understood – of the bonds that hold men and women together.

"Quality Time" earns its special status in the collection as a prefiguring story on account of its precisely calibrated and deliberate structure. The function of this structure is most visible in the opening sequence, which is subsequently revealed to be an allegorical micro-narrative of the inexorable chain of events that an initial act can set in motion and that can lead to tragic outcomes and consequences. The two opening stories, then, focus very deliberately on the anatomy of infidelity in its structural features of beginning, middle and end, but do so particularly with regard to beginnings, hence the position of the stories at the start of the collection. It is as if Ford wished to identify an unvarying and repetitive pattern of behaviour in the matter of relations between men and women, in particular the manner in which they let themselves be drawn into a dynamic of betrayal. The remaining stories in the collection will go on to expose various consequences of this initial betrayal by putting on display what Ford has termed "that multitude of tiny sins that fit under the umbrella of infidelity".[3]

Significantly, the collection closes with a story that is also self-consciously and resolutely structured according to the seemingly inexorable dynamics of cause-and-effect: if "Privacy" and "Quality Time" focus on beginnings, and only allude to, or stop short of, catastrophic outcomes, "Abyss" presses relentlessly on to the bitter end. It seems a very deliberate framing of the collection by Ford, and is a structural feature that merits close attention. "Abyss" can more appropriately be discussed in a separate chapter and as closing story (apart from its framing function and structural interest, it is also the longest story in the collection, and is, in fact, a novella). However, "Privacy" and "Quality Time", because they open the collection and because of their thematic, structural and allegorical significance, deserve more immediate consideration.

Not the least of the intriguing features of "Privacy" is its status as the collection's own version of the book of Genesis. Just as Genesis narrates an original sin in the opening chapters of the Bible, a sin that

---

[3] Jane Ganahl, Interview with Richard Ford, "Mapping a terrain of lust and lies; Richard Ford writes about the perils of temptation in 'Sins'", *San Francisco Chronicle*, 18 March 2002, Section D, 1.

destroys harmony and brings loss and conflict, "Privacy" narrates an opening infidelity that is at the origin of the subsequent loss alluded to in the story, a pattern of sin and consequence developed throughout the collection. And just as Adam and Eve are the first people and the original sinners in the Bible, so the first-person male narrator of "Privacy" is the first character and first sinner of Ford's collection – he will commit an act of betrayal that is an archetype of the betrayals in the stories that follow, from which are born the various calamities visited upon the characters. The Bible analogy, of course, is far from being forced, and is indeed quite obvious. Ford found the title of his collection in the Bible,[4] one that unambiguously introduces into his stories a moral resonance of responsibility and reckoning consistent with his commitment to a moral vision in his fiction.

In a book of stories concerned above all with the consequences of infidelity between men and women, the opening line of "Privacy" is both fitting and premonitory: "This was at a time when my marriage was still happy."[5] Given that the story is narrated from an unspecified time in the future, we might expect to learn that the events to be recounted are explicitly proposed as the source of the unhappy outcome alluded to in the narrator's first sentence. However, such an explicit causation is never established by the narrator, as if he had not understood, or did not wish to recognize, the significance of what he found himself doing back in that period of his life. What he did – in one of the resonances of the story's title – was private: not only was his wife unaware of his actions and apparently remained so, but the infidelity was committed without the willing participation of a third party. It was not, therefore, brought to light through exposure and witness; it remained private, to be acknowledged or ignored at the narrator's will.

We learn little about the condition of the narrator's ten-year marriage, apart from the important fact that it was still happy at the time of the events narrated. In seeking a context to explain the events

---

[4] The phrase, "a multitude of sins", occurs twice in the Bible, both in the New Testament. In James 5:20 one reads: "know that whoso bringeth a sinner back from the error of his way shall save the man's soul from death, and shall 'cover a multitude of sins'." In the First Epistle of St Peter the phrase occurs as follows: "[Be ye] before all things earnest in your charity for one another, because 'charity covereth a multitude of sins'" (I Peter 4:8).
[5] Ford, *A Multitude of Sins*, 3. See note 4 in the Introduction for publication details. Further references to this collection will be indicated parenthetically in the text.

to follow, the reader might be led to speculate about a certain
complacency that may have set in ("we ... were still enjoying that
strange, exhilarating illusion that we had survived the worst of life's
hardships"), or about the unrewarding working lives they were both
enduring, or, more generally, about the difficult financial and material
conditions in which they lived. The couple's daily routine seems
arduous and hardly joyful: they stay away from their unheated
apartment ("the living space [was] only a great, empty room with ...
almost no electric light" [3]) and come back, in the cold winter
evenings, merely to sleep. Yet this information seems offered by the
narrator as no more than necessary narrative setting and context, and
their trying material existence could just as easily be interpreted as
proof of the strength of their relationship. It is, indeed, the very
absence of causality that is significant: the narrator's act of betrayal
occurred simply because the circumstances presented themselves that
allowed it to occur. The narrator found himself looking out his
apartment window one night and into the apartment opposite, where
he noticed a woman undressing. It is precisely the contingent nature of
the origin of the betrayal that is important, as if the text wishes to
insist on the intractable nature of male sexuality: a man chances upon
a woman undressing, knows he can watch her undetected, and does so.

The narrator is "rapt by this sight" and uses a pair of opera glasses
to watch what he takes to be a young woman. Although he claims not
to know what was going through his mind then, he will allow that he
"was aroused" and that he "loved the very illicitness" of watching the
woman while his wife lay "sleeping nearby and knowing nothing of
what I was doing". He is spellbound at the sight of the naked woman
as she performs "a kind of languid, ritual dance" (5) and is ultimately
clear about the nature of the attraction of what he is witnessing: "It
was all arousal and secrecy and illicitness and really nothing else" (6).
Between the first night when the narrator happens upon the scene of
the woman undressing and the following nights when he stays awake,
lets his wife fall asleep, then installs himself to watch his private
spectacle, there occurs the first sin against fidelity to his wife.

Significantly, it is exactly at this point in the text, after the first
night, that the narrator records that he is "sure now that all of this had
to do with my impending failures" (5). He does not specify the nature
of these failures, although he has already mentioned that, at the time
of these events, he was "failing" (4) in his work as a writer. Yet it is

difficult to dissociate his voyeurism and betrayal from his ominous opening sentence that his marriage was still happy when he began to watch the woman undressing. This is where we may understand "Privacy" as a story about beginnings. The nights of the week that follows surely represent the beginning of the period that would lead to a happy marriage no longer being so. The infidelity portrayed here may be secretive and private in nature, and his wife may never even learn of it, but the narrator has nonetheless looked outside his relationship for the thrill of illicit sexual stimulation and, he suggests, relief from the frustrations of his life at that time. The seeds of the undoing of his marriage have been sown, the foundations for his "impending failures" have been laid.

The narrator's voyeurism ends on the night the woman is no longer to be seen when he goes to gaze at her through his opera glasses. He goes back to bed, "never thinking to look through the window again" (6). He will subsequently come across her when he finds himself passing in front of her building, will discover that she is an old woman, and will feel "oddly … betrayed". The word has finally been uttered, but it is of course the narrator who has betrayed. The story ends with the narrator announcing that, at the end of that week, his life was entering "its first, long cycle of necessity" (7), an ambiguous phrase that suggests constraint, difficulty, inevitability. As a closing sentence it stands in opposition to the opening one that spoke of a happy marriage, and seems, therefore, both to recognize that the week's events have extinguished something important and to anticipate a change, a drift into the failures already evoked.

Intriguingly, "Privacy" is the only story in the collection in which adultery does not feature, and the narrator also withholds a direct causation that would link his behaviour to suggested effects. Yet, in Ford's first and seminal story, the primary components are present – two people who have promised themselves and their moral beings to each other, who have decided to live their lives together, and who are happy; one who lets him- or herself be tempted away from that promise by the allure of another; and the hint that there will be consequences to be borne as a result of this infidelity. The remaining nine stories will offer various articulations on this habitual human drama.

As with "Privacy", the position of "Quality Time" in the collection seems related to its status as one of the three original stories that furnished Richard Ford with the inspiration and direction for the rest of the collection. "Quality Time", indeed, could be considered as the prototype story of *A Multitude of Sins*: it brings a married woman and her lover together in an affair and moves them towards what could be grave and irreparable consequences. If it is one of the more dispassionate stories in the collection, it is because of its highly determined nature: as much as it is the story of an affair, it is also a model of the infidelity-and-consequences schema of the other stories. As one of the narratives that prefigures the others, "Quality Time" seems for the author to have taken on, in part at least, the status of paradigm narrative.

The opening passages set up the moral and intellectual experiment of the story. It describes the death of a woman as witnessed by the male protagonist, Wales, as he drives to the hotel where he is to spend the night with the married woman with whom he has spent the previous five nights in the same manner. The event witnessed and the protagonist's affair become linked as the story progresses, and this interdependence gives the story its narrative and moral dynamic. As Wales watches from his car, stopped at a traffic light at a busy Chicago junction, a woman pedestrian falls down in the snow as she waits to cross the street. She gets to her feet, and, inexplicably, given the volume of traffic, the darkness and the icy conditions, begins to cross the road. In the textual equivalent of slow motion, the narrative describes her movement and gestures as she leaves the safety of the sidewalk and moves towards the potential danger of the thoroughfare. One line of cars stops for her, but a van in the next line hits the woman "flush-on" (10), transforming her in a moment from a living human being "into a collection of assorted remnants on a frozen pavement" (11). It is this brutal and abrupt transformation that, as the initial shock begins to be absorbed, preoccupies Wales as he replays the sequence of events in his mind. The woman fell, then righted and steadied herself:

> She'd been completely *in* her life then, in the fullest grip and perplex of it. And then—as he'd watched—three steps, possibly four, and that was all over. In his mind he broke it down: first, as though nothing that happened had been inevitable. And then as if it *all* was inevitable, a steady unfolding. (12)

Rather, however, than this sequence being simply the anatomy of a few dramatic and horrifying moments in which a human life is destroyed, the slow unfolding of the woman's accident as she passes from safety to her death becomes, as the story progresses, an allegory of the evolution and potential outcomes of sequences of events in life in general. Later in the evening, when he is with his lover, Jena, Wales recalls the accident's unfolding, understands it as an allegory and identifies its relevance to himself and Jena:

> So much possibility, so much chance for a better outcome had been caught in that slow motion. It should make one able to see the ends of events before they happened, to forestall bad outcomes. It could be applied to love affairs. (23)

As we have already seen, Richard Ford had long been concerned in his fiction with the consequences of one's actions. That preoccupation continued into this collection, as he notes: "These stories are about failure – failure of patience, failure to tell the truth, failure of affection – and what the consequences of those failures are."[6] In "Quality Time", the preoccupation is more with the stage directly preceding consequences, namely outcomes, understood initially by Wales in the straightforward sense of how a series of related events and actions turn out. Yet it will gain another meaning in Wales' mind as he seeks to understand what it is that Jena seems to want from their relationship.

Wales is a European-based American journalist who is back in Chicago for two months to lecture on the subject of the actual, or real events, and particularly their re-interpretation by, and their acquisition of meaning through, the narratives of mass media. Wales' case study is Princess Diana's death, the kind of event that, in Wales' view, was the "easiest to cover", as journalists "simply made up the emotions, made up their consequence, invented what was important" (16). Witnessing the wave of near-hysterical propaganda – establishment-sanctioned and tabloid-press-induced – surrounding Diana's funeral, Wales concluded that, "and this is what he wrote finally, the crux of it, the literature of the failed actuality—*someone has to tell us what's important, because we no longer know*". It is to this lecture, entitled

---

[6] Bob Hoover, Interview with Richard Ford, "Ford is story maker, not story teller", *Pittsburgh Post-Gazette*, 17 February 2002, Section E, 8.

"Failed Actuality: How We Discover the Meaning of the Things We See" (25), that, significantly, Jena is drawn, and after which she seeks out Wales and invites him for a drink. They speak about America and about global rather than personal matters, yet, learning that he would soon be returning to Europe, she takes his arm and tells him they would have to hurry if they were "going to do anything together".

The sexual promise hinted at in her suggestive phrase is indeed realized over the five nights they spend in the hotel room that Jena has taken for a week. Equally, however, the phrase's ambiguity is also revealed as Jena's calculating, controlling personality is made more and more obvious. Wales felt that Jena had attended his lecture because, like all women who, in his view, attended lectures, she wanted something, although "conceivably something innocent" (16). The immediate manifestation of her sexual desire upon Wales' arrival each evening initially suggested that sexual excitement and fulfilment were her goals, particularly as she is married to a man who, in her words, "was at his best a mild but considerate lover" (29). On the sixth evening, however, Jena wishes to talk, and it is here that we begin to discover what it was that drew Jena to Wales' lecture, and why she is anxious to have Wales listen to her now.

Jena is an artist, and has taken the hotel room for a week to paint, with her husband's agreement. Her paintings are worked-over black-and-white photographs of a couple from an earlier generation whose features have been grossly distorted, in the manner of Francis Bacon, through the use of strong, smearing colours. Wales finds them "depressing" and "unnecessary" (18). He has already understood that the couple whose features and very identity are being distorted is Jena's parents, and that her parents are Jena's obsession. They are the people at the heart of the story "she couldn't get over from her past, the completely insignificant story that she believed cooperated in all her major failures" (20), above all her unsatisfactory marriage and her lack of success as an artist. Jena reproaches her parents with their muteness, with their failure to master language and, thus, to shape the world, to make themselves and the world mean what they and the world could be made to mean. For Jena, this lack of language and the inability to construct meaning rendered them "unsuccessful human beings". Her distorting paintings are a reaction to her parents' failure to "honor their duty to order the world in a responsible way. So I have to say things with my painting, because they didn't" (21).

Wales, the journalist who specializes in rescuing failed actuality, who creates meaning from mute events for people who cannot do so for themselves, has unwittingly become Jena's chosen interlocutor and collaborator in her personal and artistic quest to extract new meaning from the failed or stunted meaning of her own past. It is this, the construction of meaning flagged in Wales' lecture title, that initially drew Jena to Wales. Meaning, particularly the meaning of our pasts, is an important theme in "Quality Time". And it is here that the mute and brute actuality of the short opening sequence returns to reverberate in the story. If this sequence, in its beginning-middle-end structure, is, as already indicated, an allegory of the progression of individual but related events towards an outcome, it is also a potential micro-narrative whose meaning, as it passes through individual stages, has to be interpreted. Wales sees the sequence as containing "so much possibility, so much chance for a better outcome", which indicates that, at different stages in its unfolding, its outcome is open-ended, capable of having different endings, and therefore consequences.

The beginning-middle-end structure of the opening sequence is analogous to the Ricoeurean narrative temporality (and that of MacIntyre and Taylor) of past to present to future, to how the interpretation of the past guides our present and future actions, and therefore the decisions and choices we make. We are reminded of what Ricoeur says with regard to meaning and temporal unfolding: "the retrospective character of narration is closely linked to the prospective horizon of the future .... narration preserves the meaning that is behind us so that we can have meaning before us."[7] The creation of meaning through the interpretation of events engages both Wales (as a journalist, but also in his attempt to understand the unfolding of the woman's death) and Jena (in her vengeful interpretation of her parents' role in her failures and in her desire to write a novel – an act of explicit narrativization – in which they would feature). The discovery of meaning equally engages Jena's husband, who has insisted that Jena and he undergo therapy in order to discover the source of an indefinable "lack" (26) at the heart of their marriage. All three characters, then, are implicated in the opening allegory of the story: how do events, but in particular their interpretation, bring us from one stage to the next and direct us towards future choices,

---

[7] Kearney, *Dialogues with Contemporary Continental Thinkers*, 22.

decisions, outcomes and, finally, consequences? This is the allegory
that also structures and directs the unfolding of "Quality Time" itself,
as Jena's manipulative personality places Wales in a position where he
is obliged to carefully consider the consequences of actions he might
take.

"Quality Time", like "Privacy", although more so, is, in part,
something of a manifesto story, a statement of artistic intent and
creative approach: *A Multitude of Sins* will be a collection of stories
dealing with the heightened reality and intensified sensations of illicit
relationships, when people, as Richard Ford puts it, "feel more real,
more alive, than they do during the happenstances of their regular
lives".[8] But it is also a time when their normal judgement is no longer
available to them, when they misread people and situations, when they
are misled by an intoxicating sense of freedom (Howard in "Abyss",
for example), when they run great risks, and, in some cases, fail to see
these risks and plunge headlong into calamitous consequences. If the
opening sequence of "Quality Time" furnishes Wales with the
meaning of a cautionary allegory that will allow him to avoid the
worst, it will not be so elsewhere in the collection. From here on, in
the emotional, hermeneutic and moral world Ford draws us into, acts,
and the meanings constructed to explain and justify these acts, will
have serious and, sometimes, dramatic consequences.

Some general comments on *A Multitude of Sins* are necessary. The
protagonists in these stories are white, urban, well-educated and
middle-class professionals, unencumbered by the bad luck, limited
opportunities and constricted lives that beset the more marginalized
characters of one of Ford's earlier collections, the Montana stories of
Rock Springs. It is as if Ford wished to place the characters of *A
Multitude of Sins* beyond material need so that their behaviour would
not be dictated by misfortune or material circumstances, but uniquely
by the moral considerations attending the choices people deliberately
and consciously make. The well-educated characters of *A Multitude of
Sins* also allow Ford to articulate a moral language to which less well-
educated characters might not plausibly have access, as Ford notes in
the interview at the end of this book.

---

[8] William Wineke, Interview with Richard Ford, "Of love and infidelity", *Wisconsin
State Journal*, 3 March 2002, Section F, 3.

A majority of the stories take place in winter, a symbolic setting for the darker and more confined worlds the characters have entered. Hotel and motel rooms feature in several stories, as do cars, streets, public spaces and open landscapes: this is the impersonal topography of infidelity, transient locations rather than personal spaces.[9] Infidelity exiles characters from the intimate spaces to which they are attached and that bear witness to the lives they have built over the years with a person they chose to build that life. With regard to the temporal ranges of the stories, all of them observe the typical, though not obligatory, delimitations of the short story, working within narrower time frames than those of longer narrative forms.

Six of the stories are narrated in the third person and four in the first person, although the narrative person does not allow the stories to be distributed into easy categories. However, the one undoubted effect of some of the third-person stories is to render their characters less sympathetic. Ford has called these stories "much more morally stringent" than his earlier ones, which produces, particularly in the case of "Quality Time" and "Abyss", characters with whom it is difficult to sympathize. Ford himself has spoken of the third-person stories of this phase of his career (which would include "The Womanizer" and "Occidentals") as being "less personable", noting that their "principal characters … are not admirable—even to me".[10] All but one of the stories deal with infidelity in heterosexual relationships, the exception being "Calling", where the conflict results from a husband and father leaving his family for another man. "Calling", indeed, is a notable example of many of the stories whose narrative dynamic is not that of an ongoing illicit affair between a man and a woman: the story's main concern is the damaged relationship between father and son, narrated from the perspective of the son thirty years after the father's abandonment of his family. In "Reunion" the narrative is devoted to a meeting between a cuckolded husband and his wife's former lover.

---

[9] The story "Dominion" captures nicely the manner in which the necessary furtiveness of infidelity, in this case of a married woman having an affair with a business associate, transforms places and space into uncongenial venues: "… saying their goodbyes in other hotel rooms or in airports, in car-parks, hotel lobbies, taxi stands, bus stops" (151).

[10] *Conversations with Richard Ford*, 202.

Richard Ford's long-time fascination with consequences translates, in *A Multitude of Sins*, into a greater interest in exploring the effects of infidelity rather than its origins. These stories, then, spend rather less time investigating the original motivations of characters involved in affairs than on the consequences on such relationships. Only "Privacy" and "Abyss" explore in detail the beginnings of betrayal; the bulk of the stories either join the affairs *in medias res*, when the initial exhilaration has worn off and the consequences of decisions taken begin to manifest themselves, or when the affair is over (as in "Calling", "Reunion", "Puppy", "Under the Radar", and "Charity"). Indeed, it is the stories' focus on endings and consequences that makes *A Multitude of Sins* such a sombre collection, and that explains the air of exhaustion that pervades a number of the stories. There is little or no joy in these stories; the dominant emotions are regret, anger, bitterness, mistrust, disappointment and sorrow, emotions directed as much at oneself as at the other. The narrator of "Reunion", for example, is unhappy with himself over the affair he had with a married woman as it contributed to the break-up of a family, while the protagonists of "Abyss" come to regret deeply, individually and privately, the damage that their affair has inflicted on them. Illusion and disillusion are never far away as characters ponder on or deal with events they have set in motion but are now no longer in a position to control. Often, all that is left to them is to comprehend that lives have been altered, sometimes beyond repair.

Apart from the two stories already discussed here, four others receive individual chapters. In a situation where, for practical considerations, some selection had to be made, each of these four stories offered a strong case for detailed analysis. "Calling" is exceptional in the collection in its examination of a father-and-son-relationship; in addition, as a story told thirty years after the occurrence of the events recounted, it engenders intriguing emotions, perspectives and themes. It is also an exceptionally evocative and powerful story. "Reunion" is of interest in that it is one of the shorter stories, but also because of the unusual perspective on infidelity it offers through the meeting of betrayed husband and his ex-wife's guilty lover. It is also classical in its short-story focus and concentration on a narrow time frame, the length of a brief, chance meeting in a public space. "Charity" is the story in which the characters are treated most sympathetically. Told from the perspective of the betrayed wife of a married couple, the story sadly assesses the incalculable damage caused by betrayal, even in a relationship in which both members wish to repair what they considered to be a good and valuable marriage. "Abyss", apart from its crucial position at the end of the collection and its status as the only novella, is distinctive in that it traces an illicit relationship from start to finish. It is clinical and unrelenting in its depiction of unbridled passion, changing emotions and irrevocable consequences. It could be seen as the emblematic narrative of the collection in its portrayal of the acts-and-consequences causality of the stages of an affair, ensnaring the protagonists in a cycle of events they are no longer able to control and that sweeps them to their doom.

Taken together, these four stories also offer different degrees of proximity to the act of infidelity and different temporal perspectives on their consequences. We witness the infidelity in "Abyss" up close, as it happens, whereas the act of betrayal in "Calling" took place over thirty years before it is eventually narrated. As for consequences, "Calling" lets us see the effects of infidelity from the distance of almost half a lifetime, whereas "Abyss" ends as one of the protagonists struggles to come to terms with the immediate consequences of the end of the affair. It has to be acknowledged, of course, that a plausible case could be made for the inclusion of any story, and that any selection includes an element of personal preference as well as the desire to highlight interesting structures, features and themes.

A Multitude of Sins presents ten stories in which characters fail people they often do not wish to fail. These characters are not always unhappy with their lives when they betray people they claim to love, but, when they betray them, they cause deep and sometimes irreparable harm. Their acts, therefore, have an ineradicable moral dimension. Ford deliberately raises the stakes of failure in his collection. Asked in an interview whether he equated failure with sin, he replied: "Yes. I'm conscious about doing that. I wanted to try to elevate the way we fail each other to that level to make it morally consequent."[11] Richard Ford is never moralizing in these stories; he is simply reminding us that we are moral beings, and that our behaviour

---

[11] "Richard Ford", *identity theory: the narrative thread,* 5.

has a moral dimension to it that we will not be allowed to escape. Put simply, *A Multitude of Sins* reminds us that we are responsible, that we will be held responsible for what we do, and that what we do defines who we are. Morality and identity, we see again, cannot be held apart.

CHAPTER 10

"CALLING"

THE NARRATIVE CURE

The adult narrator of "Calling" is looking back at events in his adolescent life that he does not wish to consider as "life-changing", but that are nonetheless important enough to impel him to tell the story of these events more than thirty years after they occurred. The events recounted deal with the narrator's relationship with his father, and with one pivotal encounter with him in particular. It is at the end of his story that the narrator minimizes the wider significance of the events he has narrated, yet everything he has just recounted – the abandonment of his mother and himself by his father and the damaging consequences for all three of them – throws into doubt this retrospective underplaying of the importance of events he experienced when he was fifteen years old. There is, indeed, more than a hint of contradiction in the narrator's assertion that the events were not "life-changing", as he also says that the decisive meeting with his father represented the "first working out of particulars I would evermore observe",[1] a clear indication of the life-long effects of this adolescent experience. If, then, the events were not "life-changing", neither were they fated to be distant and innocuous memories that mere chance or circumstance might occasionally revive.

The narrator's father left his family for another man, and left his New Orleans home to live with him in St Louis. A year later he phones his son and, taking advantage of a short return trip to New Orleans, invites him to go duck hunting with him. The narrator divides his account into three sections: the opening passages deal with the phone conversation, the son's view of his father, and the description

---

[1] Ford, *A Multitude of Sins*, 61. See note 4 in the Introduction for publication details. Further references to this collection will be indicated parenthetically in the text.

of the circumstances and consequences of his father's departure; the
second part is devoted to the duck-hunting outing; and the final
section is an epilogue in which the adult narrator brings the story up to
date, and reflects on some of the consequences of the events of that
pre-Christmas period in 1961.

As already indicated, the story begins with the father's call to his son
to invite him to go duck hunting a few days later. The details of the
phone conversation, however, are initially withheld by the narrator, as
if the return of his father to his life a year after the latter's departure
reawakens emotions provoked by the break-up of his family, emotions
so powerful that they must be immediately expressed. As if to remind
us again that we are dealing with moral fiction, with stories about acts
that have consequences, Ford has his narrator reflect immediately on
his sense of how his home and family life have been destroyed by his
father's act – the narrator says in his first sentence that his father left
his mother and him to cope in "whatever manner we could" (33).
Responsibility for the dissolute life his mother now leads is directly
attributed by the narrator to his father's departure, although the tone of
moral indignation is also directed, if to a lesser degree, at his mother.
    It is striking, too, that, after this initial forceful expression of
resentment, the narrator turns to his father's personality, an indication
that he locates the origin of the family break-up in a flaw in his
father's temperament or moral character, one, moreover – and very
significantly – that he attributes to a kind of New Orleans professional
man of that period. He describes his father initially, then, not as an
individual but as a type, by way of the latter's shared characteristics
with this generic figure, one who continues to exist and the sight of
whom today still reminds the narrator of his father. The physical
features, deportment and dress of this generic New Orleanian bespeak
a whole identity, a way of being with others and even a way of life;
most pertinently, they also bespeak a particular moral outlook. In
Ford's incisive extended profile of this figure, the milieu is seen to
shape the man, and the public face to conceal the private
prevarications:

> New Orleans produces men like my father, or once did: club-men,
> racquets players, deft, balmy-day sailors, soft-handed Episcopalians
> with progressive attitudes, good educations, effortless manners, but
> with secrets. These men, when you meet them on the sidewalk or at

some uptown dinner, seem like the very best damn old guys you could ever know. You want to call them up the very next day and set some plans going.

All is appearance, charm, public display and studied ease. But during the lunch that the admirer will hasten to arrange, the conversation will suddenly flag, and "you see this man is far, far away from you .... and you know you're nothing to him and will probably never even see him again, never take the trouble" (34). Lift away the layers of public performance to reach the heart and soul of these men, and one discovers an absence, a well-rehearsed impersonation. There is nothing to be found behind the self-protective screen of flattery and charm. This is the socio-cultural environment and moral lineage that produced a man like his father, an impression confirmed by the narrator now switching from the generic to the particular and the personal: "of course it's more complicated when the man in question is your father" (35).

The phone call that renews the son's contact with his father confirms the latter's membership of this patrician New Orleans class: his tone is sardonic and condescending, and self-consciously so, as if part of a calculated display of refined superiority. The father is portrayed by the narrator as a carefree dilettante, "handsome" and "youthful" (37) in the – as imagined by the narrator – elegant setting of his St Louis home, and enjoying the rewards of his betrayal, unconcerned at the harm he has done to his family. The text will later imply, in another of Ford's occasional barbs in his fiction at his native region, that the superficial charms of this representative of the New Orleans ruling classes is of a piece with a generalized southern mentality, which, according to the narrator's father, thrives on appearance only: "southerners get along", he reassures his son, "On looks", which, for the father, is "the great intelligence" (39). Everything we learn about the narrator's father suggests that he has adopted this maxim as a guiding principle in his life. And we are also given to understand that the emphasis on surface appearance explains the father's moral weakness.

The father's departure has had damaging consequences, and the narrator's opening sentences speak of these in a tone of moral resentment. Everyone has lost what was most important to them: mother, son and father have been thrust into disillusionments and regrets they had never anticipated would be their lot. The

disintegration of the family deprived each of them of their role and
place in life, and all three now seem destabilized in the absence of the
assurance and guidance formerly provided by the family structure.
The certainty of their life together has been replaced by transience and
mutability, visible most notably in the new living arrangements that
have replaced family life. The father is living in St Louis, far from the
life and world in which he had his place, but it is the transformations
in the family home that receive most attention. The mother is trying to
construct a singing career and has allowed – her son notes
disapprovingly – "a tall black man who was her accompanist move
into our house and into her bedroom". They drink "far too much",
play jazz records "too loud" and make "unwelcome noises until late".
The son – nicknamed Buck to distinguish him from his father whose
first name, Boatwright, he shares – can only lament that this was not
"how things were done when my father was there" (33), and he finds
the new arrangements "nearly too much" for him (36).

Buck no longer knows how to speak to either of his parents, as
neither of them can any longer play the role or enjoy the status of
parent. In the case of Buck's father, physical separation and distance
have added to this problem, but even proximity to his mother in the
family home no longer provides intimacy and reassurance. While the
focus of the story is the father, and Buck's relationship with him, the
mother does not escape her son's censure for the dissolute lifestyle she
has let herself fall into and her failure to hold together a semblance of
family life. Mother and son now walk through the family home as if
they were strangers to one other, she unable to occupy the role of
mother without a husband, and he no longer able to be a son without
his father. Buck is the abandoned offspring, adrift between father and
mother, no longer claimed by or attached to either, yet having to deal
with both in a new role that is beyond his young intelligence to
comprehend or define.

The vestiges of the family relationships are visible only in the
family members' shared fate as disillusioned victims. Buck notes that
his mother had "married *up* and come to be at ease with the society
my father introduced her into" (43). While a higher social status in
itself was clearly important in this elevation, the mother also expected
to enter a society where higher standards prevailed. She does not
reproach her husband with taking a lover, nor even that the lover was
a man; her accusation is more directed at the moral order into which

she married. It is as if, in the mother's eyes, social privilege and position bring with it a moral burden of responsibility, and it is to this heritage that her husband has proved inadequate. As she puts it to Buck at one point: "let's just say I hold his entire self against him .... He could've kept things together here. Other men do." Marrying up, in her eyes, meant being with a man of exceptional standards, hence her disappointment and ultimate charge that her husband failed "to be any better than most men would be" (44).

Buck, too, judges his father at a moral level, and is less tolerant than his mother of the fact that his father left them for another a man, although he does allow, over thirty years later, that Dr Carter was his father's "great love". But he sees his father as a man who simply could not bear being unable to "do whatever he wanted", and who could not accept that he was responsible for the "hard feeling" or "terrible scandal" (36) he caused. Buck shares what he interprets as his mother's wider reproach against his father, namely his self-serving calculation that granting himself freedom from responsibility necessarily granted others an equal freedom. Yet this is a freedom that neither wife nor son wanted, but that has become their common plight and seemingly all that binds them together. This ostensible freedom, from responsibility but also from affection, will finally work itself through the relationship between mother and son in the transmuted form of disconnection and escapism. Buck can think only of getting away from the affront to his old family life that his home has become by applying to the New Jersey school his father had attended: it "seemed to offer escape and relief and a future better than the one I had at home in New Orleans". So "impossible" (42), indeed, has life at home become that Buck sees the school as a way of "saving my life" (45). Freedom for the deserted wife takes the form of escape into alcohol and drugs, and these, along with disappointment, will kill her within a year.

In a collection of stories depicting the consequences of people's acts, the question of moral responsibility cannot be evaded. The father is the person who abandoned his wife and child, and nothing in the narrator's early portrait of his father allows mitigating circumstances. Yet, in having the father leave his family for another man, Ford introduces (but does not pursue) issues that trouble this immediate attribution of responsibility. The father was presumably either bisexual or homosexual when he married, which would suggest that his marriage was a necessary arrangement to satisfy the conventions of his social milieu rather than a willing commitment to a relationship with a woman he loved. These considerations, of course, are speculations beyond the purview of the story, yet, if the father is guilty, the source of his failure is surely to be found in the socio-cultural milieu that formed him, which serves to underline the significance of the narrator's portrait of his father's social environment.

The first part of the story sets the scene for the second and longest part, devoted to the meeting between father and son on their duck-hunting outing. Buck approaches this encounter with all the ambivalence created by his insecure situation: he is renewing contact with a man who, for most of Buck's young life, had occupied the privileged role and enjoyed the venerated status of father, but whose recent conduct has led his son to consider him "a bastard" (35). For all his ambivalence, however, Buck yearns to go duck hunting with his father, to realize a longstanding aspiration to share this definitive father-son experience, just as his friends have done with their fathers. There is a part of Buck that needs to cling to the notion of a father-son relationship and that would even aspire to recuperate and normalize his father. When his father suggests the trip Buck notes that "he didn't sound to me like some man who was living with another man in St. Louis. He sounded much as he always had in our normal life when ... we were a family" (36). And despite his father's desertion of his mother and himself, Buck's plans for the future, beginning with the school he applies to, are to a certain degree influenced by his desire to follow his father's footsteps and, unacknowledged though this ambition this may be, to emulate him.

These competing feelings of attraction and rejection bear on his decision about whether to accept or refuse his father's invitation. He records his feeling of nervousness as he considers what to do, aware that "I was crossing a line, putting myself at risk". He understands this "line" as one separating anticipation from "Disappointment" (37), yet it is also the dividing line that has cut Buck's life into two irreconcilable spheres, those of mother and father, of heterosexual and homosexual worlds, of moral and immoral behaviour, and of safe family past and destabilizing present. But it is also a line separating present and future, in that, by accepting his father's invitation to meet with him for the first time since his departure, Buck is agreeing to a contact likely to influence the nature of any future relationship with his father.

Buck is going to meet a man who has, at this point, conceivably paid a higher price than anyone for his actions. He has been expelled from the law firm his family had started a hundred years earlier and that still bears the McKendall name; he has brought scandal to his name and reputation; and he has lost his privileged place in elite New Orleans society and seems to be living in disgraced exile in St Louis. Buck, moreover, considers that his father's behaviour may also have caused the death of his (father's) mother, "from sheer disappointment" (36-37).

Everything about his father's appearance when Buck meets him at the boat dock in the pre-dawn gloom – his physical condition, his attire and demeanour – speaks of a man defeated by his fate. As Buck puts it:

> I remember thinking ... that if he'd had an older brother, this would be what that brother would look like. Not good. Not happy or wholesome. And of course I realized he was drinking, even at that hour. (46)

But the most significant aspect of his father's appearance is its utter incongruity: he has turned up to go duck hunting in dress shoes and tan topcoat, under which he is wearing "a tuxedo with a pink shirt, a bright-red bow tie and a pink carnation" (47). The father's natural milieu is that of privileged society, and, though excluded now from the official circles of the cultured New Orleans classes, he can only function in a world of soirées and formal dress. His inappropriate clothes and haggard appearance at the boat dock signify a double exclusion: his drinking indicates the extent, and cost, of his fall from grace in the eyes of the society into which he was born, and his attire cruelly highlights his incompatibility with the virile world of hunters. The duck hunting is an attempt, one suspects, to project an image to his son (and perhaps to himself) that is as far removed as possible from that which attaches to him on account of his homosexuality and the general stain of his disgrace. It is also surely a half-hearted attempt to play the role of father through what is the archetypal father-son experience in the world he used to inhabit.

But the father's attempt to inhabit both his former life and the duck-hunting world are compromised. In both cases he is condemned to exist on the periphery, present in both worlds in only a diminished, marginal form: although back temporarily in New Orleans, he cannot return to his former society, and has spent the evening with "people who were his friend now" (47), while their duck-hunting guide, Renard, makes clear his contempt for the father's hunting credentials. In this marginalized and displaced state Buck's father seems to have lost his cultural and social bearings, displaying little awareness of the absurdity of his appearance and his lack of dignity, or of the disappointment he causes his son. The text does not fail to suggest the father's double exclusion: as the sun rises on the bayou, Buck pointedly records that the "Hibernia Bank [building] where my father's office had been" (49) is visible on the horizon. Past and present, and two contrasting worlds, are juxtaposed, but Buck's father cannot find a place in either. He has, in fact, been thoroughly disempowered, and appears now to lack a vital force, dabbling in his life rather than living it, as indicated by the triviality that attends his endeavours: he no longer practises law but, instead, has taken up golf and plays "quite a bit" (57), and he goes duck hunting with his "beautiful Beretta [shotgun] over-under with silver inlays" (54), confirming the earlier image of elegant dilettante.

In the time they spend together, Buck's ambivalence with regard to his father finds little opportunity to be eased by natural, uncomplicated feelings for him. Buck is "thrilled" (49) to be where he is, yet sees immediately from his father's appearance and condition that "This was not exactly duck hunting in the way I'd heard about from my school friends" (47). However, his eagerness to have this idealized father-son experience has him believe that "this had to be some version of what the real thing felt like" (49). But Buck's youthful excitement and optimism are stifled by the father's cynicism (and by being caught in the crossfire, as he continues to be at home, between bickering adults, this time between his father and Renard[2]).

---

[2] Buck is obliged to be a passive spectator to the tense exchanges between his father and Renard. These two do not so much communicate as provoke each other and reduce each other to stereotypes. The father reveals the snobbery of his privileged class, but, like everything else in his life now, he has lost the authority to enforce the assumed superiority of that class, and is reduced to defeated silence by Renard's sexual innuendos.

When Buck, in answer to a question from his father, tells him that he is reading *The Inferno*, he has to endure his father's world-weary condescension as the latter goes on to deliver himself of Yeats' views on "stoicism, asceticism and ecstasy" (48) and of his own efforts to combine these in his life. Buck can only suffer his father's cynicism that uses him as an audience for his performance as aesthete, a performance that also has the effect of depriving Buck of expressing himself in his own way and, indeed, of communicating with his father. In a second display of cynicism, again an instance of knowingly speaking in a manner liable to reduce his son to silence, the father affects a tone of vulgar plebeian frankness as he ostensibly offers Buck sexual advice. One has the sense that the father's speech, true to type, is all performance, that his affected tones and varying language registers are so many symptoms of his own obsessions and evasions, his convoluted way of trying to give vent to, yet at the same time not disclose, his own damaged feelings.

That this is a lifetime habit of a homosexual man who conformed to the rigid sexual mores of his society, and who married rather than live out his homosexuality, is no doubt what lies behind one of his few unaffected comments to his son: "convenience matters to me very much. Too much, I think" (58). The incongruous attire, the drunkenness, the tiredness and increasing dishevelment are overwhelming expressions of the unhappy state to which a life of dissimulation and expedience has brought him. Buck is the unfortunate victim of his father's unhappiness, and is undoubtedly the only one in the latter's circle of intimates who has neither the choice nor the wherewithal to do anything but be a passive audience to his father's bitter despair. Buck is again seeing up close the kind of man his father is; he had "not always liked" the latter's "abrupt moves and changes of attitude" (54), but, as young sons do, had assumed his father to be the archetype of all men, and had accepted the model. But the father's abandonment of his family, his absence from Buck's life for a year, and the opportunity for Buck to see him up close again has him see his father in a changing light. If life as convenience is the weakness that has made his father into the man he has become, Buck resolves, in his one explicit statement of how the duck-hunting outing with his father would influence the conduct of his own life, that he would "see to it that my fault in life would not be his" (58). It is a solemn moment in the story, when paternal authority and filial submission cease to coincide – Buck's father has now become a model of what not to be.

Buck's changing view of his father is mirrored in his changing apprehension of the landscape itself, figured in the text, through Buck's eyes, as a destabilizing space where expectations and appearances are undermined: "I could begin to see now that what I'd imagined the marsh to look like was different from how it was." His senses and initial apprehension of reality prove to be unreliable guides as the stimuli of landscape, light and sound, which create "these confusing and disorienting and reversing features of where I was" (51), combine to mislead him as to his orientation and relation to the world around him. The destabilizing bayou landscape prefigures the destabilization of preconceptions and meanings of Buck's duck-hunting experience: the father's veneer of superiority and authority disintegrates, visibly so as his appearance becomes more and more dishevelled, and Buck is surprised that Renard's voice does not correspond to his father's caricature of their guide as a *yat*[3] – Renard's voice turns out to be "cultivated and mellow and inflected" (50). The account of the events of Buck's bayou experience, then, constitute something of a coming-of-age narrative, and particularly so in the gaining of harsh knowledge about others and in a loss of innocence, a coming to maturity already set in motion by the family break-up but harshly advanced by Buck's experience of his father in the bayou.

The duck-hunting outing culminates in an incident that seals the rupture between father and son, when the disappointment feared by Buck becomes a reality. Buck's father allows his son the first shot after Renard's duck call, but, as Buck aims his shotgun, everything that has been wrong about this idealized experience with his father is captured for him in the flight of a lone duck in the direction of the duck blind:

> What's the good of one duck shot down? In my dreams there'd been hundreds of ducks, and my father and I shot them so that they fell out of the sky like rain, and how many there were would not have

---

[3] In local parlance, a *yat* refers to a middle- to lower-class New Orleanian whose speech is marked by pronunciation features and vocabulary unique to New Orleans. The term is considered by some, and certainly by Buck's father, to have pejorative connotations.

mattered because we were doing it together. But I was doing this alone. (59)

Buck is left to cope with what he takes to be the derision of the two men for his having failed to shoot the duck, but it is his father's patronizing smile that enrages him, causing all the suppressed resentment against him to well up. Father and son confront each other in mutual resentment, yet looking at each other, too, as if aware that important new knowledge about the other was being given to them. The father seems to recognize that his son is still only a boy, whereas he had been dealing with him until now as if he were an adult, while the son casts off any lingering hopes he may have harboured about forging a worthwhile relationship with his father. In this momentary face-off, both assume the roles to which events, past and more recent, have brought them, and that will determine their future relationship. The father smiles sardonically at his son, and casually, "without seeming to notice", kisses him on the forehead and embraces him. The gesture is an odd mixture of affection and detachment, fuelled by whiskey and an uncertainty about how to deal with his increasingly unfamiliar son. For his part, Buck is clear that this moment signals the end of any possibility of a future relationship with this father and he begins an accusatory outburst that, however, he cuts short:

> Though I did that for myself, I think now, and not for him, and in order that I not have to regret more than I already regretted. I didn't really care what happened to him, to be truthful. Didn't and don't.

Whatever ambivalent or ill-understood emotions there may have been in the father's semi-affectionate gesture, it is too late to win back his son, who stands before him "rigid in anger and loathing" (61).

Although his father lived for another thirty years after these events and appears to have visited New Orleans regularly, father and son never saw each other again. As already noted, Buck does not wish to consider the duck-hunting events as "life-changing", preferring to view the episode as merely the final act in a relationship that had begun to disintegrate a year earlier. Yet the fact that Buck has recourse to the act of narration, and the fact that he had entertained hopes that the experience with his father would have turned out differently, call into question the perspective on events that Buck, as adult narrator, wishes to convey. Despite his anger at his father, which surged up in him over the years, and despite his father's weakness and his responsibility for his wife's death, Buck's feelings about him continued to be tinged with ambivalence. His father remained something of a model for him, as Buck ended up emulating him by becoming a lawyer. And Buck allows, too, that, after the bayou events, he "prayed quite fervently for a while and in spite of all, that he would come back to us and that our life would begin to be as it had been". This was part of a pattern of Buck's oscillating and conflicting emotions, as he would then pray that his father would die and that "his memory would cease to be a memory, and all would be erased" (62). Buck's downplaying of the significance of the bayou encounter, then, seems calculated to conceal unresolved emotions with regard to his father.

But it is above all the very existence of the narrative of these events that confirms the conflict of emotions and that belies the attempt to diminish the importance of the encounter. The value of narrative to the narrator of "Calling" may best be appreciated through Richard Ford's own comments on storytelling, and the context of these comments is particularly pertinent to "Calling". Asked in an interview about the theme of the "inherent loneliness of the human condition" in the context of a conversation about his novel, *Wildlife*, in which an adult narrator recounts the break-up of his family when he was sixteen, Ford replied:

> It's what Emerson in his essay on Friendship ... calls the "infinite remoteness" that underlies us all. But I also think that that condition is a seminal one; that is, what it inseminates is an attempt to console that remote condition. If loneliness is the disease, then the story is the cure. To be able to tell a story like that one about your parents is in itself an act of consolation. Even to come to the act of articulating that your parents are unknowable to each other, unknowable to you, is itself an act of acceptance, an act of some optimism.[4]

In the final paragraph of "Calling", adult narrator Buck both acknowledges the consoling, liberating power of narrative and states more explicitly what he has been hesitating to say in his epilogue up to then, namely that his parents' lives, and particularly his relationship

---

[4] *Conversations with Richard Ford*, 143-44.

with his father, continued to influence his life after the events of Christmas 1961, and that his own life took the form it did as a consequence of those events:

> And so the memory was not erased. Yet because I can tell this now, I believe that I have gone beyond it, and on to a life better than one might've imagined for me. Of course, I think of life—mine—as being part of their aftermath, part of the residue of all they risked and squandered and ignored. Such a sense of life's connectedness can certainly occur. (63)

One has the clear impression that the very reason this story has been told is that "the memory was not erased", as Buck had prayed at one point it would be: the conflicting meanings of these events have stayed with Buck and have never been fully resolved over his lifetime. His story is his attempt to resolve them now. Narrative is the great discourse of reconciliation, facilitating a flexible, renewable reconfiguration of events and experiences in time. Out of these endless reconfigurations, there emerges bearable stories of who we are, where we have come from and how we have arrived at where we are in our lives. Ford does not evoke the practice of psychoanalysis in the interview in which he coins the "story as cure" formulation, but his insight about narrative as therapy is supported by a substantial body of opinion in psychoanalytical scholarship and practice. One of the leading theorists of the narrative psychology and psychoanalysis movement, psychoanalyst Roy Schafer, observes that "clinical psychoanalysis is an interpretive discipline whose concern it is to construct life histories of human beings".[5] This view accords with Peter Brooks' reading of Freud: "There is in Freud's case histories an underlying assumption that psychic health corresponds to a coherent narrative account of one's life."[6] Both concur with Ford in the latter's view of the role of narrative as a response to emotional conflict and as a means to emotional well-being, realized through the curative function of the story of the self and of one's life.

Such has been the case for Buck. He had lived his life in the "aftermath" of his family's disintegration, which had remained as a

---

[5] Roy Schafer, *Language and Insight*, New Haven: Yale UP, 1978, 6.
[6] Peter Brooks, *Reading for the Plot: Design and Intention in Narrative*, Oxford: Clarendon, 1984, 281-82.

"residue" in his mind. The metaphor is hardly innocent, indicating a remainder, a heavy sediment, and is a term that rarely has positive connotations. But now he has confronted this residue of unresolved and ambivalent emotions; now he has told his story and has succeeded in moving beyond events that would not be erased. In the logic of cause and effect that he proposes to explain his release from the past – "because I can tell this now, I believe that I have gone beyond [the memory]" – he allows merely that his being able to tell his story is proof of his new-found emotional distance from these events. However, it seems more accurate to claim that he is able to go beyond these events because of his story. His narrative has reconfigured these events in such a way as to produce an enabling, curative account that has finally liberated him from confusing emotions and memories that had remained unresolved in his mind for thirty years of his life.[7]

---

[7] In the interview at the end of this book Richard Ford responds to a question about the relationship between narrative and the self in a way that is quite consonant with the idea that retrospective narrativization liberated the narrator of "Calling". Ford is not speaking about "Calling" but rather in very general terms when he says: "if we have a character who tells us a story on the page, and he's talking about a time in his life when these events took place, a series of events which started and then ended, and then later on he's looking back on it and telling it … the fact that he can tell it means that he's put a shape upon it that it didn't have at the time of its occurrence, and that it radiates out to him as an event of moral consequence because it's important enough to tell. Maybe it didn't have moral consequence when it took place, but the shaping and the ability to narrate it gives it that consequence" (Interview, 340).

CHAPTER 11

"REUNION"

TIME AND NARRATIVE

"Reunion" is a very short story, and seems quite straightforward. It focuses on the chance and brief encounter between the story's male narrator and the husband of the woman with whom the narrator had a short-lived affair eighteen months earlier. The story narrates the important details of the affair, its consequences and the narrator's retrospective feelings about the experience. When the two men meet in Grand Central Station in New York, they have a brief conversation, instigated by the narrator, during which the husband makes clear that he has nothing to say to the narrator.[1] The men go their separate ways, and the story ends. One has witnessed another small but continuing effect of infidelity, a reminder, above all to the protagonists, that the consequences of one's behaviour resonate well beyond the dramatic scenes and immediate damage that attend an illicit relationship. The dominant feeling in the story is one of regret, articulated several times by the narrator, notably in his closing remarks: "None of it was a good thing to have done".[2]

This is a fair reading of the story, and there is much relevant commentary to be made on the text along these lines. However, such a reading would be incomplete, as it would take only partial account of

---

[1] It seems likely that Richard Ford found the title of his story in John Cheever's story, "Reunion". Cheever's story begins and ends in Grand Central Station, and it, too, tells of a meeting between two men, in this case between a father and a son. Ford included Cheever's story in the short-story anthology he edited, *The New Granta Book of the American Short Story*, London: Granta, 2007. Ford speaks admiringly of Cheever's story in his Introduction, calling it "a model of short-story virtue, focus and conciseness", ix.

[2] Ford, *A Multitude of Sins*, 74. See note 4 in the Introduction for publication details. Further references to this collection will be indicated parenthetically in the text.

certain reflections by the narrator on his reasons for wishing to speak to Mack Bolger when he sees him, and of conclusions he draws as a result of their brief contact. These reflections and conclusions do not take up much space in the text and could perhaps be overlooked, but they are nonetheless there, and they frame, or function as a context for, the meeting between the two men. One can bring these two strands of the story together under the notion of the "moment". The meaning of the first strand can be said to be realized through the narrative focus on the moment, on a delimited and reduced period of time in which the meeting between the narrator and Mack takes place. The narrative offers the background information – the affair and its consequences – necessary to explain and set the scene for the meeting in the station. Much of the story is conducted by way of a retrospective summary of the events surrounding the affair, the better to build up to and intensify the reverberations of the brief contact between the men, which becomes the focus of the story and that takes up the greater part of the text.

But the very concept of the "moment" itself becomes – and this is the second strand of the story – a theme of the narrative. When the narrator sees Mack in the station concourse he is motivated to go to speak to him by an impulse to experience "a dimensionless, unreverberant moment". He understands this impulse as no more than a desire to benefit from a fleeting opportunity that presents itself, one that will allow him to establish a "contact" and to "create an event where before there was none" (67). These seem rather odd ambitions for the narrator, given that the person with whom he desires to achieve these aims is the man with whose wife he had an affair, the man who was obliged to slap him around a little when he found him in a St Louis hotel room with his wife. That the narrator fails to appreciate the incongruous nature of his impulse to speak to Mack seems to be traceable – the reservation is necessary as the link is never made explicit – to his ideas about time, specifically to his belief about the primacy of the present over the past. The second strand of the story, then, concerns the status and integrity of the present moment, or, to use the narrator's terms, it explores the consequences of conceiving the individual moment (or a short series or succession of moments) as "dimensionless" or "unreverberant" points in time.

As we will see, the two strands of the story turn out to be related, an interdependence, indeed, that informs the narrator's closing comments. The discussion to follow will explore the story's two strands separately – the moment when a woman's husband and her former lover meet, and the temporal depth and status of this moment – before considering how the end of the story reveals, not least to the narrator, why the outcome of his meeting with Mack takes the unsatisfactory turn that it takes – it does so not simply because of an understandable antagonism on Mack's part, but also because of the narrator's flawed belief about the nature of the moment and the primacy of the present over the past.

Among the structural features that distinguish the stories in *A Multitude of Sins* from each other is the temporal distance between the time of the narration and the events narrated. As we have seen already, Richard Ford is interested above all in consequences to acts, which no doubt explains the temporal distance between the moment of narration and the events narrated that he creates in a number of his stories: consequences are revealed with the passage of time, but this duration cannot be predetermined, and hindsight can radically alter the judgement on earlier experience. In "Calling", this temporal distance extends to more than thirty years, a period during which the consequences of events that occurred when the adult narrator was an adolescent have continued to be felt; in "Reunion", the period is a year and a half.

This is sufficient time, however, for the narrator to have come to an unequivocal judgement about his affair with Mack Bolger's wife: "What went on between Beth Bolger and me is hardly worth the words that would be required to explain it away." The "away" is telling, hinting at both the aberrant, inexplicable nature of the affair and the uncomfortable feelings that came in its wake and that have persisted. It is as if the narrator, with hindsight, does not recognize himself as one of the people involved in the affair, nor understand the reasons for his actions, with the result that, eighteen months later, he continues to feel disappointment and shame for doing what he did. While briefly "spirited" and "thrilling" for the two people involved, the affair was, the narrator now concludes, "an ordinary adultery" (66). This short verdict represents a damning judgement by the narrator on himself: he let himself be intoxicated by the excitement of the affair; his behaviour was commonplace, not the action of an exceptional man; and his use of the term "adultery", resonating with all the force of the Ten Commandments' prohibition, carries the narrator's own moral charge against himself. It seems as if the narrator now views his behaviour as having distanced himself from the moral person he considered himself to be, with the result that, as well as betraying his lover's family, he also betrayed himself.

In this respect, Ford's story acts as eloquent confirmation of Charles Taylor's premise about the link between morality and identity: the narrator's different perceptions of his present and previous selves is the measure of the disparity he allowed develop between his behaviour and the moral stance that constituted his moral identity. The narrator's expressions of regret articulate the moral awareness that developed in the interval between his behaviour and his retrospective assessment of that behaviour. This moral loss is expressed through the symbolic loss of "a brown silk Hermès scarf with tassels" that his mother had given him to mark the beginning of his career as a book editor, but that was left behind in his undignified exit from the St Louis hotel bedroom. The narrator is glad that his mother "didn't have to know about my losing it, and how it happened" (67), an admission of his shame and a recognition that he has betrayed a moral heritage passed on to him by his parents.[3]

The narrator's assessment of the consequences of his behaviour is most evident in the language he uses to describe the aftermath of the affair. The immediate consequence of his "ignoble" relationship was to "[cause] as many people as possible unhappiness, embarrassment and heartache", before "finally" becoming "almost disastrous to those same people" (66). This verdict is delivered with what seems to be a weary recognition of the predictable course that such behaviour entrains, as if people are forever condemned to be short-sighted, unoriginal and gullible in turning to sexual liaisons for solutions to lack of fulfilment in their lives. But Ford also wishes to suggest that the foundations upon which people build their lives may be much more fragile than they believe and that they may not withstand undue pressure. There is a kind of domino effect in the chain of

---

[3] This episode recalls a scene near the end of "The Womanizer" when Martin Austin wonders what his late father would have thought about Austin's abandonment of his wife, Barbara, and his flight to Paris to pursue another woman. Austin concludes that "ultimately his judgment would've been harsh and he'd have sided with Barbara" (80). In both "The Womanizer" and "Reunion" the parents represent the moral values of an earlier generation from which the sons have strayed.

consequences following the collapse of the Bolger marriage, as if family life alone had provided the props and stabilizers that held the family members' lives together. This support structure allowed everyone to find their place in the world and to function accordingly, both as a family and in wider society. When this structure crumbled for the Bolger family, a great unmooring occurred: both Beth and Mack, despite trying to put things back together, ended up living apart, taking younger lovers and finally deciding to divorce. Beth is now living in Paris, while Mack gave up his job, considered "studying for the ministry" (68) and working abroad as a missionary, before finally leaving St Louis and taking up a new job and residence in New York. And the children also suffered from the loss of a stabilizing family structure, with one of them being arrested for shoplifting.[4]

These were the visible consequences of the affair. But the consequences extended beyond the dramatic partings and unpredictable transitions mentioned above, and crystallized into what might be termed a residue that settled into the minds and spirits of those concerned, producing a form of enervation and impoverishment, the effects of which continue to be felt almost eighteen months later. The narrator meets with Beth for a drink about six months after the end of the affair, but it is a "nervous, uncomfortable meeting" (67), as if they no longer know how to be with each other, despite their having been, according to Beth, "so close for a little while" (68). These longer-term effects are communicated essentially through the narrator, most strikingly in the manner in which the after-shocks of the affair reverberate in the deepest recesses of his being. He comes away from his drink with Beth with the "feeling that all of life was a sorry mess" (67), and, looking back on the affair, he records that "none of it except for what we'd done in bed made me feel good about life" (69). The narrator does not merely feel regretful and ashamed about a specific set of events; his moral disappointment with himself for his part in this "ignoble" episode has contaminated his relationship with life itself. And when the narrator approaches Mack in the station, he sees that

---

[4] The effects of the marriage break-up on the Bolger family recall the fate of Frank Bascombe's son, Paul, in *Independence Day* after the break-up of the Bascombe family. We are also reminded of the unhappy consequences for all three members of the McKendall family in "Calling" when the father left the family home for another man, and of the story devoted quite specifically to the family in *A Multitude of Sins*, "Crèche".

both of them have been dispirited by the effects of the affair: "[Mack's] face looked resigned—resigned to me, resigned to the situations the world foists onto you unwilling; resigned to himself. Resignation was actually what we had in common" (70). There is a defeated air about the two of them, both of them getting on with their lives but carrying the wounds of experience, enduring life now rather than enjoying it.

The residue of the events of eighteen months earlier have also afflicted Mack in the form of what the narrator calls "something akin to exhaustion, where the words you say are the only true words you *can* say" (72). The relatively few words that Mack speaks to the narrator are indeed direct and unvarnished, and certainly truthful, but it is a weary truth, born of enervation of spirit and will, and of ruinous blows to the fundamental structures and values in his life. And just as the affair is belittled through its association with the blandness of the city in which it mostly took place – St Louis is depicted as a soulless city, "lost in the middle" of the country, an "abstraction" (66) whose lack of essence or necessity aptly characterizes the inconsequence of the affair – so the import and substance of the renewed contact between the narrator and Mack is diminished by the season of its occurrence: the narrator meets Mack just before Christmas, "when the weather stayed so warm and watery the spirit seemed to go out of the season" (65). The "watery" anticipates the attenuated status of the encounter between the two men, as well as the enervation inhabiting both of them, while the "spirit" absent from the season that celebrates the family is appropriate for a meeting that recalls the disintegration of a family.

The moral responsibility for that "disastrous" occurrence is attributed in the story to Beth and the narrator; Mack is exempted, and is said to have been "frantic to hold matters together" (67) in the marriage for the sake of the two children. The attribution of moral responsibility is communicated to an important degree through the narrator's portrait of Mack, particularly when set beside Beth's venom and the narrator's own shame and regret. The details of this portrait resonate well beyond their purely literal value, due to the setting of the meeting and Mack's status as innocent victim. When first sighted by the narrator, Mack is standing apart from the bustling crowds that criss-cross the concourse of Grand Central Station.[5] Here stands a man alone, standing outside the "shouting [of] goodbyes and greetings" (65), pointedly set apart and isolated from the excited rituals of pre-Christmas activity. This image of isolation echoes the solitariness in his life of which he has become a victim due to the behaviour of others – Mack will tell the narrator that he is "living alone" now (72). This opening image of Mack standing alone amid the passing crowds has another resonance. He is the one who has always been where he was supposed to be; he stayed in his marriage and tried to save it and keep his family together for the sake of the children. Mack did not move from where he promised to be, while his wife and her lover threw themselves into the whirl of their affair, "[crossing] the continent several times" (66) in the process. And when the affair was over, it was Beth who left the family home. Now, in the station, as the Christmas crowds bustle through the concourse "on their way somewhere" (65), there is Mack, immobile, still being there, still where he is supposed to be, this time waiting for his daughter. It is in this stoical pose, in his fidelity and dignity, that he is obliged, yet again, to submit to the narrator's selfishness and importunity.

The second telling detail of the narrator's description of Mack that serves to elevate the latter in a moral sense concerns his height. The narrator notes initially that Mack is tall, before going on to observe that he "seems to see everything from a height" and that he "seemed even taller than what he was" (65). Further on he will record that, although Mack and he were "nearly the same height", Mack "was in every way larger and seemed to look down to me" (71). In a short text this seems an exceptional amount of observation devoted to just one aspect of Mack's appearance, as well as being, in the circumstances, an unusual feature to single out. But in the context of the wider portrait of Mack as victim, one begins to recognize the attention to Mack's physical appearance as an extended metaphor of a certain moral grandeur and superiority attached to Mack in the eyes of one of the author's of his suffering. The narrator admits to feeling "sympathy" (70) for Mack and, when he finally speaks to him, finds his demeanour "extremely admirable" (72). Mack's tallness, then, represents his moral elevation, and if, as the narrator apprehends it, Mack looks down at the narrator, he does so from the heights of the

---

[5] This crowd scene is captured in the jacket photograph of the American hardback edition of *A Multitude of Sins*.

moral superiority and the injured dignity of innocent victim that the narrator attributes to him.

The portrait is fully realized when the narrator refers to Mack as an "effigy" (66). Yet the narrator has not so much constructed an effigy as sculpted a statue of Mack. Where most of the people occupying the space of the concourse are in full motion, Mack "simply stood ... staring rather vacantly" (65). He is accorded strong facial features ("his square face and prominent brow" [66]), wears an "impassive expression" (72), and his effigy is described as "good-looking" (66). In all of this, one is reminded of the idealized statues of Hellenistic and Roman art, in which flaws were suppressed in order to produce images of beauty and perfection, images that would represent, *inter alia*, superior moral qualities. Mack is described as "a tall, handsome, well-put-together man" by the narrator, who also records with admiration the perfection of the detail of Mack's attire and general appearance – his expensive Italian overcoat, the shoes "polished to a high gloss" (65), the perfect alignment of trouser cuff and shoe, his "slightly elevated" smooth chin, the cut of his hair, his tanned face. Mack has been transformed into an icon of imposing and dignified moral strength, in which his outer attractive appearance, as was the case for a long time in ancient Greek art, represents inner moral virtue. And the narrator interprets the presence of this icon as being "situated precisely there to attract my attention" (66). When the narrator looks upon Mack, therefore, he sees less a person than a monument, at once an expression of dignified moral values and a reminder to the narrator of his own moral failings. It is in this condition of statuesque representation that Mack wears an expression of "stony" unsurprise (70) and that has the narrator observe that it was "as though in a peculiar way the man I saw was not Mack Bolger" (66).

The recollection of the affair and the narrator's sighting of Mack represent the background and prelude to the moment when two men who in the recent past had been in conflict over their relationship with the same woman finally speak to each other. But the moment of the meeting has another antecedent, which constitutes the second theme of the story. When the narrator spots Mack in the station, his response, even in his own estimation, is rather curious:

I was taken by a sudden and strange impulse—which was to walk straight across through the eddying sea of travelers and speak to him, just as one might speak to anyone you casually knew and had unexpectedly yet not unhappily encountered. And not to impart anything, or set in motion any particular action (to clarify history, for instance, or make amends), but simply to create an event where before there was none. And not an unpleasant event, or a provocative one. Just a dimensionless, unreverberant moment, a contact, unimportant in every other respect. Life has few enough of these moments—the rest of it being so consumed by the predictable and the obligated. (67)

The narrator seems guilty of a number of miscalculations here. To see this potential encounter as analogous to one that a person might have with someone "not unhappily encountered" is akin to a category mistake: everything about his relationship with Mack is unhappy and will colour everything about any conversation they could possibly have. Walking across to Mack to speak to him, given what has happened between them, could hardly be anything but unpleasant and provocative. Equally, the unhappy nature of his past relationship with Mack disqualifies their potential conversation from being a simple, unimportant contact, as the narrator blithely presumes, or from countering "the predictable and the obligated" in life, as if there were no history between them to be clarified.

But the most complicated part of the narrator's reasoning concerns his desire to "create an event" and to participate in a "dimensionless, unreverberant moment". These are abstract and rather puzzling ambitions. It is as if "the predictable and the obligated" in the narrator's life so fastened him into routine, so deprived him of spontaneity and the unexpected, that any opportunity to break the hold of habit ought to be grasped. However, as the story progresses, it becomes clear that what underpins and encourages the ambition to create a "dimensionless, unreverberant moment" is a particular philosophy of both time and human action to which the narrator subscribes, one, however, that he will be obliged to revise in the light of his encounter with Mack.

What might a moment be that is without dimension, an apparently autonomous moment? The primary understanding of a moment is of a very brief period of time, a point in time, even. So a "dimensionless" moment would be one without temporal dimension, by which we understand that it is without connection to past or future time; it is delimited in time, does not expand nor extend beyond itself. That this is indeed the sense of the narrator's words is reinforced by other temporal references he makes. Looking back on his affair with Beth, he says: "I couldn't undo it. I don't believe the past can be repaired, only exceeded" (69). There is more than a hint here of a desire to leave the past behind, to move away from and beyond the reach of meanings enclosed in the past. At another point, again as he looks back to the affair, the narrator makes a quite explicit statement of his understanding of the operations of time:

> But that was now gone. Everything Beth and I had done was gone. All that remained was this—a series of moments in the great train terminal, moments which, in spite of all, seemed correct, sturdy, almost classical in character, as if this later time was all that really mattered, whereas the previous, briefly passionate, linked but now-distant moments were merely preliminary. (71)

The narrator establishes a clear temporal hierarchy here: the past is beyond meaningful engagement and constitutes little more than a spectral temporality when set beside the heft and "sturdy" materiality of the present. Seen from the present, the past is, at best, no more than a necessary facilitator of "this later time ... that really mattered". The only link the past has to the present, when considered from the fullness of the present, is as a temporal stepping-stone, as obligatory way station, which, once negotiated, fades into obscurity and irrelevance. It follows from this that an event in the present is detached from events in the past, or, to reverse the perspective, that events in the past have little or no claim on the present. It is important to emphasize that it is this very reasoning that propels the narrator to speak to Mack: if he allows himself to do so, it is specifically because of his conviction that the moments within which his conversation with Mack will take place will be independent of that past time they briefly but dolefully shared. The "series of moments" constituting the present of their meeting will stand alone, "dimensionless [and] unreverberant", autonomous events taking place in autonomous time.

Attentive readers of Richard Ford will recognize a relationship to time encountered elsewhere in his fiction, most notably in the three Frank Bascombe novels. We had cause, indeed, to consider in some detail Frank's systematic privileging of present over past in the trilogy, continuing through to the latter passages of *The Lay of the*

Land. It is worth briefly restating the arguments that may be brought to bear to counter these characters' impulse to jettison the past, as they are entirely relevant to the ambitions of the narrator in "Reunion". In the discussion on *The Sportswriter* we drew on Alasdair MacIntyre's theory of action, which insists that human behaviour is only intelligible when considered within the context of its settings and, at a more extended level, within the unity of a whole life. For MacIntyre, it does not make any sense to consider human action atomistically, that is, as actions that are disconnected from each other, that are temporally autonomous. MacIntyre insists that individual events and actions become intelligible only within the context of human agents' intentions, motives, beliefs and the settings within which these events and actions occur, all of which have their own histories. As he puts it: "'an' action is always an episode in a possible history."[6] And the intelligibility that emerges out of these temporal connections is, as MacIntyre points out, a narrative one: "Narrative history of a certain kind turns out to be the basic and essential genre for the characterization of human actions."[7]

To MacIntyre's voice might be added that of the great theorist of time and narrative, Paul Ricoeur: "time becomes human time to the extent that it is organized after the manner of a narrative; narrative, in turn, is meaningful to the extent that it portrays the features of temporal experience."[8] Time and narrative are thoroughly interdependent in so far as human intelligibility are concerned: mere succession in time is transformed into narrative configurations that capture past, present and future, configurations brought into being by the synthesizing function of narrative emplotment that brings and holds together the heterogeneous features that constitute the raw material of life experience.

We can return now to the desire of the narrator in "Reunion" to create an event and a moment that would be "dimensionless" and "unreverberant", a desire consistent with his instinct to cut the present off from the past. Yet one wonders how the narrator could even understand the event he wishes to create without reference to his own history with Mack. He could not do so, of course, no more than he

---

[6] MacIntyre, *After Virtue*, 216. See Chapter 2 for a fuller discussion of this topic.
[7] *Ibid.*, 208.
[8] Paul Ricoeur, *Time and Narrative*, vol. I, trans. Kathleen McLaughlin and David Pellauer, Chicago: U of Chicago P, 1984, 3.

could even want to have such an encounter in the first place were it not for their common history, the very history, indeed, that he has just been narrating. His very desire to create an event is intelligible only within a narrative of his own and Mack's pasts, just as the event itself, when it takes place, will be inscribed within similar, or other, narrative configurations. The productive circularity of the relationship between time and narrative proposed by Ricoeur reminds us that human experience is a temporal experience, and that the plots of our narratives confer a shape on our actions and events in time, connecting past, present, and future in creative orderings and re-orderings that explain our days and our lives to us. An event that would fall outside such temporal orderings would be, we might say, a non-event, as it would be disconnected from the history of other events upon which it is dependent for its meanings; in MacIntyre's terms, it would be an atomized event, unintelligible in its ostensible autonomy.

The two strands of the story – the moment as another episode in the history of the narrator's involvement in Mack's life; and the status, or autonomy, of the moment in time – come together in the event that is the meeting between Mack and the narrator, and strikingly so: the narrator's desire to create an event and to experience a dimensionless moment becomes the very theme of the meeting with Mack. The ground for this thematization is laid by the initial exchanges between the two men, and specifically by Mack's unwillingness to participate in a conversation, or even to accord their contact the status of a meeting or encounter. It is clear that the event desired by the narrator is precisely what Mack does not wish to sanction, as he indicates by his opening words: "Did you have something special in mind to tell me?" (70). For Mack, only an exceptional statement, perhaps an apology or an expression of regret, would warrant the narrator speaking to him. When it is clear that this is not the narrator's intention, Mack, unsolicited, offers the narrator a quick headline summary of his divorce from Beth and his move to New York, in order to satisfy what he considers to be the narrator's only motivation in coming to speak to him – vulgar curiosity. This is all that Mack wishes to say to the narrator, apart from asking him to leave as he does not wish to have to explain anything about his interlocutor to his daughter, for whom he is waiting.

In a story that is partly about a person's defencelessness against others' behaviour, there remains a part of Mack's being that cannot be touched and over which he remains sovereign: he can refuse to lend his person to the realization of whatever it is the narrator has in mind. Mack announces to the narrator that "Nothing's happened today", before continuing:

> Don't go away thinking anything happened here. Between you and me, I mean. *Nothing* happened. I'm sorry I ever met you, that's all. Sorry I ever had to touch you. You make me feel ashamed. (73)

There is a powerful sense of rejection and moral indignation in Mack's words. From the heights of his moral superiority, Mack's verdict on the narrator falls with Old Testament might in its connotations of the latter's moral impurity and uncleanliness: Mack is expressing a desire to create not only a physical but also a moral distance between them. If, in his capacity as victim of his wife's and the narrator's affair, and feeling contaminated by their behaviour, Mack has been unable up to now to maintain that moral distance, he can do so in this second encounter with the narrator. Although unaware of the narrator's curious desire to create an event, Mack asserts the sovereignty of moral being and action that remains to him, and he refuses to allow his words to the narrator to be accorded the status of an event, conversation or exchange between them. He reserves the right, as far as his own association with this episode is concerned, to name, and to accord meaning to, the moment that has just taken place between him and the narrator. With echoes of a New Testament denial of a different kind, Mack pronounces the word "Nothing" three times to deny the moment the status of an event, or, indeed, any status at all.

The conflicting views of time held by the two men, and their understanding of the relationship between present and past, now also come into play. The narrator privileges the present, wishes to move away from the past and to accord it an inferior status as mere preliminary time, a time of intrinsic obsolescence. For Mack, on the other hand, the present is not independent of the past, nor is time constructed of autonomous moments. For him, the past is the continuing time of betrayal and suffering, of which the narrator's appearance is an unhappy reminder. Mack would fully subscribe to MacIntyre's notion of the non-atomistic nature of action and to Ricoeur's premise about the narrative features of our temporal experience, what Ricoeur calls the "pre-narrative structure of experience",[9] by which he means the events, actions and experiences in time that call for the intelligibility of full narrative configuration. Mack's apprehension of the narrator in the present is intelligible to him, and painfully so, as an experience immediately inscribed within the history of the collapse of his marriage, the end of his life with Beth and the break-up of his family.

The story will come down on the side of Mack, beyond even his elevation to the status of superior moral figure and dignified innocent victim. Mack turns away from the narrator to greet his daughter, transforming the narrator into a non-person, consistent with the non-event of their contact. It is as if, in Mack's eyes, as he turns his gaze to his daughter, the narrator has ceased to exist. It is left to the narrator to agree belatedly with Mack's interpretation of temporal experience and to return to the centrality of the theme of time in the story: "I had, of course, been wrong about the linkage of moments, and about what was preliminary and what was primary. It was a mistake, one I would not make again" (74). We recall that the narrator had said that the past time of the affair constituted "linked but now-distant moments [that] were merely preliminary". The narrator had considered "linked" and "linkage" to indicate a connected series of moments in the past, moments, however, that are now thoroughly consigned to the past, to be exceeded by the fullness of meaning in the "sturdy" present. He has learned otherwise – his meeting with Mack has caused him to see that the past is not the "preliminary" or inferior time he had believed it to be. His belated acceptance of the continuing relevance of the past represents the end of any last hold-out for redemption in the present: "None of it was a good thing to have done" is his final verdict on the affair. Not for the first time, a male character in Richard Ford's fiction has found that the past can return with formidable force, that it can, indeed, exceed the present.

---

[9] Paul Ricoeur, "Life in Quest of Narrative", 29.

CHAPTER 12

"CHARITY"

MARRIAGE AND IDENTITY

Richard Ford has said of "Charity" that he "thought it was the most, in a way, healing story" in his collection. It was also, of the ten stories that constitute *A Multitude of Sins*, the last one he wrote. When he tried to write another, he found that all he "had left for the book was meanness".[1] It was as if all the empathy he had at his disposal for characters caught up in the unforgiving consequences of marital failure was bestowed on his protagonists in "Charity". While there are occasional flashes of anger and resentment from a wife having to deal with the consequences of her husband's affair, the story is indeed suffused with a spirit of understanding and forgiveness as Nancy Marshall strives to save her marriage and renew the strong bond that had made that relationship, in her eyes, close to perfect. As noted in Chapter 9, Ford found the title for his collection in the Bible, and it is possible that he took the title for this particular story from the specific message of one of the two biblical references to "a multitude of sins". In I Peter 4:8, one reads: "[Be ye] before all things earnest in your charity for one another, because 'charity covereth a multitude of sins'".

Consonant with the other biblical occurrence of the collection's title, Nancy seeks to bring her husband Tom back from the error of his ways as the latter struggles to find hope and direction in his life after the traumatic event that triggered his disorientation and subsequent betrayal of his wife.[2] It is undoubtedly one of Ford's goals in the story to explore the consequences of infidelity in a marriage characterized

---

[1] "Richard Ford", *identity theory: the narrative thread*, 2.
[2] James 5:20: "know that whoso bringeth a sinner back from the error of his way shall save the man's soul from death, and shall 'cover a multitude of sins'."

by love, commitment, responsibility and respect. Are the bonds created between two people by the practice of these virtues strong enough to save a relationship when these virtues are no longer fully respected? Are the unquestionable decency of a man and a woman and their will to revive the spirit of their marriage sufficient to overcome infidelity? And can a marriage go on as before in the wake of such an infidelity, and indeed be reinvigorated by it?

The story is narrated in the third person, but from Nancy's perspective. It is told from the present of an early-September weekend break that the couple, who live in Harlingen, Maryland, take along the south Maine coast, but it alternates, for most of the text, between the present of the Maine weekend and Nancy's recollection of the past, both of her happy marriage and of recent events that had undermined that relationship. It is only in the latter part of the story, as their time together in Maine moves them towards a resolution of the crisis in their marriage, that the story unfolds fully in the present of the events as they take place.

In Nancy's eyes, being married to Tom Marshall had been the experience that had most enriched her life and helped her find her place in the world. As Tom went about his domestic tasks of fixing and creating ("He had the disposition of a true artisan"), she would marvel at her good fortune, watching him "admiringly, raptly, almost mystically, as if to say 'how marvelous and strange and lucky to be married to such a man'".[3] Their marriage was characterized by the mutual understanding that they functioned no longer as two individuals but as a couple, and particularly so when, early in their married life, their son was born. Tom had hoped to become a lawyer, but had renounced his ambition and had become a policeman in order to more quickly earn a living. Nancy had raised their son, and, that task accomplished, had started law school, a decision enthusiastically supported by Tom, both emotionally and materially. And when she became a public defender, he "didn't gripe about the low pay and long hours, which he said were the costs of important satisfactions and of making a contribution".

Both, then, in turn, displayed selflessness and civic responsibility, signs of their mutual support and shared values. This harmonious life,

---

[3] Ford, *A Multitude of Sins*, 182. See note 4 in the Introduction for publication details. Further references to this collection will be indicated parenthetically in the text.

however, was threatened by tragedy when Tom's police partner was shot dead and Tom was injured as they questioned a suspect in a robbery attempt. Tom never settled into his new office-bound reassignment and left the police force soon after. But he put his creative talents to use in inventing and making children's toys, and was soon modestly successful, which, along with Nancy's winning more and more cases and their son being promised a job upon graduation, allowed Nancy to say of that time that "their life on earth seemed as perfect as ever could be imagined" (183).

Yet recorded within Nancy's evocation of her marriage before Tom's affair are small discordant facts and asides to which she herself is not alert, but that suggest themselves as at least potential sources of dissatisfaction and regret in Tom's life. He had had to abandon his ambition to become a lawyer, while Nancy ultimately became one, "a reversal in their careers" that the text records, although it "seemed ironic but insignificant". And while the text notes that Tom "liked police work" (181), Nancy herself found that he "was more like a high-school science teacher, which Nancy thought he should've been". She also notes that Tom had "never been truly 'cop-ish'" (182), while Tom himself will remark late in the story that he "was never a very good policeman" (208), all of which suggests a man who had spent over twenty years in the wrong job, an incongruity that even a strong sense of duty and responsibility might be hard put to suppress.

Nancy ultimately arrives at the logical conclusion of her own reflections when she observes that she "had never figured out why he'd stayed a cop so long except that he'd never thought his life was his own when he was young, but rather that he was a married man with responsibilities" (182). It is a comment that reveals both insight and blindness on Nancy's part: she understands the strong sense of duty that made her husband the man he was, the man she so admired and respected, yet does not see a possible source of discontentment and frustrated ambition in the role accorded to Tom in their life together. It is significant that one of the reasons cited by Tom to explain his affair was "his age-related feelings of under-achievement" (185). Nancy seems to have managed not to pay attention to, or to miss altogether, the fact that her husband was not fulfilled in his life.

This life, "as perfect as ever could be imagined", is gravely harmed by Tom's affair. It is not simply the fact of his affair that disturbs Nancy, but also that he had it with "a pretty little airhead with no personality" (183) and that he let it continue for months, well beyond the point when Nancy believed a man like Tom would see that "there was nothing ... to be interested in" in a woman like Crystal. But Tom went beyond that point and did not stop until Crystal's boyfriend "blew Tom's cover". Nancy's idealization of her husband and marriage was rendered hollow and even foolish through Tom's infatuation, just as her knowledge of her husband and failure to appreciate his potential dissatisfactions were called into question. Tom attributed his behaviour to a reaction to "suddenly being off the force after half his life", but also to the experience of "his new life". This latter explanation confirms the suspicion that Nancy had blinded herself to a certain reality, as Tom speaks of his having felt the need to "celebrate" the "pure exhilaration" of his new circumstances, in which "acts took place outside the boundaries of convention, obligation, the past and even good sense" (184). While sounding suspiciously self-serving, Tom's explanation also points to a sense of his having wished to unshackle himself from the duty and responsibility he had carried for twenty years. Nonetheless, once his affair is exposed, his desire is to repair his marriage if Nancy can forgive him, in which case "he could promise her that such as this would never happen again" (185).

Not for the only time in this collection an affair is seen to have a contaminating effect on the relationship it troubles. The idealistic language of purity and goodness in which Nancy conceived her marriage with Tom stands in stark contrast to the language she uses now to characterize Tom's affair. The nature of Tom and Crystal's relationship is understood by her through one crude term only: Nancy notes that Tom was not constrained by his new lover's intellectual and emotional limitations and that he "managed ... to fuck Crystal in her silkscreen studio on an almost daily basis for months" (184). And when Tom ends his confession to her after she confronts him with her knowledge of the affair, she finds herself saying to him: "Why don't you just fuck *me* tonight?" She immediately recognizes silently that the "word *fuck* was provocative but also ... slightly pathetic as an address to your husband" (186).

Her use of the term in this context, however, is a measure of the degree to which Tom's affair has corrupted her marriage: what Nancy views as the purely instinctive and mechanical act between Tom and Crystal now sullies her conception of her own lovemaking with Tom. This coarsening of her view of her marriage points to an even deeper malaise that has infiltrated the very foundations of their life together, beyond even issues of trust and infidelity, honesty and deception: in focusing again on the consequences of acts, Richard Ford in "Charity" explores the damage caused to Nancy's sense of identity, to her fond, long-held understanding of her husband and to her fixed image of her marriage, all of which have been altered and undermined by Tom's affair.

Nancy's sense of identity was inextricably bound up with her status as a happily married woman. She recalls how she would watch Tom admiringly as he carried out "some typical Saturday-morning project". Such moments of quiet observation and complete immersion in her husband's simple daily expression of his being and values constituted her "most pleasing vision of her married self". Tom had also provided a moral example that had formed her personality and identity, by drawing her away from the "too selfish" younger person she had been: being married to him "had allowed her to learn the ordinary acts of devotion, love, attentiveness, and the acceptance of another" – acts, it is noted, that "she'd never practiced when she was younger" (182) Nancy's sense of herself, then, is deeply troubled by the revelation of Tom's affair, and she continues to be disturbed that Tom could have been with her for over twenty years and then turn for comfort to a morally and emotionally inferior woman, whom she thinks of as Tom's *"retarded girlfriend"* (186). Nancy feels demeaned by association, seeing in Tom's relationship with Crystal a reflected value of herself. And when Tom moves out of the family home in the winter before their September Maine vacation, and continues to live away from Nancy, his absence further corrodes her sense of self. No longer sustained by the certainty of her role and place in life, she experiences her abandonment and isolation as "an *ebbing*, something going out of her, like water seeping from a cracked beaker, restoring it to its original, vacant state" (195). It is as if Nancy is slowly being emptied of the vital elements of her very identity.

If Nancy has come to discern a certain grandeur arising from her new condition and if she begins to observe the emergence of a new sense of who she is, this new identity is born out of her abandonment and draws its strength from her isolation and from her "being alone and getting on with things" (195). The new fragility in Nancy's identity is compounded by an insight she has into herself as she listens to Tom's attempts to articulate his feelings about his affair. She sees

Tom as a man who "wasn't ... distanced from what he felt", whereas she finds in herself a gap between her words and their meanings and consequences. She had "never exactly recognized this about herself, and now considered the possibility that it had just become true, or been made true by Tom's betrayal". Whatever the origin of this dichotomy between intention and meaning, desire and utterance, and utterance and consequence, that often left her wondering "how she could get out of doing the very things she said she desired", she feels it as a new vulnerability in herself in the context of Tom's confession. A disturbing question now hangs over her identity:

> But what was it, she wondered, as they left the restaurant headed for home and bed? What was that thing she was? Surely it was a thing anyone should be able to say. There would be a word for it. She simply couldn't bring that word to mind. (187)

Her husband's affair has prompted a questioning about her own self, and has revealed an ambivalence at the heart of her being, an ambiguity in her utterances and an unnamability in her identity. This is the disquieting burden she carries with her on her vacation to Maine.

If Tom's affair has necessitated a revision of Nancy's sense of self, so too has it obliged her to reconsider her image of Tom, and here, too, the nature of the revised image is revealing. The image of a diminishment of Nancy's own being, expressed through "ebbing" and "seeping", becomes one of death itself as Nancy looks at Tom while he confesses his affair: where she normally saw Tom's "craggy, handsome face", she now sees something "more like a skull, a death's head" (185-86). The only appropriate expression, then, for the magnitude of the loss threatened by Tom's infidelity is death – death as a severe spiritual lessening of self in Nancy's case and as a threat to the identity through which she has always understood her husband. And just as one crude term, for Nancy, characterized Tom and Crystal's relationship, so now does a single word attach itself to Tom and define his identity, and risks establishing a moral hierarchy between them: "she was not an adulterer and he was" (187). Tom's twenty-year fixed identity has had to be re-evaluated, with the result that, whenever he visits Nancy in her house after he had left home, she finds herself trying "to decide anew" if he was indeed the man she had always taken him to be, or "if he was just a creep or a jerk she had unwisely married, then gradually gotten used to" (193).

An inevitable consequence of the diminution and alteration in Nancy's sense of self and of her questioning of the identity and character of her husband is a revision of her image of the couple constituted by Tom and herself. Her idealization of her marriage ill prepares their relationship to withstand a grievous blow to the values upon which the relationship rests, and makes its fall from grace all the harder to absorb. Ruminating upon the details of the affair and listening to Tom's confession, Nancy has the disagreeable thought that the "humiliating, dismal disclosures" she has been listening to imply that "your life was even more like every other life than you were prepared to concede". Nancy is letting herself be directed by the notion of self-image, in which one is concerned, to quote Charles Taylor, that one's "image matches up to certain standards, generally socially induced".[4] Nancy is being punished here for a certain smugness that had her see her life and relationship as superior to others', superior certainly to those of "airhead" Crystal and her "hillbilly boyfriend" (185). Since the revelation of the affair she has been forced to reckon with this inferior other life and relationship, and, for a period of time and measured against the criteria of fidelity and trust, sees it as little different from her own.

As Nancy begins her important weekend holiday with Tom she is prey to conflicting feelings and desires and to great uncertainties about her and Tom's ability to reanimate their marriage. She has concluded that Tom is sincere in his regret, that he "*was* all the things she'd always thought him to be" (194), that she wanted her marriage to survive and that she was able to forgive Tom without great difficulty, deciding that "betrayal had to mean something worse that hadn't really happened" (195) in their case. For all that, however, the winter of Tom's departure had turned to spring, and still he stayed away, seemingly "able to adjust to being alone and even to thrive on it" (194). The imagery of diminishment returns as Nancy observes that "the entire edifice of their life was beginning to take on clearer shape and to grow smaller" (195). The altered shape of their relationship is the new configuration of separation, isolation and reduced attention to the other, the antithesis of their earlier life together. If the

---

[4] Taylor, *Sources of the Self*, 33. For a discussion on the distinction between identity and self-image, see the chapter on "The Womanizer".

protagonists' identities have essentially been articulated through their marriage and their moral and emotional roles in a valued relationship, it is little wonder, as Nancy concludes, that the "uncertain emotional territory" upon which they now stand "might put to the test exactly who they were as humans, might require that new facets of the diamond be examined" (194). In saving or losing their marriage Nancy and Tom will either reaffirm the identities they have forged together, or reinvent themselves in order to face into the future alone.

The opening scene of the story takes place on the first night of the weekend in Maine. It is a short scene but sufficient to indicate the awkwardness and uncertainty that now troubles the once-easy relationship between Nancy and Tom. They are in the bedroom of a B&B in Freeport, and Nancy is standing watching customers entering and leaving the L.L. Bean store. Tom moves behind Nancy and begins to make love to her. An innocent remark from her about the activity across the street discourages Tom and he climbs into bed and immediately falls asleep. Nancy would have been happy to make love, but her innocent remark is misinterpreted by Tom, and neither of them has the assurance to overcome the misunderstanding, out of fear of overstepping the limits that now constrain and regulate their relations. Throughout their time together in Maine – from this Thursday night until the story ends on the afternoon of the following day – they manage only momentarily to get beyond the emotional legacy of Tom's affair and to rediscover the complicity and intimacy that used to characterize their relationship. Otherwise, the atmosphere between them is marked variously by over-sensitivity, misunderstanding, emotional distance, doubt, resentment and foreboding.

Maine and its geography feature strongly in the story, functioning at both a literal and figurative level. The state has great significance for Tom as a place he might come to live in, but its landscapes and towns also provide a series of metaphors for the condition of Nancy and Tom's relationship. At a literal level the state has become the focus of Tom's hope for personal renewal. The Maine holiday was his idea: a notion he has about the "primary" experience of the ocean and "something hazy about the country having started here" had "all of a sudden 'made sense' to him" (191), as if were driven by a private mythology of a return to origins, of wiping the slate clean and beginning again.

But it is only as they explore their surroundings that Nancy realizes that Tom had proposed the vacation to allow him the opportunity to check out the feasibility of living in Maine. Feeling unable to tell Nancy directly what is on his mind, yet knowing that he will ultimately have to do so, Tom's intentions are discernible only through his demeanour. He takes great interest in real estate office windows displaying houses for sale, and his mood begins to change as he eases himself into the Maine landscape and appraises the opportunities that life in the state might present. Although not yet revealing his intention, Tom tells Nancy that he regrets not having considered Maine as a home twenty years earlier, an indication that he does indeed nourish deep disappointments with regard to his life, a dissatisfaction that was brought into brutally sharp perspective by the shooting. As he explains to Nancy just before he confesses his hopes for a new life in Maine, he has been "disappointed about life" since the shooting. Since then, everything has seemed "so damned congested" and he has been unable to "keep anything simple. So I just made it more complicated" (209).

It is here that the story earns its title in a sense other than that of a will to forgive: it is charitable also in that Tom's infidelity is attributed to a traumatic event and not to the self-interested motives found in other stories.[5] Yet even with this charitable perspective Tom displays the tendency so familiar from other male characters in Richard Ford, that of looking beyond one's present life and difficulties and towards the somewhat tenuous hopes held out by the untested schemes of one's fantasies: Frank Bascombe in *The Sportswriter*, Martin Austin in "The Womanizer" and Charley Matthews in "Occidentals" are the examples that spring readily to mind. In Tom's case, escapism has its source in the self-image and comparative evaluation of one's life of which Nancy was guilty earlier, although this time Tom views himself as the inferior figure when he contrasts himself to others: he sees

---

[5] In this respect one might contrast Tom with Martin Austin in "The Womanizer". In the latter story the issues are much more clearly of a moral nature: there are no mitigating circumstances in Austin's case – he is simply a womanizer who systematically lies to his wife and who seems to consider his trips abroad as an opportunity to have brief sexual encounters. While Tom Marshall does indeed betray his wife, it is made clear that this is because the shooting seems to have completely undermined the foundations upon which he lived his life. This causes him ultimately to lose his way morally, but the story invites understanding rather than condemnation of Tom's confusions and reactions.

others as making "fewer mistakes" than he does and of having a "firmer grasp of things" (207). The unreality of Tom's ambitions for a new life in Maine are evidenced in the vague wish-list of possible expansions of his toy-making activities that he blurts out to Nancy, culminating in an unlikely fallback position: "I could be a cop if it came to that" (210).

Understandable though it may be in his case, Tom is yet another male Richard Ford character who runs way from responsibility for his life instead of facing up to it. And, as is often the case in Ford's fiction, it is women who have a more lucid view of life's realities and responsibilities: Tom's fantasy is countered by Nancy's calm realism, which sees beyond the pretty summer settings to the harshness of life in Maine in winter. Nor is she impressed by the self-satisfied punning on the state's name ("Mainiac Markdowns", "Roof Maine-tenance" [190]) and a certain coy conceit she detects in the way the local population speaks of itself in the local press, an example of an entire state's concern with its self-image.

At a metaphorical level the Maine landscape is used extensively to communicate Nancy's emotions and to chart the evolution of the couple's relationship. The uncertainty that besets the relationship is announced in their disorientation as soon as they drive from Freeport to Wiscasset on Friday morning:

> They'd imagined leaves would be turning, but they weren't yet because of all the summer rain.
> They were also not able to tell exactly how far anything was from anything else. The map was complicated by quirky peninsulas extending back south and the road having to go up and around and down again. The morning's drive from Freeport had seemed long, but not much distance was covered. It made you feel foreign in your own country. (191)

It is not difficult to read their geographical disorientation as an extended metaphor for their emotional disorientation: things are not turning out as they expected; the steadfastness of their relationship is now complicated by trying twists and turns; their trial separation is lengthening but has not brought them closer; and they are both now inhabiting unfamiliar emotional territory.[6] Nancy in particular is confused by her situation with regard to her surroundings. She does not understand the local idiom of "down-east"; she does not know in which direction she is facing when she looks out the car window; she cannot locate Nova Scotia; and she finds the map of Maine misleading as distances are difficult to calculate. Tom, in contrast, having planned the trip, has little problem finding his bearings and is more assertive in the direction he wishes them to take.

The map-reading, too, functions as an extended metaphor, this time for the rearrangement of their lives after Tom's affair and the planned trajectory of their relationship as they sought initially to move beyond the early emotional distress. Nancy's bafflement about her whereabouts on their journey expresses her inner confusion about the course and organisation of their lives in the aftermath of the affair, just as it expresses Tom's growing confidence. She notes now that "since he'd been away, he seemed healthier, calmer, more hopeful, though the story was somehow that he'd moved a mile away to a shitty apartment to make *her* happier" (197). Just as Nancy cannot read the map of Maine, she has misread her own relationship and is as bewildered by the topography of Maine as she is by that of her marriage.

They spend the greater part of their day in the town of Belfast, and observations on the town resonate metaphorically as commentary on Nancy and Tom. Their arrival in the "inconspicuous middle of Belfast" also situates them with regard to the indistinct condition and course of their marriage. Nancy notes that Belfast is a "town in transition. From what to what, she wasn't sure" (201), echoing the shifting state of their relationship, but also Tom's remark that he "[likes] the idea of transition" (203) and Nancy's own observation that "Tom liked the idea of transforming yourself" (189). The air of foreboding and fatalism surrounding their future together is conveyed in Nancy's reflection that Belfast was a town "waiting quietly for what would soon surely arrive" (204) and in the observation that preparations were being made "for a long winter" (208). The pollution of the town's bay by a poultry factory, leaving it "inert" and "sterile" but also "ready for profitable alternative uses" recalls metaphorically

---

[6] Ford's use of geographical metaphors in "Charity" recalls a similar device in "The Womanizer" and "Occidentals", where the protagonists' cultural lostness is communicated through their sense of disorientation in Paris.

the corruption of their marriage by Tom's affair, its harmful aftermath and Tom's desire to re-invent himself in Maine. Nancy apprehends the fate of the Belfast bay explicitly in metaphorical terms, seeing in its pattern of decay and possible recycling "the way all things became". And as if expressing a desire for her relationship to move beyond its present state of stagnation, whatever the outcome, she concludes that even the "presence of an awful-smelling factory or a poisonous tannery or a cement factory" in the town "could almost seem like something to wish for" (204-205).[7]

The Maine vacation instigates a revision of both Nancy's and Tom's identities, obliging both of them to redefine who they are, and Nancy to further consider the image she has of her husband. The opening scene of the story on the first night in Maine not only conveys the unease in Nancy and Tom's relationship but also suggests the beginnings of a transformation of Nancy's identity. As she watches the "customers ... streaming in and out" (179) of the L.L. Bean store across the street she is naked and standing at the window. Two bus drivers are smoking on the opposite side of the street, but are unable, Nancy believes, to see her. When her misunderstood remark discourages Tom and he stops his initial lovemaking gestures, she realizes that the "two bus drivers she believed could not see through the shadowy trees were both looking right at her". Nancy decides that she

> didn't care if two creeps saw her naked; it was exactly the same as her seeing them clothed. She was forty-five. Not so slender, but tall, willowy. Let them look. (180)

While dismissing the possibility of the drivers seeing anything personal or intimate about her, she nonetheless knowingly continues to leave herself open to their gaze, and it is they, and not her, who finally move away.

---

[7] The Belfast restaurant in which they eat also functions metaphorically in the text. They come across a chowder house that Nancy "already knew" (201) they would find; its sign outside is "so picturesque and clear and pristine as to be painful", but everything inside is mediocre and disagreeable; and a sign inside announces that "in a week the whole place would close for the winter" (202). In these reflections one can read the inevitability of the course of their relationship, the superficial appearance of a happy couple on holiday, the reality that this appearance hides, and Nancy's generally pessimistic mood about the outcome of things.

As the story moves on to recount past events, this behaviour of Nancy remains puzzling: nothing we learn about her from the narrative of her ideal and idealized married life with Tom conforms to this somewhat exhibitionist moment in the B&B. But the window incident occurs in the post-affair period, when Nancy's comfortable notions about her identity and place in life have been deeply undermined. As she is being watched by the drivers, she is conscious of her physical features that might be attractive to men: despite her disclaimer, she is fully aware that the men are looking at a desirable woman's body and that she is making that body available to the eyes of watching men. This tableau of a woman in a window knowingly presenting her body to the outside male gaze has echoes of red-light-district window display, a suggestion reinforced by the sexual act Nancy had begun to perform with Tom while standing at the window, and indeed by the (perhaps hypocritical) reaction of the drivers who "[shake] their heads" (181) before moving away. We will learn later, too, that, during their separation, Nancy had "considered the possibility of having an affair—a colleague or a delivery boy" (193), another hint about her new accessibility. Her highly ambiguous availability to the male sexual gaze, then, suggests an awareness on her part that her identity as a faithful married woman is loosening and that she will need to step outside the cocoon of married life and – notwithstanding a certain ambivalence on her part – step into the public gaze, where her sense of self will be influenced by how she understands herself to be perceived through the gaze of others.

A further incident on the Friday reveals Nancy's new preoccupation with her identity, articulated again through the dynamics of seeing and being seen. As a tour bus passes by her and Tom in Belfast she wonders how she might appear to those who may be looking at her, enough to make her want to say to them that "whatever you're thinking about me, you're wrong. I'm just as out of place as you are." Nancy mentions to Tom about this sensation of "[being] seen, but to understand you're being seen wrong" (205). That her preoccupation with being seen does indeed reveal a wider awareness about her identity in the wake of Tom's affair and his leaving home is confirmed by a further thought, as Tom puts his hand on her shoulder: "too bad, she thought, the tourist bus couldn't come by when his arm was around her, a true married couple out for a summery walk on a sunny street. Most of that would be accurate."

"Most", but not all: it is precisely an insufficiency that now characterizes her relationship with Tom and that is at the heart of the disturbance in her identity, the insufficiency that this vacation will either overcome or deepen. It is Nancy herself who articulates the sense of uncertainty of identity of which she is now aware and that the gaze of the bus passengers reveals to her: does knowing "you're being seen wrong" mean "you're not inhabiting your real life?" (206), she wonders to Tom.

The upheaval in Nancy's life and identity is communicated through another extended metaphor: this story of transformation and transition takes place as Nancy and Tom are on a journey from their home to a destination quite far away, and then in a car as they drive from place to place. They have a depressing argument in the car, recalling, ironically, the remark that "In the car, who they really were became available to the other. Guards went down. They felt free" (191). Nancy is relieved when this movement comes to an end with their arrival in Belfast, and it is to her that the conception of their journey in metaphorical terms is attributed:

> She felt happy being on foot where normally you'd be in the car, she preferred it to arriving and leaving, which now seemed to promote misunderstandings and fractiousness of the sort they'd already experienced. She could appreciate these parts of a trip when you were *there*, and everything stopped moving and changing. (207)

Nancy is wistful now for the sense of permanence and constancy that her marriage had once conferred: in both her life and identity, there is no longer a "*there*" in which to restore that sense of security. But it is precisely the sense of transition represented by Maine – as well as the travelling to and within it – that appeals to Tom, to his desire to cast off his past life and identity, and to his yearning for a return to a mythical state of pure beginning. He tells Nancy that, for his part, he would like to inhabit his life "more" (206), an idea he expands upon when Nancy finally forces the truth out of him about his interest in Maine: "I know too much about myself where I am, and I'd like to find out something new before I get too old" (211). The holiday weekend, then, is understood by both of them as a moment of suspension between two possible destinations – they will either find a new harmony to allow them to go back to their marriage, which is where Nancy wishes to go, or they will face into the unknown of a new life in Maine, which is where Tom wishes to take them.

The pull in different directions represents the sundering of their once-unified identity, and becomes the focal point for Nancy in the bitter argument they have in the car. Tom's talk about the need for "readjustment" in their relationship has Nancy angrily articulate, once again in trenchant single words, the changing view she has of her husband: she calls him a "stupe" ("old Chicago code to them. An ancient language of disgust" [200]) and wonders if he is becoming a "bullshitter" (201). It is as if Tom's changing identity has suddenly become utterly clear to her, and she begins now to notice small but significant changes in him that widen the gulf between them. She is struck, for example, by his table manners:

> Years ago, he'd possessed lovely table manners, eaten unhurriedly and enjoyed everything. It had been his Irish mother's influence. Now he was itchy, interested elsewhere, and his mother was dead. (203-204)

Yet this change in Tom had occurred over time, another sign that Nancy had perhaps been taken in by her idealized view of her marriage and had been misreading her husband and their relationship for a considerable time, a possibility that is now dawning on her: in relation to Tom possibly becoming a "bullshitter", she wonders: "How had that happened?" (201).

In her new lucidity, a precise new identity for Tom is emerging. She finds herself having to remind him during their argument that he is "a grown man" (200), and when he finally divulges his Maine plans to her, she observes that Tom sometimes "could be like an extremely earnest, extremely attractive boy" (211). It is as if her husband is indeed being transformed before her eyes, but in a regressive movement, returning to a fantasy-filled, responsibility-free world of childhood, to his mythical state of pure origins. In the final conversation between them, toymaker Tom's new identity seems sealed in Nancy's eyes: his plan to move to Maine "was a certain kind of boy's fabulous dream". Their trajectories have once again been reversed. As in their careers, their preferred future domicile and their being together or apart, so now in age and identity: as Nancy ponders the implications of a "boy's fabulous dream", she feels "heavy-bodied, older even than she'd felt before" (212).

In the final, lengthy section of the story Nancy is effectively alone. The couple find a motel room in Belfast and Tom falls asleep immediately. For the second time in the story Tom's response to disappointment (on this occasion to Nancy's unenthusiastic response to his Maine plans) is to escape into sleep, instituting a separation that will remain for the rest of the story. Nancy's solitude is accompanied by a silence symbolizing the end of communication between them, the silence between two people who have nothing left to say to each other that could change the course of events. Nancy's emotions range from anger to comprehension as she takes stock of her life, but the residual feelings are those that have her conclude that "in all probability life with Tom Marshall was over". Her overriding sense is of having been used by Tom through his manipulation of the trip "for the sole purpose of having her reject it so he could then do what he wanted to anyway", all of which, for her, confirms Tom's new identity as "an overexuberant child" and as not being "a grownup" (215). Nancy's interlude in the motel room represents the end of the period of suspension in which Tom and she have been hovering during the weekend.

In a deliberately understated story (unlike some others in the collection where violence either threatens or occurs), Nancy's epiphany is not accompanied by dramatic acts but by small shifts of perception and discreet but significant gestures, and rendered by a highly symbolic ending. So it is that Nancy, as she had already done at breakfast that morning, looks at the local newspaper's dating-exchange listings of men and women seeking partners, a perhaps unconscious gesture indicating her own new availability, and itself an echo of the window scene in the B&B. As she reads the listings the thought comes to her that they represent a "generalized sense of the possible, of what lay out there waiting" (213). And it is indeed by way of a literal turning to "out there" that Nancy begins to ease herself away from the orbit of her marriage: she becomes aware of noise from outside and is drawn to look out, where she sees a man in a wheelchair and a little girl playing with a kite. She recognizes them from having seen them earlier in Belfast, yet her reaction now is unusual – "A coincidence of no importance" (214) is how the text records her thought. But why should the unremarkable second sighting of people in a small town even rise to the status of possible significance, if not for Nancy's readiness to read significance into it? The scene she witnesses as she looks out the window is the repeated failure of the man in the wheelchair to launch the kite into the air. But each failure prompts a renewed attempt to launch it, in a demonstration of patient resolve to overcome frustration and adversity.

It is in the moments following the witnessing of this scene, as she sits again in the gloom of the motel room, that small but important re-evaluations about her identity occur. She recalls "being misidentified" by the tourist-bus passengers in Belfast and how she liked the feeling this gave her, "as if she was especially credible when seen without the benefit of circumstance and the encumbrances of love, residues of decisions made long, long ago". She had also, however, associated this feeling with "not inhabiting [her] real life". Nancy has not yet brought these random thoughts and sensations together into a coherent account of selfhood, but one discerns the beginnings of a profound re-evaluation, and even renouncement, of the identity accorded to her for over twenty years through her marriage to Tom. And it is surely this very identity that is at the origin of the disturbing unnamability she had discovered in herself as Tom was confessing his affair, this gap she identified between what she desired and what she said and the consequences she had to bear as a result.

The cause of this unnamability, this disquieting paradox at the core of her sense of self, exposed particularly through the gaze of others and in her sensitivity to that gaze, is located firmly now somewhere in her marriage: she finds that she is "especially credible" when shorn of "circumstance and the encumbrances of love", and "More credible, certainly, than she was here now, trapped in East Whatever, Maine, with a wayward husband on his way down the road" (215). These thoughts about herself have the effect of wresting her away from her present life and from her identity as a married woman and as part of a couple, and have her consider herself more as an individual, one now liberating herself from that life and the role it accorded her.

These reflections on her identity are those that precede, and no doubt trigger, the final, symbolic exclusion of and break with Tom. For one pivotal moment she wants to wake him to share a hopeful thought with him, but then does not do so: "for an instant", at this precise moment of decision, "she seemed to understand *slightly* better the person she was—though she lacked a proper word for it" (217). The unnamability at the heart of Nancy's self remains, but she has nonetheless glimpsed a future reconfiguration of her identity. She leaves her sleeping husband and walks "out there", moving from the cocooned space of her marriage symbolized by the darkened motel room to the vast open expanse of light and space and water, outside to the man and child and their attempts to launch their kite.

With regard to his short stories Richard Ford has noted: "I kind of load up the end. I make the end be really full."[8] And speaking specifically of the stories in *A Multitude of Sins*, he has said: "These, I think, were the most 'written' of anything I've done. I did a lot of hard writing on them."[9] The end of "Charity" is indeed loaded in a highly literary manner, and in such a way to allow the narrative be regarded as the healing story Ford believes it to be. The man in the wheelchair has succeeded in overcoming the obstacles dealt him by fate – in a way Tom has not yet done – and has launched the kite, which was "dancing and tricking and had gained altitude" (217). The launching of the kite from the earth into the sky becomes an overarching final metaphor for the journey that awaits Nancy, should she have the courage to launch herself alone into a new life. The man asks Nancy if she wants to fly the kite:

> Nancy felt embarrassed. Seen. It was shocking. The spacious blue bay spread away from her down the hill, and off of it arose a freshened breeze. It was far from clear that she could hold the kite. It *could* take her up, pull her away, far and out of sight. It was unnerving .... And then, she thought ... that she would take the kite ... yes, of course, and fly it, take the chance, be strong, unassailable, do everything she could to hold on. (219)

The relevance of the individual elements of the metaphor to Nancy's situation as she faces into life without Tom – the challenge, the possibilities, the dangers, the leap into the unknown, the uncertainties, the need for self-belief and determination – is self-evident. Of greater interest here is the return to the issue of identity, by way of the motif of the gaze and the exposure it occasions. As she walks towards the man and the child, but, more pertinently, as she walks out into the open and the light, and away from her marriage and the security of identity it conferred, Nancy is exposed – as she will be

---

[8] "Richard Ford", *identity theory: the narrative thread*, 6.
[9] Jeff Baker, Interview with Richard Ford, "Life Readings & Writings: Imagining the Possibilities", *The Oregonian*, 8 March 2002, Arts and Living Section, 6.

in the future – to the gaze of others, a scrutiny that she finds "shocking". She is deeply conscious of this gaze as it probes her being for signs of the person she is. This is the person and identity that must now be constructed as she faces into the future alone.

The story is healing in so far as Nancy leaves Tom still thinking well of him, feelings that allow her, by the end, to turn to thinking about herself and her future. For all that, however, "Charity" is hardly an optimistic story. It recounts the failure of a marriage that should not have failed, as it was a marriage, in Nancy's final verdict on Tom and herself, between two "basically decent people" (216) who were convinced, in Nancy's words, that "They loved each other" (189). Nancy had wondered at one point earlier in the day, as she reflected on all that was good in her marriage, about what "all these reserves of tender feeling and kind regard actually *come to*? And not come to?" (189). By the end of the story she has found an answer to both of these questions. For her and Tom, these feelings come to thinking kind thoughts about each other, but they do not come to their being able to live with or be married to each other anymore. From this perspective, one might choose to see "Charity" as the most disconsolate story of them all.

CHAPTER 13

"ABYSS"

THE FALL

In the table of contents for *A Multitude of Sins*, "Abyss" is the last story listed. It is also set off from the other nine stories because of its status as a novella.[1] The title of the story is even more forceful when isolated and surrounded by white space in this initial presentation of the titles, as if the organization of the story titles on the page functions as an overarching metaphor for the collection – at the end of infidelity there awaits an abyss. The presentational build-up is carried through in the novella itself: Ford's liking for strong endings to his stories is given full expression in the calamitous conclusion to "Abyss" and, therefore, to the entire collection. In overall terms, the story has an archetypal feel to it, that is to say that Ford seemed determined to use it to explore and forcefully insist on the premise that guided the writing of the entire collection, namely that acts of infidelity have consequences.[2] Through its resolute beginning-middle-end narrative structure, "Abyss" traces the unfolding of an affair from its first moments to the immediate aftermath of its shocking conclusion, in an exercise of teleological storytelling whose overriding concern is to

---

[1] It is Richard Ford himself who so justifies the isolation of "Abyss" in the table of contents ("Richard Ford", *identity theory: the narrative thread*, 3).

[2] As already pointed out in this study, the consequences of human action have interested Ford for almost his entire writing life, and continued to do so during the writing of these stories. It is still a message he seeks to communicate to his readers. In an interview to coincide with the publication of *The Lay of the Land* he uses a line from a story by Irish writer Frank O'Connor to illustrate his point: "A line like that at the end of O'Connor's story, it wants to say, life is very important. Pay really close attention to it. Because your acts will have consequences" (Belinda McKeon, Interview with Richard Ford, "Remembrance and Release", *Irish Times*, 16 September 2006, Weekend Review Section, 11).

produce a cautionary tale with the starkest of messages: very bad things can happen when you ignore your conscience and forget what is important in your life.

Somewhat like "The Womanizer", "Abyss" has the instructional force of a biblical parable. If the opening story of *A Multitude of Sins* only anticipates the consequences of infidelity, the final one carries us through to infidelity's bitter end and aftermath. Another feature that obliquely connects the first and last stories of the collection – and that also recalls the biblical resonance of the entire collection – is adultery: "Privacy" is the only story in the collection not to feature adultery, whereas "Abyss" could accurately be described as an anatomy of an adulterous liaison. The term "adultery" features in the text (244, 256), and fittingly so, as the story, more than any other in the collection, focuses on a relationship motivated above all by sexual desire for a person other than one's spouse.

The novella has a two-part temporal structure reflecting the two essential phases of the relationship: the attraction and excitement of the early days as real estate agents Howard Cameron and Frances Bilandic begin their affair in the towns near where they live and work, followed by the development of the affair when they transport it to the Phoenix sales conference of the company for which they both work, the period when sexual attraction and pleasure are revealed to be an inadequate defence against growing mutual irritation.

Frances and Howard meet at the company banquet at which they are both awarded the title of Connecticut Residential Agents of the Year. When they speak to each other for the first time, they experience what Frances considers to be a "large, instinctual carnal attraction" for each other. She experiences this magnetism as animal-like in its primitive intensity, and this will be a recurring motif that Ford will employ in the story to underline the aggressive, ruttish sexuality that propels Frances and Howard towards each other. Convention and appearance prohibit an immediate expression of lust, so their dinner-table chat has at once to respect propriety yet advance them far enough within the delimited time of eating dinner to establish what, if anything, they intend to do about their mutual attraction. Their conversation, therefore, driven uniquely by the pulsations of sexual desire, becomes an exercise in dissimulation, as truth-telling becomes the first victim of their desire. They circle around each other and their intentions through a form of code they both employ, advancing in their complicity in stages, initially through "exchanging snickering asides about the other winners' table manners" and other deficiencies, moving on to the sad stories of friends and family, which, they agree sagely, offer a salutary lesson about "life's brevity and the need to squeeze every second for all its worth", before, as the end of the meal approaches, getting on to the general topic of sex. These rapid transitions are possible because they both know what they want. Although speaking in their allegorical code, "sex infiltrated their soft-spoken conversation like a dense, rich but explosive secret".

The initial moral issue in the story, then, as they circle hungrily around each other, is one of truth. Their disingenuous conversation could be seen as no more than a modern form of age-old courtship rituals were it not for the fact that both of them are married. The greater truth that is sidetracked, then, is that of the lives they have chosen to live and the people with whom they have chosen to live them. These commitments are quickly reconsidered and reconfigured as the urges of sexual desire demand that Howard and Frances take a distance from their spouses. Yet, equally, in this initial period of decoding the feelings of the other, they cannot afford to repel the other by being too explicitly available or by appearing morally unattractive. So it is that they need to walk a fine line between honour and availability: "They each spoke lovingly about their spouses, but not that much."[3] But as their sexual desire is encouraged by the coded expression of it in the other, they detach themselves increasingly from their spouses and their marriages, with both agreeing that "Marriage shouldn't be a prison cell. The best marriages were always the ones where both partners felt free to pursue their personal needs."

Individually, silently, they seek out deficiencies in their own lives to justify the direction the conversation is taking. Frances is impressed with how relaxed she is with Howard after two hours, something she had not achieved with her husband Ed "in six years" (225), while Howard finds motivation in his father's health problems for the view that "life had to be seized". And because both are absolutely clear about what they are doing – Howard refers to their increasingly explicit conversation as "a game" (226) – and about what they hope will be the outcome of this "instinctual carnal attraction", their moral

---

[3] Ford, *A Multitude of Sins*, 224. See note 4 in the Introduction for publication details. Further references to this collection will be indicated parenthetically in the text.

sensibilities need to be deflected or redirected. Both, therefore, seek moral justification for their intentions. Frances considers that she works "her tail off" selling in the grubby end of the real estate market, which authorizes her to "wander into some fun" with Howard. Howard, for his part, decides that many people choose an "alternative avenue" in which to "squeeze" the most out of life. "Why fight it?" (227), he concludes. Both, therefore, feel obliged to rationalize their behaviour with an ostensibly moral rationale, the first sign of the loss of truth and the suppression of the voice of conscience.

A month will pass before they give themselves up to their "furious passions" (223), something they will do on three further occasions before the Phoenix conference. The co-ordinates of their relationship are established in this two-week period of their first sexual encounters. The moral co-ordinates are those of a relationship in which the body is the unique site of exchange between them, where the moral self or personhood of the other is virtually an irrelevance, and where the clear understanding exists that the body of one is placed at the disposal and pleasure of the other. Their affair is nourished, not by lovemaking that arises from a fusion of emotional, aesthetic, moral and physical attraction, but by the insatiable craving to copulate, an affective terrain mapped by a coarse language of physical exertions and primitive pleasures.

Howard conceives of their couplings in terms of "screwing", considers that "Frances gave fucking a new meaning" (233), and is drunk with the demands of her "flat-out, full-bore sexual appetite" (234), which fills his mind with images of orgasm and explosion. That they both conceive of their relationship in purely physical terms is underlined by Frances after their first illicit sexual encounter when she tells Howard in the motel car park that she is not in love with him, then a few moments later presses her hand "flagrantly" (237) against his penis, cautioning him to save his sexual appetite for her in Phoenix. Howard concurs in depriving them of moral and affective responses as he reduces them both to the sum of their sexual sensations, which were not in his view "the kind of experience that ever led to marriage, or to any lasting importance" (234).

If their coupling is a purely physical act with the goal of sexual pleasure, it nonetheless leads to new emotions in Howard that bring about a transformation in his sense of self. Once again, one might usefully call upon Charles Taylor's distinction between moral identity and self-image. Taylor speaks of "the essential link between identity and a kind of orientation. To know who you are is to be oriented in moral space, a space in which questions arise about what is good or bad, what is worth doing and what not."[4] But Howard is now too intoxicated by his sex with Frances to have any thought about good or bad, right or wrong. He has substituted his identity as loyal husband and married man with the conceits of self-image: the outward orientation towards the good has been replaced by an inward turn towards self-regard, where people are preoccupied, as Taylor asserts, with "[striving] to appear in a good light in the eyes of those they come in contact with as well as in their own".[5] Here, all is ego and vanity. Howard now sees himself anew, preening himself in the knowledge that Frances makes him feel that "among all men there *was* no one like Howard Cameron": only he can satisfy her insatiable appetite because he has the sexual "equipment to do things properly". He glories in his new self-image of a man capable of such things, and compares himself with those "other men [who] couldn't cut the mustard" (234) in satisfying sexually demanding women.

Driven though they are by their sexual attraction and appetite, Howard and Frances cannot isolate themselves completely from a moral context, one that impinges on them at different moments. Howard is aware of the value of his marriage, and considers that it "might be one of those rarities" (236) in life (like his parents' marriage) that worked out even "halfway well" (235), in which case one was fortunate. Paradoxically, it is the very value he places on the marriage he is betraying that has him assert that he has no intention of making Frances "number two" in his life. For her part, Frances becomes troubled at one point by the face of a woman that her conscience constructs out of the night-time clouds over Phoenix, a face she takes to be that of Howard's wife, one expressing hurt and disappointment. Both, then, need to inure themselves to incipient guilt, Howard by reassuring himself that Frances and he knew "what they were doing" (236) and that it was not serious, and Frances by insisting on the essential goodness of both Howard and herself: "True, he was ready to cheat on his wife back in Pawcatuck; but he also seemed like a decent family man with a strong sense of right and wrong, and no real wish to do anybody harm. She felt the same"

---

[4] Taylor, *Sources of the Self*, 28.
[5] *Ibid.*, 33. For a fuller treatment of these issues, see the chapter on "The Womanizer".

(231). One notes in Frances' articulation of moral awareness the echoes of Taylor's formulation with regard to identity as an orientation in moral space, within which one is obliged to choose between "what is good or bad, what is worth doing and what not". Howard and Frances need at once to acknowledge the moral issues and to counter them if they are to preserve their self-images as moral beings, and if they are to continue to enjoy the sexual pleasures their affair procures them.

Their private moral accommodations, however, are counteracted by their awareness of public disapproval. Society's censure of their illicit relationship is manifested through the Weiboldt Company for which they both work. From their first complicit conversation at the awards banquet to their clandestine motel meetings, and then to their late-night hotel-room trysts at the Phoenix conference, their employer's code of conduct makes them aware of their transgression. Although the company's disapproval would take the form essentially of a material rather than a moral loss (they would lose their jobs if exposed), the company's stance functions in the text as a continuing reminder to Howard and Frances that their affair is both blameworthy and dangerous: "Office romances ... now landed you in federal court for polluting the workplace with messy personal matters" (229).

The protagonists, in fact, are enmeshed in a curious circularity. It is, in part, their very sense of the restrictive and coercive nature of the public moral code that governs their lives that has them seek the release of illicit sex, but in so doing they risk incurring the wrath of their culture's public morality (one topic of their coded conversation on sex at the award's banquet is the Puritans' detrimental influence on sexual attitudes in America). Howard marvels that he "[feels] so free now" as a result of his sexual relationship with Frances, to the point that he insists to her that what they have represents his "real life" and that it is "as real as marriage" (232), as if he sees societal arrangements and conventions as a barrier to self-fulfilment.[6] Yet, for all the sense of freedom that unsanctioned sex may bring them, fear of

---

[6] Howard's "real life" formulation is exactly the one used by Martin Austin in "The Womanizer" as he attempts to convince Joséphine that his interest in her is not "a sidetrack" but, rather, that it represents "real life" (24). What is common to both characters is the manner in which they justify themselves and their affairs at the expense of their married lives.

public exposure envelops their affair in furtiveness, and imbues the story with an atmosphere of foreboding and fatalism.

The second phase of the story consists of the trip Frances and Howard make from Phoenix to the Grand Canyon. Where the first phase recounts the early sexual excitement of their affair, the second charts the quick decline into bickering and then mutual loathing as the thrill of sexual conquest and excitement begin to wear off. Now is the time they begin to see beyond the body of the other, when they discover instead the person of the other in all its moods, habits and even physical features; it is also the time of discovery of the moral being of the other person. Their pounding sexual urges had up to then concealed the person, restricting the being of the other to a purely instrumental, means-to-ends role of sex object. The car trip to the Grand Canyon, however, confines them together for long periods as full human beings, with no recourse to the distractions and concealments of sex. The occasional sympathetic thought for the other is now lost in silent mutual recrimination as they begin to deal with the first consequences of the mistake they have made. The narrative perspective switches back and forth between the two, a dynamic of reproach and regret that propels the imprisoned characters beyond the point where their affair could have a positive outcome, an evolution captured in the metaphor of the car journey into the desert.

The disaffection and mutual irritation emerges in petty fault-finding that characterizes their changing views of the other, most notably in spiteful thoughts each has about the other's physical appearance. It is ironic that the body of the other, so exalted when their sexual attraction was at its height, is so quickly demeaned when that attraction is no longer adequate to conceal their differences, and when all they have to offer the other is their moral being. And it is indeed the view each has of the moral being of the other – the view of where the other person "stands", the formulation Taylor uses to articulate the link between identity and moral orientation – that thoroughly undermines their relationship. Frances finds she dislikes a kind of opportunistic and cynical passivity in Howard, a calculated withholding that allows another, more courageous, person to fail before he steps in to profit from that failure. She comes to see him, too, as someone who is probably dishonest in his dealings with clients while all the time projecting a contrary image of himself; Howard, in her eyes, is not "much better" than a "con man" (239). Pointedly, she measures herself against these moral deficiencies and affirms that Howard would do things that "she would never do" (238). For his part, Howard sees Frances as obsessed and pushy, "driving buyers crazy" with her relentless selling tactics; she has become "hateful" to him (244), and has metamorphosized in his eyes into "a different person" (245).

The story could be said to be structured according to the changing value attached by the protagonists to, first, sex, and then to wider personal and moral values. As the latter begin to take precedence, the hitherto purely sexual nature of their relationship is called into question. On the way to the Grand Canyon they spend the night in a motel, and duly have sex. Afterwards, Frances thinks about the "hard way" of Howard's sexual approach, how "he wanted to take her too fast too violently", and she tries to rationalize this as a kind of intimacy, before having to conclude that his sexual approach was a response to what she had said to him: "I just want to get fucked." This was not intimacy, she sees, but simply his letting her "*employ* him— that was the word—become the implement for what she wanted fixed, emptied, ended, ridded—whatever". She had "invented" Howard sexually, "turned him into someone she had a use for" (258).

The sexual and moral dimensions of their relationship are juxtaposed by Howard when he asks Frances if she "could ever be married" to him. Her evasive but negative response has him pronounce that their relationship was "just barb-less fucking. Fuck-and-release" (266), which, of course, is what they sought when they emptied their relationship of personal, emotional and moral dimensions from the start. As they arrive at the Grand Canyon Frances' mind is invaded by the "displeasing mental picture of Howard whamming away on her" (268) in the motel, an image that now has her question her own judgement, just as it exposes the dehumanized nature of their relationship. In that regard Howard will later recall that he "hardly ever said" Frances' name (274). The brute physicality of this relationship no doubt gives rise to Frances' thought that, in their growing mutual detestation, Howard might physically "[pose] a threat" to her (267), and she considers for a moment calling the police and denouncing him as a stalker, or simply pushing him out of the car. The violence of her thoughts is unsurprising, as it is no more than a natural consequence of what has been, in its unbridled carnality, a sexually aggressive relationship.

The state that their relationship has now reached is captured metaphorically in a scene Frances witnesses between a rat and a snake; one senses, although it is not made explicit in the text, that Frances has her relationship with Howard at the back of her mind as she watches the scene, particularly in her fascination with the behaviour of the rat. In their motel car park a rat harasses a snake, the two hissing and dancing around each other until the snake gains the cover of scrub ground. Ford has chosen two of the most reviled of creatures, and the immemorial symbolism attached to them, to represent aspects of his two generally unattractive characters and their relationship – the inability to share a common space; their profound difference in nature; the antagonism that characterizes their exchanges; the fear that exists between them; the chasing of one by the other (Frances is taken by the rat's surprising aggressiveness as it seeks to be rid of an "enemy" that was its "physical superior" [256], a relation of physical force that mirrors that of Howard and Frances, as the text constantly underlines); and the instinctive animal behaviour of the two protagonists, which in turn suggests the degrading transformation the affair has wrought on both of them. In a story intent on depicting the moral (and other) consequences of infidelity, the scene is unforgiving in its implications.

The greatest source of resentment and disenchantment between the characters arises from their thoroughly opposing sensibilities, another sign of irreconcilable differences as persons, and revealed most pointedly in their divergent reactions to the desert environment, and ultimately to the Grand Canyon. Frances' reaction is mystical and spiritual, Howard's literal and practical. Her reverent and mystical reaction to two Indians they pass on the road ("Those were our ancient spirits" [253]) stands in stark contrast to Howard's flippant cynicism to other Indians they see, who, he suggests, would strip their car and kill them if they had a breakdown. Despite their inhabiting the same space and experiencing the same landscape, their different sensibilities do not allow them to focus on the same aspects of that experience. Howard sees the desert only as an empty space being thoughtlessly filled up by encroaching civilization, which brings "big gas stations, shopping malls, half-finished cinema plazas, new franchise restaurant pads, housing sprawled along empty streambeds that had been walled up beside giant golf courses with hundreds of sprinklers turning the dry air to mist" (241).

In the same vein, he approaches the Grand Canyon as just another place with traffic and too many people, an insidious standardization wrought by the juggernaut of civilization, transforming the Grand Canyon, in Howard's eyes, from a natural wonder to a depressing cultural phenomenon: being at the Grand Canyon, for him, is like being at an airport. Once again in Richard Ford, the nightmare vision of America on the move is being depicted, recalling the apocalyptic scenes in *Independence Day* as Frank Bascombe gets snarled up in night-time holiday traffic as car-ensconced Americans bulldoze their way to the coast. American civilization, for Howard, is all about constant movement: "We're supposed to think where we are *does* matter. But it's like a shark's life. Dedicated to constant moving" (268). In much the same way as Nancy in "Charity", Howard feels undermined by the perpetual movement, and longs for the stability of pause and repose, either in Phoenix or at home. Howard's reaction to his desert experience confirms him in his innately conservative view, that of wishing things would not change and of clinging to what he knows, hence his dislike of the ravages of capitalist civilization, his preference for stability over movement and his sensitivity to the call of home. It is a conservative sensibility disliked by Frances, for whom Howard was "genetically hard-wired to like things how they were" (238).

Frances, for her part, is "exhilarated" by the desert landscape, and she too contrasts this experience with home and her life there. Unlike Howard, however, she senses "a spirit" being released in her that she had "never realized was there", and contrasts her elation with the "dragging, grinding minutiae" (265) of her daily life of work, housekeeping and social entanglement. As she gets nearer to the Grand Canyon she has already entered a different mode of being and sensation, sensing a profound liberation of force and spirit taking place in her. She understands her attraction to the power of the Grand Canyon as being a form of mystical call, an awakening of a dormant spiritual affinity. As she takes in the vista that finally opens up before her eyes she counters Howard's comically practical and literal view that the Grand Canyon is "empty" (272) with the reflection that it is "full of healing energy", although she is otherwise so affected by her experience that she is unable to articulate her feelings, is unable to "say it right" because what she sees "has its own language" (273).

Frances' reaction to the Grand Canyon reminds Howard of their sexual act the previous evening, and of how "she'd fixed her eyes on his face when she took him in", causing him to wonder whether "she was looking at the canyon the same way now" (273). Sex, of course, is Howard's essential point of reference where he and Frances are concerned, and his measure, therefore, of gauging the intensity of Frances' union with nature and of the sense that she may be undergoing an epiphanic, life-transforming experience (the term "religious experience" is twice employed during this scene to indicate the intensity of Frances' experience, in both cases from Howard's perspective). His linking of the sexual act to Frances' communion with the Grand Canyon, however, is sanctioned by an earlier observation by Frances herself:

> ... adultery was the act that *rid*, *erased*, even erased itself once the performance was over. Sometimes, she imagined, it must erase more than itself. And sometimes, surely, it erased everything around it. It was a remedy for ills you couldn't get cured any other way, but it was a danger you needed to be cautious with (256-57).

Frances' spiritual merging with the Grand Canyon has the purifacatory power of this view of adultery, containing within it the potential for release, self-forgetting, self-transformation and renewal.[7]

---

[7] This Grand Canyon scene recalls another literary text where a woman has an intense spiritual experience with the desert described in sexual terms. There are, in fact, a remarkable number of correspondences between "Abyss" and Albert Camus' short story, "La femme adultère". Camus' story recounts the epiphanic experience in the desert of Janine, a French woman living in Algeria at the end of the Second World War. She lives cooped up in a small city apartment with her husband, Marcel, who does not love her and who is interested only in his business. Marcel brings her on a business trip, which involves an uncomfortable and tense bus journey into the desert. Janine feels trapped, alone and distant from her husband, and cannot stop the melancholy thought that her life has been wasted. They speak little, and, when Marcel does so, it is usually to be dismissive of the native Arabs, their silent and mysterious fellow passengers. When they arrive at their destination, Janine brings a reluctant Marcel to look at the desert from atop an old fort. There, she stands transfixed and speechless as she takes in the vast empty expanse of light and space, and she experiences a great and profound loosening as the tension in which her life, habit and boredom has imprisoned her slowly begins to unravel. Her impatient, irritable husband, seeing nothing but empty space, drags her away. But, that night, Janine,

The journey, literal and figurative, that Frances and Howard set out on together comes to a definitive end as they look at the Grand Canyon. As Frances strains away from her existing life and towards the "healing energy" of grandiose nature, Howard is pulling in the other direction, back towards the familiarity and reassurance of his life at home. The bond of mutual sexual attraction that brought them together at the start seems derisory in the face of the spiritual incompatibility that divides them now at the end of their journey.

Frances herself pronounces the obvious truth about them and implicitly announces the end of their relationship as they look into the Grand Canyon and attribute different meanings to what they see: "I understand. You think it's empty. To me it's full. You and I are just different" (272). This is a simple truth, but too belatedly understood. Their animal-like carnal attraction has bred a relationship that has been a moral catastrophe for both of them, and this in two senses: first, because of the effects of the relationship on them as moral beings responsible to those with whom they have committed to share their lives, and, second, because of the effects on themselves as moral beings whose actions define who they are. The common denominator between these two moral failings is the lies they must tell and the lie they are obliged to live out, the accumulated effect of which is a serious inner conflict for both of them. In Flagstaff both of them go off to phone, and lie to, their spouses. As Frances speaks to Ed, she is burdened with regret and guilt at the moral abyss she is sinking into:

> That absolutely wasn't how life should be, she thought. Life should be all on the up-and-up. She wished she was here alone and there weren't any lies. How good that would feel. (248)

Where Howard is concerned, his lying to his wife is a betrayal of something that he realizes he values deeply. He knows he is married to "the right person" and "why being married was so good": the institution of marriage "took you to deeper depths, and you felt serious things you wouldn't otherwise feel" (249).

---

hearing the call of the desert, slips out of the conjugal bed to commit the act of adultery with nature, from where the story gets its title. She runs to the top of the fort and consummates her union with the spirit of the desert, which is rendered by Camus, explicitly and sensually, as an act of lovemaking. Janine, the adulterous woman, experiences this act as an ablution and purification, relieving her of the burden of others and the anguishes of her life.

The further they drive into the desert and the longer they spend with each other, the greater the lies they have to commit against the truth of their lives as married people with responsibility to others. Neither of them is able to deal with the freedom, or absence of framework, that their affair allows, although both had marvelled in it at the beginning. Both of them end up regretting the loss of the structure of protection and guidance conferred by their normal lives as married and working people. Frances finds the loss of the points of reference that structure and delimit her life "disorienting" (246), while, in Howard, this sense of loss takes the form of thinking nostalgically about the award he received as agent of the year, a recognition he had disdained the evening he received it in a display of machismo to impress Frances, but that he now values as a token of the safe and rewarding life he is in the process of destroying. The increasing estrangement from the moral framework represented by their normal, married lives causes a crisis of identity in both of them. Immediately after witnessing the scene between the snake and the rat, in which she clearly sees a message about herself and Howard, Frances is subject to serious doubt about the person she is becoming:

> She felt strange waiting here. Not really like who she was, the little agent from Nowhereburg, Connecticut—*specialist* in starter homes and rehabbed condos. Daughter. Wife. Holder of an associate's degree in retail from an accredited community college. In a way, though, this guy was exactly right for her, as wrong as he was. Aren't you always yourself? Is anybody you want *ever* wrong for you? (256)

Charles Taylor conceives of an identity crisis as "an acute form of disorientation, which people often express in terms of not knowing who they are, but which can also be seen as a radical uncertainty of where they stand. They lack a frame or horizon within which things can take on a stable significance."[8] Frances' "disorienting" loss of a "frame or horizon" has produced her crisis of identity. The roles and relationships of her normal life are the stabilizing points of reference through which she knows who she is and against which she now seeks to measure the extent of her divergence from that identity. Where she "stands" now is in an illicit sexual affair that seems to her to represent the antithesis of everything she understood herself to be. What, she

---

[8] Taylor, *Sources of the Self*, 27.

wonders, does the choice she has made to occupy this moral space, and with the particular man with whom she chooses to occupy it, say about who she is? Frances tells Howard of waking up in the desert motel during the night and of looking intently into his face: "I had no idea where I was. I really didn't even know who *you* were" (262). This incomprehension is a literal one, but it resonates more strongly in its metaphorical sense: one reads Frances' moment of deepest disorientation as an expression of her disbelief and dismay at the moral identity of the person she is with, and the moral space to which her association with this person has brought her. Is it possible, she wonders, that, through her choice to be with Howard and to do what she is doing with him, she is no longer herself?[9] This is the ultimate dramatic consequence of her affair: as well as betraying others, Frances wonders now if she is not also betraying herself.[10]

Howard's crisis is not as concentrated into one moment of self-interrogation, nor articulated so explicitly, yet he suffers from a similar sense that he is endangering something fundamental and important about himself that relates to his understanding of the person he is. As he looks across from his desert motel to a "white clapboard chapel" with a "white picket fence" (260), clearly a reproduction of the New England church style so familiar to him, beside which is a (damaged) sign that reads "*CHRIS* DIED FOR YOUR SINS", he is reminded of his family's Christian ancestry and his father's attachment to that tradition, and has a certain premonition of his own moral ruin. The chapel triggers in him a great unease about what he is getting drawn into through his affair with Frances:

> … what this crummy little chapel made him consider was that life, at best, implied a small, barely noticeable entity; and yet it was also a goddamned important entity. And you could ruin your entity before

---

[9] Howard will also reflect on this scene, as he was awake when it took place, although he pretended not to be. In their recollections, both of them associate the other with an animal, which recalls both the animal-like nature of their sexual relations and the text's identification of them with the snake and rat. But the motel scene also raises the identity question again: as Frances acknowledges, one's identity is articulated in part through the people with whom one chooses to associate. The misrecognition of each other as an animal is a profound measure of the alienation of self experienced by both of them by virtue of their choice to associate with a person they misrecognize.

[10] This is the most dramatic consequence for her as a moral being. In literal terms the ultimate dramatic consequence of her affair is, of course, her death.

you even realized it. And further, it occurred to him, that no doubt just as you were in the process of ruining yours, how you felt at the exact moment of ruining it was probably precisely how this fucked-up landscape looked! Dry, empty, bright, chilly, alien, and difficult to breathe in. So that all around here was actually hell, he thought, instead of hell being the old version his father had told him about under the ground. (260-61)

Howard feels a strong urge to get back to Phoenix, to where his life at that moment, represented by his profession, is located. He has let himself inhabit an "alien" moral landscape that is carrying him away from the life and tradition through which he knows himself, and that risks carrying him towards ruination: to remain in this physical and moral landscape could lead to "something awful—despair you wouldn't escape from" (261). Even before they reach the Grand Canyon Howard and Frances have reached the stage where only the truth can save them from themselves and each other, yet, bound together by mutual fear and physical desire, neither feels able to speak that truth. An episode in the car on the way to the Grand Canyon encapsulates in turn the lie at the heart of their relationship, the crisis of identity they are both experiencing and their desire to hide themselves from each other: they begin to communicate jokingly to each other in Japanese-accented English ("We want buy condlo-min-lium long time" [251]). Such has been their difficulty in speaking to each other amicably that they must don the masks of concealment and distortion and speak, once again, in code in order to find a terrain upon which they can communicate, but doing so as other than themselves.

Generally unattractive though the protagonists are, there is nonetheless a pathos in the fate that befalls them, and particularly so in Frances' case: as she seeks to have a photograph that will capture "just me and the canyon" (273), the source of the spiritual energy, she slips and falls to her death. Her fall could hardly be rendered in a more understated or undramatic way – in the space of a moment she is simply no longer there, a disappearance marked only by her tiny and unapt words, "Oh my" (274). It is a fall rendered prosaic in the sheer randomness of its occurrence, a mere momentary loss of attention. It could be read simply as a stupid accident that ends Frances' life, bringing loss and grief to some, and leading to embarrassing questions

for Howard. However, Frances' fall and death need to be read within
the very particular context in which they occur. This is a novella in a
collection called *A Multitude of Sins*, the stories of which deal with
infidelity and its consequences; it is the last and longest story, the one
to leave final impressions and communicate accumulated wisdoms
and truths; and it is itself a story about adultery and its consequences,
and is so in a way that is more explicit, single-minded and teleological
than any other story in the collection. All of these factors confer a
certain emblematic status on the story. One might add that it is also a
story written by an author who wants his fiction to display a moral
vision and to depict moral consequences.

It is in this wider context that the terrible punishment meted out by
Ford to his characters needs to be considered, and it is precisely this
wider context that directs one to the biblical resonances of the story.
Frances' fall into the abyss recalls the original Fall, particularly as Eve
in Genesis is tempted by a serpent, recalling the rat and snake scene
that Frances witnesses: Frances clearly identifies with the role of the
rat, leaving the role of the snake to Howard, a role sanctioned by
Frances herself, who considers that Howard, as we have noted, is not
to be trusted, no more than the serpent in the Fall story.[11] And
Howard, of course, also tempted Frances into betrayal. In addition,
Adam and Eve are made aware that the punishment for eating from
the tree of knowledge of good and evil is to "die the death".[12]

The other, more obvious biblical resonance concerns the Seventh
Commandment prohibition of adultery (a term becoming somewhat
outmoded, but one used in this story). Both adulterer and adulteress
are promised death in the Old Testament[13] (although, as has often
been pointed out, the prohibition was much more restrictive on
women than on men: a married man could have sexual relations with
an unmarried woman without committing adultery, as adultery in the
Bible refers to sexual relations between a man and a married woman).
In Old Testament terms, both Frances and Howard have committed

---

[11] As if to confirm the respective attribution of roles in the rat and snake scene,
Howard is associated with the snake yet again as he moves to peer into the abyss of
the Grand Canyon after Frances' fall: "But after only four cautious steps (a snake
seemed possible here) he found himself at a sudden rough edge and a straight drop
down" (275).
[12] Genesis 2:17.
[13] Leviticus 20:10: "If any man commit adultery with the wife of another, and defile
his neighbour's wife, let them be put to death, both the adulterer and the adulteress."

adultery, one of the most serious of crimes. So if Frances is the victim in Ford's story, it is in keeping with the generally more severe attitude towards female sexuality in the Old Testament, considered as bewitching and corrupting.[14] Yet, if there were to be punishment meted out in the story to only one of the characters on the basis of fewer mitigating circumstances, Howard would be the more fitting victim: he is happy with his wife and marriage, and had no reason to betray these, apart from his sexual desire. By contrast, Frances at least had the excuse of being married to an embittered, unpleasant husband, unable to work after an accident, and who unloads all his bitterness onto her.

"Abyss" is a story about acts and consequences. Many of the stories in this collection, of course, can be seen in this way, but "Abyss" is so in a very focused manner. It is also a story that is relentless in its binary logic – there is cause and effect; there are acts and consequences; there is a before and after; there is innocence and guilt; there is safety and vulnerability. With Frances' fall, Howard crosses a line: he leaves the time of acts and enters the time of consequences. He climbs over the wall separating the pathway from the Grand Canyon proper to confirm his worst fears that Frances has fallen. Thoughts of his own fate have him jump back over the wall to the path: "Whatever was bad had occurred on the other side. Now he was here. Safe" (277). He is wrong, however: he can indeed hop back over the wall but not back in time, to when acts were still without serious consequences, to when he was still relatively innocent and relatively safe. In his initial refusal to accept that he has entered this new uncertain realm, he wrestles with ways in which he might keep himself safe by not reporting Frances' death, but his acts have lodged him irrevocably in the world of consequences. The voice of conscience is finally allowed to recognize that he is now on the wrong side of the line, his moral sense no longer blocked by the pulsations of sexual desire: "he *had* made crazy mistakes of judgment, mistakes of excess, of intemperance, of passion, of nearsightedness, of stupidity. Of course, they'd all seemed natural when he was doing them" (279). He now passes his own verdict on himself: he was guilty of Frances' death ("*He* did it" [280]), and must now accept the consequences and hand himself up to the moral order he has offended.

---

[14] Proverbs 6 and 7.

Like Martin Austin in "The Womanizer", a novella with which, in its careful depiction of the stages of moral decline and in its resemblance to a parable, "Abyss" shares many features, Howard has brought himself to a state of near-perdition. The various connotations and resonances of the term – loss, spiritual ruin, damnation, the fate of the sinner – describe the despair and moral ruin he finds himself in, recalling the "hell" he had glimpsed earlier as he looked at the alien desert landscape and the "crummy little chapel" with its sign linking sin and sacrifice. "Abyss", however, offers an even smaller chance of salvation than "The Womanizer". Whereas the latter novella continues on to the point where Austin can see a path back to his wife, to "everything good", "Abyss" leaves Howard as he contemplates the enormity of his loss.

In this sense, Howard's hopping back over the wall to what he sees as the safety of the path has another resonance. The wall is the metaphorical boundary between his old and present identities – his crisis of identity is, in Taylor's terms, a crisis of moral identity. In losing his ability to distinguish between, as Taylor puts it, "what has meaning and importance … and what is trivial and secondary",[15] Howard has placed himself firmly on the wrong side of the boundary, and it is from here, where the story abandons him, that he now contemplates his ruin. It is from this lonely space of moral exile that he looks back to his version of Martin Austin's "everything good", to the moral and emotional framework of his married and working life, full of tiny pleasures and reassuring habits. He yearns now to be "at home, or waking up, lying in bed, thinking about the day when he would sell a house, eat lunch with a friend, call his mother, drive to the playground, shoot baskets, then return at dusk to someone who loved and understood him" (279). Nor is the damage, in a story and a collection about consequences and responsibility, limited to the protagonists. Howard thinks, too, of Frances' husband and his own wife, of "lives that now were affected, possibly spoiled, unquestionably made less good, even made impossible" (282).

One senses everywhere in these final pages, in the pitiless inventory of the harm inflicted by Howard's and Frances' acts, that Richard Ford, in the last of these overtly moral tales, wished to be brutally clear in his cause-and-effect logic about acts and

---

[15] Taylor, *Sources of the Self*, 28.

consequences. He goes so far, indeed, as to have Howard articulate explicitly the awareness of that logic, as he is driven away from the Grand Canyon: "What you did definitely changed things, he thought .... Even this view down the mountain was changed because of what had happened; it seemed less beautiful now" (285). The consequences are not simply that Howard will lose his job and will have to face his wife and family – his very experience and apprehension of the world have been altered. It is as if he will henceforth be able to experience life only through the mediating screen of his own moral failing.

It is fitting that both story and collection end on a reflection that links acts and consequences, and morality and identity:

> ... [Howard] understood that in fact very little of what he knew mattered; and that however he might've felt today—if circumstances could just have been better—he would now not be allowed to feel. Perhaps he never would again. And whatever he might even have liked, bringing his full and best self to the experience, had now been taken away. So that life, as fast as this car hurtling down the side of a mountain toward the dark, seemed to be disappearing from around him. Being erased. And he was so sorry. And he felt afraid, very afraid. (285-86)

The further Howard ponders the consequences of his acts and his responsibility for what happened, the bleaker his thoughts become. His sense of an altered apprehension of and relationship with the world are merely symptoms of a greater metamorphosis he is undergoing: standing now on the wrong side of the moral boundary, he sees his very identity – the "full and best self" he had constructed in the life he had lived until his affair – as lost to him. The person he has been, intellectually, emotionally and morally, no longer exists. It is in this sense that Howard feels that life is "disappearing from around him" – his old life has disappeared. In their reckless pursuit of sexual pleasure Frances and Howard have each committed a form of suicide: Frances' infidelity led her to fall into the abyss of the Grand Canyon and lose her life, while Howard fell into the abyss of moral sophistry and lost his old life and the identity that went with it.

We are reminded again of the story's biblical echoes in the manner in which the final passage recalls an earlier moment when Frances thought of adultery as an act that "*erased*", not just "ills" but possibly "everything around it". As we have just seen, their adultery has indeed led to such an obliteration. In the final lines of the final story of a collection called *A Multitude of Sins*, a title drawn from the New Testament, the Old Testament injunction against adultery rings out loud and severe: "But he that is an adulterer, for the folly of his heart shall destroy his own soul: He gathereth to himself shame and dishonour, and his reproach shall not be blotted out."[16]

---

[16] Proverbs 6:32-33.

CONCLUSION

The Frank Bascombe trilogy reminds us that one of the indispensable functions of literature is to confront us with difference, one of the effects of which is to draw us away from lazy and complacent thinking. Mention of the suburbs triggers commonplaces about white middle-class enclaves, smugness, uniformity, shopping centres. But in the midst of all of this, and not at all incongruously, there can be a reflective man living his life the best way he knows how, and who is curious enough about the way he finds himself living it to need to reflect upon that experience. Such is Frank Bascombe, living an unremarkable existence in an utterly familiar world, and with no larger ambitions than to want to like his life and to be reasonably happy, admissible expectations in a nation that enshrined the pursuit of happiness in its Declaration of Independence.

For all that, one might wonder if this is the most promising terrain for great literature, and particularly so when this life and character are rendered in an unironic, realist mode. Richard Ford, however, has found a language and an idiom to raise the generally unexceptional experience of suburban daily life out of its apparent banality and into a literary form of deceptive complexity and impressive philosophical substance. The trilogy presents us with an examined life in what might have seemed the most unpropitious of settings, and reminds us, as the novels weave their intricate patterns of intellectual, emotional and moral commitment, that an ordinary life is a truly extraordinary affair. An inquiring and reflective narrator is allowed the time to scrutinize his thoughts, actions, reactions, relationships, desires – in short, all the raw material of experience – in the attempt to carry out the greatest of human undertakings, that of understanding one's own life.

In granting such an elevated place to thought and reflection, Richard Ford has created something of a Cartesian character and narrator. It is the productions of Frank's prodigious mind that render his life, and the trilogy, exceptional; remove, or seriously reduce, Frank's musings, and our fascination with him would be greatly diminished. Although Frank might appear to demote himself in his transitions from reflective man of letters to sportswriter to real estate agent, he remains true to his Cartesian identity as thinking and meditative subject, and is as contemplative at the end of *The Lay of the Land*, facing the possibility of his own death, as he was at the beginning of *The Sportswriter*, as he stands in the Haddam graveyard mourning the death of his son.

Of all the raw material of Frank's daily existence presented over the three novels, there is no doubt that its most important component is his relationships with others, a dimension of human experience that is accorded a similar prominence in the other texts examined in this book. It is through these relationships that Richard Ford elaborates the moral vision of his fiction. Solitary though Frank may be for much of the trilogy, it is nonetheless a solitude constructed in relation to others and that originates in an ambivalence in Frank about the desirability of being close to others. Ultimately, however, he cannot avoid being brought into intimate contact with others, and it is in these relationships of intimacy (as is the case in the narratives of *Women with Men* and *A Multitude of Sins*) that the moral dynamics of affection and estrangement are explored.

In all of this, it is the relationship between men and women that most engages Richard Ford. In choosing to examine so microscopically the fault-lines of this fundamental relationship, in choosing to consider the condition of the love that is supposed to bring and hold men and women together, Ford knowingly and willingly enters a world where a moral language cannot be avoided. As he puts it: "those things that people do with each other – betrayals and failures; failures to be sincere, to be faithful, to be sensitive to each other – that's ground-level morality. That's where the boot hits the ground when it comes to understanding what goes on with us."[1] Another defining feature of Ford's treatment of his vital subject is that he writes about love unironically and uncynically, itself an expression of his moral approach. Characters fail love in Ford's fiction, and, in so doing, fail themselves and others. Failing oneself and others, indeed, could be a definition of what it is to fail love. Ford does not hesitate to confer on this failure the moral status of sin, although such judgemental language never finds its way into the fiction as the voice of a condemnatory author or narrator. Such judgements occur in the

---

[1] Interview with Richard Ford, *The Sunday Times*, 1 October 2006, Features, 12.

stories, of course, but they come from the characters themselves as they face the consequences of their acts. One thinks of Martin Austin ("The Womanizer") and Howard Cameron ("Abyss") as they contemplate, in shock and remorse, the damage they have wreaked on others, but also on themselves. Ford's fiction is moral, but the author is not moralizing; his narratives are instructive and illuminating, but never didactic.

Out of such a lengthy and considered fictional exploration by Ford of relationships between men and women, there emerges a certain number of insights into the failure to love, and that may be articulated in moral terms. The most grievous and recurring fault of characters is the failure to take full responsibility for their own and others' lives. Another way of saying this is that characters do not take full responsibility for their own moral identities. Time and again the force and relevance of Charles Taylor's insight into the connection between identity and morality – identity as knowing where one stands, as knowing what is important and what is not – is brought home. This connection is manifested through characters' acts – what they do comes to define their moral identity. The loss of one's moral identity becomes a loss of self, which is the terrible fate that awaits, in particular, Martin Austin, Frances Bilandic and Howard Cameron. In "The Womanizer" and "Abyss" these characters stray from their moral identities, culminating in either the literal or metaphorical death of self. The failures that contribute to the ultimate loss of moral identity are many – characters do not adequately know themselves; they fail to see the effects their behaviour is having on them; they lose sight of what is important in their lives; they take themselves and others for granted; they become selfish and self-absorbed; they confuse moral identity with the vanity of self-image; and they rationalize their betrayal into something other than it is, into something of no great importance and devoid of possible consequences.

It is here that two of the characters' great misjudgements are exposed: these men and women, in their self-absorption, lose the capacity to appreciate that their behaviour may have consequences and that they cannot control the consequences of their behaviour. This is the dominant sense of both "Privacy" and "Quality Time": the private betrayal in the first story was clearly the seed of later, greater betrayals, while the opening allegory of "Quality Time" prefigures the uncontrollable momentum of events that may sweep characters beyond the point where they can recuperate their old lives. In departing from their better selves, characters lose their moral orientation and rush towards disaster. It is only in the fate that Ford visits upon his wayward character that he manifests an implicit moral judgement: the harshest punishments are reserved for characters guilty of the greatest infidelity and irresponsibility, or with the fewest mitigating circumstances, most notably in "The Womanizer" and "Abyss".

Richard Ford likes to quote the following lines from Emerson's essay, "Self-Reliance": "Power ceases in the instant of repose; it resides in the moment of transition from a past to a new state, in the shooting of the gulf, in the darting to an aim."[2] Narrative, of course, is the discourse of transition, and Richard Ford uses narrative momentum to situate his characters in the hazardous territory of transition and change, an unstable emotional and moral space to which characters are seen to have brought themselves by their deliberate choices. And it is in this unfamiliar territory – with his characters exposed and vulnerable – that he conducts his moral experiments. Many of the novels and stories catch their characters either in dangerous moments of transition or in their aftermath, when they are either leaving or have left the safety of the known and the knowable. Richard Ford's fiction, therefore, is a fiction of the mutable, a fiction, indeed, whose very dynamic is the instability and unpredictability of lives and identities being wrenched into new and unfamiliar forms.

Richard Ford writes both novels and short stories, and both genres have been examined in this study. The short stories, for the most past, consider the shorter- or medium-term consequences of betrayal and point to longer-term effects ("Calling" is the explicit exception to this, although "Privacy" announces eventual long-term consequences). The novels of the trilogy employ narrative time-frames quite typical of short fiction (they take place over the restricted period of a few days), but together they expand out to the vaster temporality of what feels like a whole life, although the trilogy covers, in fact, about a twenty-year period. However, it is reasonable to speak in terms of a life as this is the metaphorical, if not the actual, temporal range of the trilogy.

---

[2] Emerson, *Self-Reliance*, 29.

With each successive book Frank's beliefs and decisions, his evasions and choices, are available to a new scrutiny. By the third novel a new configuration of Frank's life emerges in the various roles he has fulfilled (husband, father, lover, and so forth). But the most powerful and moving configuration is that drawn by the arc that reaches from the pre-history of *The Sportswriter* to the latter pages of *The Lay of the Land*, an arc not previously visible as it is a temporal arc that needed to be completed, but also because it is an emotional arc whose development had been concealed by Frank's refusal to acknowledge it. Time itself comes to be one of the trilogy's most important themes as Frank is finally forced to reckon with a past knowingly and systematically avoided, but that now envelops him in resurgent and previously unattended grief at his son's death. In constructing *The Lay of the Land* on the foundations of the two previous novels, Richard Ford brings to the forefront and accords a new gravity to themes deeply implicated in time, those of personal identity and selfhood, the unity and coherence of a whole life, and loss and decline. The interconnection of the three novels also accords them the definitive identity of a trilogy, of three novels indissolubly linked by the exchanges between present and past, as in life itself.

Richard Ford also writes about America in his fiction, most explicitly in the latter two novels of the trilogy. The judgement on contemporary America was already quite severe in *Independence Day* in its depiction of a segregated country, individualist in the extreme, practising an exclusionary form of independence and allowing a laissez-faire economic doctrine divide its citizens and atomize its society. During a holiday that celebrated the founding of the union, the vista presented in *Independence Day* is one of disunion. Twelve (fictional) years on, the portrait of America in *The Lay of the Land* is even grimmer. The divisions on display in *Independence Day* are now more entrenched – the very notion of a coherent social body is profoundly called into question in a society portrayed essentially as little more than an economic entity, in which communities are structured and managed according to the dogma of free-market liberalism. And the notions of a union and a republic are even less tenable by the third novel.

In both novels America seems, in some respects (though not in others), to have detached itself from its history, just as Frank had

detached himself from his own personal history, and with a striking
coincidence of effect in the manner in which the past, insufficiently
unacknowledged, comes back to blight the present. In the case of
America this is most notable in the unresolved race issues in
Independence Day and in the propensity for gun violence in *The Lay
of the Land*. The American nation was forged from an extraordinary
energy, courage and thirst for freedom, but also from ruthless
oppression and violence. These legacies of nation-building feed into
the novels through the portrait of a nervous, fearful country, one
revelling in its wealth and the pleasures of the free market, but one
that seems to have lost a sense of direction and a sense of a noble
national vision. Although *The Lay of the Land* is set in 2000, it was
written between 2002 and 2006. The vision of the country articulated
through the values of the Republican administration of that latter
period, founded on, *inter alia*, military power and corporate freedom,
influenced the portrait of America in the novel, as is evident from an
interview Richard Ford gave to coincide with the publication of *The
Lay of the Land*:

> It's real bad in America just now. It's shameful how our government
> is conducting itself at home and abroad. I think it's dangerous for the
> world. I always think of myself as a patriot: I believe in the principles
> that the country was founded on; at least the ones that didn't exclude
> blacks and minorities. But now those principles are being deeply and
> profoundly eroded. The education system is failing us, the electoral
> process itself is being eroded, minorities are being overlooked, large
> corporations are running the country. It's disgusting. And I love my
> country.[3]

The trilogy does not examine Americans abroad, but Ford had already
done so some years earlier in "Occidentals", which offered an image
of American identity entirely consistent with that delineated in the
trilogy and with the sentiments expressed above by Ford. The
egregious American couple in "Occidentals" (Rex and Bea) blunder
their way through a foreign culture with all the delicacy of the worst
kind of colonizer: they practise the racism and xenophobia, and the
cultural stereotyping and assumed superiority, of Lester in *The Lay of
the Land*; they display an isolationist and exclusionary attitude to

---

[3] *Ibid.*, 12.

those not like them that is consonant with the portrayal of these failings at home in *Independence Day* and *The Lay of the Land*; and they instigate a cultural segregation and exhibit a hostility to the other that is also depicted extensively in the latter two novels. No reasonable person would for a moment reduce America uniquely to these expressions of national arrogance; neither does Richard Ford, as the appeal and sympathy of many of his characters testify. Yet as the most technologically advanced, militarily powerful and economically influential country the world has ever known, America has a special responsibility to itself and to others that, Ford makes clear, it only fitfully assumes.

It seems inevitable that Richard Ford will most readily be associated with the Frank Bascombe trilogy, notwithstanding that he has published three story collections and three other novels, and is capable of writing successfully in different literary genres and styles. It would be a mistake and an injustice to let this body of work be overshadowed by the novel trilogy, a body of work in which one finds the same density of theme and exploration, the same seriousness and felicity of style, that distinguishes the Frank Bascombe books. Yet the trilogy will be the likely point of departure in considering Ford's legacy. And this is not unreasonable, given its impact and achievements, among which the powerful cumulative effect of three long novels devoted to a single character, the appeal and extraordinary range and depth of that character, the generosity of spirit of the novels, the command of different emotional and literary registers (the latter two novels, in particular, have moments of wonderful comedy), the idiosyncratic literary language that Ford has fashioned for his narrator, the exploration of contemporary American cultural life and values, and the novels' winning, quintessentially American, expansiveness.

But Richard Ford is not finished yet, although he says he is finished with Frank Bascombe. Thus far, Ford has published the trilogy novels at roughly ten-year intervals. As we leave Frank in *The Lay of the Land* he is fifty-five and still alive. One hopes that the author, at some time in the future, may again begin to hear the first-person narrating voice of his most genial and accessible character, and that he might envisage a way of bringing Frank into whatever experiences and insights old age would have to offer. This would be a fitting and deserving conclusion to the life of a character long ago begun but that seems too fruitful, and still too full of potential, to be laid to rest just yet.

INTERVIEW WITH RICHARD FORD

Brian Duffy: You said in an interview that finding the title *The Lay of the Land* was important for you in guiding you in conceiving the book. Why was this so?[1]

Richard Ford: I always like to have a title early in the writing. I mean, I don't know all that much about what the book will be at that point. But a title can often have a certain tone to it, even a certain explicitness that can be the first solid guide I have in the writing. If I find a title early enough, and I don't always find it before I start – in the case of *The Lay of the Land* I did – I can write within its spirit. I didn't dream up "the lay of the land"; it's a standard idiom in American speech. But when I heard it, I thought, "Ooh gee, for some reason that sounds just exactly right for what I'm thinking about. I wonder if I'm writing a book which really does satisfy the definition of a book about how the American landscape lies, and, beyond that, how the American spiritual landscape lies." So my then-possible title provoked me to think about what my intention might actually be. And the way I then conceived my intention was fairly consonant with that title.

BD: There's a sense of stocktaking in the title.

RF: Yes, I seem to remember two, or at least one, moment in the book when Frank accuses himself of taking stock, and scolds himself for doing that. He thinks of stocktaking as a kind of literary cliché and probably bad luck. And yet, as is true with this book in general, a lot of the things that are literary clichés turn out to be things that Frank inescapably does, because cliché or not, they turn out to be reliable –

---

[1] In order that the final text of the interview represent as faithfully as possible the author's views, Richard Ford and I agreed that the interview process should consist of two stages: first, the interview itself, and, second, the review by Richard Ford of the interview transcript, at which time he would be free to amend the transcript in whatever manner he wished. This was indeed the procedure we followed. The interview took place in Richard Ford's home in Maine in May 2007.

"Misery doesn't want company", for instance. "Don't look a gift horse in the mouth." He, humorously I thought, makes a case for the validity of conventional wisdom.

BD: I was wondering if, before you found your title, you considered calling it *Thanksgiving*, following the model of *Independence Day*.

RF: I did, but I never really thought it was right. I didn't want to be confined by such a specific metaphor, which is to say to be a book *only* about giving thanks. That seemed potentially mawkish and not inclusive enough for all the material I wanted to put in the book. I thought that if I had a title with a somewhat broader scope I could talk about Thanksgiving, but also talk about all the other things I had in mind.

BD: By the time you came to write *The Lay of the Land* you had built up a huge fund of experience and a wide network of relationships for Frank. I am interested in what guided you at the planning stage in reaching certain editorial and creative decisions as to what to retain from the previous books and what to reject, particularly where his family members, Ann, Paul and Clarissa, were concerned.

RF: Well, I was very specifically concerned – and I could show you my notes to that effect – that I not repeat things, events, concerns that were in the other books. So I didn't want to dwell too much on Paul, and I didn't want to dwell too much on talking about the State of New Jersey *per se*. I didn't want to dwell on what was by then for me the well-rehearsed history of Frank's divorce from Ann. I did want to write about Clarissa because I felt like Clarissa had been given insufficient attention in the prior books and was possibly a source of what could be good writing. So in the main those were my motives. And then, without really caring much who it would be, I wanted to resurrect some people from the prior books, from back, from the eighties, just to make the books connected and in sequence, and also (again) to give myself a resource of interesting writing. It turned out, then, that I could resurrect Vicki's father, Wade, very easily. That interested me. I liked the idea that Wade, back in *The Sportswriter*, was a very clearly defined character, but could be, in a new book, equally clearly defined, but almost entirely unrecognizable from who he was before – except of course that I would insist he was the same person. One of my "intellectual" concerns in this book was the issue of character, anyone's character – not characters in fiction – and whether or not we humans actually have characters that develop as we get older, or if we are as time goes by remarkably or even entirely different people. Because I made characters up all the time and used that word, "character" as a dominating force in western literature had become of heightened interest to me. It's one of those moral notions we all take for granted. So, I just wanted to put these issue of "character" in play in a book and see what I could write – or, if you please, see what I could have Frank say. Beyond Wade, though, I don't think I really did take up anybody else in any through-going way.

BD: The sense we have of Wade at the end is almost of a pathetic figure. Age above all is what has got to Wade – he really is diminished in all sorts of ways

RF: Yes, he is.

BD: The portrait of old age is actually quite harsh in the book.

RF: It's certainly played for jokes. And Frank semi-seriously says some harsh things about getting old. Those things he says don't accurately reflect what I think, though. It's frequent if not usual that I make Frank says things that I don't necessarily agree with. I wanted him to be provoking to the reader, to initiate a passionate conversation.

BD: We come away from meeting Wade feeling ... uncomfortable almost. You don't pull back in presenting the ...

RF: ... no, my general view is, "Let's not get old".

BD: I know, it's a terrible time, I think.

RF: (Laughing). Well, it can be.

BD: And Wade covers it up through wearing these fancy clothes, but he is just diminishing within his clothes ...

RF: ... he smells bad ...

BD: ... he's not pleasant to be with.

RF: I never saw my parents get old. They died before they could. But I have seen lots of other people get old and sick and tired of being alive, and it, in my view, isn't to be desired.

BD: I've noticed when people ask you questions at your public readings – I'm always surprised at the confusion between author and narrator.

RF: People are often – Americans particularly – made very uncomfortable by the truth of an imaginative gesture. They're much more comfortable by factuality and with truth being not something made up but something granite-like. Americans don't like to operate in that part of the ether around themselves. They don't want things to *become* truth, they want things to exist as truth prior.

BD: In all three Frank Bascombe novels you go to great trouble to capture the contemporary physical American landscape, both natural and man-made. In *The Lay of the Land* you record in particular the changing nature of these landscapes. Beyond wishing to locate your characters firmly within a specific historical and cultural moment, are there other motivations in your striving to capture the configurations of the American landscape, in what is a very visual dimension of *The Lay of the Land*?

RF: Well, there are. As you suggest, I do want to do what Toulouse-Lautrec said he wanted to do with his scene-painting, namely to create a sensuous background in front of which the principals persuasively can act out their lives. I think that characters are seen to be more plausible when they can be plausibly put into an environment that is itself plausible. That said, I don't have a very romantic view about the environment. I don't, for example, believe that the landscape of New Jersey or the landscape of Montana or the landscape of Paris has really much of anything much of importance to do with the behaviour of the people in it. In other words, I don't think place itself has a germinal aspect. I think people mostly do what they do for reasons that they alone are responsible for. So it isn't as though the landscape forms them in any particular way.

BD: Yet Charley Matthews in "Occidentals" uses Paris in the little narratives he recounts to himself in his attempt to become something other than he is, to change his life. Paris is very important in that. There's a real exchange between city and character …

RF: … there is, but I think he fails. He wants that to happen, but it doesn't. You can't escape yourself.

BD: He has to leave Paris.

RF: Yes, indeed. The other aspect of it, writing about place, or scene-painting, is – it gives me an opportunity to write descriptions and to force the reader through sentences which I think are themselves felicitous. Because I think that one of the virtues of literature is to suffuse readers with beautiful, interesting, well-chosen language, and that fundamentally scene-painting is mostly about language, and even though the reader may try to formulate a picture based on the description in his or her mind, it's all language. I think that's quite wholesome. Such writing brings the reader both to the putative place and to the fact of place being made of language in a way that substantiates life, reifies life. The moral address to the reader is, "Pay attention, pay attention, this is probably all your life is. And language can bring it to you more formidably."

BD: One of the intentions of *The Lay of the Land* seems to have been that it would function in some ways as a document, and Frank even has thoughts along these lines when he wonders what future scientists might make of the nature of contemporary American culture when considering, some time in the future, its artefacts. You go to great lengths to record both the contemporary American cultural experience and choice. You seem to want to capture the whole texture of the American experience. I was wondering if you approached the book in part with the mindset of the "scientist" that Frank evokes at one point?

RF: No, I didn't. I think I approached the book exactly the way I approached its predecessors, which was to try to write an interesting novel. But I think one of the advantages of this book, one of the advantages gained by me being as old as I was when I started it, and the advantage gained by having these two prior books already in place, and by having, as you say, a rather burgeoning storage of cultural information in my brain, was that this book freed me, somehow or other, to widen the book's aperture, and to take more in. And along the way of taking more in I just fell victim, or fell heir, to all kinds of images which were spinning around in my brain which maybe the other books didn't let me use quite as much – the literal image, for instance, of the scientist who years later will sift back through the detritus of a civilization trying to figure out what it was like back then. That was an image that had been in my brain forever, partly owing to the fact that I have this friend, at the University of Chicago, who's an ancient near-eastern historian – one of my early friendships when I was beginning to be a writer. And that's what this fellow did, and still does today. The whole little riff in the book about finding blood-spattered uniforms comes from him. I remembered how we used to joke about what people will think about civilization, our civilization, decades, centuries on. But it wasn't ever really my conscious intention for the book to be, or for Frank to be, that kind of documentary point man. It was just something that was there in my brain, which, when I got stuck for something to write about on a Tuesday afternoon, I wrote. That's a much better story, I think. And, it's the truth.

BD: And also, of course, it's precisely what you were saying earlier, that the title you picked allowed you to do this because this is part of the wider notion of "the lay of the land".

RF: It's a capacious title, yes, it is.

BD: America in *Independence Day* was explored in an important way through the influence of the economy on the lives of your characters. You develop this line of investigation in *The Lay of the Land* by establishing commerce as a defining American value and activity. Yet you present a picture, particularly in the early pages of the novel, of shoppers pinballing from shop to shop, in thrall to the very activity of shopping, without quite knowing if they want to buy anything, or what they want to buy ...

RF: ... and that they couldn't find what they want if they tried...

BD: ... exactly. What you seem to be portraying is a society that is completely enslaved to consumerism. It's not a very optimistic picture of contemporary America. These people are just spending money, this is what it's about, this is the contemporary American experience.

RF: It is, and I believe that that's completely accurate, that America is a country anaesthetized by consumerism, right to the point that we have become insensate to moral concerns that lie somewhere – and not very far – beyond the perimeters of consumerism. That's what *The Lay of the Land* purports to be true – at least in so far as it wants to provoke a conversation with the reader.

BD: And it also, as Frank at least speculates, is producing an enervated culture, and is sapping the very fibre of the republic.

RF: The moral fibre. Particularly sapping the moral fibre that would be involved in self-criticism. When you have the possibility of further anaesthetizing yourself with a new blender, or a new set of snow tires, or a new flat screen TV, that can become a lot more attractive than finding fault with yourself for doing irreparable harm to the globe, irreparable harm to other countries, for letting your politicians lie to you, for letting the rich run rough-shod over the poor.

BD: But was America ever any different? You read back to the Founding Fathers, and commerce was right at the heart of the American Revolution. Is there anything new?

RF: Yes. One thing that's new is the outsized effect that we have on the rest of the world. That's new. But, internally, no. Freedom and the pursuit of happiness were always our guiding principles. And, as guiding principles, they have their firmest expression in commerce.

And as anybody can read in history, the whole idea for the American Revolution was based on commerce. So that we could quit being a captive client state to Britain and become a client of many other countries.

BD: Yes, so that these wealthy landowners could get on with the business of making a lot of money.

RF: That's right.

BD: There's a much less benign view of the role and impact of the economy in *The Lay of the Land* than in *Independence Day*, it seems to me. Frank describes the economy as the "malign force" that spurred the outbreak of greed in Haddam in the early nineties as real estate prices soared. Do you agree that there's a more critical view of the impact of economic forces in *The Lay of the Land*?

RF: Yes.

BD: What happened in the ten years between the two books to lead to this harsher view of economic impact?

RF: Well, what happened was … in a market economy, rises in prices are always a moral good. But in a frame of reference that's not totally dominated by market concerns, there are other parameters for measuring moral good. Ridiculously high prices pushed Frank outside of the commercial parameter and into one whose route to morality was different. You might call it the "common sense" parameter – which sounds to me like Frank. Frank finally decided that the price of housing in Haddam was just morally repulsive. It's a reflex, a gagging feeling in ourselves, that we have to pay attention to. That's the directive we get from ourselves that something is not right. Even though there may be countervailing and culturally significant arguments which say, "Well, you're being ridiculous, go buy a new car, go buy a timeshare in the Bahamas, don't think about that stuff". But when you're having that gagging reflex you have to pay attention to it.

BD: That's the moral reflex.

RF: Yes. And what commerce wants to do is completely subvert that impulse in yourself by saying, "No, no, no, no, no – don't pay attention to that aspect of yourself, get on with the business of making more money, everything will be fine". Well, it isn't.

BD: *The Lay of the Land* sets up a form of ideological confrontation between two visions of the evolution of a society and communities. On the one hand, there is the view represented by the merchant classes and Republican town fathers of Haddam, and by the "Dollars For Doers" business group in Sea-Clift, namely that a community is essentially an economic entity to be managed and developed like a branded product. On the other hand, we are offered the vision of Frank and of other inhabitants of Sea-Clift which would say that a community should be allowed to grow at its own speed and according more to quality-of-life criteria. There is a very strong ideological, and therefore political, confrontation that you set up in the book ...

RF: ... I'm married to a city planner, of course ...

(laughter).

BD: ... well, that's true ...

RF: ... we sit around the table and we talk about these very things every day ...

BD: ... ah, so that's what it is. But you do seem to want to challenge this view of communities that are constructed and managed as purely economic entities. It's a portrait of a society that sees itself as needing to be managed only according to laissez-faire economic principles.

RF: Yes. You know, in America we've been hearing for decades about running government like a business. We've been hearing it, or whether we've been hearing it or not, it's being said and supposedly happening. It's a commonplace perception of how well commercialism serves a society. Only it doesn't. It's the sour inheritance of Reaganomics, the trickle-down economy. It's the Republican's paradigm for a thriving society. But not enough trickles down. I suppose in that way, it *is* like a business.

BD: Capitalism, of course, is predicated on such a hierarchy.

RF: It just doesn't work. I mean, if it did work, we wouldn't have poor people, we wouldn't have crappy schools, we wouldn't have kids killing each other, we wouldn't have literacy going down. We're all of us inured to the prospect of a permanent lower class in this country, despite the fact that such a class gives the lie to every single economic principle that "government being a business" is based on.

BD: While *The Lay of the Land* is extremely funny at times, the overall atmosphere is nonetheless tense, anxious and sombre. Contemporary America is portrayed as being riven by sectionalism, leading in turn to the advanced stage of atomization on display, depicted as being even more widespread than it was in *Independence Day*. Within families, Americans are breaking up into individuals, and, within wider society, the country is fragmenting into groups. My question is this: are the old, strong bonds of family and of American national identity failing to hold Americans together, causing them to break away from each other in search of other sources of meaning and identification? The thing isn't holding together anymore.

RF: The middle isn't holding. It's an outgrowth, and maybe even a natural outgrowth, of the ways – for one – in which America has always replenished its populations through immigration; it's an outgrowth of the Civil Rights movement in the sixties; it's an outgrowth of diversity politics, in which, to gain purchase in the society, minorities, or other groups, Christians for instance, or white supremacists for instance, band together much more fiercely to have political purchase in the society. So, in a sense, the liberalism of the sixties, the egalitarianism of that period, has allowed these kinds of things to happen. And there hasn't been much civic guidance, particularly since Reagan (and you'd get that guidance in public education) to restrain the misuse of those good liberal principles which invest everybody with a singularity, and with the expectation of political potency. It does seems to me to be pretty natural, and it's malignant, because it'll finally eventually cause this country to tear apart.

BD: Although you portray this comically at times – I think of the 5-K roadrunners who form a little group of their own and who glare at Frank as he's driving past, simply because he isn't one of them. OK, there's an old couple, Wally's parents, who are sixty years married, they're together, but elsewhere everyone is separating from each other. It's a bleak vision of America.

RF: It is a bleak vision of America, indeed it is. There is a force in America that wants to identify the other as your adversary. There's no doubt about that. The person different from you is your adversary. I'm not talking about on racial terms. I'm talking about on much more generalized commercial terms, really. And that gets expressed by a litigiousness in the society, it gets expressed by a feeling – and again I credit Reagan with this – a feeling that no one should be discomforted about anything, and that no one should be made share the blame for anything that happens that turns out bad. I just noticed the other day … I said something in the public press which was reported widely, which was completely mild, about bloggers over here. I don't know much about bloggers over here, since I don't read them (although I've been interviewed by them). But I was just comparing what I did know about bloggers to what I did know about newspapers, and I said that I thought that newspapers were generally more responsible than bloggers. Well, I became anathema on blogs, that afternoon. And, you know, God forbid that anyone should criticize or fail fully to appreciate anybody else like that. This feeling that no one should be responsible for anything but his very singular self further atomizes people. There becomes no way for someone to say, you know, "I disagree with what you do, and here is why I disagree with it, and I wish you would take this into consideration". Nobody does that in America except on extreme radio, which isn't a dialogue, just a rant. Frank's antidote for it, whether it's a successful antidote or not, is – as he's driving around America and he sees this wasteland of commercialism that has become our streets – he tries to affirm things. He tries to say, "You know, commercialism is ugly, but it has its pluses. It's not always pretty but it is always progressive." Most Americans would take an ambiguous view of that, but, in Frank's case, what he's trying to do is take responsibility for those things in the culture, even if he doesn't like what those things are, and basically say, "This is the way it is because I must want it that way. Even if I don't like it as much as I'd like to, this is an outgrowth of something that's me." That seems to me to be the first step of taking individual responsibility for the things that you see around you that you don't like, rather than for isolating the forces outside yourself and making somebody else responsible. Kurt Vonnegut, when he died a couple of weeks ago, was remembered in the *New York Times* with a little poem, in which the speaker in the poem decried the state of modern existence in America, particularly the kind of things that we've just been talking about – a sort of metastasis of commercialism in America. And he comes to the end of the little poem, and the speaker says, "And we must conclude about the people who lived here that they didn't like it very much". I don't want that to be the case in America, I don't want scientists centuries on to look back on us and say, "We didn't like it here very much. Look at what we did to it."

BD: The other fracture in American society that is portrayed in the novel is that between the individual and the wider culture. Personal well-being and the pursuit of happiness seem to have become purely private affairs, detaching themselves from the social, and even from the American republic itself. The interesting thing in *The Lay of the Land* is that Frank is a liberal and is committed to the notion of a society and to the values of the republic. Yet he seems to feel increasingly isolated from his culture and his country, and even feels the need to protect himself from these, and he feels estranged from the republic. Do you recognize that detachment between the citizen and the wider society?

RF: Yes.

BD: There's a kind of a privatization of experience.

RF: It's an outgrowth of things that started in America in the eighteenth century. It's an outgrowth of what we deem to be federalism, in which the society as a whole is represented by the federal government, but as much as possible is enacted by the individual states. That sense of reciprocity between the larger culture and its governing organs has, I think, grown more dysfunctional over time. And I think that was the way it was always imagined, that the federal government would in fact be not a last resort but a least resort – this, so that citizens and even states could be left alone to pursue happiness however happiness was understood.

BD: Absolutely. The republic almost didn't come together at all over this very issue, over the insistence on states' rights.

RF: Exactly.

BD: One wonders sometimes how the colonies ever managed to come together at all. It could so easily have become six or twelve different countries.

RF: It *was*, that's what it was. The colonies, South Carolina and Massachusetts and Delaware, all thought of themselves as individual little chartered states, separate though contiguous, that's all. Their sense of isolation, their sense of their own soleness was furthered by a common goal of each wanting to be rich. They simply chose to give up parts of their independence in order to further that goal of prosperity. Which is why, of course, the republic tore apart in the 1860s – for economic reasons.

BD: It wasn't about abolishing slavery?

RF: Well, it was, but slavery was a façade behind which there was a lot of money changing hands, and the South was threatening to take a lot of money out of the hands of the northeast bankers and the northeast merchants – if the South successfully seceded and could trade their cotton with France, for instance. But, again, to get back to the eighteenth century, to our Founding Fathers – it was also understood that citizens out in the states (and there weren't as many states then, so it seemed probably less a daunting affair in 1779 than it would become), but citizens weren't expected to take part in the civic life of the republic except once every four years, which is pretty much how it is to this day. People were supposed to vote on representatives and then go back to making a living. We have a hugely uninformed electorate in America, susceptible to being lied to, because nobody really thinks that the culture or civic well-being of the whole country is ever his or her responsibility. The country operates entirely on slogans, it operates entirely on received wisdom, it operates entirely on misapprehensions of history – which is what Americans have time for and all they think they *should* have time for.

BD: Does that then strengthen local politics? Is that the other side of the coin, the good side? If we can't identify with national government, with the federal government, we can at least identify with where we live, with my little corner. Does it work that way?

RF: It works that way to a certain extent, but there is reluctance toward government even on the lower scale, which is why you can have a state like Maine being a fairly moderate-to-liberal state and have two Republican Senators. Because there's a dysfunction there someplace, in the individual's sense of responsibility to the government that represents it and how much we ought to expect government to represent us. Americans do not want to be interested in government, which is why we have this isolated political class, these professional politicians – because individuals don't much migrate out of their home towns and become, in an instinctual way, citizen politicians.

BD: But Americans don't want to be *governed* either.

RF: No, they don't. I mean, look over here at the state next to us, New Hampshire, whose state motto is "Live Free or Die". That could as well be the motto for every state in the Union.

BD: To move away now from the political side of the novel – is the anxiety and tension at the heart of the novel not ultimately due to the failure of love? In Frank's life alone, his relationships with Sally, Ann and Paul are all scarred by what we might call love's failure; and the unhappy condition of a number of other characters offers further evidence of an absence of love. Is this not the great calamity that you are portraying in the novel?

RF: I don't think it's love's failure. I think rather it's love's frailty. I mean, there's a moment in the book which I was very thrilled to get to write (and I had to be lead to it by my editor in a way), toward the end of the scene in which Frank and Paul have this calamitous battering of bodies together. One of the things Frank says to Paul in that scene out of immense exasperation with his son is: "I love you." And that seemed to me ... if I could make Frank say it, then it was true, in spite of all. If I'd written it and it hadn't seemed to belong or been otherwise wrong, then maybe it wouldn't have been as true as I wanted it to be. But I felt it was. Later, when Sally writes to Frank, from wherever she is when she writes it ...

BD: ... Maidenhead ...

RF: ... from Maidenhead. She says, "What is it we have between us?". She says, "It isn't this, it isn't that, it isn't this, it isn't that. Maybe love is the only thing that unites us." So I – who wrote that – don't think the book's about love's failure at all. Love and its expressions are under attack by all these other forces that we've been talking about – the forces that tend to drive people from each other, or to blame others, the forces that tend to cause us to look away from ourselves in seeking satisfaction and redemption. Whereas love is standing out there for us, waiting to console us, waiting to redeem us; but we don't look for it, don't imagine it, don't express it. But it isn't love's failure.

BD: I'm just thinking of the relationship between Ann and Frank. Ann comes back to live in Haddam after the death of her second husband. She's not sure why she comes back, she thinks it might be to live again with Frank. She thinks she may have loved Frank, but she's not sure if she loves Frank. Frank is horrified at this, of course, but there seems to be a great confusion between them about love, on both their parts, as to whether they ever loved each other ...

RF: ... and Frank concludes that he didn't ...

BD: ... that's right ...

RF: ... and if he did, certainly not enough.

BD: And yet he often proclaimed that he did over the course of the novels. Ann, who has always seemed a very steadfast, solid character who, you would think, knew the person she loved or didn't love ... *she* doesn't seem to know if she loved Frank, or she doesn't know now if she loves Frank, or not. So, is it that they don't know what love is, or know how to love each other?

RF: I think that we inherited the concept of love, often without any proper training for it, and so love gets agglomerated into all of these other swirling forces that are around us – commerce, even the desire for affluence, self-individualization. I mean, it's not new to the world that love is often mis-identified. I'd just go back to the idea of its frailty. Is Ann good at deciding what she loves? No, she's not. They were children when they married. And, as Frank said, things sorting out the way they did, with Ralph dying, deprived them of a perfectly good chance of realizing quite early on that they didn't love each other and shouldn't be married at all. But as far as Sally is concerned with Frank, as far as his kids are concerned, I think Frank loves them in ways that are very estimable, because they are not blinkered by his own frailties, they're not blinkered by *their* frailties as human beings. But love, I think, persists between them fully. This is causing me to talk about these characters as if I didn't make them up, as if they had existences apart from me. And I don't like to do that.

BD: I suppose it's a necessary kind of shorthand for talking about fiction. Regarding Frank and Paul's relationship ... they really are quite hostile to each other for most of the novel. That changes toward the end. You're right, Frank does say that he loves Paul, on two occasions, but he's pushed to it, it's almost in anger that he says that he loves him. One wonders why he could never manage to say this beforehand. It takes Jill, Paul's girlfriend, to act as intermediary between the two of them, so that they can hear how fond they are of each other, particularly in a conversation she has with Frank. They seem to be afraid to utter the language of love.

RF: Well, I just think that's the modern condition. Or maybe it's just *the* condition. I mean, Hamlet ... (laughing) ... Lear. I think the failures of children to properly identify with, and to express their affection for, their parents is an long-established subject. And I don't think again it's love's failures, it's *our* failures, in which case a book like mine becomes a kind of – alas, I keep finding myself writing things like this all the time – a cautionary tale. And based on my book I don't feel that one needs to expand the view of relationships between parents and children outwards throughout the whole American society. In my case, for instance, I had wonderful parents who loved me depthlessly, and I had nothing but high regard for them and they had nothing but love for me. So, it could very well be that – I have a lecture which I give sometimes – it could very well be that growing up in a loving environment allowed me to more fully appreciate what I had, and to fear what I didn't have – enough to make that a subject for literature.

BD: The political expression of divided America is given an important place in the novel by way of the August Inn scene where Frank ends up in a fight with a customer and in a nasty argument with the barman. The scene depicts yet another confrontation of ideologies and values in contemporary America, this time between liberals and xenophobes, or, more generally, between the values of Democrats and those of Republicans. We expect political division, of course, but why did you choose to give political division this particular character of meanness, of violence even?

RF: Well, it wasn't so much a thing I planned to do. It's typical of me just to put people into a situation and see what I intuitively make them do. And so, when I see what I intuitively make them do, I either then leave it or take it out and change it. In this instance I put them there, these five or six people in that bar, and what grew out of my putting them there was something that I must have thought was plausible. I must have thought it was something I was willing to keep and have the reader think is somehow apposite to what's going on in American culture at the time.

BD: The year 2000 and the whole election-recount backdrop.

RF: That's right. As you say, xenophobia, racism. I had all of them, had all of the constituents for a wonderful little psychodrama there, which is punctuated at the end by Mike Mahoney walking down the stairs, and suddenly the bartender is so alarmed to see this little Tibetan walking into this snuggery for old Republicans that he's brought to venom by it.

BD: Yes, he calls him a "coolie", I think, he's really vicious in his insults.

RF: Well, that's not unusual in America. Listen to right-wing radio.

BD: Such overt racism?

RF: Oh, no. It's not typical, but it's not unusual. But, again, let me stress the fact that I didn't set this all up to illustrate a point. I just put them there and then stirred it up, and decided to keep what I brewed.

BD: So what you're saying is that the novel, your writing, emerges as you write words on the page, as you write sentences, as you give characters lines, as you describe some kind of interaction, the thing just grows out almost without you trying it to grow out in a particular way.

RF: No, not that last part. I am trying to make it grow, but in many instances I know exactly what I mean to take place. But what I think is my failsafe here is that I'm putting into play in these situations recognizable and important forces, moral forces that I'm interested in. If I was just putting trivial forces into play, then I would end up not keeping what I wrote. Almost a counter-example is the Marguerite episode, in which Frank goes into Marguerite's house, trying to be a Sponsor to whatever she needs to have sponsored. I actually had to scratch my head a long time in writing that scene to try to figure out what I was getting at. I finally figured it out. It was probably the hardest scene in the whole book to get right. It was a scene I literally worked on until the last minute on the last day when this book was in my hands, a year ago last August. I still was tuning it, trying to get my own understanding of the scene into alignment with what the scene was doing. But in the scene with Bob Butts and the bartender in the August Inn, there I knew what the moral polarities were. I didn't know how it would turn out, but that seemed to me to be the grounding on which the scene was set. I felt good about however it turned out.

BD: So within the overall idea of what you think or hope the scene will achieve, it nonetheless can take different forms?

RF: It could take a variety of different forms other than the one it does take. And that pretty much happens with me writing a sentence, and seeing how I like that sentence.

BD: Or seeing what that sparks off, perhaps?

RF: That's right.

BD: So it could be an adjective that might send you one way, it could be a particular phrase that sends you a particular way?

RF: That's right. I'm at ease with that notion of composition. It may turn out to be entirely contradictory to what my glimmering ideas for the scene were at the beginning, it may turn against my original plan, and I don't mean to say "it" turns against. *I* am the one doing the writing, *I* am the one doing the determining. *I* am, of course, still the one doing the deciding and sometimes the erasing and the taking out. It isn't as though the scene or some unseen force ever takes over, or that the characters write their own scenes, or that I relinquish in any way my responsibility. It's just that I start to write a sentence and I'm writing a sentence in a kind of spiritual consonance with what I think is at issue in the scene. You write a sentence – and I could show you manuscripts in which I crossed this out, took that out, wrote through this or that. And so I'm just feeling my way. I can't think all writers don't do some version of that. I guess it's interesting to people because it seems to leave a considerable bit to chance, and yet can still turn out to be excellent. It's a process of relinquishing control and then re-establishing it. It's quite exciting – one of the few parts of writing that is.

BD: And you're also, to go back to what you said earlier, being faithful to the greater principle that literature is language.

RF: That's right. And subject to all of the mutability that language has inherent in it, all the subjectivity.

BD: That's the adventure, too.

RF: It is.

BD: Frank has not always been well served by his optimism, but in *The Lay of the Land*, in the difficult circumstances in which he finds himself, he emerges, to my reading at least, as admirable and steadfast …

RF: … to me, too.

BD: Previously it was Frank who hovered around others, withholding and being evasive; now it is others who hover around, aggravate and pull at Frank. You seem to agree that the novel has evolved in this way. Was it a conscious decision that you took to make Frank a more morally admirable character in *The Lay of the Land*?

RF: Yes, I think I wanted him to be more clearly admirable, and I had going for me circumstances which could bring out and clarify that sense of moral goodness. Which is to say he's ill, he's been poorly served by another wife and can be buoyant about it, he is at a time in his life when taking stock is almost inescapable, and his kids are driving him crazy. My notion of a character who's good, or happy, is a character who has things to overcome, and does. I mean, part of the thesis of this book is that Frank is looking for something for which he can give thanks. And that, I think, is fundamentally an affirming point of view. I don't know if I could have told you five years ago that I'm trying to write a book in which Frank looks like more of a positive moral integer than I had thought him to be before, because I think I always thought of him as a positive moral integer anyway. I think writing novels is fundamentally affirmative. Writing novels, reading novels, is fundamentally an act of acceptance of the world around us. And so even if my characters, in *A Multitude of Sins*, for instance, seem sometimes to be beleaguered, they sometimes seem to be morally deeply ambiguous, they seem sometimes to be morally corrupted, I tend to let them exist in the more affirming ethers of the larger effort of the book. I think, for instance, that Dostoyevsky must have felt the same way when he wrote *Crime and Punishment*. How to write an execrable character like Raskolnikov in a book that means fundamentally to be affirmative of humankind but which involves a man murdering someone, and murderous impulses? So I would have always said that Frank was a positive character, because he was involved in a large positive operation, which was me writing a book of which he's the centrepiece. But, yes, in this other book, this third book … I'm perhaps more than usually looking for a vocabulary for affirmation. Wallace Stevens said, "We gulp down evil, choke at good". So I'm trying to make good not be something we choke on.

BD: There were hints in *Independence Day*, particularly by way of his "winces", that Frank was not immune to the odd shaky existential moment. Yet we tend to see him as a character firmly rooted in his life and as one getting on with the more or less comprehensible business of living it. So it comes as something of a surprise to learn that Frank, back in Haddam in the nineties, had suffered a crisis of identity, a sense that he lacked an inner essence, a sense that Frank Bascombe didn't mean anything, didn't stand for anything very much. You've touched on this earlier, but could you say something about what led you to develop this part of Frank's personality, this existential shakiness which is not what we would associate with Frank's rootedness in his life?

RF: It's probably just something I personally thought about which I finally just externalized and gave to Frank. For a long time – I don't mean to make this sound profound – for a long time I have noted discrepancies between my behaviour and the models for my behaviour, and particularly the expectations of other people about my behaviour. That led me to believe that the whole notion of character *per se* was possibly a dubious notion, and maybe even in fact a made-up notion, that it was a convenience that our ancestors gave to themselves in an attempt to make them seem reliable to themselves and to others, making them seem to possess an identifiable essence – that we have good character and therefore we are representatives of God. I just began to realize that I didn't find any of that to be true – about me – that the notion of human beings having a character just seemed to me to be completely spurious, based on my own behaviour, and based on the behaviour of people I saw around me, which isn't to say that people around me don't claim to have characters. They mostly do. Sometimes even *I* claim to have a character, as a sort of a shorthand meaning something else. You say you have a good character, by which you mean that faced with an alternative I would choose to do no harm rather than harm. But I just found this concept to be trickier and trickier – especially, as we were saying, in the political sphere. So I just sort of decided to put it into Frank's life and vocabulary to see what it would occasion me to say, and one of the things it occasioned me to say was that, "Yes, we all experience this lack of moral identity, we all experience this failure of being plausible to oneself, and even to others, and that possibly puts us in a position to try to rectify that". As though we *could* rectify it. And if I could make rectifying one's character seem within the grasp of human beings, then I would have done the world a favour. Rather than just saying that we are, in Darwinian terms, just the product of all the trivial things that made us. We can actually put a new face on that if we want to. But first of all we have to face the fact that we're basically just a sort of a little insular system of impulses.

BD: How do we reconcile that with the need for us to exist as moral beings over time? Time and character, time and identity, are inseparable. You have lived sixty-odd years. People, as you say, talk about you in ways that ... well, they feel they can identify who you are, perhaps they feel they could predict how you might react in particular circumstances. What *does* allow us to hold ourselves together as a moral being over time?

RF: Well, I think the accumulation of our observed behaviour – your past, your present, and what you hold to be possible for you in the future. It all comes down to something very basic: have I done more good than bad in my life, and am I liable to do more good than bad in the future, and am I, at any given moment in life, more on the good side than the bad side? And I think that that's all we have of character – we have memory and history, we have present awareness, we have a sense of future. That's what character is to me. As much as anything else, character is the awareness of this self.

BD: I don't know if you're familiar with Paul Ricoeur, and his notion of a narrative identity. His response would be – and it's not dissimilar from your own – is that we tell the *story* of the self that embraces past, present and future. We recuperate the past in order to project ourselves into the future, and in order, too, to situate ourselves in the present. It's a vast, whole temporal embracing that stories allow. You've talked about this before with the idea of the story as cure. I think you have a notion that storytelling helps us to hold ourselves together. Do you agree with this idea of the story of the self?

RF: I'd hesitate to say I really understand that. What I understand about the virtues of stories is decidedly lower case. Looked at almost in English 101 terms – I'll externalize this – if we have a character who tells us a story on the page, and he's talking about a time in his life when these events took place, a series of events which started and then ended, and then later on he's looking back on it and telling it – the fact that he can tell it means that somehow he's survived it. The fact that he can tell it means that he's put a shape upon it that it didn't have at the time of its occurrence, and that it radiates out to him as an event of moral consequence because it's important enough to tell. Maybe it didn't have moral consequence when it took place, but the shaping and the ability to narrate it gives it that consequence. I mean, James said, "Art makes life, art makes importance". That's how we know, it's through art, and one of those arts is narration.

BD: That would be what Ricoeur would say. It's not story with a big "s", it's several stories, because we constantly configure and reconfigure ourselves ...

RF: ... yes ...

BD: ... and it's through a series of little narratives that we constitute what you might call character.

RF: Right. And that's why I tell these novels in the first person and present tense. Who is this man again?

BD: Paul Ricoeur. A French philosopher, he died just a couple of years ago. He wrote a three-volume work called *Time and Narrative*. It's a wonderful work.

RF: Maybe I don't need to read it; maybe I've already done that ... (laughing)

BD: ... yes, maybe you've done it in the novels.

RF: I've read a lot of philosophy over the years, but I've only read the philosophies that I felt most kindred to.

BD: I was struck because ... isn't it Emerson you've cited before in the quote about the story as cure?

RF: Yes.

BD: I was really taken by that because I was using Ricoeur for something else at the time, and I just saw affinities between you and Ricoeur.

RF: And Merleau-Ponty. I've read him. And Kierkegaard. All of us American novelists are required to read Kierkegaard. But I never wrote a line in my life trying to illustrate something I'd read. Sometimes I plucked a line out of something and stuck it in a book because it seemed apposite at the moment, and I was shocked to see that was true for Buddhism – the closest I could come to having a personal philosophy or religion is Buddhism. But I'm like the Dalai Lama, occasionally I have to watch the BBC and eat meat. (Laughter)

BD: You're probably just as well not to be writing novels according to ideas.

RF: Not me, no.

BD: Because that produces bad novels, I think.

RF: And it wouldn't be any fun either.

BD: It's hardly a novel for a start, I don't think. What I mean is, it's not fundamentally about language, it's not literature as language.

RF: It's not an experiment.

BD: To get back to *The Lay of the Land* ... Frank has always preferred the present to the past, and has lived his life accordingly. This desire to ignore his past could be said to be the source of many of his problems in the earlier novels. But, in *The Lay of the Land*, time, and Frank's past, come back at him with a vengeance – the day of reckoning arrives. Just to stay with Ann and Paul for the moment and their respective relationships with Frank, did you see it as a form of moral obligation to force Frank to confront a past for which he had often not taken responsibility, and from which he had often tried to run away in the previous books?

RF: I would hate to be a person who admitted to any moral obligation. Novelists don't have any of that. That would be the last thing on earth I would probably do.

BD: Even with your characters?

RF: *Particularly* with my characters. I'm much more inclined to recognize moral obligation in my private life, but with my characters, never. They're just there to be manipulated. But I – and you can decide the difference between what I'm going to say and moral obligation here – I just had the subject that you just mentioned available to me. I'm thinking about whether I'm going to put potatoes or turnips in my stew, and I choose turnips instead of potatoes because I like turnips better. Well, when I look about at all the possible constituents of what I could put in my novel, there's Ann waiting to be taken up, and my reason for taking her up is her availability and the possibility, which I feel in some way that I can't describe, the possibility that I might be able to write things, make events happen, and put them in Frank's vocabulary in ways that would be interesting. If I put them in that little closed room together, I think to myself, "Oh boy, oh boy, oh boy, I can't wait to see what I'll make them say". Now that may be a sense of moral obligation. But, if it is, then that satisfies my understanding of moral obligation, which is to say, moral obligation mostly has to do with availability. Which is a fairly amoral view of moral obligation. (Laughing)

BD: In your returning in *The Lay of the Land* to Frank's relationship to his dead son, Ralph, you bring us back to the opening, graveyard scene of *The Sportswriter*, which has the effect of bringing Frank's whole adult life as explored in the three novels back into play …

RF: … which was my intention …

BD: … yes, the books start with Ralph and they come back to Ralph. Frank now sees that all his strategies and concepts were just so many ways of not accepting the absolute finality of his son's death …

RF: … which is the passage in that book that I am most pleased by.

BD: Yes, it's a lovely passage. It's very, very strong. You really get a thump of emotion when you read that towards the end of the novel. Yet you burden your character with this insight, in a sense, because you have him say that his life is based on a lie. That's quite a burden of guilt and regret to inflict on Frank at this late stage of his development.

RF: Yes, I thought so, too. And, in fact, when I wrote it, it was – for me – such a burden and such a strong passage that I had to break it up into parts. I didn't have it happen all in one flow of emotion and event. I had to have Frank go to sleep thinking this, and wake up and think it some more.

BD: Yes, he has to absorb this.

RF: That's right. In fact, when I was writing it, I thought, "This seems almost too much". As you say, I burden him with it, I inflict it on him, but I inflicted it on him for reasons that I felt were, for me, as close to inevitable and inescapable as anything I have ever written. I mean, I knew I wanted to make these novels come around, but when I did it, I thought, "My God, what a huge thing to do", to make *this* be plausible. But I think I did it *there* as kind of a penultimate moment in the book, so I would have time to make him survive it. I didn't do it at the very end because, in my own sense of the book's syncopation, at the penultimate moment was where it seemed the most logical to come. But again, you know, I had him walk out of that bar, in the rain, and go sit in his car ...

BD: ... and he can't find his keys ...

RF: ... he can't find his keys, he's stuck there, and I had him – and this is as close to the actual writing as I could say – I had him sitting at that bar and starting to cry, and I got him out in the car, and I'm still making him cry, and I thought to myself, "What could it be both in my imagination, and what could it be in Frank's history" – that I'm entirely responsible for – "what could make him be crying this way?".

BD: You didn't know at that stage?

RF: No. I mean I knew that I wanted to have that whole issue of Ralph come around. I didn't have exactly a template for it. But I felt, "What would it be? What could I make it be?". And, I thought, "Well, yes, it's that". But I'll say this: if I had written it and I hadn't liked it, I'd have taken it out. And in actuality I did write it and I didn't altogether like it, so I kept it as kind of provisional for a time, till I had Kristina read it, and then I read it two or three times and then my editor read it and didn't make any adverse remarks about it. It took me a while to make it seem permanent in the book because I knew it was one of those moments in the book when I really was manipulating the intelligence of the book in a way I thought didn't even *seem* organic. It was really me pounding down on something that I had elected to pound down on – you used the word "burden" – and I didn't know if it was persuasive or not. But, once I got reconciled to it, then I realized I had the rest of the book, maybe at that point a hundred more pages to make it fit.

BD: I see ... how would Frank deal with this epiphany, which is one of the literary conceits that he sneers at ...

RF: ... that's right.

BD: This *is* an epiphany.

RF: That's right. It is an epiphany, but it's at least, it seems to me, an epiphany of his own imagining. When I can think of epiphany as something that one imagines, as a connection one makes for oneself, and then tries afterwards to believe and to hold to, then I'm a little more able to be persuaded by it. This, I realize, violates my most fundamentally held premise about my characters – that I make everything happen. *They* don't. But in this case, in this particular scene, I was about as close to my character as I've probably ever gotten.

BD: But he *feels* it as well. It's a very emotional scene. It comes from Frank's guts, almost ...

RF: ... that's right ...

BD: ... this just wells up and out.

RF: Right

BD: It's emotion as well as imagination.

RF: But he *makes* it, though. Whatever it was that was responsible for that welling, and that tumult in his gut, is something that he gives the sense to. I mean, I can say in the most obvious way, in the hands of another person it might have been something else. It could have been assigned to some other force. It just so happened that I assigned it to that force, and that's what it becomes. You know, it's that very nature ... when we were talking earlier about how Americans are so resistant to the truths of fiction because they are not factual and actual, it's that fact ... I have him feel the tumult which I kind of share with him and then I assign to him the interpretation of that tumult to be this, and that's what it then becomes – that's what drives Americans crazy. It seems to be the heart of moral relativism. For which they have only one antidote, which is God, which they feel like is not imagined but which is ordained.

BD: Frank, being an intelligent and reflective character, has been able, over the three novels, to conceptualize and intellectualize his avoidance of the past, namely through his concepts of mystery, literalism, factualism, and the temporal demarcations of the Existence Period and now the Permanent Period of *The Lay of the Land*. In so far as this intellectual edifice finally collapses through the intrusion of simple human emotion in *The Lay of the Land*, are you trying to say something about a balance between the rational and the emotional in the understanding of our lives?

RF: I wouldn't be surprised. I mean, it would be the thing that probably has motivated me throughout my entire writing life, the contiguousness and sometimes adversarial relationships – but certainly the distinct relationships – between the cognitive powers and the sensuous, intuitive ones. I think that that's, from the beginning of my writing life, what I've been up to. I don't know if you know *A Piece of My Heart*, it's got two narrators, and I was aware even in my twenties when I was writing these two narrators that they were representatives: one of a sensuous, intuitive, non-cognitive way of approaching the world and understanding the world, and the other of a cognitive one. In writing all these novels and stories, I've tried to bring these life forces into closer connection and have tried to make them synthesize in some way. But, in the process of making them synthesize, I probably always come out on the side of the cognitive, because I think the two of these things can be ... it's Lawrencian in a way, or it's like Lawrence, who was one of my heroes. Nobody ever asks me about Lawrence. They always ask me about Walker Percy and Faulkner, and people like that ...

BD: ... and Emerson ...

RF: .. and Emerson, right. It's not that I think that this is what the world is all about – it's just what *I*'m all about, that's just what these *novels* are about. The world is about a whole lot of other things than that.

BD: Frank has been a great vehicle for that, in fact, because he is a strange mix between the two ...

RF: ...I suppose ...

BD: ... he does tend to intellectualize a little too much, it seems to me, in the early novels ... but as the past comes back ... well, maybe he allows his emotions to come through in the end, and he's probably better for it. The relationship of characters to their pasts is a recurring theme in your writing. Frank favours either ignoring or forgetting the past, but elsewhere in your writing this proves impossible for characters: Jena in "Quality Time" is weighed down by what she sees as her parents having been "unsuccessful human beings"; the adult narrator of "Calling" feels obliged, thirty years on, to narrate events from his adolescence; and the narrator of "Reunion" finds that the past is not so easily relegated to a lesser status in terms of its meanings and relation to the present. On balance, you seem to be suggesting that we cannot but carry our pasts around with us, and that we can't escape our pasts. The past seems to be a burden for a lot of your characters.

RF: I think that one of the things that Frank says at the beginning of *The Lay of the Land,* or maybe it's in this little passage about character ... he says that our pasts can only be exceeded, which is to say, they can't be escaped. You can possibly be aware of your past and understand what its hold on you is, and essay to live beyond it, or to live something that the past, in a way, makes possible for you. But in my understanding of the past, and I grew up in a past-laden, past-ridden, past-corrupted world, you can't ever really get away from it. But you can try to do something better with it than everybody else does with it, you can try to do something with it that is more hopeful than its most minimum possibilities. This is probably the answer that will identify me as a southerner. Too bad. I guess you can't escape that either.

BD: Some of your characters have difficulty doing this …

RF: … yes …

BD: … getting away from their pasts.

RF: Well, probably over the scope of all these books and stories that you just mentioned, it's a whole constellation of possibilities that's illuminated. Frank, probably being the most optimistic character I have ever tried to write, is the person most likely to get away with that, whereas the characters in "Quality Time" and in those stories in *A Multitude of Sins* are less adept at it.

BD: Although even Frank, in trying to get away from it, as we said … it kind of comes full circle at the end.

RF: At least that's what he imagines. He imagines that to be true. He makes up that epiphanal seeing-through, and then decides that the way to exceed the past is to accept it, and then to think if that acceptance doesn't create a boundary beyond which one can operate.

BD: That interests you a lot, in fact. You talk in several stories about this notion of whether there are, or are not, eras, and of characters trying to demarcate their pasts.

RF: Sartre says that to take something that was part of life but not noticed, give it a name, elevates important bits of our existence to the level where we can think about them. That's what I did, or had Frank do, regarding his middle fifties – a period of life that might've gotten classified as "middle age", but not very usefully. When I call it the Permanent Period and give it all sort of attributes, I'm just fulfilling Sartre's requirement.

BD: The Frank Bascombe novels are long novels, each covering just a few days. *The Lay of the Land* uses the expression the "examined life" on more than one occasion. What I'm getting at here is a possible connection between this slow narrative tempo of the novels and a moral dimension. Was the narrative tempos you adopted for the novels a conscious one in order to facilitate the examined life? Does the temporality of these novels favour, do you think, the examined life by focusing heavily on the moment?

RF: I think it probably does favour the examined life. However, these are all fictively imagined circumstances and fictively imagined lives. I don't think that anybody would think that she or he could live a life of any kind proceeding on the way that Frank does – having to narrate your every wince and gulp and joy on a minute-to-minute basis, even if it's not really minute-to-minute, although a lot of it is minute-to-minute. That said, I can't say that I figured out the time-scale for these books as a way of promoting or as a way of representing life as a more meditative life. No, I think it just worked out that way. I think I was in the grip of – in choosing to narrate the books this way – I was in the grip of several books that I had read that I really liked: *The Moviegoer* by Walker Percy, *Something Happened* by Joe Heller, and *A Fan's Notes* by Frederick Exley. Those books were all told in the first person – two of them in present-tense verbs – and they just hugely affected me. So I was just in the grip of those books that I liked very much, and what I did with my own once I made that narrative decision just came quite fortuitously. I'm not quite so calculating as to be able to do that. Another writer might lay claim to it, but I'm not able to do that.

BD: The temporality of the Frank novels is very effective as it does allow you to draw in the reader to Frank's reflective and meditative mode, although you have often said in the past that what brought you to this two- or three-day timeframe was the holiday concept. That brought you to this narrative tempo, then, more than anything.

RF: That's right. Certainly, it's that to a large extent. I knew from reading *Ulysses* – although I don't like *Ulysses* very much – but I knew from that book that you could encapsulate a short period of time in a rather long period of narration. So it wasn't unknown to me that this was possible, even though I would hesitate to say that *Ulysses* had influence on me. But, I mean, maybe in some sublime way I understood that to be treated to the interior of a character for a concentrated period of time could potentially be pleasurable. It wasn't an outlandish idea.

BD: As in the previous novels, you send Frank out into America, which allows him to take the country's pulse. This time, however, it's generally an unhappy experience for him. There's an atmosphere of foreboding in the days before Thanksgiving, and, on Thanksgiving

Day itself, events speed up and sweep Frank along. I read this accelerated momentum of events on Thanksgiving Day in which Frank is caught up as a metaphor for the way things are spinning out of control in this society. I wondered if this was what you were trying to suggest in the rushed and fevered atmosphere of the events of Thanksgiving Day?

RF: No. I have been told by people that they thought that the third part of the book … Jeff Eugenides told me that he thought the third part of the book dragged a little bit. I never thought it did, I never thought it dragged, not that it has to be a perfect novel, and not that he isn't entitled to his opinion, because he certainly is, he's a very smart boy. No, I was in fact wanting to quicken the pace of the reader's passage through time. Just to get on with things. But I had no wish for the pace to be a correlative for something that was perceived to be happening in the wider world. Again, I'm not that calculating.

BD: What led me to that thought was the way the day ends for Frank, in the shooting. Frank seems to be led by events on that morning. He's constantly chasing after the day …

RF: … true …

BD: … and chasing after things, and then it all speeds up and speeds up, and suddenly he's shot. Maybe it's just that you're not aware of all the effects of your books …

RF: I can't be entirely, I don't think – though I try to be. I was vaguely apprehensive about having him be shot in the manner that I did. Though it was always in my mind that it happen that way. But when I got to the appointed moment – following simply what felt to me like the natural rhythms of part three – when I got to the part at which he was going to be shot, I tried to slow the speed of the scene down, because I guess I was aware of thinking, "Well, maybe this is happening too precipitously for the reader, maybe I've missed some beat someplace back in the book". But once I wrote it (and I don't know that I ever got over the sense of its being a little precipitous), and when I went back over it and over it and over it, I couldn't see anything that I wanted to do differently. I couldn't see anything that I felt was in my power to change. I liked it the way it was. I've since thought of one little tiny thing that I could've done differently but it would have been just a matter of inserting a very small detail early only, something that nobody would have paid any attention to when it took place. So, in other words, I could have laid in something that could have been more foreshadowing, but then I thought, "You know, this book starts with a shooting, it's got a shooting in the middle, it's got violence throughout, it has explosions". And so the fact that this could be suddenly visited on Frank ... this kind of thing's happening in the society all the time. It really was true in the interior validity of the book, as well as the exterior validity of the world outside the book.

BD: Completely. And in *Independence Day*, too. The threat of violence is there ...

RF: ... yes ...

BD: ... when I totted them all up I was surprised, because it didn't strike me when I first read *Independence Day*, but when I went back to it and took note of all the allusions to violence, of violent acts ... and then you take it through to *The Lay of the Land*, it's there all the time.

RF: All the time. I was aware of that. I was aware of it in a kind of indirect way, which is to say, I didn't wilfully put those things there. It was just that in the attempt to describe the environment that Americans live in, to try to pluck this up and pluck that up out of the landscape, and out of the audio landscape, I was just always hearing sirens. There were just always explosions, guns going off ... it was just there in the real world.

BD: ... and lights flashing ...

RF: ... there were always police officers nearby, there was always somebody with a gun. That was just something that came naturally into the book without my planning to say that. But once I saw what was happening I thought, "Well, that's just probably indigenous to American culture".

BD: It's another view of the "cultural literacy" that Frank speaks about ...

RF: ... right, it is ...

BD: ... the McDonalds around the corner, the cop with a gun.

RF: Yeah, you always know you're going to find a cop with a gun. There's almost no place you can go in America anymore without running into sirens, without running into people with guns, sometimes the gun's drawn, without running into somebody trying to steal something from you. That was just there. I just acknowledged it the same way you'd put a mountain into a novel set in Montana.

BD: I understand everything you say, and yet this is a novel which takes place at Thanksgiving, and it brings us back to the beginnings of the country, which were violent. White settlers came and they basically began a campaign of violence to clear the land of people who got in their way. You were obviously deeply aware that you were bringing America back to its origins; you seemed to be saying something about Thanksgiving and what it's supposed to stand for.

RF: Yes, that's right. It doesn't change very much in that regard. America's still a place where those who're vulnerable to dispossession are dispossessed.

BD: To move now to the end of the book: one could say that *The Lay of the Land* allows a truer, or at least an alternative, meaning of Thanksgiving to emerge in the final chapter. The official Thanksgiving is dismissed by Frank on several occasions. But in the chapter entitled "Thanksgiving", the events of which take place after official Thanksgiving, there's a new atmosphere and a gentler contact between people, and it is here that Frank proposes that love is the word that Sally had been looking for to describe "the natural human state for how we exist toward each other", and Frank has found, too, that the existential necessity is simply "to live, to live, to live it out". So the book ends affirmatively, affirming life and affirming love. You like affirmative endings in the Frank books, this is the third one. You really wanted to end with this affirmation?

RF: Yes, I did, but it has a harsh undertone. Even though affirming those things that the book articulates, even though that's at the end of the book, it's still the case that this is a book that took place the year before 9/11. It's very much the fact that with Frank saying "to live, to live, to live it out" is affirming, it's also insulating yourself from all of those things going on around him – politics, violence, the pre-9/11 world that's a lot like the post 9/11 world.

BD: Oh, completely. It's a personal affirmation, it's not a cultural one at all …

RF: … no, it's not …

BD: … he's isolated from a lot. It's almost as if he is saying, "*Here* is where I will find peace", at the personal level. It's pessimistic about America …

RF: … absolutely…

BD: … it doesn't apply to America, in fact.

RF: No, it doesn't. In fact, that's the state of mind that existed in Frank's life, or in the life of anybody who's like Frank at the point at which the World Trade Center buildings were bombed. It's that state of inward-gazing, that state of attempting self-satisfaction, that state of personal insularity from the news, from globalism, from all of those things that's made America so vulnerable.

BD: Before some of your characters get to the point of acting upon their understanding of what is happening in their lives, they are seen on occasions as having first to reach that stage of understanding. In other words, your stories quite often focus on the construction of meaning itself. This is very explicitly the case in "Quality Time" …

RF: … my favourite story in that book …

BD: … but also in the retrospective construction of meaning in "Calling", and in the stories of the self – past, present and future – that Martin Austin and Charley Matthews tell themselves as they negotiate experience. Are you conscious of this theme in your writing of how people construct meaning for themselves?

RF: Yes, I am. But I don't think it's very different from any other first-person narration in which one talks about life as it has been lived, in an attempt to construct a version of life that's acceptable. You know, John Gardner wrote in his book, *On Moral Fiction*, that life is all conjunctions: this and this and this and this and this, whereas art is all subordinations: this *because* of this, this *in spite* of that, this *attendant* to that, always through the agency of adverbial and adjectival and subordinating constructions. That's what novels provide us about life.

BD: Connections.

RF: Right. Put another way, Ruskin said composition (artistic composition) is the arrangement of unequal things. And really, for me, that's what I'm doing. I'm arranging unequal things, and saying that this is unequal to that, or that's superior to this, this is different from that. That's really what I'm doing. Connecting and appraising.

BD: It's storytelling, isn't it?

RF: Well, it can be. It's art, anyway. We're dependant on James: storytelling (he said art) is making importance. Whereas otherwise it's just this and then this and then this and then this …

BD: … just a succession of things …

RF: Yeah, out to the end of our lives. So art tries to say, "No, we'll put this frame around it, we'll bring things into better focus, we'll say that this is more important to that, and this is accomplished by that, and this is the agent to that", and in so doing meaning is made.

BD: And this sends us *back* to that … Frank at the end … the end is the beginning…

RF: … right …

BD: … of the three novels, when Ralph's death suddenly comes back to Frank …

RF: … looms up in his life. Yes. When James says that art makes importance, he might as well have said that art makes meaning.

BD: Yes, out of this endless succession, without links.

RF: Right.

BD: When I read your fiction, I am always struck by the detail and nuance in the construction of your characters. You don't try to construct your characters on just one or two ideas. You fill up your characters and your scenes to an impressive extent with new thoughts …

RF: … often competing ideas …

BD: … competing ideas, new ideas, you want to move things forward, this scene or that character forward. You seek, it seems to me, to render both a fullness of intellectual and emotional experience but also to push your characters to the limits of their intelligence, and your own, for that matter. You fill up and fill up your scenes with impressive detail and achieve an exceptional density of rendered thought and experience. It leads to a very rich construction of character.

RF: Bob Hughes, the art critic, was writing about the American painter, Fairfield Porter. And he wrote of Porter that the pieties of abstract impressionism of the fifties were unpersuasive to him, who was more or less a realistic, representative painter. And this was so because the pieties of abstract impressionism did not comply with Porter's sense of how art represents life and conveys its density. And so, for me – for me, not necessarily for anybody else – to be interesting, art has to convey a version of life's density …

BD: … of lived life, as you have referred to it elsewhere …

RF: … lived life, yes. Lived life is very dense, and it's not very consistent and it's not very well ordered, and it is full of competing details and competing ideas, and full of competing impulses. And so for me to do that in a novel, I'm going to have to somehow get that much detail onto the page.

BD: And it's often contradictory detail, too.

RF: Yes. But I take my consolation from Emerson there. What does he say? ... "A foolish consistency is the hobgoblin of little minds." He knew life was full of contradictions. So, yeah, I think the same. We in ourselves somehow reconcile in order that we not be like my friend Sam Shepard's character in *Kicking a Dead Horse* – so we're not stuck in a hole someplace, so that we will actually be able to tread on a little.

BD: Some of your male characters – for example Martin Austin, Charley Matthews, then Howard in "Abyss" – seem lost in their own lives. Another way of coming at this is through a theme that seems to be important to you, namely that of belonging, articulated in your stories through these male characters not having a sense of belonging, but portrayed also in the exploration of infidelity as a form of exile ...

RF: ... yes ...

BD: ... as a loss of belonging ...

RF: ... yes ...

BD: Could you just say a little about your notion of belonging?

RF: Well, I don't know that I have a very well-developed notion of belonging. I mean, I know that belonging can take some shapes that are classically recognizable. It can be in love, you can be in love with someone, and remain in it and have a sense of belonging. Or you can be attached to a place and its history and that will give you a sense of belonging. My own sense of belonging is entirely expressed in marriage, and not so much in marriage the institution, but with Kristina. And you can create situations in your life, or your life can create situations for you, in which you become a satellite to your own sense of belonging, you're away from it. And that can be a dire feeling, a dire situation. I think that there are impulses in us all, whether we act on them or we don't, that drive us away from belonging, because there's something about belonging – this gets back to *The Lay of the Land* – that seems quite, almost too permanent. As Frank says at the end of *The Lay of the Land*, "Permanence is a pretty scary situation". I think that's one of the things that happens – we get into a situation that could last us out forever, and it scares us to death, so that we act in obstreperous ways.

BD: I'm thinking of the character of Martin Austin, who loses touch with his own life, with his own better self, with his marriage ...

RF: ... yes ...

BD: ... and you have him over in Paris, in a place he shouldn't be ...

RF: … yes …

BD: … and Joséphine says in that story, "You cannot live a long time where you don't belong". She had been in America and she had to come back to France for that reason. That seems to be the central metaphor of Paris, and of Martin always being someplace he shouldn't be. He's lost in his life, and at the end he's really in a state of near-perdition, in fact.

RF: Yes, I thought so, too.

BD: It's like a parable, a moral tale, a cautionary tale.

RF: It's the story in that book that most people who like that book like the most. It's the first one I wrote, of those long stories. I just credited it all to solipsism, to what it is that busts you out of the places that protect you and relationships that console, and that are love relationships. It's an infatuation with yourself, one's impulses, one notions, appetites.

BD: That's very much his case, yes.

RF: Yeah, I think in all three of those stories that all three of the principal characters are solipsists.

BD: Yes, Charley also. He's really lost in his life, too.

RF: Yes.

BD: He's apart from everything in his own life. He neglects Helen …

RF: …yes, he let's her die …

BD: … he lets her die. He's just not there because he's too busy fantasizing about being a great writer in Paris. He's lost touch with his own sense of what he might be able to achieve in his life.

RF: Exactly. Americans don't like stories like these. But the French like them. Maybe they know something Americans don't know. Maybe they're less apt to be stubborn idealists about human behaviour.

BD: "Europeans", maybe?

RF: Yeah, the French like them very much, and I know the Germans like them very much. They seem to most of my friends who like these books, in Germany and France, to be true to a certain view of life. But Americans don't like views like that.

BD: A couple of final questions. You set all the stories of *A Multitude of Sins* in a world of white, middle-class professionals. Why did you do that?

RF: I did it for this reason – that's one thing I can be held responsible for. They were white, I guess, because I'm white, and I didn't have a

sense that race was involved. I made them white because – for me – that neutralized other issues. And I made them professionals because I wanted a chance to articulate at a high level of intellection the things that I felt needed to be articulated. I wanted the stories to have a high level of discourse with their readership, particularly, say, with a story like "Calling". At the end of "Calling" the narrator says [RF reads from *A Multitude of Sins*]: "So that when we are tempted, as I was for an instant in the duck blind, or as I was through all those thirty years, to let myself become preoccupied and angry with my father, or when I even see a man who reminds me of him, stepping into some building in a seersucker suit and a bright bow tie, I try to realize again that it is best just to offer myself release and to realize I am feeling anger all alone, and that there is no redress. We want it. Life can be seen to be about almost nothing else sometimes than our wish for redress. As a lawyer who was the son of a lawyer and the grandson of another, I know this. And I also know not to expect it."[2] I have to have somebody who can say that persuasively. I could've had an African-American do that, of course. But it was easier for me not to – in a story where there was already enough going on that was hard.
BD: I see. Which your characters in *Rock Springs*, for example, couldn't say.
RF: As eloquent as I force them to be sometimes, I couldn't get them to say that. Or in "Quality Time", when Wales decides he's not going to tell Jena about what he had seen [RF reads from *A Multitude of Sins*]: "Wales had expected to tell her about the woman he had seen killed, about the astonishment of that, to retell it—the slowing of time, the stateliness of events, the sensation that the worst could be avoided, the future improved by a more gradual unfolding. But he had no wish now to reveal the things he could be made to think, how his mind worked, or what he could feel in response to events."[3] I had to have somebody, some character, who in my view is capable of holding thoughts like that in his head.
BD: Yes, he's a journalist, he's also lectured on "Failed Actuality" …
RF: … yes …
BD: … and he's reflected deeply on the whole media frenzy and mythification surrounding Princess Diana …

---

[2] Ford, *A Multitude of Sins*, 61-62.
[3] *Ibid.*, 31.

RF: ... exactly. And if you like that story, then I have you in my thrall, because that's a very demanding story.
BD: It is. The opening scene in particular, which functions as a little allegory of some of the things that happen later on ...
RF: Yes, absolutely.
BD: ... about how meaning unfolds ...
RF: ... that's right ...
BD: ... how meaning is constructed, which is back to what were saying earlier.
RF: Exactly.
BD: My last question is about "Abyss", which is a particularly unforgiving story.
RF: (Laughing) At least it's funny.
BD: I must have missed those bits! You seem to have set out deliberately not to hold back ...
RF: ... yes, that's true ...
BD: ... and even, it seems to me, to give vent to strong emotions that motivated the story. The characters are not likeable; their mutual attraction is based on nothing more than primitive sexual desire; you have them both betray their spouses; and you reserve terribly harsh fates for both of them. In that the story takes an act of infidelity from its beginnings through to its consequences, it could be said to encapsulate the concerns of the entire collection, and indeed to be an exemplary moral tale. What did you wish to achieve with this novella that was perhaps different from what you wanted to explore in the preceding stories of the collection? It's also the final story, of course – it ends with this, this is what the reader is left with
RF: Well, I wanted to be able to say what the consequences of these acts are. Howard says at the end [RF reads from *A Multitude of Sins*]: "But those things didn't matter. Peering out the windshield at the flat, gray desert at evening, he understood that in fact very little of what he knew mattered; and that however he might've felt today—if circumstances could just have been better—he would now not be allowed to feel. Perhaps he never would again. And whatever he might even have liked, bringing his full and best self to the experience, had now been taken away. So that life, as fast as this car hurtling down the side of a mountain toward the dark, seemed to be

disappearing from around him. Being erased. And he was so sorry."[4] I wanted to be able to write that.

BD: The vision there is as harsh as at the end of "The Womanizer'.

RF: Yes, it is.

BD: They have nothing left, almost. Martin Austin perhaps begins to see at least that he has failed, that he has a chance, but it's really bleak.

RF: I wanted to be able to say that the things that you do in your life matter, and that you can live your life in such a way that you can get completely and forever lost. My own feeling through so much of my life was that I can always recover, I could recuperate, I could do things that turned out badly, people around me could do things that turned out badly, but that things could finally reconstruct themselves and turn out, you know, OK. But I realized either before I wrote those stories, or in the writing of them, that that faith wasn't really substantiable. You can *not* recover. For me, without a religion, without a sense of foreboding, without a sense of promise about a future, it leaves one wanting for a sense of consequence to one's acts. That's one of the things that religion does for you, it promises a consequence to your behaviour. So I had to make up a sense of consequence, which would say to a readership, "You know, if you do things that are bad enough, you're not going to get out of it". In this view, art becomes the religion.

BD: And you'll pay the price *now*.

RF: And you will pay a price that this story will articulate for you when you yourself may not have ever been able to articulate it. And the story'll be useful for doing that for you.

BD: And it's not going to be at the end of your life …

RF: … no, no …

BD: … like at the Day of Judgement …

RF: … it can be when you're thirty-five, and you can be lost forever.

BD: And the two characters we have been speaking about, Howard and Martin Austin, are ruined.

RF: Seemingly. At that point they have bottomed out. Ruined, I don't know. I prefer the vocabulary of my stories to the borrowed one of "ruin". "Ruin" doesn't tell us enough.

BD: The question is, will they learn from what has happened?

---

[4] *Ibid.*, 285-86.

RF: Well, then I went on and wrote other books, I went on and wrote this long Frank Bascombe book, so I guess I think that an act of acceptance is potentially an act of redemption, and that if you have enough time left you still have time to recover yourself.

BD: Thank you very much, Richard.

RF: Thank you.

Bibliography

Primary Literature

Richard Ford

Books (in order of publication)
A Piece of My Heart, New York: Harper and Row, 1976.
The Ultimate Good Luck, New York: Houghton Mifflin, 1981.
The Sportswriter, New York: Vintage, 1986.
Rock Springs, New York: Atlantic Monthly Press, 1987.
Wildlife, New York: Atlantic Monthly Press, 1990.
Independence Day, New York: Knopf, 1995.
Women with Men, New York: Knopf, 1997.
A Multitude of Sins, New York: Knopf, 2002.
The Lay of the Land, New York: Knopf, 2006.

Play
American Tropical. Actors Theatre of Louisville. Produced November 1983. Published in *Antaeus* 66 (Spring 1991), 75-80.

Screenplay
Bright Angel, Hemdale Productions, 1990.

Edited (in order of publication)
The Best American Short Stories, New York: Houghton Mifflin, 1990.
The Granta Book of the American Short Story, London: Granta, 1992.
Eudora Welty: Complete Novels (with Michael Kreyling), New York: Library of America, 1998.
Eudora Welty: Stories, Essays, and Memoir (with Michael Kreyling), New York: Library of America, 1998.
The Granta Book of the American Long Story, London: Granta, 1998.
The Essential Tales of Chekhov, London: Granta, 1999.
The New Granta Book of the American Short Story, London: Granta, 2007.

Essay cited
"What We Write, Why We Write It, and Who Cares", *Michigan Quarterly Review*, XXXI/3 (Summer 1992), 379-80.

Interviews cited
Baker, Jeff, "Life Readings and Writings: Imagining the Possibilities", *The Oregonian*, 8 March 2002, Arts and Living Section, 6.
Birnbaum, Robert, "Richard Ford", *identity theory: the narrative thread*, http://www.identitytheory.com/people/birnbaum37.html (31/05/2005).
Ganahl, Jane, "Mapping a terrain of lust and lies: Richard Ford writes about the perils of temptation in 'Sins'", *San Francisco Chronicle*, 18 March 2002, Section D, 1.
Gbadamosi, Gabriel, *Night Waves*, BBC Radio 3, 27 September 2006.
Hoover, Bob, "Ford is story maker, not story teller", *Pittsburgh Post-Gazette*, 17 February 2002, Section E, 8.
Kanner, Ellen, "A Multitude of Sins: Errors of omission are the stuff of real life", http://www.bookpage.com/0202bp/richard_ford.html (26/06/2006).
Lyons, Bonnie, "Richard Ford: The Art of Fiction CXLVII", *Paris Review*, 140, Fall 1996, 42-77.
McKeon, Belinda, "Remembrance and Release", *Irish Times*, 16 September 2006, Weekend Review Section, 11.
Ross, Michael, "The final chapter", *Sunday Times*, 1 October 2006, Features Section, 12.
Salusinszky, Imre, and Mills, Stephen, "An Interview with Richard Ford", *Heat Magazine*, 15, 2000, 165-74.
Treisman, Deborah, "Frankly Speaking", http://www.newyorker.com/archive/2006/08/28/060828on_onlineonly02 (12/01/2008).
Wineke, William, "Of love and infidelity", *Wisconsin State Journal*, 3 March 2002, Section F, 3.
(Unattributed), "Ford assesses America's house", *Toronto Star*, 29 October 2006, Section C, 7.

Secondary Literature
Bone, Martyn, "New Jersey Real Estate and the Postsouthern 'Sense of Place': Richard Ford's *Independence Day*", *American Studies in Scandinavia*, XXXIII/2 (2001), 105-19.

Brooks, Peter, *Reading for the Plot: Design and Intention in Narrative*, Oxford: Clarendon, 1984.

Duffy, Brian "The Story as Cure in Richard Ford's 'Occidentals'", *Mississippi Quarterly*, LIX/1, 2 (Winter 2005-2006, Spring 2006), 225-41.

Emerson, Ralph Waldo, *Self-Reliance and Other Essays*, New York: Dover, 1993.

Folks, Jeffrey J., "The Risks of Membership: Richard Ford's *The Sportswriter*", *Mississippi Quarterly*, LII/1 (1998-99), 73-88.

Guagliardo, Huey, ed., *Perspectives on Richard Ford*, Jackson, MS: UP of Mississippi, 2000.

Guagliardo, Huey, ed., *Conversations with Richard Ford*, Literary Conversations Series, Jackson, MS: UP of Mississippi, 2001.

http://www.whitehouse.gov/news/releases/2006/11/20061116-8.html (7/12/2006)

Kearney, Richard, *Dialogues with Contemporary Continental Thinkers: The Phenomenological Heritage*, Manchester: Manchester UP, 1984.

King, Desmond, *The Liberty of Strangers: Making the American Nation*, New York: Oxford UP, 2005.

Leerssen, Joep, *Mere Irish and Fíor-Ghael: Studies in the Idea of Irish Nationality, its Development and Literary Expression prior to the Nineteenth Century*, 2nd edn, Field Day Monographs 3, Cork: Cork UP in association with Field Day, 1996.

Leerssen, Joep, *Remembrance and Imagination: Patterns in the Historical and Literary Representation of Ireland in the Nineteenth Century*, Field Day Monographs 4, Cork: Cork UP in association with Field Day, 1996.

Leerssen, Joep, "The Allochronic Periphery: Towards a Grammar of Cross-Cultural Representation", in *Beyond Pug's Tour: National and Ethnic Stereotyping in Theory and Literary Practice*, ed. C.C. Barfoot, Amsterdam: Rodopi, 1997, 285-94.

MacIntyre, Alasdair, *After Virtue: A Study in Moral Theory*, 2nd edn, London: Duckworth, 1985.

Nash, Gary B., *The Unknown American Revolution: The Unruly Birth of Democracy and the Struggle to Create America*, New York: Viking, 2005.

Newsweek, 18 September 2000.

Pageaux, Daniel-Henri, "De l'imagerie culturelle à l'imaginaire", in *Précis de littérature comparée*, eds. Pierre Brunel and Yves Chevrel, Paris: Presses Universitaires de France, 1989, 133-161.

Putnam, Robert D., *Bowling Alone: The Collapse and Revival of American Community*, New York: Simon and Schuster, 2000.

Ricoeur, Paul, *Time and Narrative*, vol. I, trans. Kathleen McLaughlin and David Pellauer, Chicago: U of Chicago P, 1984.

Ricoeur, Paul "Life in Quest of Narrative", in *On Paul Ricoeur: Narrative and Interpretation*, ed. David Wood, London: Routledge, 1991, 20-33.

Ricoeur, Paul *Oneself as Another*, trans. Kathleen Blamey, Chicago: U of Chicago P, 1992.

Said, Edward, *Orientalism*, London: Penguin, 2003.

Schafer, Roy, *Language and Insight*, New Haven: Yale UP, 1978.

Slotkin, Richard, *Regeneration Through Violence: The Mythology of the American Frontier, 1600-1860*, Hanover, NH: Wesleyan UP, 1973.

Taylor, Charles, *Sources of the Self: The Making of the Modern Identity*, Cambridge, MA: Harvard UP, 1989.

The Declaration of Independence and The Constitution of the United States, Introduction by Pauline Maier, New York: Bantam, 1998.

Walker, Elinor Ann, *Richard Ford*, Twayne United States Authors Series, New York: Twayne, 2000.

INDEX

Lightning Source UK Ltd.
Milton Keynes UK
25 January 2011

166365UK00001B/182/P